Teaching Literature
to Adolescents

Lawrence Erlbaum Associates, Inc., Publishers
10 Industrial Avenue
Mahwah, New Jersey 07430
www.erlbaum.com

Cover design by Tomai Maridou

Visit www.teachingliterature.org

Library of Congress Cataloging-in-Publication Data

Teaching literature to adolescents / Richard Beach … [et al.].
    p. cm.
  Includes bibliographical references and index.
ISBN 0-8058-4195-4 (pbk. : alk. paper)
1. Literature—Study and teaching (Secondary)—United States.   I. Beach, Richard.
PN70.T34 2005
807.1'273—dc22
                                         2005050378
                                             CIP

Books published by Lawrence Erlbaum Associates are printed on acid-free paper, and their bindings are chosen for strength and durability.

Printed in the United States of America
10 9 8 7 6 5 4 3 2 1

Brief Contents

Contents

4   Using Drama to Foster Interpretation: How Can I Help   67
Students Read Better?

5   Leading Classroom Discussions of Literature: How Do I Get   86
Students to Talk About Literature?

6   Writing About Literature: How Do I Get Students to Write   101
About Literature?

Preface

Welcome to *Teaching Literature to Adolescents*. This volume is designed to provide preservice English teachers with current methods of teaching literature to middle and high school students. These methods are based on social constructivist and sociocultural theory of learning that emphasizes the value of engaging students with alternative perspectives portrayed in literature, perspective-taking that is extended through writing, talk, and drama activities involved in responding to literature. These methods are also based on the need to provide students with critical lenses for interrogating the beliefs, attitudes, and ideological perspectives portrayed in literature.

These methods also draw on the research on literary response conducted by the four authors, research that highlights the need to not only recognize the influence of individual differences in students' construction of the meaning of a text, but also how the social context created by a teacher serves to foster growth in students' ability to interpret texts.

This volume draws on many of the ideas in an earlier textbook, *Teaching Literature in the Secondary School*, by Richard Beach and James Marshall, published in 1991. This new book has been entirely rewritten to address some of the developments in teaching literature that have occurred since 1991:

• An increasing focus on a social constructivist and sociocultural theory of literacy learning that emphasizes the need for students to acquire social tools of language, narratives, genres, talk, writing, drama, and images through participation in specific contexts. Students best acquire these tools through actively employing them in purposeful activities you create.

• An organization of the literature curriculum around topics, themes, or issues, with a particular focus on inquiry instruction related to exploring students' own questions, issues, or concerns, around, for example, the portrayal of power in literature. Although *Teaching Literature in the Secondary School* was organized largely around genre forms, this revised edition focuses more on organizing instruction around topics, themes, or issues.

• The broadening of critical perspectives employed in analyzing texts. *Teaching Literature in the Secondary School* focused primarily on a reader-response approach, whereas this text promotes the need to employ a range of different critical lenses, including reader-response approaches, to foster critical analysis of race, class, and gender in literature and how students' own stances shape their construction of text meaning.

• The increased infusion of multicultural literature into the largely White, male, Western high school literature canon and an increased focus on how writers portray race, class, and gender differences. For a study of teaching multicultural literature to high school students, see Beach, Thein, and Parks (in press).

• The use of drama as a tool for enhancing understanding of texts in which students interpret texts through assuming characters' roles and perspectives.

• A broadening of different ways of writing about literature through informal and formal writing tools, and hypermedia interpretations of literature through texts, images, sounds, video clips, as well as writing stories, poems, and drama to help students understand literature through creating it.

• The importance of integrating critical analysis of film and media texts with study of literature so that students learn to apply critical lenses to both print and film and media texts.

• The ongoing integration of quality young adult literature into the curriculum, particularly at the middle school level, to foster student engagement with reading.

• An increased focus on students who have difficulty succeeding in literature classes due to reading difficulties, disparities between school and home cultures, attitudes towards school and English, or lack of engagement with assigned texts or response activities.

ORGANIZATION OF THE VOLUME

This volume begins with a discussion of the larger purposes and goals for teaching literature (Chapter 1), followed by a discussion of the need to consider individual differences in working with adolescents, particularly in terms of providing them with young adult literature choices based on their reading interests (Chapter 2). It then formulates a model of planning literature instruction based on considering students' needs and ability; defining specific objectives related to learning interpretive strategies or critical lenses; selecting drama, talk, or writing tools; sequencing tasks; and evaluating learning (Chapter 3).

Tools for Responding to Literature. Based on the concept of teaching tools for responding to texts, Chapter 4 describes uses of drama tools for helping students learn to interpret texts. Chapter 5 discusses talk tools for fostering discussions of literature in small and large groups, as well as online settings. And, Chapter 6 discusses informal and formal writing tools for writing about literature, as well as integrating writing of literature with writing about literature.

Teaching Interpretive Strategies. Chapter 7 provides specific teaching techniques for teaching narratives—oral anecdotes, short stories, and novels. Chapter 8 discusses the use of interpretive strategies for teaching poetry, myths, fables, and essays. Chapter 9 applies the material in Chapters 7 and 8 to examples of teaching interpretation of canonical texts.

Teaching Critical Lenses and Media Analysis. Chapter 10 discusses methods of teaching critical lenses (reader-response, deconstructionist, feminist, Marxist, poststructuralist) for analysis of literary and media texts. Chapter 11 describes further methods for analyzing a range of different types of media texts, as well as studying film adaptations of literature.

Evaluating and Reflecting on Teaching Literature. The final two chapters focus on methods for evaluating and assessing learning of literature through observing and analyzing students' uses of drama, talk, and writing tools (Chapter 12) and reflecting on one's own teaching as a professional and ways of enhancing professional development (Chapter 13).

ORGANIZATION OF EACH CHAPTER

Each chapter is organized around a specific question English educators frequently hear in working with preservice teachers—questions such as "How do I decide what to teach?" "How can I help students read better?" "How do I get them to write about literature?" "Do I have to teach Shakespeare?"

Every chapter begins with a case narrative depicting a preservice teacher's experience coping with a particular issue related to teaching literature. The narrative or description serves to frame discussions of how to address the issue it portrays. For example, Chapter 5 begins with a description of a preservice teacher having difficulty leading a discussion; the chapter then provides teaching techniques for leading discussions. Preservice teachers can discuss their reactions to these case narratives as well as share their own related experiences, as part of an inquiry-based approach to framing questions and issues that need to be addressed in a methods course.

Many of the chapters also contain teacher narratives or lesson plans that demonstrate how a teacher implements the methods presented.

All chapters end with either a portfolio reflection activity for use in contributing to a teacher portfolio employed in a teacher education program or an action research project in which preservice teachers conduct a small-scale, qualitative study on some topic related to their teaching or classroom observations.

LINKS TO THE *TEACHING LITERATURE WEB SITE*

Each chapter ends with a reference to the Teaching Literature Web site that is designed to be used in conjunction with this volume (http://www.teachingliterature.org/).

This Web site contains recommended readings, resources, and activities, as well as links to Web sites and PowerPoint™ presentations. One of the advantages of this site is that its information is continually updated with new links, resources, and books, so that it does not become dated. We also want to make this an interactive site—something that you could model for use with your students—by inviting your participation on the site blog. In sharing your reactions to the volume, as well as your own experiences in observing and engaging in teaching literature, you are contributing to a community of preservice English teachers using this site. We also invite you to attach teaching units to your messages so that we can include them in the unit databases under the generic categories.

This site contains two basic types of information: chapter links and generic links.

CHAPTER LINKS

For each of the chapters listed on the left side of the home page, there are the following:

- Chapter activities for use as assignments in your methods course or as teaching activities in your own teaching.
- Further readings that include relatively current books and articles on topics addressed in the chapter.
- Web links to sites related to the topics dealt with in the chapter.

- Literary texts that include lists of poems, short stories, novels, or plays (only included in chapters about these genres).
- PowerPoint presentations that include PowerPoint™ presentations in Web format, PDF files, and the original presentation for download and your own use.

GENERIC LINKS

For each of the generic topics across the top of the home page, there are activities, further readings, Web links, lists of literary texts, units, and PowerPoint presentations related to the following generic categories: American literature; British literature; multicultural and world literature; poetry; drama and speech; Shakespeare; young adult literature; mythology, fantasy, and science fiction; nonfiction; critical lenses; story response and writing; assessment; censorship; professional development; and media and technology. Some of the same material appears in both the chapters and the generic categories.

ACKNOWLEDGMENTS

We would like to acknowledge the ongoing, long-term assistance provided by Naomi Silverman; without her support, this volume would never have been completed. We would also like to thank Erica Kica, Associate Editor at Lawrence Erlbaum Associates, Inc., as well as the reviewers: Christian Knoeller, Purdue University; Cynthia Lewis, University of Iowa; Linda Miller Cleary, University of Minnesota; George E. Newell, Ohio State University; and Anna O. Soter, Ohio State University.

Richard Beach would also like to thank three graduate students at the University of Minnesota who worked on the Teaching Literature Web site design: Beth O'Hara, Kazue Oda, and Tamela McCarthy. Deborah Appleman would like to thank Emily Meisler for her cover design; Tim Klobochar, Martha Cosgrove, Matthew Jabaily, and Harry Jackson for their lesson plans and teaching insights, Lois Marek for her able production assistance and John Schmit for his astute reading and much, much more. Susan Hynds acknowledges the help and assistance provided by Kelly Chandler-Olcott, Cari Sue Palma, Lydia Preczewski, Melissa Porter, Mandi Tice, and Trina Nocerino. Jeff Wilhelm would like to acknowledge Michael W. Smith; George Hillocks; his teaching colleagues, Tany Baker and Jamie Heans; and his student Elizabeth Skoro; for their help with the ideas in this text.

About the Authors

Richard Beach, Professor of English Education, University of Minnesota, Twin Cities. He is the coauthor of *Inquiry-Based English Instruction: Engaging Students in Literature and Life* (Teachers College Press, 2001) and *Journals in the Classroom: Writing to Learn* (Christopher Gordon, 1996), and author of *A Teacher's Introduction to Reader Response Theories* (National Council of Teachers of English, 1993).

Deborah Appleman, Professor and Chair of Educational Studies and Director of the Summer Writing Program, Carleton College, Northfield, Minnesota. She is the author of *The Breakfast Book Club* (Heinemann, 2006); *Critical Encounters in High School English: Teaching Literary Theory to Adolescents* (Teachers College Press, 2000); and coeditor of *Braided Lives: A Multicultural Literature Anthology* (Minnesota Humanities Commission, 1991).

Susan Hynds, Professor of English Education, Syracuse University, Syracuse, New York. She is the coauthor of *Literacy Lessons: Teaching and Learning With Middle School Students* (Prentice Hall, 2003), and author of *On the Brink: Negotiating Literature and Life With Adolescents* (Teachers College Press, 1997) and *Making Connections: Language and Learning in the Classroom* (Christopher Gordon, 1994).

Jeffrey Wilhelm is Associate Professor of English, Boise State University, Boise, Idaho. He is the author of *"You Gotta Be the Book": Teaching Engaged and Reflective Reading With Adolescents* (Teachers College Press, 1997) and coauthor of *Imagining to Learn: Inquiry, Ethics, and Integration Through Drama* (Heinemann, 1998) and *Strategic Reading: Guiding Students to Lifelong Literacy, 6–12* (Boynton-Cook, 2001).

1

Goals for Teaching Literature: What Does It Mean to Teach Literature?

Chapter Overview

- Purposes for teaching literature, illustrated with a narrative about Tanya's instruction.
- Different theories of teaching literature: transmission, student-centered, sociocultural learning theory.
- Sociocultural learning theory: implications for teaching literature.
- How purposes and goals for teaching literature shape instruction.
- Practices constituting a literature curriculum: perspective-taking, constructing social worlds, explaining characters' actions, making connections, posing questions, problem solving, rereading, applying critical lenses.
- Using tools to foster learning of literature.

What does it mean to teach literature? You may have a good sense of what it means to be a student of literature, but now that you're going to be on the other side of the desk, you are now having to think about how to teach literature—selecting texts, planning response activities and units, leading discussions, formulating writing assignments, evaluating students' interpretations, and so forth.

Underlying all of these choices are your beliefs and attitudes about the larger purpose and value for teaching literature—why you're doing what you are doing. You will ultimately need to formulate your own sense of purpose and value as a means of making decisions about what kinds of texts you select, how you will foster student participation, the role you adopt in the classroom, what criteria you employ in evaluating students, and how you justify what you do to your students, the school, parents, and to yourself. Formulating your purposes and value for teaching literature ultimately reflects your theory as to how one best learns literature and what it means to learn literature. With this in mind, read the following case about Tanya, and think about how her beliefs and attitudes about teaching shaped her teaching techniques.

CASE NARRATIVE: TANYA BAKER'S GOALS
AS AN ENGLISH TEACHER

Tanya Baker is a high school English teacher. She loves her job. She parks her red truck in the parking lot each morning and hefts her bag full of books and papers onto her shoulder. As she enters the building, she gives a wide smile to her colleagues in the office and in the hallways as she makes her way to her classroom in the west wing of Brewer High School.

Her classes are engaging and fun, yet rigorous and challenging to students. She is always trying new teaching techniques like using critical theories, drama, and various technological applications with video and computers to teach literature and help kids to interpret and respond to their reading.

Her students genuinely enjoy her and hang out in her room between classes and after school. She often works, at her students' request, with the literary magazine, school newspaper, or Junior Exhibition—a talent show the juniors put on to raise money for the prom.

Tanya is also a leader in the wider profession of English teaching. She's a lead teacher in the University of Maine's Professional Development Site program. She provides in-service assistance to teaching peers, participates in learning labs demonstrating her own and others' teaching innovations, and often takes on one or two student teachers. She codirects her local Maine Writing Project site, an affiliate of the National Writing Project. She presents regularly at conferences and institutes on the regional, national, and international level. She has written several articles, coauthored a volume, and is now conducting a teacher research study she hopes to turn into another volume.

She recently completed her master's degree in literacy education, and is now turning her attention to doctoral work.

By any measure, she is a motivated, highly successful, and professional teacher.

Yet several years ago, after only 5 years of teaching, Tanya felt like a failure and was ready to quit. If she had, her school, her future students, and the profession would have lost a very valuable member.

What was it that was bugging her?

This is what Tanya has to say:

> I was teaching for a while and I was really struggling. I thought teaching was transmitting information and my kids didn't understand the information I taught—and they didn't care about it either. So it was clear: one of us has to be fixed. Either I'm not doing a good job or they aren't. And I couldn't see how to fix either of us.

Tanya maintains that experimenting with drama in education techniques for teaching literature saved her career:

> When I started using drama strategies I moved off the center of the stage and stopped lecturing. I started working with the kids. I became much happier with my teaching and had more fun with my kids. But it was much bigger than that. I realized through using the drama that it wasn't me or the kids who were deficient. The drama made me see that I'd been working with a deficient theoretical model of teaching. I realized that I shouldn't be delivering information or letting

kids do whatever they want. I realized that I needed to be explicitly guiding them to be able to do new things. The drama work showed me how to use the sociocultural model of teaching and learning—though I didn't even know what that was at the time. Later, I made the connection to Vygotsky—and that made me see that no one was broken; if the kids can't do something, teach them. And teach them in an area in which the teacher and students can play, and build, and learn together. In that realm, anything the kids don't know how to do I can help them do. And enactment strategies for teaching provided me with a way to help them. It made me see that learning happens in the interaction and relationship between me and the students, is shared by me and my students, and that there is always something a teacher can do that teaches and transforms them, that helps them to take the step beyond who they already are and what they can already do. And doing that transforms the teacher, too. That's how drama saved my career—by helping me rethink the theory behind what I do.

In turn, I began to experiment with new ways of assisting kids to do the kind of work that both they and I could value. The new methods I experimented with fed my theoretical understanding of how teaching and learning could work through joint productive activities—through participation as a community in projects of making meaning that we all cared about. And my new theoretical understandings helped me adapt and develop new ways to teach that were fun, contextualized, and useful to my kids. So really, in a funny kind of way, it's practicing theory in more wide awake ways that has helped me become an effective teacher. In fact, it's what kept me in the profession. Who knows what I would be doing now if I hadn't found my theory?

I used to think my job was to teach literature, which is a very teacher/text/information-centered view. Now I see my job as teaching kids HOW to read literature, which is a more sociocultural, teaching and learning-centered view.

Interestingly, Tanya teaches in a fairly traditional school with traditional expectations. Yet she has been able to meet the curricular and assessment expectations in very creative ways. She basically teaches the same material as other teachers, but in a way that reorganizes the material into issue-related themes.

In thinking about Tanya's reflection on her theories of learning, what theories did Tanya reject, and what are the features of the theory she embraced? What theories are in play and competition anyway in the field of English teaching? And how does Tanya's theory inform what she decides to teach, why she decides to teach it, and how she actually does teach it? These are questions we take up at the end of this chapter, after we have had the chance to review the theoretical landscape of teaching and what it will mean to you as a teacher.

WHAT DOES IT MEAN TO TEACH LITERATURE?

The field of education in general, and of literacy education in particular, is politically and theoretically charged. Debates rage about how to best teach, what to teach, how to prove students have learned. Legislation, such as the federal No Child Left Behind Act (United States Department of Education, 2002), and many more local state-level laws, have implicitly endorsed and mandated some ideas and theories over others.

Often, such mandates seem to occur within a vacuum, and assume that everyone would agree on definitions of learning, ideas of what content and processes should be learned, and the best ways to assess learning. But nothing could be further from the truth. And nowhere are such issues more contended than in the areas of teaching reading and literature.

As Tanya's story points out, teaching is a theoretical act, and theories, whether explicitly or implicitly held, have huge and powerful effects—on what we do, how we do it, and how we determine if we are successful, and in Tanya's case, how effective she felt herself to be, and how happy she was in the classroom.

In this volume, we stake a very clear theoretical position about teaching and learning, and about what constitutes a text—or "literature." The main questions we address in this chapter are as follows: What IS "teaching"? and What IS "literature"?

We believe that the theoretical positions we use to inform the teaching we describe and champion in this volume are the most powerful and effective ones. Our belief is based on our experience as learners, teachers, and researchers, and on our careful reading of the data about learning to read and respond to literature available in the research base. But we want to be clear that there are other theories—and in fact, a different theory is currently winning in both the legislative and practical arena of classroom teaching. We believe that this is to the detriment of both teachers and learners. Now, because the field is contentious—we could be wrong—but we are pretty sure we are not! At any rate, we begin by outlining the three major learning theories at play in American schools and in current debates. We then show how theories of learning to read, and of reading literature, map onto these three theories. As we do so, we argue our claim for one of these theories. This is the theory that underlies the instructional practices we suggest throughout this volume. Indeed, it is the theory that the authors of this volume, like Tanya Baker, have come to embrace and that has enlivened our teaching.

DIFFERENT THEORIES OF TEACHING LITERATURE

In thinking about different theories of learning literature, it is useful to consider three larger notions of learning that have shaped instruction in all subject matter areas for the past 50 years: transmission theories, student-centered theories, and practice-oriented theories (Beach & Myers, 2001; Wilhelm, Baker, & Dube, 2001).

Transmission Theories.   Most of us share a mental image of how the traditional English classroom is organized. All students are reading the same text, usually a novel. They are seated in straight rows, and the teacher is either reading to them or questioning them about their reading. Everything that goes on in the classroom revolves around the teacher as the all-knowing expert who imparts knowledge to students.

Transmission theories frame learning in terms of acquiring facts and knowledge about literature—the characteristics of the short story or Romantic poetry—or critical concepts used to analyze literary text—the difference between metaphor and simile. The primary focus in terms of teaching is how to best impart knowledge to students assumed to be empty vessels dutifully waiting to be filled up with the knowledge you provide them through lectures or presentations, what Freire (1973) refers to as the "banking model of education." You then give students tests to determine if they can replicate what you taught them.

One problem with this transmission model is that it focuses simply on a "knowing that" aspect of learning literature—whether students know that there is a difference between a first person and a third person point of view. Simply having knowledge about literature—knowing the difference between a metaphor and a simile—doesn't necessarily mean that he or she knows how to insightfully interpret literature.

The transmission model is reflected in literature curriculums in which the primary focus is on coverage of different literary periods, historical backgrounds, biographical information about authors, literary concepts, or genre characteristics, as reflected in literature textbooks. In her book, *Teaching Literature*, Elaine Showalter (2002) notes that given the easy availability of many texts, teachers experience the need to have to cover all of literature. She challenges that need by noting that "obsession with coverage and content is one of the main barriers to good teaching . . . instead of aiming for comprehensive coverage, we have to think about what students need to read in order to establish a basis for further learning . . ." (p. 13).

Another limitation of the transmission model is that instruction revolves primarily around the teacher as the center of instruction. The "Direct Instruction" approach in teaching reading—teaching specific comprehension skills or strategies—often results in the teacher modeling specific skills or strategies designed to foster desired "correct answers." Similarly, a "New Criticism" literary critical approach assumes that the meaning is "in" the text and that the teacher's job is to model ways of teasing our specific meanings of figurative language used in the text without having to refer to authorial intent or one's subjective experience.

All of this positions students to assume relatively passive, dependent roles. Although you as teacher certainly play a central role in scaffolding and modeling ways of interpreting literature, students need to be more actively engaged in practicing responding to literature with peers and they will not have that opportunity if they are passively watching the teacher perform. And, the student is totally dependent on the teacher's instruction; if the student doesn't respond positively to the teacher or fails to keep up with instruction, then the student is at a disadvantage.

Student-Centered. A second theory of learning derives from the Progressive Movement in education in the 1920s that challenged the teacher-centered model. Proponents of a student-centered theory of learning argue that students should be able to make their own choices for what and how they would learn. If students have choices, they are more motivated to want to learn. For example, if students could choose whatever texts they wanted to study, they would then be more engaged with those texts than having to study assigned texts.

Although it is certainly important to provide students with choices and to be concerned about their motivation to learn, one problem with this theory is that it leaves the responsibility for learning up to the student, so if the student sinks or swims, that's the fault of the student. This points to a larger limitation of this theory—that it fails to recognize that learning is inherently social—that we learn through participation in social contexts or communities.

Sociocultural Learning Theory. A third theory of teaching is based on sociocultural learning theory which posits that learning is primarily social. Based on the work of Lev Vygotsky (1978), it argues that we learn to acquire uses of certain practices and tools that serve certain purposes in social groups or communities. Through participation in these groups or communities, people acquire uses of these practices and tools that are then internalized and developed over time. Brazilian street children who are engaged in the practice of selling candy on the street learn to make complicated math calculations as a tool to help them succeed in their work (Lave, 1988). Over time, they become increasingly effective at selling candy simply through engaging in that practice.

Practices are ways of thinking, knowing, and being and knowing, for example, the practice of greeting someone. We may not be consciously aware of using them, yet we know that we're deliberately employing certain practices to achieve certain objects of value in a social world. Students learn these practices not as isolated, autonomous participants but through participation in a joint, collective activity motivated by a purpose or object (Cole, 1996; Engestrom, 1987). Members of a soccer team learn the practices of "laying back on the ball" or "swarming the net" as collective activities designed to achieve the purpose of winning the game. The practices they acquire in the world of their soccer team transfers for use in other worlds. What is being transferred is the use of a practice across different contexts and worlds.

Sociocultural learning theory therefore emphasizes the importance of creating a social community that supports learning literature. As a literature teacher, you are socializing students into what could be called a literary community of practice reflected in the practices of a highly engaged literary book club (Edelsky, Smith, & Wolfe, 2002). In this community of practice, students assume the identities of careful readers who acquire various practices involved in interpreting and producing literature.

Most secondary students are not familiar with what it means to be participants in this literary community of practice; they are still outsiders who need an opportunity to participate in an apprenticeship in such a community. Your job is to socialize them into membership into this community—to show them what it is like to be the kind of person who values participation in a literary community of practice. For example, one teacher, Karen Smith, continually provided her fifth- and sixth-grade students with information about literature itself, for example, in studying a fantasy text, noting that " 'When you get into a fantasy like *Tuck Everlasting* a lot of people say that in order to get into it and enjoy it you have to do what they call suspend disbelief. You have to accept the fantasy world and then you buy into it and then you start believing' " (Edelsky et al., 2002, pp. 21–22). Also, Karen engaged in "tourguiding"—giving highlights of her response practices in her "trip" with a text: " 'it's kind of like that foreshadowing, where we know all along' " (Edelsky et al., 2002, p. 23). She also engaged in "lifting the level" by validating students' responses as being aligned with valued practices. After a student described how rereading the prologue helped her understand the story, Karen stated, "'so it almost sets a mood or a time, doesn't it,'" noting the value of the student's rereading and modeling the use of literary terminology (Edelsky et al., 2002, p. 25). She also provided "support and empathy" for students in ways that positioned them as members of the same community through sharing her own difficulties in interpreting the text. After a student noted that she was confused by a certain episode, Karen noted, "'that WAS a hard part, I kinda circled that part too' " (Edelsky et al., 2002, p. 28). By acknowledging that she and the students shared the same challenges, she is implying that they are becoming members of the same community of practice which values the work of literary analysis.

Another central idea in sociocultural learning theory is that learning occurs within certain developmental boundaries of what Vygotsky (1987) called students' *zone of proximal development* or ZPD. The ZPD refers to their developmental "zone" of sophistication within which students will be able to employ certain practices without undue struggling on their part given the current level, but still, by stretching to the upper level of the zone, improve on the use of their practices (see Table 1.1)

Modeling and Scaffolding Practices Within Students' ZPD.   To help students improve in their use of practices, you model or scaffold the uses of those practices by demonstrating your use of practices to achieve certain purposes. You then do a hand-over, letting students engage in the practice themselves with your assistance, employing an "I do, you watch, you try, I watch" sequence.

TABLE 1.1
Students' Zone of Proximal Development

Upper level	_____
Current or familiar level	_____

In modeling or scaffolding practices, it is essential that you consider your students' ZPD so that they will understand your modeling and scaffolding, while challenging them to grow and develop beyond their existing ZPD. In planning her 11th-grade American Literature courses, which she teaches to three groups a year, Tanya is continually thinking about her students' ZPD:

> Since I can't do everything, I have to make choices about what seminal concepts and strategies of reading literature are most important for my students to learn. I make this judgment based on several factors: what will motivate and engage my students, what is possible for them to learn, what is significant and usable in their current and future lives. I also want to make sure that they really learn what I decide to teach, so I consider carefully how I can devote the time and rigor to teaching them well enough so they will be able to move through their zones of proximal development and be transformed in their abilities to read, think, write and problem solve.

Middle School Versus High School Students. The ZPD also reflects differences in students' developmental level. For those of you who plan to student-teach at the middle school level, your instruction will be based on the developmental abilities and interests of early adolescents. Much of the "middle school philosophy" revolves around addressing those abilities and interests as opposed to simply a focus on teaching academic subjects in preparation for high school—as was often the focus of the junior high school. In considering early adolescents' ZPD, you need to recognize that they may not as readily infer abstract themes or apply critical lenses to texts with the facility of high school students. On the other hand, you do not want to underestimate their ability to grapple with abstractions or lenses, assuming that you develop activities that engage students with the themes or lenses.

And, the ZPD influences your text selection. In working with middle school students, you consider the fact that young-adult novels portray experiences and address themes in a manner consistent with early adolescents' thinking and interests. Early adolescents are not all that interested in complex psychological character motivations; they are interested in exploring alternative worlds—as reflected in their reading preferences for story-driven adventure, fantasy, mystery, or science fiction novels.

Ability Ranges in a Classroom. Determining your students' ZPD may be a challenge when you have a wide range of different ability levels represented in one class—with some students who are having difficulty reading a text and others who, as avid readers, have little difficulty. You may therefore need to develop different kinds of activities—some that address the needs of your struggling readers and some that serve to challenge your avid readers.

Providing Choice. Another central tenet of sociocultural learning theory is the importance of engagement in learning (Smith & Wilhelm, 2002). People are more likely to be engaged in an activity with they have some sense of ownership in or responsibility for planning and participating in that activity. In planning her units, Tanya believes that students are more likely to be engaged if they have some choice about what they will study and the texts they will read. If students choose a particular topic or text for a classroom activity, they then have a sense of ownership and responsibility for completing an activity because they were part of planning that activity. For example, Tanya presents her students with six unit choices that could be pursued throughout the year, and asks students to choose four. Sometimes they choose the two for the first semester, and then wait to choose the next two.

The choices change from year to year, but currently they are as follows:

- Race: What is the effect of race on being an American?
- Wealth and Poverty: What is the role of money in American culture and identity?
- Gender: What difference does being female (or male) make to being an American?
- War: What is the experience of being at war for Americans?
- Self and Community: How do we balance personal and cultural interests in American lives and culture?
- Civil Rights: How do we work for change, to procure and preserve civil rights, in the American context?

Tanya explains that all of these units intertwine, and she can cover major canonical pieces of literature in each one. Any four choices allow her to cover the history of American culture and literature without using a historical approach. For example, during the self and community unit, the class explores how the Federalists and Republicans debated these issues in the Continental Congress, the writing of the Constitution, through the early years of our country to this very day. Students can read Joseph Ellis on how this debate informed the famous dinner party between Madison, Jefferson, and Hamilton, and how the Burr–Hamilton duel was informed by this debate. She can also focus on the Transcendentalists, read Thoreau or Hawthorne. And she points out that if the kids don't choose this unit, she can incorporate these same American struggles and literary texts into the unit on War or Civil Rights:

> The great thing about all of these units is that they are all issue oriented. There are multiple perspectives around these issues. Kids are interested in the debate. And we can't fall into the information-centered trap of playing "guess what the teacher already knows." And instead of the kids doing my work, I am helping them to learn how to read so they can do their work: making tentative conclusions about important personal and social issues, staking their claims and identities, and figuring out how these decisions should inform how they live, vote, problem solve, etc. And all the units are so flexible that I can teach the students anything I would want them to know, but this teaching will be in service of helping them construct their own understandings and stake their own claims.
>
> The units can be done in lots of different ways too—and what you learn one year can be incorporated the next. It really keeps me fresh. For example, sometimes we do some short readings together, and then I let them choose a text to read in a small group through literature circles. In my most recent race unit, I encouraged one group to read *Beloved* by Toni Morrison. This text is conceptually and procedurally harder than almost anything else I've ever taught. But I had some kids for whom this text was in their ZPD. Other groups read Walker's *The Color Purple* or Thurston's *Their Eyes Were Watching God*. A few others read sections of *Black Boy* or *I Know Why the Caged Bird Sings*, and I could help select the sections based on their interests, questions and needs. And since I had some struggling readers, I also offered the choice of *Roll of Thunder, Hear My Cry*, a YA text that is of extremely high quality and that

really engages kids. So each group worked through their text with some assistance and activities from me, and they knew they would have to teach the rest of the class about how the African-American experience was presented in their book. We concluded the unit by reading Huck Finn together, and then debated whether Huck Finn should be in the American literature curriculum. We bring in the perspectives of characters and authors from the literature circle studies to consider what they might say. We also consider the value to us of the various texts, the ends they can be made to serve. It's always lively, but I wouldn't do this if I wasn't sure there were different perspectives and ethnic groups represented in the class.

Engaging Students Based on Collective Experiences. Although a student-centered approach focuses on individual students' interests—which can lead to 30 students doing 30 different things, a sociocultural approach engages students in joint, collective activity built on achieving a shared goal. Just as in organizing any social event, fostering collective activity requires fostering some initial buy-in from students in terms of them, as a group, actually wanting to engage in an activity. This requires you "frontload" a unit with a topic, theme, issue, concern, or experience that initially engages them as a group. For example, in her wealth and poverty unit, Tanya built an interest around studying *The Great Gatsby* by selecting the topic of dreams:

The centerpiece of this unit is always *The Great Gatsby*. This can be read in lots of ways from lots of possible angles. We used it to examining wealth and Americanism. I wanted the kids to explore the effect of money on people who have it, and people who don't have it. I want my kids to examine this central question: How does money affect your conception of who you are, and your identity as an American? How is or has this conception been different in different times and places across our history?

I have to do a lot of macro-planning, because *The Great Gatsby* is a difficult text to read. It uses sophisticated language, lots of description that makes implied points, symbolism, and leaves inference gaps. It's not a straightforward text and my kids will need help reading it.

But I think this is a great text and I would teach it even if I wasn't expected to, because I think our question is an essential one to consider as an American, and I think this book is a great text to use to explore this. Also, it really appeals to my students if I do it right.

I frontload this particular unit by exploring dreams. I want the kids to think about their dreams, what they would do to achieve it? How will they monitor their progress and know they are on track? How do they know if the dream is worth the effort? *The Great Gatsby* is about great themes like money, power, love and sex. But it doesn't offer pat answers. It asks all these essential questions in conflicted, debatable ways without being didactic.

So, on the macro-level of planning, I have to consider my conceptual and procedural goals. I want my kids to deal with the essential question and our sub-questions about dreams and money. And I know I will have to teach them about seeing complex implied relationships and making inferencs. So I'll have to work on that in regards to seeing textual patterns and understanding symbolism. Once I have these goals, which might be different with different groups, I then think about how to sequence instruction so I can assist various students through their ZPD step-by-step, building competence through each activity we do and each text we read.

In sociocultural theory of teaching, the primary focus is not simply on the teacher or on the student but on creating social activities or communities in which students acquire various practices and tools constituting learning literature. Student motivation and engagement with learning is no longer an individual matter, but now is a function of the quality of the activity or community created in the classroom.

In summary, a transmission model of teaching literature focuses on imparting knowledge about literature to students. A student-centered model focuses on letting students respond to literature in terms of their own interests and needs. A sociocultural model focuses on helping students acquire practices and tools through participation in social communities.

THE WHY TEACH LITERATURE SHAPES THE WHAT AND HOW

Each of these models values certain teaching techniques and roles over others. In your own teaching, you will continually be making decisions about how to best foster student learning. Those decisions are based on what you value in terms of "what works." And, what you believe "works" reflects your preferred teaching model and what you think is important in teaching literature—the larger purposes and goals for teaching literature. In other words, our decisions reflect our theoretical orientation and beliefs about the ultimate purpose for teaching literature.

For example, in a study of two high school literature teachers working in the same department in a small town in New Mexico, Don Zancanella (1998) found that they subscribed to quite different reasons for teaching literature, reasons that shaped what they taught and how they taught. One teacher, who is also the department chair, teaches an 11th-grade American Literature course that focuses on authors such as Hawthorne, Twain, and Fitzgerald. Students write in-class essays and devote a lot of time preparing for college admissions tests such as the SAT's and ACT's. When asked to provide a rationale for what she does in her class, the teacher noted the following:

> Knowing that most students are going to have to have some kind of post-secondary instruction, whatever they decide to do—they're going to have to be able to do at least short research papers—so they're going to have to be able to do that correctly. They should be able to write an opinion paper. And they need a sound vocabulary. In fact, they need a good vocabulary to do well at all on SAT's or ACT's. These are some of our department's aims. (Zancanella, 1998, p. 103)

This teacher's purposes revolve primarily around preparing students for college—consistent with what she perceives to be the needs of the largely White, middle-class students in her American Literature course. In contrast, another teacher teaches Southwest Literature and Creative Writing, a course that attracts a more diverse population. In this course, students read authors such as Rudolpho Anaya, Jimmy Baca, Denise Chavez, M. Scott Momaday, and Leslie Silko. They devote a lot of time to writing personal narratives, poetry, and fictions related to what they are reading. In class, students write about and discuss the texts in small groups based on questions that encourage them to make connections between the text and their own cultural backgrounds and experiences. This teacher describes his purposes for his instruction:

> I want them to see that they have things to write about. Most of the authors we read have backgrounds very similar to theirs and that's evident in the literature itself. So it shows the students that they have something to say . . . I want them to have some sense that the world of books and of people in books have something to do with them. I don't think a lot of kids really feel that very clearly or deeply. (Zancanella, 1998, pp. 100–101)

This teacher has a very different purpose for teaching literature. He wants his students, many of whom are Hispanic and Native American, to perceive some relation between their lives and the literature they are reading. And, he wants them to experiment with forms of writing that encourage them to write about their experiences, as opposed to the traditional literary critical essays.

Activity: Reflect on Your Own Learning Experiences in Literature Classes

- Write a story about a positive and powerful learning experience—a time when you learned something new inside or outside of school. What was your motivation? What assistance was provided by the environment, materials, peers, a teacher? What teaching methods were used? What difficulties were encountered and how were they overcome? What theory of teaching and learning was embodied?
- Write about a negative learning experience.
- Write about a positive reading experience. What were the conditions that were present that made it positive?
- Write a personal theory statement about your personal philosophy of effective teaching and learning—in general, or of literature in particular. What do you most want for your students? What do they have to know before they leave your classes?
- Given the two teachers' very different purposes described by Zancanella (1998), in thinking about your own purposes for teaching literature, with which of these purposes would you align yourself?

Activity: Observing Literature Instruction

In your practicum or student teaching observations of literature classrooms, do some journaling or notetaking—either in the midst or after classes. Focus on questions such as the following: How is motivation attended to or not and with what effect? What is the quality of relationships between teacher and student, student and student? How are these relationships organized around learning, or not? How are materials and methods employed to assist students? How is sequencing employed, or not? What theory of teaching and learning seems to be dominant? Are there other competing theories at play?

PRACTICES CONSTITUTING A LITERATURE CURRICULUM

What then are the practices that are involved in teaching and learning literature?

Perspective-Taking. One of the central practices involved in learning literature, and one we emphasize in this volume, is the ability to adopt different perspectives of characters, roles in a drama activity, peers, one's audiences, teachers, and larger ideological or institutional perspectives. Adopting different perspectives is a challenge for adolescents who often assume that their perspective is the only perspective, what David Elkind (1998) described as "adolescent egocentricity." They have difficulty recognizing that others may perceive the world differently than themselves. As a result, they assume that everyone's continually watching them as if they were on stage, leading to self-consciousness about appearance and behavior.

Part of perspective-taking involves experimenting with the uses of new social languages and voices (Gee, 1996). For example, in a drama activity, when a student takes on the role of a "mad scientist" based on a science fiction text, he or she is adopting a language of science and fantasy to construct that role. When students employ alternative, hypothetical, "what-if" languages portrayed in fantasy or science fiction literature, they begin to perceive their lived worlds in a new and different light (Blackford, 2004).

By adopting characters' perspectives or roles in a drama activity, students assume the voices of others whose perspectives differ from their own in terms of race, class, gender, age, or historical period. They adopt the perspective of Richie Perry, an African American from New York City, fighting in Vietnam in Walter Dean Myers' (1988) *Fallen Angels*, and reflecting on the first death of one of his platoon members.

> I wrote Mama a letter all about how Jenkins had get killed. Then I tore it up and decided not to tell her about it. It would only get her upset. Instead, I told her more about Peewee. I didn't want to tell her about Jenkins for another reason. I didn't know how I felt about it. In a way I was really sorry for Jenkins, but there was a small voice inside me that kept saying that I was glad that it wasn't me that was killed. I didn't want anybody to see me putting that in a letter. (p. 46)

In adopting Richie's voice, a student is experiencing the perspective of someone who is both sensitive and fearful over being in a very dangerous world far away from his familiar home.

Constructing Social Worlds. In responding to literature, students are constructing text worlds as social worlds. In constructing these worlds, they are defining the roles, norms, beliefs, traditions, and purposes constituting the meaning of characters' actions based on their knowledge of the historical and cultural forces shaping a world (Beach & Myers, 2001). Given the popularity of computer games, such as $Sims^{TM}$, students are accustomed to the notion of participating in alternative virtual worlds and learning what it means to be successful in those worlds based on the rules of the game (Gee, 2003).

To understand characters' actions in Harper Lee's (1988) *To Kill a Mockingbird*, students construct a text world based on an understanding of White–Black relationships in the segregated South, the Civil Rights Movement, the world of the rural small town, and the law. Or, in constructing the world of Jane Austen's (1983) *Pride and Prejudice*, they construct a text world based on knowledge of the class structure and women's roles in early 19th-century England.

In his student teaching, using *The Things They Carried* by Tim O'Brien (1998), Corry Lund describes how he encourage students to perceive their own secure suburban worlds from the perspective of a character who is questioning his world related to coping with the Vietnam War:

> I tried to get them to imagine what it might be like if they had gone through his experience, how they might have been changed their outlook on the world. And we talked about you know, how at the beginning of the book, Ellie is very secure in his beliefs about the world. I mean he looked around at the world. He had a very, very strong faith and belief in God, you know, God was in control and God was good, and towards the end of the book, he starts to question those things and you know I applied it to them, and said, I'm sure that most of you feel the same way, that you know that the world is a place where bad things happen to you. And they're aware that they live in Apple Valley, a very privileged community. They don't have a whole lot of major worries about money or violence or crime, or anything like that, and um, you know, I tried to get them to imagine what it might be like for a 15 year old going through this experience and you know that is what compels him to write this, to write his memoirs.

Students also construct text worlds based on ideas about race, class, gender, and regional or national identity. Tanya begins the year with "frontloading" activities to help her students stake their claims and beliefs about different notions of being American, and different positions around current events:

> I want the kids to put their opinions out there so, first, they can see they have beliefs about the issues that we will study, and second, so we can discuss and debate these now and throughout the year, using the texts we read as a way to converse with characters and authors. At the end of units and the year, we return to these activities to see what's pushed their thinking or rattled their cage, so they can see that literature is part of the grand conversation about how to live and shape our cultural life together.

Explaining Characters' Actions.   Another practice involves explaining characters' actions—formulating reasons or motives having to do with characters' beliefs, traits, and goals, as well as the larger social and cultural meanings of those actions. For example, in responding to *I Know Why the Caged Bird Sings,* students interpret Maya Angelou's (1969) actions as reflecting her development of strong beliefs about race by witnessing her grandmother's challenges to a racist system.

Inferring Symbolic and Thematic Meanings.   Another practice has to do with inferring symbolic meaning—that language, signs, images, gestures, dress, behaviors, actions, and so forth, represent larger meanings. Making these inferences requires students to apply their literary know-how—that they need to go beyond the literal to infer implied meanings that serve some larger purpose. In reading *Hamlet*, they know that the ghosts represent the previous misdeeds committed in Denmark that Hamlet needs to address.

They also learn to infer implied thematic meanings. Interpreting thematic meanings often involves inferring the value assumptions underlying story development. For example, underlying the typical comedy story development in which conflicts and tensions are resolved at the end is the value assumption that institutions can restore themselves (Frye, 1966). Underlying the murder mystery novel is the assumption that crime doesn't pay.

What's important in teaching students to infer implied meanings is that they need to recognize that there are not certain official meanings endorsed by the teacher, but that there can be multiple, alternative implied meanings. In planning her instruction for teaching *To Kill a Mockingbird* (Lee, 1988) in student teaching, Heidi Murphy emphasizes the need for students to generate their own interpretations:

> I introduced an overhead that had all of the themes up and we said, you know, well what evidence do you see of heroism in the novel and what, you know, what might be an example of gender in this novel and how that affects the characters. So I kind of introduced them that way and I throw it up every couple of days and then about the last week that we were working on the novel, I had them choose a passage from the novel that is related to one of the themes they kind of liked or they . . . or that spoke to them in some way to share with the class and discuss how that name related to that passage. And so then, again, you know, when they were involved and they got to choose a passage, then they were able to understand the themes better because they could learn from each other again and they also were in charge of looking for the themes in the book.

Making Connections.   Students are also making text-to-text and text-to-world connections, drawing on their knowledge of other texts as well as their lived-world experiences. Given the basic learning theory of the need to move from the familiar—what students already know—to the unfamiliar, new practices they are learning, you build on familiar practices, tools, and experiences within their current ZPD to help them acquire new practices, tools, and experiences. Prior to or during reading of a text, you provide students with other related texts with similar character types, themes, issues, cultural perspectives, or techniques, asking them to define the similarities and differences between these texts and the current text they are reading. Or, you have them connect the text to specific events or experiences in their own lives, while helping them recognize the differences between their lives and those portrayed in the literature.

One of the challenges you face in making connections is that students may simply not have read much literature or may bring cultural background experiences that differ markedly from those portrayed in the literature. You therefore need to select related texts and experience based on what you know about your students. For example, in her notion of "cultural modeling," Carol Lee (1993) builds on African American students' familiarity with the symbolic meanings of "doing the dozens" to help them infer implied meanings in literature. The teacher of the Southwest literature course builds on his Hispanic and Native American cultural experiences in selecting authors who portray these experiences.

In thinking about unit design, Tanya is continually considering connections with texts and experiences that will benefit her students:

> If I am going to teach in a way that is consistent with my beliefs and theoretical model, I have to teach my kids from their current state of being and understanding. So I have to get a sense, if I don't have it already, about what they know about wealth, and how well they can inference. Most of my students, and our national assessments show this to be true across the country, aren't very good at making inferences, or figuring out an author's generalization, and justifying either of these with facts and details from the text. So it's worth doing, and everybody is going to need help. But some kids will need more help than others, so I have to keep that in mind.
>
> Once I have a sense of where my kids are, I'll consider what initial texts and activities to use to get them started. In sequencing, you want to start with shorter, easier, more visual and accessible texts and move to increasingly longer, harder, less concrete and accessible texts. As Michael Smith says, sequencing should move kids from close to home to far from home. You have to start your journey at home, but you want to travel as far as you can, and I want to provide the support necessary for a successful journey.
>
> I like to start this unit journey with two wonderful children's books. I think using children's books is really important. Everybody can read them, they work well in sequences, they provide concrete, visual experiences that can scaffold conceptual and procedural development, and there are so many wonderful pieces of children's literature.
>
> The books I use are *Henry Hikes to Fitchburg* and *Henry Builds A Cabin*. These are books about Henry David Thoreau by D.B. Johnson. It's great for the kids to learn about Thoreau, and the books require some inferencing and judgment on the part of the readers. In the first book, Thoreau says that hiking to Fitchburg from Concord will take "less time" than the train. What he means is that when you consider the time and human energy you will spend working to earn the train ticket, that it is actually faster and cheaper to just walk there! He challenges a friend to work to earn the money for a train ticket to Fitchburg then to buy the ticket and take the ride. Henry will leave on his hike and they will see who gets there first.
>
> This book asks students to consider the question: what does money cost us? We talk a lot about the time and convenience students might get from owning a car versus the time and energy they spend buying and maintaining it. Is it worth it?
>
> Early in the unit I also like to read a recent YA biography of Dorothea Lange. I think it's important for the kids to know her historically important work with the WPA photographs and Japanese internment photos. This can be applied to our conceptual goals about wealth. But her life is interesting to debate. She basically left her children motherless as she went around

taking photographs. Is it OK that she ignored her family to pursue her dream? What if her work had not been so successful? What if she were a man?

Posing Questions, Problem Solving, Rereading. In his volume on teaching literature, *The Literature Workshop*, Sheridan Blau (2004) argues that much of the literature he considers worth teaching is difficult for beginning literature students: they struggle in the initial readings. Given this difficulty, students need to learn to how to admit to and then grapple with what they do not understand about a text through posing questions based on what puzzles or mystifies them, for example, why does Bartelby in Melville's (1967) story, "Bartelby the Scrivener," just sit there and do nothing? Or, in reading a mystery story, students engage in problem solving to sift through the often contradictory clues, red herrings, and false leads. By defining what they do not understand, they may then reread or revise their initial readings to formulate new interpretations. As Blau notes:

> Experienced readers know that their first vision of a text may be entirely misdirected or so minimal as to appear worthless. . . . But they also know that such a reading is merely a zero draft, a starting place for a series of rereadings that will gradually yield an increasingly more adequate and illuminating sense of a meaning that they are constructing to reconstitute the text in front of them. Inexperienced readers may regard all encounters with difficult texts to be worthless, because they have never progressed beyond the inchoate and apparently pointless zero draft represented by their first reading. Thus, based on their experience, they will declare quite accurately that for them the reading of poetry (or most other challenging texts) is an utterly worthless enterprise. (p. 54)

Blau (2004) notes that as a beginning teacher, he assumed that he needed to give the impression that teachers know everything there is to know about a text. He then devoted hours to preparing to teach the text, the result being that the teacher learns a lot, but the students learn little. Now, he recognizes that his students need to be involved in this process whereby both the students and the teacher admit to and grapple with difficulties in a text:

> In a classroom that cultivates a disposition to uncover and examine problems in learning and understanding, students learn to look more honestly and critically at the state of their own understanding, to make distinctions between what they do and don't understand, and to note qualitative differences in the kinds of understandings they themselves possess. (p. 57)

In this inquiry-based approach, students and teachers formulate and address questions, concerns, dilemmas, wonderings, hypotheses, or hunches about texts, topics, themes, or ideas (Beach & Myers, 2001; Holden & Schmit, 2002). Having a question, concern, issue, or dilemma about which they have no simple, easy answer means that they use their responses or writing to engage in an inquiry investigation. Characters are often caught in dilemmas created when different characters adopt competing dilemmas; for example, when Romeo and Juliet are caught between pleasing their families and continuing their relationship (Mosenthal, 1998).

Central to inquiry instruction is that learning revolves around the students' and teachers' questions that then frame their inquiry about a certain phenomenon. To some degree, inquiry instruction involves adopting a stance of critical interrogation, of challenging status quo beliefs.

In organizing her teaching, Tanya finds students more engaged with challenging questions:

I find it is more interesting to kids to organize the course around an issue or inquiry question. In the case of my American literature courses, we ask the question "What does it mean to be an American?" I tell the students that everything we do will help us to explore variants of this question: what does it mean to us to be Americans? to different people in groups in America or outside America? What are the costs and benefits of American culture and its influence on world culture and politics? The history of American literature contends with all these questions, and there are always popular culture and current events materials that I can use so that kids can see that the big literary questions asked in the past, and the debates on which this country were founded are all alive and kicking. In other words, the kids can see that this course is about us, our culture, and our current concerns. And they are encouraged to bring up their own variants on this question. It considerably enlivens literary study to make it about the kids and their concerns.

And, if students are struggling with a difficult text such as *The Great Gatsby* (1991), Tanya provides them with other texts that contain portrayals of related themes:

If my kids were struggling with the inference strategies, I might use some more YA short stories to help them. But usually they are progressing well. I usually lead the sequence up to a reading of *The Great Gatsby* by watching the video of Fitzgerald's short story "Bernice Bobs Her Hair." In this story, although everyone is wealthy, there are still insiders and outsiders, and the climax of the story changes who is inside and outside. I ask the kids to make inferences and judgments based on the story itself, and the visual cues offered by the video. Then we typically read "Winter Dreams" which I see as a prototype for *The Great Gatsby*. So it's a great intro to the themes and inferencing demands of Gatsby.

Applying Critical Lenses.   Another practice involves critically analyzing texts by applying different critical lenses to texts: semiotic, feminist, Marxist, deconstructionist, postmodern (see Chapter 10). In applying these lenses to critically analyze texts, students are analyzing larger aspects of cultural and institutional themes of power, hierarchy, and control.

This practice reflects a larger critical pedagogy approach that values critical analysis of the beliefs and ideologies portrayed in texts and in institutions shaping their lives (Edelsky, 1999; Fleischer & Schaafsma, 1998; Freire, 1973). In this approach, the teacher's role is to demonstrate ways to not only interrogate beliefs and ideologies associated with institutions portrayed in texts, but to also link that interrogation to addressing and acting on injustices inherent in these institutions. For example, in responding to the novel, *Catherine Called Birdy* (Cushman, 1994), a group of eighth-grade girls in an afterschool discussion group expressed a strong concern about the subordination of the main character, Catherine, who is forced into marriage at an early age (Beach & Myers, 2001). As one student reported in a written log, "they were appalled that girls were told who they must marry. They were also disturbed by the fact that Catherine's father beat her regularly. They were upset by the lack of opportunity for women during this time period." This concern led them to also consider the subordination of women in the contemporary world. Working in pairs, the students investigated issues of single-sex classrooms, women in the military, the Equal Rights Amendment, girls, sports and Title IX, mail-order brides, comparing women in different cultures, historical women, women during war, the media and women, the glass ceiling, and super moms. One group examined the issue of idealized portrayal of body weight in advertising. The students then presented their findings to a group of sixth-grade girls, something that served to change the eighth graders' perspectives on the need to address and change gender attitudes.

TOOLS FOR USE IN LITERATURE LEARNING

How do students acquire these practices? How do you motivate them to want to learn these practices? Let's return to the example of computer games. Many students are motivated to play games, particularly games involving online chat, because they are participating in social communities with other players. In these communities, they are recognized for their skill in learning the tools involved in playing the game successfully (Gee, 2003).

Learning to become community members in a literature class involves learning to employ various practices through the uses of certain tools—language, talk, writing, art work, and digital media—that help students learn the practices involved in interpreting and producing literature. Based on his sociocultural learning theory, Vygotsky (1978) defined tools as language, signs, images, or texts that are used to achieve certain purposes or outcomes of activities. A speaker makes a request in order to garner some information. A writer uses narrative to illustrate a point. A photographer uses an image of poor people to portray poverty. A web designer uses a web page to provide information. The meaning of each of these tools is defined by its purpose or outcome.

As Vygotsky (1978) argued, without a sense of its social purpose, a tool has no meaning. By itself, a hammer has no meaning. It is only when the hammer is used as a tool to pound in nails that it has a meaning. By itself, a fiberglass pole has no meaning. It assumes meaning when it is used to fling a pole-vaulter over a bar (Wertsch, 1998). People learn to use tools as serving various social uses. As Vygotsky argued, learning evolves from social interactions and collaboration which is then internalized as inner dialogue: "every function in cultural development appears twice: first, on the social level, and later on the individual level; first between people, and then inside . . . all the higher functions originate as actual relationships between individuals" (p. 46).

Vygotsky (1978) described the ways in which tools mediate the relations among speakers, writers, and readers and their purposes, objects, or outcomes. By mediate, he meant that a tool serves to connect the speaker or writer to an audience or reader to achieve a larger purpose. As a teacher, your use of "teacher talk" language mediates the relation between your role as teacher and your purpose in facilitating student discussion—your language connects your purpose with your role as teacher.

Without understanding their purpose, tools are meaningless. Simply giving students access to different tools does not mean that they know how to use them in some purposeful way. When Short and Kauffman (2000) gave elementary students a range of different tools to use as part of inquiry projects, they observed that the students often could not perceive their play with these tools as linked to the purpose of their inquiry projects:

> Students' play often seemed purposeless. They did not connect their play with sign systems to either personal or class inquiries—it was just a time to "mess" around. . . . The heart of the issue appeared to be that they didn't know *why* they were being given time to play with these sign systems—the play was not connected to the curriculum or their lives. (p. 12)

We discuss purposes for using various tools throughout the volume. Drama tools (Chapter 4) engage students in simulated contexts or situations where they can enact different roles, identities, and perspectives. Talk tools (Chapter 5) involve students in sharing their verbal responses to literature. Writing tools (Chapter 6) involve students in informal and formal writing about a text. And, digital media tools (Chapter 11)—chat rooms, hypermedia productions, and so forth—involve students in both social exchanges and media productions.

USING TOOLS TO FOSTER PRACTICES: TANYA'S USE OF TOOLS TO TEACH *THE GREAT GATSBY*

To illustrate how teachers use different tools to foster practices, we cite Tanya's description of how she uses a range of tools—talk, drama, and writing—to foster interpretation of the novel. As you read her description, think about how she is using different tools to engage students in learning certain practices:

Since Gatsby is a tough text, I not only want to be sure I've assisted the kids through my sequence to a place where they can be successful with it, I also want to carefully microplan my unit. I'll have a good idea by now with where they are and what help they will need, but I have to be responsive and willing to cut out support they don't need, or to provide more support they do need. In other words, plans are never set in stone, especially at the micro-level. You have to be ready to roll with the punches and surf on the crest of the future's breaking wave. It's like being the coach in a basketball game. You have to adjust your strategies to your players and the game situation.

Because I know my kids will need concrete assistance, I plan to use lots of drama and visual activities to assist them with seeing patterns of details and inferencing from these. In Chapter One, I want my students to start inferring and generalizing about characters and settings in ways that are founded on textual details. Four of the five major characters are present, and the difference between East and West Egg is introduced.

To frame all of the drama work we will do, I use a mantle of the expert drama strategy and tell the students that they will be playing the role of detectives at a detective agency. They are to keep dossiers on the major characters of the book, particularly Gatsby. We've been hired by a wealthy and influential client and it's our job to find out who these people really are and what they are up to. We'll have to make a report by the end of the book before Nick reveals Gatsby's story late in the novel. I have them get together several times during our reading to compare notes, and we do lots of drama work throughout to help them see evidence and make inferences about these details.

For example, to help my students out with during the first chapter, I use a drama technique known as hotseating. Drama techniques are a perfect fit with my theoretical orientation because they are participatory, transactional, active, developmentally appropriate, and can help move the kids from concrete details to abstract inferences and judgments.

Students are divided into groups and each group is responsible for filling out a hotseat sheet that asks them to list and then infer from details about their assigned character's clothing, physical description, demeanor, spoken exchanges, what others say about them, etc. They then must list interview questions they would like to ask the other characters who will be hotseated.

Each group chooses a student to sit in the hotseat as that character. The other group members can act as alter egos (an inner voice that reveals what the character is really thinking, should they have a reason to withhold or twist information) or as the character's brain or lifeline (providing assistance to answer particular questions). When done, the groups write up a dossier statement about the characters of the "suspects."

Another thing I do in Chapter One is to ask the students to visualize and draw the two houses, i.e. Tom and Daisy's and Gatsby's. Visualization is essential to good reading, and sometimes my students don't know what details to use to visualize, or they skip over the description. Visualizing also makes you slow down and consider the importance of details.

Typically, I'll read aloud and ask them to sketch out the two homes. Then we compare our drawings to each others and ask what details we attended to or not. We can then amend our sketches. We then compare the sketches of Tom and Daisy's house to that of Gatsby and ask how the sketches are tied to textual details, and what is revealed by the houses themselves and by comparing them. So this helps us to read the description carefully, identify essential details, how we determined details were important, and how to make inferences based on these. If my students need continued help, I might also have them sketch out the Valley of Ashes, or the

Eyes of T. J. Eckleburg in much the same manner. Visualization is all about deciding what's important, inferring significance, and creating a literary world that we can participate in.

I also assist students to visualize and infer by showing some short movie clips, like of the shirt scene when Gatsby shows Daisy all his shirts. I might start by asking kids how they would stage this scene, and maybe even doing some short moving tableaux. Then we watch the scene and critique it.

Symbolism is important too, and many of the events and objects and settings we visualize in Gatsby have symbolic import. So I'll teach the students to read symbolism in the context of our reading and our inquiry about wealth. So that reading symbolism isn't decontextualized, but is embedded in and in service of our current project.

If some kids have trouble, I will work individually or in small groups with them, highlighting important details for them and asking them to make the inferences by seeing connections. I might have some kids reading on their own, some in groups, and some in a group with me, depending how much assistance they need. They are all getting the same procedures, and we are all reading the same text and engaged in the same democratic project, even though different kids are doing different kinds of work and getting different levels of assistance. Though I often have kids reading different texts, I find it is easier to teach procedures and strategies of reading when everyone is reading the same text. Since certain texts demand certain kinds of interpretive operations, texts like Gatsy invite us to learn to visualize, infer, and read symbols in the context of our reading project.

Understanding unreliable narrators is another interpretive move I might want to help students master during this book, and I really like Michael Smith's sequence to teach this.

At the conclusion of our reading, I ask the students to return to our essential questions and the opinionairre. They write an essay using evidence from the book and elsewhere and their own life to address the question of Wealth and Power.

I often download U.S. budget and census data from the internet so we can discuss what our budget says about how the government feels about wealth and wealth production, or what our society values based on the earnings of different professions, or different ethnic groups, say NBA vs. WNBA players. What can we do to change or influence economic problems? What can the government do? What are the costs and benefits of these various actions? What would be necessary to our success? It's interesting to me that you can't consider any of our unit questions without considering them all, and the big question about American Character that runs through them all. In this way, too, every unit becomes a resource for the next unit, because we know things and have staked opinions that can be used as resources for understanding. And we also use our home resources and our own experience to engage, so the message is that these texts are about you and me and the world we live in. My kids often write about whether Gatsby was a romantic or a stalker, what were the rewards and costs of his or other people's obsession? What other dreams could he have pursued? How else could he have used his money? And of course we can apply this thinking to our current day.

As a final project, I ask the kids to write movie proposals. Why is Gatsby an important story to tell today and how would they tell it? Who would they cast as movie characters and why? Make a poster promoting the movie, and film an essential scene. I have them present their proposal and this scene to the class, who act as a screening board, to whom they have to justify why they did it this way, and what purpose and work will be done through this version of Gatsby.

TANYA'S LITERATURE INSTRUCTION: ISSUES RELATED TO TEACHING LITERATURE TO ADOLESCENTS

The interview with Tanya introduces several important issues that we pursue throughout this volume.

First, What Must We Know to Teach?

Tanya makes a case for what we might call the *3 Ms*: motivation, methods, materials. She argues that to teach students how to read and write, we need to know their needs and interests. In Chapter 2, we describe the importance of knowing about adolescence in general and your students in particular so that you gear your instruction to meet your students' needs and interests so that they will be engaged with your instruction.

She also draws on a wide range of tools and teaching techniques to assist her students to learn new practices and to engage with the conceptual content of the unit. General knowledge about providing assistance through sequences is complemented by more specific techniques to promote visualization, drama techniques, assistance to notice and interpret symbolism and unreliable narrators. All of her tools and techniques are contextualized to assist in the pursuit of the unit inquiry and the comprehension of Gatsby as part of this inquiry. Each tool and technique is chosen in very wide-awake and strategic ways to "do work," that is, to assist students to learn something that they need to know, both now and in the future.

She also draws on her knowledge of materials—young adult literature, popular culture texts, films and film adaptations of literature, other texts by Fitzgerald, and so forth, in creating her unit.

Second: How Do I Know What I Know and How Do I Get Them To Go With The Flow?

As we discuss in more detail in Chapter 3 on planning, you need to consider the order and structure for what you teach. Tanya's thinking about how to plan her unit also introduces the ideas of macroplanning and microplanning and macroscaffolding and microscaffolding, which can usefully serve as templates for planning instruction. She starts with organizing units around unit themes and problem orientations; she then considers how to use various teaching interventions to assist students text by text and activity by activity to learn procedures of reading and thinking that they do not yet know.

In her Gatsby unit, she organizes her instruction around an initial problem statement related to students' understanding of certain conceptual, affective, and procedural goals. She then is frontloading the unit with activities designed to motivate them and to apply their prior knowledge and experience. She is selecting other literary and popular culture texts related to the novel. She is continually intervening with various tools to help students acquire certain practices. And, all of this leads up to a culminating project in which students demonstrate what they have learned.

Third: How Do I Know What They Have Learned?

As we discuss in Chapter 13 on evaluating and assessing students, teachers are also continually determining what students understand and don't understand, who is ready to move on and who needs more help, what is working and not working, and what kind of interventions they might try next. Teachers use assessment to document student learning and make it visible to all their various stakeholders, from the student himself or herself to parents, school board members, and citizens in the community, in ways that show learning in actual accomplishment. And, teachers are continually reflecting on and revising their instruction based on what they learn from successes and shortcomings. They learn from students how to teach students.

All of this requires moving beyond just thinking about your own performance in the classroom—how I will teach to them—to attending to students' learning—how they are learning with me and what they are teaching you.

Action Research and Portfolio Addition:
Studying Teachers' Methods Versus Your Own Methods

As part of your practicum or student teaching observation, observe several different teachers, and, if possible, talk to them about what they believe is important in teaching literature. Then, create a portfolio entry in which you identify the model(s) that best characterizes the different teachers' approaches. Describe how these teachers' adherence to a particular model shapes their instruction—the practices they emphasize, the techniques they employ, the tools they use, the texts they select, and the way they organize or sequence their curriculum. Then, reflect on how or why your own instruction would be similar to or different from these teachers—if you had to emulate any one of these teachers, which one would you emulate and why?

Online Additional Activities, Links, and Further Reading

Go to the textbook Web site, Chapter 1, for additional activities, links, and further reading.

2

Understanding Students' Individual
Differences: Who Are My Students?

America created the teenager in its own image—brash, unfinished, ebullient, idealistic,
crude, energetic, innocent, greedy, changing in all sorts of unsettling ways. A messy, some-
times loutish character who is nonetheless capable of performing heroically when neces-
sary, the teenager embodies endless potential not yet hobbled by the defeats and compro-
mises of life. The American teenager is the noble savage in blue jeans, the future in your
face.

—Hine (2000, p. 10)

Chapter Overview

- The students we teach: Adolescents then and now.
- Getting past the "reading sucks" syndrome.
- Engaging kids and avoiding the censors.

CASE NARRATIVE: READING THE READING LIVES OF TEENAGERS

At the beginning of each day, Allen strides slowly into the noise and chaos of his middle school classroom and takes his usual seat in a large overstuffed armchair in a remote corner of the room. An unusually tall blonde boy, Allen rarely engages with other students at the beginning of class, preferring instead to survey the room with a mix of what looks like amusement and contempt. While the other students push and shove their way to desks, throw backpacks on the floor, and yell "hellos" and insults to each other, Allen quietly hides his face in a book. Only when his teacher asks the students to move into small groups does he slouch over to one of the tables. As he sits down, Bruce shouts, "I don't want to sit with him!" Allen shoots a sharp rebuff, and there is a moment of strained silence as their classmates shift nervously in their seats. The teacher intervenes, telling both boys that insults are not allowed in her classroom.

After separating them, she gets out her grade book and makes notes as students choose whether they will be attending a teacher-sponsored literature circle or working independently on various literacy projects. Today, Allen is not required to attend the literature circle (he hasn't used up his two "passes" yet), so he stakes out his territory in the big stuffed chair, pulls a book off the shelf, and zones out for the remainder of class.

As Allen's teacher, what would you make of this scenario? Is Allen shy or antisocial? Is he a "typical" adolescent or a ticking time bomb? Is he an avid reader or a social outcast? Should you keep an eye on him, protect him, attempt to bring him out of his silence, suggest a book he might like, or leave him alone, hoping that adolescence will some day give way to adulthood and he will grow out of whatever may be troubling him? He is, perhaps, the quintessential model of what Thomas Hine (2000) calls "the noble savage in blue jeans, the future in your face" (p. 24).

As a literature teacher, perhaps the first thing you might notice about Allen is the book that continually covers his face as he settles into the big stuffed chair. The cover changes, but the posture and the preference for solitary reading rarely does. After a few weeks and a bit of worry over his antisocial behavior, you may decide to make a connection with him, leaning over the chair and whispering something like, "Gee, Allen, you always seem to be reading. What kind of books do you like?" His answer may surprise you: "I hate reading. I just do it to get out of doing stuff in here." Failing to hide the depths of your disappointment, you hold your breath, waiting for the two words you just know will come next: "Reading sucks!"

Allen is just one of the several thousand teenagers you will encounter in a lifetime of teaching, and you can bet he won't be the last to say those all-too-familiar words. As you might imagine, you'll barely scratch the surface of your questions about Allen just about the time he is ready to leave your classroom at the end of the school year. One thing is sure, however: you can't wait until he grows up before you teach him to read critically and passionately, to love reading and do it for a lifetime. You have only this short time, and you'd better make the most of it.

Allen and kids like him are a constant reminder of how hard it is to read the reading lives of adolescents. In describing our century-long vacillation between fascination and confusion with the adolescents, Thomas Hine (2000) remarks as follows:

> Our beliefs about teenagers are deeply contradictory. They should be free to be themselves. They need many years of training and study. They know more about the future than adults do. They know hardly anything at all. They ought to know the value of a dollar. They should be protected from the world of work. They are frail, vulnerable creatures. They are children. They are sex fiends. They are the death of culture. They are the hope of us all. (p. 11)

These contradictions all play a part in how adults treat teenagers, and eventually, how adolescents learn to see themselves. As you'll soon discover if you haven't already, getting teenagers like Allen past the "reading sucks syndrome" involves far more than simply putting good books in front of him and hoping they'll work their magic. Before we consider strategies for motivating kids like Allen, we need to understand a bit more about this perplexing period called adolescence. This chapter will begin with current and historical conceptions of adolescence as a unique developmental period, before examining the many ways that teachers can create literature curricula with adolescents in mind.

UNDER CONSTRUCTION: DEVELOPING IDENTITIES
IN ADOLESCENCE

Like everyone, adolescents carry contradictory beliefs about themselves, continually asking "Who am I?" Much of learning to be an adolescent involves learning to be somebody. Looking back at your own adolescence, you can remember what a difference it made if your peers thought you were "cool" or "uncool," "geeky," an "Aberzombie," or a "metrosexual." At the same time, your adolescent students can appear to be strangely oblivious about how their words and actions affect others in the classroom, the shopping mall, or their home. They struggle with where they belong in the social order of school and community. At various points in the day, they might adopt stances as "jocks," "goths," "punks," "rappers," or "drama queens," only to lose these postures in the company of parents and other adults. They carry catalogues and trading cards in their purses and backpacks, read magazines, and belong to online chat groups; these activities each have distinct "discourses" that function as "identity kits" (Gee, 1996) to mark them as belonging (or not) to particular groups. For most contemporary adolescents, these "discourses" encompass everything from the way they speak to the clothing they wear and the content of their MP3 playlists. There are, figuratively speaking, many verbal and nonverbal "languages" in the world of adolescence, and teenagers must constantly code-switch from among these different discourses to develop not one, but a host of identities, in the midst of an ever-changing array of social situations.

What Do We Mean by "the Self"?   For decades, we have believed that adolescents are basically egocentric, developmentally doomed to a concern with themselves above all others. As English teachers, we have tried to build on this intense concern with self through literature units such as "The Individual and Society" or "Who Am I?" We assign coming-of-age books like *Vision Quest* (Davis, 2002), *Annie John* (Kincaid, 1997), or *When I Was Puerto Rican* (Santiago, 1994), and hope our students will "find themselves" in a Louden, an Annie, or an Esmerelda. We ask our students read *The Diary of Anne Frank* (Frank, 1948/1989) and hope that they'll speculate about whether they would have had the courage to shelter the Frank family as Miep Gies did or if there are parallels to the Holocaust in today's world. We ask them what it means for a character like Holden Caufield in *The Catcher in the Rye* (Salinger, 1991) to resist the conformist demands of the depersonalizing and shallow elements of society, only to end up in a mental hospital, or for Jerry in *The Chocolate War* (Cormier, 1986) to stand up for his convictions, only to be emotionally and physically abused in the end. We invite them, through literature and other language activities, to define their own sense of self and to resist the false fronts that seem to accompany their teenage years and sometimes get them into trouble.

But what do we really mean by "the Self"? It's a question that postmodern scholars have been asking as they challenge the notion of a stable, essential identity. Cultural anthropologists, for example, tell us that identity is not a singular, unchanging construct, but is continually constituted through social and cultural practices in different contexts. As Kenneth Gergen (1991) argues, identity is "an emergent by-product of persons in relations, each drawing upon his or her conversational resources (i.e., his or her networks of relationships) as the moment unfolds" (p. 149). In other words, an adolescent girl who gets an A on her math quiz may feel secure in her identity as "a good student," only to feel like a complete nerd 2 hours later as she trips over her feet in the cafeteria. The voices that surround her are not always harmonious. Her parents think she is the most beautiful girl in the world, whereas in her opinion, her braces and gawky frame mark her as a "dweeb," a "nerd," definitely nobody's party date.

CREATING CURRICULA FOR ADOLESCENTS:
BALANCING SAFETY AND CHALLENGE

Our literature units on "Self Versus Society," "Overcoming Adversity," or "Coming of Age" operate out of a comfortable fiction: the notion that true selves can be found, that positions within (or against) society can be firmly staked out, and that there are magical, irrefutable moments when we know beyond a doubt that we have "arrived" at adulthood. No wonder our students mistrust our definitions of what it means to grow up. Or perhaps they don't mistrust them enough, because our particular experiences are never the same as theirs, and we can never gain complete access to their worlds.

Deborah Britzman (1998) has argued that *The Diary of Anne Frank* (Frank, 1948/1989) is often presented in classrooms as a story of an individual's triumph over the forces of evil in society. However true this characterization of the volume may be, focusing on this theme skirts dangerously close to ignoring its aftermath: the fact that Anne, her mother, and sister died of neglect and disease in a Nazi concentration camp just shortly before they would have been liberated in the Armistice.

As teachers, we are always negotiating the fine line between protecting adolescents and equipping them for life's sober realities—between helping them to "grow up" and avoiding a cookie-cutter mentality that penalizes those who don't or won't grow up in White, middle-class ways. Do we really mean it when we urge them to pit themselves "against society" and become their "true selves"? Are kids like Allen free to be their "true selves" in your classroom, when those "selves" resist your every effort to make them avid readers and productive citizens? And while we're asking questions about the self, we might also ask questions about what it means to "grow up" or "come of age" in today's society.

FOREVER YOUNG: COMING OF AGE
IN CONTEMPORARY SOCIETY

Most of us are probably aware that *adolescence* is a relatively new concept in the scheme of things. Near the dawn of the 20th century, Granville Stanley Hall (1904) wrote the volume that attempted to "scientifically" classify every biological and psychological facet of adolescence from the raging of hormones to the potential for mental disturbance. Perhaps because of its massive size and its focus on minutiae, this now-famous book languished in libraries for several years before being resurrected by some to become a sort of last word on the care and control of those disturbing teenagers. A long-time admirer of the prewar German Youth Movement, Hall based much of his volume on the notion that adolescents should be mentally and physically stimulated by activities that divert them from their more animalistic tendencies. Hence, the birth of "civilizing" organizations such as the boy scouts and the juvenile justice system as an antidote to the immense and dangerous energies of America's youth.

One glance at our popular media reveals that many of Hall's ideas about adolescence are still alive today. Although his work has been largely discredited by contemporary psychologists, American society still tends to vilify its youth. We set up a kind of "we–they" dichotomy between adults and adolescents. We cringe when we run into them in shopping malls or in the streets. This "we–they thinking" not only objectifies youth, but can create a sort of undeclared war in the classroom. Titles and headlines in popular newspapers and magazines echo and contribute to this vilification: "Who Are These People, Anyway?"

(1998), and "The Age of Innocence Isn't What It Once Was" (1999). Annette Fuentes (1998) writes as follows:

> In the past two decades, our collective attitude toward children and youth has undergone a profound change that's reflected in the educational and criminal justice systems as well as in our daily discourse. "Zero tolerance" is the mantra in public schools and juvenile courts, and what it really means is that to be young is to be suspect. Latino and black youth have borne the brunt of this growing criminalization of youth. But the trend has spilled over racial and ethnic boundaries—even class boundaries, to a degree. Youth, with all its innocence and vulnerability, is losing ground in a society that exploits both. . . . Adults aren't merely puzzled by young people; they're terrified of them. (p. 25)

According to Fuentes, current public sentiment seems based on ideals of containment and confinement, where juveniles can be tried as adults in the court system but not treated as adults in the court of public opinion. In such an atmosphere, it becomes difficult to know where to begin helping students to "grow up" or "come of age" through literature. Yet, fictions about what this means are often perpetrated by much published literature and popular media for adolescents, and too many teenagers, like Allen, are aware of these fictions. Take, for example, MTV's new reality series for teens, "Laguna Beach." The Web site description begins as follows: "It's one of the wealthiest beach communities in the world and MTV has unlimited access to the tight-knit power clique of eight rich, beautiful teens who live there. Their lives intertwine in ways you won't believe, until you drop in . . ." (accessed from http://www.mtv.com/onair/dyn/laguna_beach/series.jhtml). A jump to the "episodes" page reveals some disturbing messages to teens about what it takes to be accepted in the world of Laguna Beach. The description of episode 101, "A Black and White Affair," begins as follows:

> Their senior year is winding down and the kids from Laguna Beach are just getting started for their summer of fun . . . and drama. Lo, LC, Morgan and Christina are the most popular senior girls in school. The four get together one gorgeous afternoon to discuss how they can begin their last summer together. They decide on a fashion-themed formal at the luxurious Surf and Sand Hotel and they call it "A Black and White Affair." Now it's time to figure out who should be on their guest list, and of course, who should not. (accessed from http://www.mtv.com/onair/dyn/laguna_beach/episode.jhtml?episodeID=79288)

The description of a later episode, entitled "Eighteen Candles," begins as follows:

> It's just days before Spring Break and Christina and Morgan are planning to vacation in New York City. Before Christina leaves, her mom surprises her with a birthday gift: an audition with a Broadway casting director. . . . Afterwards, Christina and Morgan arrive in New York City. The girls check into their hotel and admire their view of Times Square. Later that night at a diner, Morgan asks Christina, "What if you do get the part—are you going to move out here?" (accessed from http://www.mtv.com/onair/dyn/laguna_beach/episode.jhtml?episodeID=79292)

It's disturbing that any teenager with access to MTV can gain electronic, if not material access to this hyper-sexualized world of privilege and shallow self-indulgence. As literature teachers, we can try to counter these unrealistic images with texts that invite students to reflect on the role of cultural and social expectations and what it means to "come of age" in contemporary society. But where to begin? There are literally thousands of classic and current coming-of-age novels, stories, films, other texts. To begin a list here would be a book-length task (although there are some good suggestions in the volume's Web site under Chapter 2. You will also find additional links in the generic categories at the top of the Web site). Most books marketed to adolescents have some sort of coming of age theme implicit in the larger plot. Writers of adolescent or young adult fiction typically present the struggle to grow up as a universally defining characteristic of adolescence, one that resonates with all readers. Yet, the very phrase "coming of age," especially when applied to an entire genre of texts for and about young adults, is fraught with contradictions between what seems to happen in books and what students like Allen know happens in their "lived worlds." It is simply not as easy to grow up as the books make it seem.

To much of society, adolescents are in a perpetual state of "becoming." Nancy Lesko (2000) calls this an "ideology of emergence" (p. 3) where adolescents are viewed as biologically and emotionally inferior to adults, in a state of "coming into" themselves, yet paradoxically, never arriving, at least not during the period we call the teenage years. These seemingly contradictory beliefs about adolescents are further complicated by a host of social and political factors. For example, Lesko (2000) argues that we need to "consider how race and gender are intricately woven into the norms for and into the concept of developmental stage, or maturity" (p. 12).

From a psychological view, David Elkind (1979) argues that there are currently few societal markers against which adolescents can measure their growth:

> There is little or no place for adolescents in American society today—not in our homes, not in our schools, and not in society at large. We have, in effect, all but eliminated this age period as a distinct stage in the life cycle. . . . The larger society offers few places for young people to "hang out" and socialize with their peers. In contemporary society, therefore, we effectively ignore the unique needs of the age group who are no longer children, yet who have not yet attained full adulthood. (p. 3)

Mass marketers and advertisers capitalize on the adolescent preoccupation with "self," creating an avalanche of product lines specifically geared to this easily definable segment of the consumer market. Movies, television shows, and books generate a host of related (and highly lucrative) product lines from trading cards, games, and action figures, to iconographic images on T-shirts and backpacks. Ask any group of adolescents (or adults, for that matter) to look at their clothing and belongings for evidence of advertising logos on everything from the jeans they wear to the notebooks they carry. Teenagers are not merely the target of advertisement, they are, quite literally, walking advertisements themselves. Because being "an individual" in adolescence most often means fitting within rigid peer-defined norms about dress, mannerisms, and even reading practices, magazines, for example, are rife with advertisements and content geared to both reflect and create trends that only teen-targeted consumer goods and services can satisfy.

Magazine subscriptions, for example, are only a small fraction of a publication's total revenue; in fact, if everyone subscribed to magazines, they'd go out of business, because subscriptions are far lower than newsstand prices. The real power behind the scenes and between the covers of magazines is the advertiser. What gets chosen as the "hot" wardrobe item or the favorite music video depends on which companies contribute the most to a magazine's advertising revenues.

Thus, a kind of vicious cycle is perpetuated: teens (at least those with discretionary income from afterschool jobs or generous allowances) spend an incredible amount of money to be unique "individuals," but how "uniqueness" and "popularity" play out in terms of what's hot or what's not depends entirely on the advertising budgets of a relatively few multinational corporations.

Although advertisers and mass marketers seem to treat adolescents as a distinct group, our young people lack the social and cultural markers that, in other societies or historical periods, might have helped them to find direction and purpose. Security guards in arcades and shopping malls have no trouble identifying teenagers, but teenagers themselves have few resources for defining themselves within and against a backdrop of a society that simultaneously infantilizes and vilifies them. As teachers, we are caught between wanting to help our students mature into secure and responsible citizens, and realizing that, for students marginalized by race, class, ability, or culture, definitions of "maturity" are fluid, slippery, and sometimes dangerous. This makes issues of book selection and curriculum planning complicated and tricky, to say the least.

LESSON PLANNING: THE MULTIPLE MEANINGS OF "GROWING UP"

Karen, a ninth-grade teacher, begins a unit on "coming of age" by showing the film *Whale Rider* (Caro, 2004). After comparing Pai's experience with their own experiences growing up in their family, community, and neighborhood, students join one of four small book clubs that meet on Mondays and Fridays. Because hers is a suburban school with limited racial and cultural diversity, Karen tries to select books that portray coming of age in different cultural contexts. This year, for example, the reading-club books are *Beka Lamb* (Edgell, 1986), *The Curious Incident of the Dog in the Night-Time* (Haddon, 2004), *Kaffir Boy* (Mathabane, 1998), and *Girl Interrupted* (Kaysen, 1993).

Because the books are relatively short, students typically finish them in 3 weeks, reading outside of class during days when Karen is sponsoring other activities. During each phase of their reading, book clubs have different tasks. In their first couple of meetings, students are asked to simply jot down reactions during or after their reading, then boil their reactions down to five or more questions, ranging from questions of fact (e.g., What is autism?) to questions of value (e.g., Should Susannah Kaysen have been institutionalized?) to questions tied to their own curiosity or confusion (e.g., Why don't American kids have the freedom to roam around town that Beka seems to have? How did Mark Mathabane's early school experiences influence the person he became?). Students write their questions on five or more index cards, shuffle the pile, then discuss them informally.

Somewhere near the middle of their reading, groups are asked to generate some questions about the culture, historical period, or social issues portrayed in their novel, then conduct a miniresearch project on their questions. Group members make short presentations about their findings and discuss how "coming of age" in their book differs from or is similar to coming of age in their social worlds. After the novels are finished, groups make a presentation to the whole class about the theme of "coming of age" as it relates to the protagonist and setting of the novel. Presentations must include references to the text and information from their outside research as well as a visual and verbal component. Students can create PowerPoint™ slide shows, write and perform original scripts, engage in panel discussions, or use other forms of presentation.

These are just a few of the ways that teachers can help students like Allen get past the "reading sucks syndrome." Yet, even when we set up book clubs or opportunities for independent reading, we are often the final arbiter of what our students read, and rightly so. As such, we should be ever mindful of the overlap between our textual tastes and those of our students.

WHAT TEENS READ: WHAT TEACHERS TEACH

Where kids like Allen are concerned, our job often has little to do with choosing books and designing lesson plans. We shuttle among many roles with kids like Allen: disciplinarian, confidante, mentor, task master, colearner, and hopefully, fellow reader. One thing is true, however: we cannot begin with our agendas and goals; we must begin with Allen—who he is and how he defines himself as a literate person (or not). Each day we must connect with kids like Allen, as well as those who are not so obviously on our radar screens. Whether students marginalize themselves or are shunted to the margins for other reasons, we must seek them out in spare moments, in the hallways or at the classroom door. Sometimes a passing comment ("Hey Allen, are you *really* a Dolphins' fan?" or "Wow, Emily, I noticed those drawings in your journal. Can you help me with the bulletin board?") can be an invitation to shy, resistant, or reluctant students to join the classroom circle. Enticing Allen to move from a "reading sucks" posture to a "reading rules!" (or, at least, a "reading's not so bad") position often begins with humor or sometimes a bit of blatant bribery: "Okay, Allen, if you find (and read) one book you enjoy this marking period, I'll buy you a Powerade from the teacher's lounge." It helps to get yourself out from behind your desk and position yourself as a coreader and colearner: "Emily, I noticed you were reading *Speak* (Anderson, 1999). I haven't read it. Should I?" Where reading is concerned, if you want to lead a horse to water, you have to seek out the horse wherever it may be hiding.

For a reality check, it's often a good idea to ask teenagers at informal social gatherings what they're reading at the moment. When Susan asked a friend's middle school daughter about her reading preferences at dinner one evening, the girl replied, "We never read the Newberys. Teachers love 'em, but they're wicked boring to kids!" Sad but true, books that fulfill our teaching goals and are safe from the censors are not always so engaging to teenagers. Although Holden Caufield (Salinger, 1991) may have regaled us with his wry cynicism and shocking vocabulary, he'd probably bore most contemporary teenagers to tears. A glance at the "young adult" sections of most libraries and bookstores are little help either. Most often "young adult" books are more appropriate for early adolescents than for high school students, who prefer to read books written for adults (which, unfortunately, often have passages that might be objectionable to parents and other school personnel). Even the advice of our professional journals and books is not always helpful. For example, in her study of adolescent girls, Blackford (2004) discovered that, contrary to popular professional wisdom, young girls don't always gravitate toward books with strong female characters. Moreover, they often bring expectations from modern fantasy and gothic novels to reading of more classic texts like *The Scarlet Letter* (Hawthorne, 2004), and are distressed when the book violates those conventions by revealing Hester Prynne's paramour early in the book.

Visiting teen-sponsored Web sites or "Listmania" book lists created by teenagers on Web sites like Amazon.com is sometimes a good way to identify texts that reluctant adolescent readers will read. Although we might be justifiably suspicious of how these book lists get created (How does a teen's list make it on the Amazon Web site? Are all the books appropriate for our particular students?), they can be a great starting place for creating our own summer or vacation reading lists. Not surprisingly, these teen-created lists often include a healthy mix of classic and contemporary books, from *Alice in Wonderland* (Carroll, 1971) to more contemporary titles like the *Sisterhood of the Traveling Pants* (Brashares, 2003), *Angus, Thongs and Full-Frontal Snogging: Confessions of Georgia Nicolson* (Rennison, 2001), and *The Virgin Suicides* (Eugenides, 1994).

The recent popularity of books, movies, characters, and television shows, such as *The Lord of the Rings*, *Harry Potter*, "Buffy the Vampire Slayer," and "Quantum Leap," speak volumes about teenagers' voracious appetite for fantasy, gothic, and science fiction books. Novels by J. K. Rowling and Philip Pullman fly off bookstore and library shelves as soon as a new book in the series rolls off the presses. It's noteworthy that six of the ten books chosen by teens in the 2004 survey sponsored by The Young Adult Library Services Association (YALSA), a division of the American Library Association, were science fiction or fantasy (see the Web site for YALSA links).

Publishing trends and opinion polls such as these tell us a couple of important things. One is that young people today, as they did in past decades, often enjoy escaping from the mundane and frightening world of "real life" into the reassuring peril of science fiction and fantasy. Another is that series books are as popular today as Nancy Drew and The Babysitter's Club were once upon a time in the dim recesses of our youth. It's okay if our students get stuck on Rowling's Harry Potter books or Melinda Metz's "Roswell High" series. They'll probably forget the books themselves, but they won't lose the feeling of getting hooked into a world of stories and familiar characters that adult lifetime readers often experience. Teens responding to the "Teen Week Read" survey in 2004 listed their top 10 books read "for fun" the previous year; not one of their titles on the following list is typically taught in schools (see http://www.smartgirl.org/reports/2734196.html):

10. *Chicken Soup for the Teenage Soul*
 9. *All American Girl*
 8. *Hatchet*
 7. *Cat in the Hat*
 6. *Alice Series*
 5. *Sisterhood of the Traveling Pants*
 4. *Princess Diaries* and *A Child Called "It"*
 3. *The Lord of the Rings*
 2. *Holes*
 1. The *Harry Potter* series

It should be mentioned that middle-grades children from the ages of 12 to 14 constituted the largest group to respond to the "Teen Reads" survey. In an earlier survey of high school students, Wilder and Teasley (1999) discovered only 5 of the 20 most popular books chosen by their adolescent respondents that are commonly taught in schools. These were *Of Mice and Men* (Steinbeck, 1993), *Night* (Wiesel, 1982), *Things Fall Apart* (Achebe, 1996), *To Kill a Mockingbird* (Lee, 1988), and *The Lord of the Flies* (Golding, 1959). It's noteworthy that the remaining 15 books are probably more similar to the choices made by adult pleasure readers than by classroom teachers, and only a few authors (Angelou, Hinton, Lowry) are typically taught in schools. Wilder and Teasley also noted that, much like adult pleasure readers, "Apparently, once some students identify an author they like, they go on a 'binge,' reading lots of books and then finding it hard to choose a favorite among them" (p. 44).

Although none of these surveys claims to be representative of all adolescents, it is interesting to view Wilder and Teasley's list against "the best young adult novels of all time" list, compiled from a survey of 78 adults, including English teachers, authors of young adult literature, college professors, librarians, and publishers, conducted by Ted Hipple and Jennifer L. Claiborne (2005).

Although some authors such as Paulsen, Lowry, Sachar, Hinton, Myers, and Angelou make it on the lists of both adolescents and adults, the contrast between adolescent and adult preferences is rather striking. It would appear that the books chosen by adults might

TABLE 2.1
High School Students' and Adults' Favorite Literature Titles

High School Student Favorites (Wilder & Teasley, 1999)	Adult Favorites (Hipple & Claiborne, 2005)
1. Andrews, V. C., *Flowers in the Attic*	1. Cormier, *The Chocolate War*
2. Angelou, Maya, *I Know Why the Caged Bird Sings*	2. Lois Lowry, *The Giver*
	3. Laurie Halse Anderson, *Speak*
3. Grant, Cynthia D., *The White Horse*	4. S. E. Hinton, *The Outsiders*
4. Grisham, John, *The Firm*	5. Gary Paulsen, *Hatchet*
Hinton, S. E., *The Outsiders*	6. Louis Sachar, *Holes*
5. Jackson, Sheneska, *Caught Up in the Rapture*	7. Walter Dean Myers, *Monster*
6. King, Stephen, *The Shining*	8. Chris Crutcher, *Staying Fat for Sarah Byrnes*
7. Lowry, Lois, *The Giver*	9. Virginia Euwer Wolff, *Make Lemonade*
8. McMillan, Terry, *Disappearing Acts*	10. Karen Hesse, *Out of the Dust*
McMillan, Terry, *Waiting to Exhale*	11. Paul Zindel, *The Pigman*
9. Myers, Walter Dean, *Hoops*	12. Walter Dean Myers, *Fallen Angels*
10. Patterson, James, *Kiss the Girls*	13. Francesca Lia Block, *Weetzie Bat*
11. Sapphire, *Push*	14. Chris Crutcher, *Chinese Handcuffs*
12. Sinclair, April, *Coffee Will Make You Black*	15. Christopher Paul Curtis, *The Watsons Go to Birmingham—1963*
	16. J. D. Salinger, *The Catcher in the Rye*
	17. Robert Cormier, *I Am the Cheese*
	18. Jerry Spinelli, *Stargirl*
	19. Robert Cormier, *After the First Death*
	20. Nancy Garden, *Annie on My Mind*
	21. Chris Crutcher, *Ironman*
	22. Mildred D. Taylor, *Roll of Thunder, Hear My Cry*

lack relevance to the lives of contemporary teenagers much as *Silas Marner* (Eliot, 1981) did in years past. We might wonder if, perhaps, there is now a "canon" of young adult titles lying around in school book rooms or teachers' bookshelves from the last time they took a course in adolescent literature. Although many of us may have fond memories of reading Salinger, Cormier, and Taylor, the works included in the titles listed by Hipple and Claiborne may seem incredibly dated, and in some cases, juvenile to present-day adolescents. There are also recent titles that might better fulfill our curricular objectives than those on this list. For example, there are now books about gay teens that don't end with negative consequences (the firing of two favorite gay teachers in Annie Garden's classic early novel); M. E. Kerr's *Deliver Us From Evie* (1995) and almost any book by Sandra Scoppetone come to mind immediately. And although adult readers may enjoy the multi-genred texture of Walter Dean Myers' (1999) *Monster* or the nuanced California patois of Francesca Lia Block's (1999) *Weetzie Bat*, many students may have trouble making their way through Myers' shifting genres, Weetzie's breezy slang, or Block's tangled prose. Finally, it's sobering to realize that, even after years of attempts to include a multicultural mix of authors and protagonists in the literature classroom, only 4 titles (and three authors) of the 23 on Hipple and Claiborne's list—roughly one fifth of the total number of texts—were authored by people of color.

Of course, relevance isn't all. There are surely times when you need to push adolescents past John Grisham and Terry McMillan to classic and contemporary classic literature that they might not seek out on their own. When choosing from among our personal favorites, however, it would be good to remember the lessons we can learn from adolescents themselves. Here are just a few.

- Notice how many science fiction, fantasy, and gothic novels make it on the lists of teenage, as opposed to adult favorites.
- Series books, from the *Babysitter's Club* to *Harry Potter*, have not lost their universal appeal, although these are not mentioned by adults.
- Think about how important it feels to read books intended for adults, perhaps borrowed from a parent on a vacation or recommended by an admired adult role model. Grisham and McMillan may even be on our secret list of "beach books."
- Whether we like it or not, adolescents, and a great many adult pleasure readers, are plot driven (Hunt & Vipond, 1992). Clever twists of phrasing and literary devices are less important than suspense and fast-paced action for a good many adolescent readers. Although we may see Karen Hesse's *Out of the Dust* (1999) as a terrific chance to combine our love of poetry with an interdisciplinary unit on the Great Depression, our students may not find it as gripping as, say, Hesse's *Stowaway* (2004), about the voyage of Captain James Cook, or *Phoenix Rising* (1995), about the consequences of a nuclear meltdown.

This does not mean holding popularity contests where text selection is concerned, but it's good to remain humble when choosing books for adolescents. As adults, we are always mentally "role playing" our students in terms of what they might profit from and enjoy; sadly, we're probably wrong more often than we are right in even our most educated guesses. It's important to balance whole class reading with opportunities for independent or "free choice" reading, book clubs, and other activities that more closely mirror the reading practices of lifetime pleasure readers.

HOOKING KIDS ON PRINT: DEVELOPING SELECTION CRITERIA

Regardless of the many forms of text available to contemporary adolescents, we believe firmly that print literature can be taught in ways that are anything but passé. There are, in fact, many reasons why teachers should not give students total license where book selection is concerned. You might begin by exploring your (perhaps unspoken) criteria for choosing books and other print materials. In fact, try developing these criteria with the help of your students. A good place to start might be with a set of criteria developed by teenagers themselves. In 2001, six pilot groups of teens met to brainstorm the criteria by which books could be selected for the "Teens' Top Ten Books" survey sponsored by the American Library Association (see the Web site for the Teens' Top Ten: http://www.ala.org/ala/yalsa/teenreading/teenstopten/teenstopten.htm).

1. Appeal and Involvement—Books should have a "lasting and universal" appeal, an attractive cover, and high degree of personal, emotional involvement.
2. Literary Quality—Books should be substantive and not "fluffy." They should offer unique perspectives and ways of thinking.
3. Characters—Characters should be old enough to understand the problems and concerns of teenagers. They should be realistic, compelling, and distinctive.
4. Content and Style—The subject matter should be relevant to teenagers, with good descriptions, vivid imagery, and an appropriate (not condescending) tone.
5. Plot—The plot should have a good blend of action and description with a satisfying (not necessarily happy) ending.

6. Genres—The final list should contain many different genres on topics that appeal to a variety of teen readers.

BEYOND WORDS: ENLARGING TEXTUAL CHOICES

Visual print literature has undergone a sort of shape shifting, as graphic novels such as *Elfquest* (Pini & Pini, 2003) and *Maus* (Spiegelman, 1993) have replaced the comic books that were popular among teenagers and children several decades ago. It's not unusual to see teens reading graphic novels, or trading playing cards, based on Japanese anime movies. Electronic fiction and nonfiction is also rivaling print literature as e-books become more available and popular. Production companies such as the Pixar division of Disney have further fueled adolescents' interest in animation and graphic narrative. A visit to the many Web sites devoted to anime and Japanese manga (see the Web site) reveals an array of popular manga, ranging from "classic" series such as *Mai, the Psychic Girl* by Goseki Kojima (1996) and *Lone Wolf and Cub* by Kazuya Kudo (2000) to the more recent *Dragonball* series by Akira Toriyama (2000). The following is noted by blog critic Bill Sherman:

> [O]ne of the *big duh* stories in the comics industry over the last year has been the growing popularity of Japanese manga in the U.S. marketplace. Where mainstream American comics companies have been limping along with readerships that are but a fraction of what they used to be, the manga audience just seems to keep growing bigger and bigger, fueled in part by anime and toy tie-ins, but also by the fact that Japanese publishing companies seem to have a much broader view of audience age- and interest-range than the superhero-stuck Yanks. Go into any chain bookstore, head for the Graphic Novels section, and you'll probably find at least half of the offerings are Japanese—or a bastardized imitation like Marvel's *Mangaverse* series. . . . Picked up the first three issues [*Shonen Jump*] at my local Kroger's. Prior to its appearance, the only comics titles that have appeared in the grocery store's magazine racks in last few years have been *Mad* and Archie Comics digests. I can see why smaller pamphlet comics are generally less appealing to a larger store (too easy to swipe; too quick an in-store read; too difficult to keep track of). *Shonen Jump* is phone book size, and two of the three issues I've bought were sealed in plastic to discourage kids from taking the freebie cards inside. Much easier to manage, I bet. (accessed from http://blogcritics.org/archives/2003/03/04/125927.php on 10/12/2004)

In light of the myriad of texts available to contemporary teenagers, we might well wonder how traditional print literature can compete. This is a legitimate concern—one echoed by the American Library Association in its 2000 report of an online survey conducted by SmartGirl and the ALA, that found that "[o]f the 3,072 young men and women surveyed (ages 11–18), nearly half (43 percent) said they enjoyed reading for fun, but did not have time to do so" (SmartGirl & the American Library Association, 2001, p. 6). In 1999, the president of YALSA, Mary Arnold, reported the following:

> With all the things they are doing—sports, clubs, after-school jobs and more—today's teens are strapped for time and find it hard to set aside the time to read. . . . We want to help change that. As librarians, we are trying to find creative ways to help teens find the time to read the books and magazines they want to read. We also welcome parents' and teachers' assistance in this effort. (accessed from http://www.smartgirl.org/speakout/archives/trw1999/trwsummary.html)

MAKING ROOM FOR READING

Let's face it. Whether in the form of comics, graphic novels, or even electronic texts, reading is a zero sum game. Lankshear and Knobel (2002) have argued that the greatest demands of the millennium are not so much on our ability to access information, but the attention we must selectively devote to an avalanche of textual material from sources ranging from the Internet to television, to a burgeoning print industry. Part of getting a piece of their attention involves creating a space where reading practices go beyond the mundane and resemble the out-of-school literacies that a good many adults enjoy.

Angela, a veteran middle school teacher, has created such an atmosphere. She describes her classroom as a cross between Barnes & Noble and a train station. Students come and go at the sound of a bell every 80 min; there is constant noise and chaos in the halls and outside on the playground. Yet for those 80 min, her students can find a space where reading is supported, privileged, and made more enticing by the ready availability of books, music, and comfortable furniture. Beyond these physical accouterments (however enticing they may be to students), there is a sense that reading is something to be shared, books are to be recommended, trips to the library are as exciting (well almost) as a trip to the Gap or Forever 21. Maren shouts to her cousin Ebony, "Oh, you just gotta read that one! I read it last month! It's great!" (this, in response to Ebony's protests that *Jubilee* (Walker, 1999) is almost 800 pages long). Jake (shy in English class, but a regular visitor to the principal's office for his offenses) sidles over to his teacher's desk and asks to be helped in selecting a book for independent reading. Elizabeth already has her book—a copy of *The Lovely Bones* (Sebold, 2002), purchased (and approved in advance) by her mom at Borders. Willie asked for a library pass, and Robert has persuaded Angela to let him read a complicated gaming manual as part of the "nonfiction" reading requirement that every student must fulfill at least once each marking period.

As a way of creating excitement for reading, Frank, an urban high school teacher, asks his students to do periodic author studies on favorite books, locating critical reviews (preferably by other teenagers), author biographies, and interviews. In addition to author studies, Frank's students periodically do syntheses of critical reviews, write critical essays, and design their own web pages focused on favorite authors and books.

CHALLENGING THE OBVIOUS: CRITIQUING THE WORLD AND THE WORD

Many of us correctly believe that reading choices should embrace a variety of critical perspectives and enlarge students' understanding of issues such as race, class, and gender. We work hard to choose authors and protagonists representative of a broad array of cultural and ethnic perspectives; but there's a danger of construing this to mean a kind of Noah's ark philosophy of literature selection (two books each to represent every race, culture, ethnicity, and so on). In fact, no one text can (or should) speak for a broader representation of culture. In a sense, we are all "multicultural," and this goes for authors and protagonists as well as readers. There is a common tradition in secondary schools, however, where one or two texts are expected to bear the burden of cultural representation. When *Roll of Thunder, Hear My Cry* (Taylor, 1991) or *To Kill a Mockingbird* (Lee, 1988) are chosen as "the" texts by and about African Americans in a curriculum, or when Langston Hughes becomes the sole spokesperson for the Harlem Renaissance, the result is not a broader representation, but a kind of misrepresentation of the diversity, nuance, and variety of cultural, racial, ethnic, and other influences represented in our literature choices. Similarly, if we wish to connect classic literature with our students' popular culture, we must be careful not to let our own assumptions carry the day. Kids can be just as tuned out to hip hop as they can be to *Silas Marner* (Eliot, 1981).

Reading Teen Culture.   Cari Sue's experience as a student teacher in a suburban classroom demonstrates just how one adolescent's view of popular culture can be alien or passé to another. In her attempt to connect *Romeo and Juliet* with popular music, she encounters some unexpected resistance. She writes the following in her teaching journal:

> At first glance, the class was homogeneous but as I looked closer I realized that there were the cliques of students that seem standard to the high school experience: "the preps," "the nerds," "the 'bad boys,' " "the goths." I realized that I didn't notice these groups until the students expressed opposition. . . . The first time I noticed tension was when Suzanne [my teaching partner] did her lesson on the balcony scene in *Romeo and Juliet*. . . . I noticed when Suzanne played the "Hero" song, one group of female students were enthusiastic and sang along with the music. These students, lead by one female in particular, are usually outspoken in class and could be identified as class leaders (whether positively or negatively). They look and act like typical, white middle class girls we see on mainstream television—giggly, concerned with clothes and "cute boys," they are very much entrenched in the extracurricular culture of school, though they do participate in class. . . . Their behavior contrasted sharply with another group of students led by one female in particular. This group is not as "mainstream" as the first: they wear baggy jeans and skater style clothing; they decorate their bags with buttons and stickers for hard-rock bands. These students participate in class but are more erratic turning in assignments.
>
> When the first group started singing with the music, one usually outspoken female from the second group said something like, "This is disgusting" and expressed hatred for Enrique Iglesias. She also directed animosity toward the singing students, asking them to stop singing in a sarcastic tone. . . . In a following lesson the students shared projects in which they made a popular culture connection to *Romeo and Juliet*. The student who was resistant to the "Hero" song had the opportunity to share a hard rock song that she connected to the play. Although the student may have felt "excluded" during the "Hero" activity, she still knew that her experience, opinions and feelings were valued because she had space to share "her" music.

If she had more time in her short student teaching placement, Cari Sue might have asked her adolescent students to critique their notions of popular culture in particular, and "popularity" in general as it relates to adolescent culture. Books like Edward Bloor's (2001) *Tangerine* provide opportunities for adolescents to figuratively "see" through the blind eyes of Paul, the story's protagonist, questioning larger issues such as racism and class consciousness. Just as it's important to choose books with complicated visions of what it means to be Black or female or American, it's also important to undercut some of the myths about adolescents presented earlier in this chapter—to enable adolescents, through their reading, to come to terms with their complicated lives and cultures.

Cliques are a painful reality for adolescents, and they're portrayed in a number of novels and stories. The literature classroom can provide an opportunity for bringing social conflicts such as those Cari Sue experienced to the fore. You might start by showing excerpts from a popular movie satire about teenagers such as *Mean Girls* (Michaels & Waters, 2004) or *Ten Things I Hate About You* (Lazar & Junger, 2004). From a discussion of stereotypes about teens portrayed in the opening scenes of these movies, you could introduce a book like *Speak*, by Laurie Halse Anderson (1999), in which Melinda, the main character, sarcastically discusses the various cliques in Merriweather High School. As students are encountering these texts, they could explore topics such as the portrayal of teens in popular movies and television shows, the existence of cliques in contemporary society, the role of athletics and extracurricular activities such as cheerleading in determining social status, and many other aspects of teenage life.

Race and Representation. Regardless of how homogeneous a classroom may look, there's no such thing as a "monocultural" classroom. Just as each person is a special amalgam of many cultures, each classroom represents far more than what appears in a quick glance at the faces and clothing in the typical classroom. Mandi, a preservice teacher in a city school, soon comes to know this in a powerful way. Although the school in which she teaches is racially diverse, her advanced placement class fails to reflect this diversity. She writes the following in her teaching journal:

> When I first met the class I would be teaching, an advanced English block of sophomores, I wondered how race issues would play out in the classroom, as all but [one of] 13 students [in this particular classroom] were white. The other student was Mexican-American. I was especially interested in teaching our multicultural unit, as many of the cultures we read about were absent from the classroom.
>
> After reading Alice Walker's "Everyday Use," . . . [o]ne girl wanted to know "why black people always complained about how hard they have it, when white people in today's society had nothing to do with slavery. It was our ancestors." Another girl wanted to know "why we have to read about other cultures anyway?" She said that she shouldn't be "made" to read about any culture except ones that SHE found interesting.
>
> With the previous comment, came many nods and voices of agreement. At this point, the girl who began the conversation said, "How come we can't read about white people? We never just get to read about people like us." I was kind of shocked, as most high school curricula are composed of "dead, white authors." Not only was I surprised, but I was confused. Why did it seem that these white students felt so threatened by having to read something from another culture that was not their own?
>
> While I was pondering my self-posed questions, the girl continued to speak, and made a very honest point. "I am saying these things, because I CAN. If there were black students in here, I wouldn't be able to say them. In a way, I felt sorry that in a school where approximately half the population is black, there wasn't one single black student to join in the conversation. It would have been interesting to see how the conversation would have played out, had there been a different make up of students.

Mandi's questions should ring true for most of us who have ever tried to introduce literature by people of color in a primarily White classroom. Like Mandi, we should be more than a little alarmed at her student's apt observation that there are no kids of color in an advanced placement class where White students constitute only half the school population. Sadly, the silent tracking system of "advanced placement" classes often intensifies the isolation of racial and ethnic minority students, even within "diverse" schools like this one.

At the same time, we must realize that words like *minority*, *diversity*, and even labels like *Black* and *White* are slippery when it comes to understanding students and choosing "multicultural" literature. In Katelyn's city classroom, for example, the lines between race, class, and culture are often blurred. She observes the following:

> I have come to really dislike the term, "minority" after this placement because it has a connotation that does not reflect reality. Students who are African American, Native American, Puerto Rican, Spanish etc. are not the minority everywhere and that is true at Tubman High . . .
> I think that these placements are providing me with something that I have been craving: realis-

tic diversity. . . . Some of the white kids dress more 'gangster' and some dress and act 'preppy,' still, this works both ways. Some of the black students dress preppy and some dress gangster. Yet, they "call each other out" on things. For example, one of the white boys was dancing, and he had no rhythm. One of the black girls said "you dance like a white boy" and that was completely normal for her to say. The students realize there are cultural differences, but they all get along and know whom they are. I commend their upfront yet casual recognition of differences because despite the multiplicity in the class, there is respect among the students. . . . I may be really idealized in my thinking, but I feel that generations below us are unconsciously (possibly consciously as well) slowly tearing down the racial walls that our society has constructed. Also, going into city schools after being exposed to only the white middle class schools, I can not help but observe how well students work together and how little race matters in the class room at Tubman. . . . Do not think I am claiming that race is not an issue in America, I am just playing around with some of the things I have been observing.

As English teachers, we find ourselves on the horns of a dilemma: On the one hand, as Cornell West (1997) argues, "race matters" always and everywhere for students of color; on the other hand, racial generalizations about anyone or any body of literature are always inaccurate and partial. We can't conclude that all Black kids will enjoy reading Alice Walker or all Chicano kids will be drawn to Gary Soto. This is about as silly as assuming that all White kids will like Shakespeare. Yet, we bear a responsibility to students who have traditionally been left out of the classroom canon. Students like those in Mandi's advanced placement class chafe at the prospect of reading texts outside their cultural comfort zone, yet fail to realize what it would be like to go through most of their formal schooling seldom seeing themselves in the mirror, as their classmates of color have done on a daily basis. Students like Mandi's need to be enticed out of their monocultural mindset just as those in Katelyn's class deserve to been seen for more than their race.

You might begin by asking students to consider how race, culture, and ethnicity are treated across several texts and time periods. A delicate consideration of novels like Twain's (1981) *The Adventures of Huckleberry Finn* and Wright's (1998) *Black Boy*, Morrison's (2000) *The Bluest Eye*, and a more contemporary novel like James McBride's (1997) the *Color of Water*, can be an occasion to consider whether racism is still alive in contemporary society or whether Mandi's observation about the younger generation being less concerned about race is actually true. A critical reading of Sherman Alexie's (1994) *The Lone Ranger and Tonto Fistfight in Heaven* alongside the film *Smoke Signals* (Estes & Eyre, 1999) can lead to a consideration of how Alexie uses the character of Thomas Builds the Fire as a sort of trickster figure, portraying stereotypic images as a subtle and wry critique of larger social stereotypes. Comparing these texts with traditional trickster legends and stories would broaden students' understandings of irony and satire as well as teach them about the clever nuances of oral texts from many time periods and cultures.

Challenging the Canon. You might ask students to analyze how book lists get created or examine the literature selections in textbooks and anthologies, noticing what proportion of selections are by authors of various races and whether works by women and authors of color are typically shorter than those authored by White men. In his critique of the Modern Library's list of the 100 best English-language novels of the 20th century, Kevin Dettmar (1998) discusses many possible reasons why James Joyce's (1993) *Ulysses* was named number 1, including the fact that Christopher Cerf, chair of the Modern Library's advisory board, is closely connected with Random House, the company that publishes both Joyce's novel and the Modern Library series. Students could explore what literary works typically appear on such lists, as well as library shelves and bookstore displays, discussing questions such as "What is classic literature?" "What political issues influence the canon?" "How and why are books chosen or censored by school systems?" and a host of equally provocative questions.

Broadening Definitions of Difference.   Often, race gets presented in popular discourse as the primary marker of difference in society. There are many other areas of difference that can be addressed by literature teachers. Presenting texts with family structures that challenge the stereotypic two-parent household would be one important consideration. Books like *Jacob Have I Loved* (Paterson, 1990), *The Notebooks of Melanin Sun* (Woodson, 2003), and *Weetzie Bat* (Block, 1999) allow students to consider how American culture has changed to reflect widely divergent views of what it means to have (and be) a family.

Gender, History, and Culture.   There are many opportunities to pair classic and contemporary texts such as Hawthorne's (2004) *The Scarlet Letter* and Halse Anderson's (1999) *Speak*, for example, in terms of how women then and now are made to bear the brunt of guilt for violating social norms. Students might also consider gender roles through books like *Wifey* by Judy Blume (1989) and *Awakening* by Kate Chopin (1982), with dramatic literature such as *Hedda Gabler* by Ibsen (1990). Definitions of growing up or coming of age are also complicated by gender expectations. Male coming-of-age stories such as Baldwin's (1985) *Go Tell It on the Mountain*, McCourt's (1999) *Angela's Ashes: A Memoir*, and Mathabane's (1998) *Kaffir Boy: The True Story of a Black Youth's Coming of Age in Apartheid South Africa* might be compared for their portrayals of what it means to "grow into manhood." Along similar lines, students could compare female coming-of-age novels such as Alvarez's (1991) *How the Garcia Girls Lost Their Accents*, Dillard's (1988) *An American Childhood*, Gibbons' (1997) *Ellen Foster*, and Lorde's (1983) *Zami: A New Spelling of My Name*, in terms of their portrayals of female coming of age.

Reading for the Real World.   There are a great many opportunities to connect nonfiction (primary source documents and personal accounts) with fiction to engender a deeper understanding of historical events such as the Holocaust. Pairing a classic text such as *The Diary of Anne Frank* (Frank, 1989) with a memoir such as *Anne Frank Remembered* by Miep Gies (1988) and the movie *Anne Frank: The Whole Story* (Kappes & Dornhelm, 2003) would be a good way to portray this event from different perspectives. Connecting these texts to the plethora of information on current atrocities and genocides around the globe could bring immediacy to the topic of injustice in present-day society. Historic events such as the Japanese internment could be studied through movies like *Snow Falling on Cedars* (Gutterson, 1998), books like *When the Emperor Was Divine, a Novel* (Otsuka, 2003), stories like "After the War" (Wakatsuki Houston, 1990), and primary source books like *Through Innocent Eyes*, a collection of writings and art by young people in the Poston Internment Camp (Tajiri, 1989).

Engaging students in critical reading practices such as these is more than a motivational strategy. It is true that, with a relative abundance of leisure time and discretionary income when compared with teens at the turn of the century before "adolescence" was created, today's adolescents need to feel as if they "count" in American society. In a world that may seem altogether treacherous and frightening, it's easy to dismiss adolescents as useless at best and dangerous at worst. All the more reason to remember our responsibility for making them not only more literate individuals but critically informed and productive citizens of our future world. They are, after all, in Thomas Hine's (2000) words, "the hope of us all" (p. 11).

Action Research: Studying Students' Reading Interests and Preferences

In working with students, it is useful to determine their reading interests and preferences so that you can provide them with books they would want to read based on these interests and preferences for particular genres, authors, topics, or themes (Finders & Hynds, 2003). One of the limitations of determining interests and preferences with a reading-interests inventory based on lists of genres, topics, or themes is that it may only provide you with very general information. An alternative is to interview individual students about texts they enjoy reading, reasons for their enjoyment, and possible other kinds of texts they may want to read if they could.

For an action-research project, interview some students about their interests and preferences, and reasons for their interests and preferences. Analyze the differences in their reasons in terms of differences in students' reading ability, previous reading experiences, attitude toward reading, knowledge of alternative literary genres, access to books, influence of peers or teachers, or interest in certain topics or themes. Then, draw some implications for books you could provide these students based on your findings and reasons particular students may enjoy these books.

Online Additional Activities, Links, and Further Reading

Go to the textbook Web site, Chapter 2, and the generic link, Young Adult Literature, for additional activities, links, and further reading.

3

Planning and Organizing Literature Instruction: How Do I Decide What to Teach?

"Would you tell me, please, which way I ought to go from here?"
"That depends a good deal on where you want to get to," said the Cat.
"I don't much care where—" said Alice.
"Then it doesn't matter which way you go," said the Cat.
"—so long as I get somewhere," Alice added as an explanation.
"Oh, you're sure to do that," said the Cat, "if you only walk long enough."
—Carroll (1971, p. 60)

Chapter Overview

- Defining goals.
- Different ways of organizing the literature curriculum.
- The planning model (questions for planning instruction).
- Devising units and a sample unit.

In this chapter, we describe some of the basic aspects for planning literature instruction. We start at the overall curriculum level of your basic goals for teaching literature and then focus on your course or unit objectives and then on objectives for specific, daily activities to demonstrate that your larger purposes and goals shape your more specific objectives.

Good literature teaching is purposeful and the result of careful planning. It doesn't simply just happen, although we like to believe in the magical and mysterious nature of teaching. Although teaching is both an art and craft, both that art and that craft need to be directed to the learning goals you have for your students. Before you begin to plan your lessons, it's important to think through what you want to accomplish with your students through teaching literature. Therefore, our planning chapter begins with our goals for teaching literature.

GOALS

Clear goals and purpose are central to good teaching. It is important for you to explore your reasons for teaching literature and be mindful of those reasons. But outlining goals abstractly is one thing; consider what can really happen in the context of the classroom in the following case narrative:

CASE NARRATIVE: WHEN GOALS COLLIDE

Janet never felt like a reader herself when she was a teenager. She was provided few reading choices and always felt insecure about getting "the right interpretation" of whatever text the class was studying. She was a star lacrosse player in high school, and that took up most of her free time, so there was little left over for pleasure reading. It wasn't until college that Janet encountered a professor who made literature come alive and inspired her to become an English teacher herself. As a new teacher she wants to give her 11th-grade students the love of reading that she never had as a teenager. Her university methods courses provided a plethora of ideas for teaching literature to adolescents—from literature circles and workshop approaches, to opportunities for independent reading and an array of texts that appeal to a range of adolescents. She designed the classroom to accommodate an approach to literature teaching designed to promote engagement and enjoyment, with comfortable furniture, tables for small group work, and bookshelves filled with paperbacks for students' independent reading. Unfortunately, all of her 11th-grade students must also take the statewide reading test at the end of the year. The test consists of short reading passages followed by multiple-choice items. Recently, when the reading test scores fell across the state, a group of parents publicly humiliated a teacher in her building for not teaching to the test.

As a relatively new teacher, Janet is terrified of this kind of parental censure; yet she realizes that reading encompasses far more than the narrow range of skills required by high-stakes tests. Furthermore, there are several students in her city classroom who lack the motivation for coming to school at all, much less the motivation for reading. Some of her more academically successful students, on the other hand, would be bored by the kind of basic instruction that her nonreaders desperately need. How does she reach all students in her diverse classroom, inspire a love of reading, and still equip all students with the necessary skills for passing those standardized tests?

In Janet's case, she must address the urgent needs of her students, many of whom are self-proclaimed "nonreaders" as she was in high school. She must provide engaging experiences for her more avid readers, all the while attending to the mandates of her district and state department of education. She juggles among these goals daily, knowing full well that for many of her students, just sitting down to read a book is a significant accomplishment that no amount of test preparation can promote.

In the following section, we offer some ways of organizing a literature classroom that allow us to pursue our myriad and sometimes contradictory goals.

WAYS OF ORGANIZING A LITERATURE CLASSROOM

The goals you choose for teaching literature reflects your beliefs as to what you value in learning literature and how you plan to organize your literature curriculum. If you value having students know about authors, literary periods, and key texts, you may organize your curriculum around a chronological survey format similar to that found in literature text-books. If you value students engaging in sharing critical analysis of texts, you may organize your curriculum around providing critical lenses and opportunity to formulate critical analyses in class.

To formulate goals, you need to be aware of a variety of ways to organize the literature curriculum. Today, we seem to have more opportunities to choose which method of organization best suits our instructional context. Later we summarize some of the primary methods of organizing texts.

As we can see, each method of organizing texts has its own instructional advantages and disadvantages. We encourage you to play with a variety of these approaches instead of marching lockstep through a yearlong course of study that is organized in a single way. The method of organization you choose should be a principled and intentional choice that affects your goals. If you want to expose your students to great works of literature, the chronological, author study and genre approach might be the best way to accomplish that goal. If you want to have great discussions about timeless themes or topical issues, a more thematic or topical approach would be more appropriate. Of course, many of these goals overlap, which is why you will probably find yourself synthesizing a variety of approaches as you plan your instruction.

CASE NARRATIVE: MOLLY'S THINKING ABOUT GOALS FOR HER LITERATURE INSTRUCTION

This kind of rich thinking about goals is what Molly, a veteran teacher in a suburban school, must do each year of her teaching. Although we often want to believe that teaching becomes automatic over time, Molly knows that each year she must begin anew, considering the vast array of needs, experiences, and abilities in her classroom. Molly has been teaching a long time, over 20 years. You'd think she had her lesson plans in the bag—or at least safely ensconced in a file folder somewhere. She's taught nearly every major novel one could think of and has an encyclopedic list of student-tested and approved short stories. Yet when Molly asks herself "how do I decide what to teach?" her answer is always, "it depends entirely on who my students are."

For example, Molly is currently preparing to teach a class called "Enriched American Literature." One might think that certain aspects of planning what to teach are simply predetermined by the kind of class it is—Molly knows she'll use American literature. She also is invited to assume something about the students' ability levels because the class is labeled enriched. But let's hear what Molly has to say as she begins to think through her planning:

This Enriched American Literature class is composed of twenty-two students ages sixteen and seventeen. In our high school, students enroll in "enriched" classes by student and parent selection. Approximately twenty-five per cent of the junior class selects "enriched" English. In this particular class there are eighteen girls and four boys, reflecting the common imbalance between males and females in high-level English classes in our school, and nation-wide. I keep this in mind as I am selecting texts and activities and navigating class discussions, but it is an uphill battle. There are three students of color; English is not the first language of one student. All students expect to go on to college and see themselves as capable and committed students. They are not cynical or disenchanted or discouraged. One of the less typical students is an extremely intelligent boy who is disorganized, preoccupied with his computer interests, and has turned in little work assigned outside of class first quarter. He's become interested in the books we've been reading, and actually began completing work. He was so surprised at his success it has expanded his involvement in class discussions. The more difficult and abstract the work becomes, the more engaged he is. Two students don't participate in discussions unless invited. Even their parents agree they are capable introverts who contribute when asked; I make sure each of them says something every day of discussion.

The class is beginning to jell after the usual mixing up of classes at semester time. They like each other and genuinely want to find out what their classmates think about the topic at hand. They have settled in to the higher expectations of junior year and are motivated to do their best work, partially to satisfy colleges. Students expect interesting and challenging work in this class, and they can be witty and playful in their work.

As you can see, this is a nuanced and knowledgeable appraisal of students. Although Molly's classroom makeup is very different from Janet's, both teachers must consider a variety of factors that we encourage you to keep in mind as well, the size and gender makeup of the class; the cultural, linguistic and ethnic background of students; the student ability level and motivation; and the previous coursework students bring to the class.

Although their classrooms are very different on the surface, there are factors Molly and Janet both must consider. As in Janet's case, some content and skills goals for Molly's course are determined by the district (American literature) and two state standards (Academic Writing and Literary Arts Interpretation). Molly noted the following:

> Within those parameters I include literature from a wide range of time periods, races, classes, genres, perspectives, and themes. Writing, the writing process, and oral communication are integrated into all of the students' work. In addition, my commitment to integrating higher order thinking skills into students' learning is at the center of my planning and instruction. Striving to challenge my students and extend their reading and analytical skills, I include literary theory as one of the tools through which students can comprehend literature, understand their own thinking, and understand their world.

Here Molly acknowledges that teachers usually work within systems of goals and expectations larger than their own. Molly has to consider school and district curricula as well as mandated state standards. (We discuss this in more detail in Chapter 13 on evaluation.) Molly also wants to choose literature that is varied and textured, representing a wide range of student experience. Therefore, although the course is called American Literature, Molly resists relying solely on predictable canonical texts.

In addition to thinking about texts and the context of the curriculum, Molly has another core concern as she asks herself what she should teach. Simply put, she considers what she wants students to learn. But for Molly the answer to that question is not necessarily about the content of the curriculum; rather, it's the intellectual and interpretative practices she wants her students to be able to acquire through literature.

In defining these goals, you need to go beyond simply thinking about possible activities or topics you want to include in a unit or course to defining what students will learn from engaging in these activities or topics. Saying that you want your students "to respond to images in a poem" simply states the nature of your activity. You are not defining the larger purpose for why you are doing that activity. To define your purpose or objective, you need to consider what students will be learning from responding to the images in a poem—that, for example, they are learning to understand that images have symbolic meanings.

Thinking about goals therefore encourages you to articulate what you want students to take away from their experiences in a unit or course. For example, you are planning a ninth-grade unit course on The American Short Story. You ask yourself, what do I want students to learn from this course. You may define your goals in terms of specific interpretive strategies or critical approaches you want students to acquire through the course. For example, in teaching a number of different short stories, you want students to learn to infer character traits, beliefs, agendas, and goals from their actions and dialogue across the different stories. Setting that as one overall learning goal means that you can then define specific activities to help students learn to make these inferences, as well as a final evaluation that determines whether they have actually achieved your goals.

ACCOMMODATING FOR INDIVIDUAL DIFFERENCES IN PLANNING ACTIVITIES

In planning activities for a class, you are considering how to accommodate your activity for the particular group of students with a range of individual differences. It is difficult, of course, in working with a large group of students to accommodate for all individual differences. However, you may still consider ways in which your activity at least attempts to accommodate for as many of the following individual differences as possible.

Reading Ability.   Students range considerably in their reading ability within a class. Knowing something about their reading ability will help you in selecting texts that are either not too difficult or too easy for the majority of your students. In some cases, you may simply assume that students' reading ability will not be a factor and overestimate their ability to interpret relatively difficult texts.

Unfortunately, students are often labeled as reading at a certain "grade level" based on scores on standardized reading tests. One problem with such labels is that students may vary considerably in their reading ability in terms of differences in type or genre of a text, their knowledge about the text's content, their purpose for reading, and the larger context constituting the reading activity.

You can garner some rough sense of students' level of reading ability by providing them with some short stories with engaging content that are written at different levels of difficulty. By asking students some basic comprehension questions, you can then ascertain differences in the degree to which students readily understand a less difficult story—for example, one written for young adults, versus a story that is more difficult.

Student Interests. You also need to build on students' interests in certain leisure time or extracurricular activities—sports, music, films, television programs, computer games and chat, magazines, hobbies, travel, and so forth, as well as particular school subjects— social studies, art, science, math, music, second languages, and so forth, or types of reading interests defined by genre—adventure, science fiction, romance, mystery, fantasy, realistic and problem novels, and so forth. To discern students' interests, you can create interest inventories in which they respond to prompts such as, "my favorite leisure time activities," "what I most enjoy doing after school," "my favorite school subjects," "the types of reading I enjoy the most," and so forth. This will provide you with both a composite sense of the group's shared interests, as well as individual differences in interests.

For students with a strong interest in arts or drama, you can employ mapping, artwork, or drama to engage students' uses of these different intelligences. For example, students with a propensity for visual and spatial intelligences should have the opportunity to create collages, maps, diagrams, or "body biographies" of characters (Smagorinsky & O'Donnell-Allen, 1998). Students with a propensity for bodily-kinesthetic intelligences could engage in drama or tableaux productions portraying their interpretations of texts. In his student teaching, John Awsumb had his students respond to photos as an entrée into the world of *To Kill a Mockingbird* (Lee, 1988):

> I put photos on the overhead of maybe some downtrodden people, and then have them take that photo and try to write their story in their own words, and how they think this person wound up that way. And actually the photo was a very famous one, it's a *Life Magazine* picture of the woman in the Hoover era with the two kids, you know, really depression era. That was kind of scaffolding for *To Kill a Mockingbird*. Kind of give them the depression times.

Using Technology to Accommodate for Individual Needs. You can use technology tools to accommodate for individual differences in student learning by providing additional support for your students or by varying instructional design to accommodate for individual differences in learning (Rose & Meyer, 2002). For example, CAST, the Center for Applied Special Technology, is an organization focusing on the use of technology to address learning diversity that provides teachers with various online tools for accommodating to these differences, particularly differences in reading ability (see the Web site for related links).

THE PLANNING MODEL

In this chapter, we propose a planning model based on a series of questions that you are continually asking yourself as you plan activities using certain teaching techniques based on the metaphor of taking your students on a journey:

- Where am I going?
- Who am I going there with?
- How will I get there?
- How will I show them where to go?
- How will I know I have arrived?

You will not just be posing these questions in a chronological order; these questions are recursive in that you're continually posing them questions of yourself, but not in any set order.

WHERE AM I GOING?: DEFINING LEARNING OBJECTIVES FOR SPECIFIC ACTIVITIES

As with developing objectives for a unit or course, you are also defining learning objectives for each of the specific, daily activities you include in your unit or course designed to address the following question: Where am I going?

District, State, and National Curriculum Standards.   In formulating your unit or course learning objectives, you also need to relate them to local school district, state, or national standards. Many schools' English curriculums are organized around standards derived from district, state, or national standards. Go to the Web site for examples of state literature standards and the National Council of Teachers of English literature standards.

Specificity of Objectives.   It is also important that you formulate your objectives in specific terms so that they will be useful for you in defining specific learning activities. An objective such as "my students will learn to interpret a story" does not provide you with much direction in terms of learning activities. A more specific objective, "my students will learn to identify violations of social norms constituting unusual character behaviors to infer the theme or point of a story," provides more specific direction for planning activities.

Defining Learning Objectives in Terms of Interpretive Strategies and Critical Approaches.   In defining objectives for specific activities, you select a specific interpretive strategy or critical approach you want students to learn. The following are some statements of objectives based on the interpretive strategies and approaches described in this volume.

- Emotions—Students will identify the emotions they experience and reasons for those emotions associated with different characters or text worlds.
- Defining narrative development—Students will define the causal relations between unfolding story events, as well as predict story outcomes based on knowledge of prototypical genre storylines.
- Character actions as social practices—Students will infer characters' social practices based on inferences about patterns in characters' actions.
- Constructing social and cultural worlds—Students will explain or judge characters' actions in terms of the purposes, roles, rules, beliefs, traditions, or history operating in social worlds or cultures.
- Elaborating on connections to other texts—Students will reflect and elaborate on connections between the current text and similar images, characters, story lines, or themes from previous texts.
- Positioning and stances—Students will define how they are being positioned to respond according to certain invited stances and negotiate or resist those stances.
- Voices, language, and discourses—Students will identify characters' uses of different voices and social languages in terms of the discourses and ideological stances operating in the text.

- Applying a Marxist lens—Students will identify characters' practices that reflect power differences related to the class structure operating in the text world.

- Applying an archetypal lens—Students will critically analyze the archetypal use of symbolism, character prototypes, narrative patterns, and themes related to underlying cultural values.

- Applying analysis-of-gender lens—Students will critically analyze the portrayals of characters' social practices and cultural worlds as reflecting ideological assumptions about gender differences.

FIVE TYPES OF TEACHING TECHNIQUES: SELECTING AND SEQUENCING, IMMERSING AND FACILITATING, MODELING, ORIENTING, AND FACILITATING

Once you have formulated objectives, you then need to decide on what teaching techniques will fulfill your learning objectives. We have organized these activities in terms of five types of teaching techniques: selecting and sequencing, immersing and facilitating, modeling and scaffolding, orienting and socializing, and reflecting.

These five types of teaching techniques address our previous questions: (a) Who am I going there with? (b) How will I get there? (c) How will I show them where to go? and (d) How will I know that I have arrived? They are not sequential, but are more recursive in nature—they continually intersect with each other. And, the first four all revolve around reflecting—the fact that you are continually reflecting about teaching for each of these techniques (Yancey, 2004).

Selecting and sequencing addresses the following question: Who am I going there with? This involves choosing those interpretive strategies and critical lens you want to employ that will achieve your goals given the particular group of students you are working with and then selecting tasks or creating contexts involving the uses of discussion, writing, and computer tools that will best help students acquire these strategies and approaches. You also need to take into account the variation within your class in students' ZPDs—the fact that some students will have more difficulty than others given differences in their prior knowledge and experience. This means that you then need to consider some variations in your activities to accommodate for these differences or shoot for some middle ground (Smagorinsky, 2002).

Another essential component for planning literature instruction is to determine those resources that you will have available for use in your teaching. Resources include such things as class sets of books and textbooks, videos, magazines or journals, DVDs, or Web sites that you would use as texts in your units. Before you plan a unit, you need to know whether there are adequate number of books available in the school's book room, as well as what resources are available in the school's media center. For example, you are teaching two short story literature classes with 11th graders, with 30 students in each class. You need to first determine if there is an appropriate short story anthology for that grade level and whether there are 60 copies available for students. If such an anthology is not available, or if there are too few copies, you then need to consider other options.

Selecting Texts Based on Students' Reading Interests and Preferences. In selecting texts, you need to consider a number of factors associated with students' reading interests and preferences. You use this information to select "teachable" books you anticipate will be appealing to students, but that also have high literary quality. You may also be selecting books to recommend to students as part of a free-reading or individualized reading program.

Students also have quite different reading interests that will influence their interest in or response to specific texts. Some students who are avid readers have clearly defined reading interests. Contrary to the popular notion that adolescents "don't read," a national survey conducted by the National Education Association (2001) found that 42% read "primarily for fun and pleasure" and 49% read more than 10 books a year.

There are several different ways to determine students' interests in or preferences for certain types and genres or specific authors or titles. One of the most basic, obvious ways is to ask students about what they enjoy reading, either in terms of genres or texts. You can create surveys to gather this information or talk with them in individualized conferences. You can list optional genres or literary types (romance, mystery, realistic young adult novels, science fiction, adventure, horror, biography, historical fiction, short stories, etc.), or list familiar authors and ask students to check, rank order, or rate based on those that they prefer or enjoy. One problem with eliciting this information is that they are basing their preferences on their actual reading experience, as opposed to hypothetical or potential reading experiences. It may be the case that students might enjoy science fiction, but because they haven't read much science fiction, they have no clear sense of whether they would enjoy science fiction.

One strategy for addressing this issue is to create what are called fictitious annotations that represent different genres. To do so, you make up abstracts of hypothetical story summaries that represent prototypical features of a particular genre. Students can then check off, rank order, or rate these abstracts and not be biased by their own prior reading experiences.

It is also important to recognize that interests change over time given shifts in interest in certain genres or authors reflecting general trends in interests. In a study comparing the same high school students' interests in 1982, 1990, and 1997, Lisa A. Hale and Chris Crowe (2001) found that interests shift over a 15-year period. Mystery and horror books were increasingly popular, popularity related to reading of authors such as Stephen King, Mary Higgins Clark, Michael Crichton, and V. C. Andrews. Romance and love stories declined over the same period, as did science fiction, adventure, true life, humor, and fantasy. However, romance and love stories, as well as mystery, remain most popular among girls, whereas boys prefer adventure, sports science fiction, and humor.

Popular young adult authors include S. E. Hinton, Lloyd Alexander, Piers Anthony, Avi, Rebecca Baldwin, Frank L. Baum, Cynthia Blair, Judy Blume, Terry Brooks, Frances Hodgson Burnett, Ellen Conford, Caroline B. Cooney, Susan Cooper, Robert Cormier, Lois Duncan, Louise Fitzhugh, Fred Gipson, Virginia Hamilton, Carolyn Keene, Norma Klein, Madeleine L' Engle, Ursula Le Guin, C. S. Lewis, Anne McCaffrey, L. M. Montgomery, John Neufeld, Robert C. O'Brien, Christopher Pike, Ellen Raskin, Wilson Rawls, Willo Davis Roberts, Ouida Sebestyen, and Cynthia Voigt. This research points to a gap between required literary genres taught in classrooms and students' preferred genres, as well as the fact that, for younger secondary students, young adult literature is often not taught in schools, particularly at the high school level.

For middle school students, you need to be particularly concerned about the readability level—the degree to which the language, plot development, and sophistication of ideas will be too difficult or complex. On the other hand, you also should not underestimate some students' ability to tackle difficult texts.

Setting Up an Individualized Reading Program.   Based on the information you gather on students' reading interests, you could set up an individualized reading program or what is often referred to as "sustained silent reading" (SSR), in which you devote several weeks or 1 day a week to having students simply read self-selected texts. A central goal of such a program is to foster a positive attitude toward reading through allowing students to choose their own texts to read and to gain satisfaction from that reading. The very fact that students make their own choices provides some incentive for them to read a text, as opposed to assigned texts. This does not mean that they necessarily need to complete the text—they also need to learn to reject texts that they may not enjoy and choose another text.

In setting up your program, you need to provide students with a lot of optional choices of texts. It is important to help them learn how to make selections based on their prior reading experiences and defined interests. However, finding texts consistent with students' own interests can often be a challenge. Making choices about literature, as opposed to nonfiction, is often difficult, because readers may not have a clear idea as to whether they would enjoy a particular text.

To introduce books to students or to engage them in topics, you or the media specialist can do book talks in which you briefly summarize or abstract the story line of the book, along with some particular aspect of the book that would make it appealing.

It is also important that you have a lot of current paperback books available in the classroom or in the media center. Establishing a close, working relationship with staff in the media center is critical because they can assist you in making books available. You can often purchase these books at local warehouse discount outlets or ask students or parents to loan you books. And, you should provide choices from a wide range of different genres in addition to novels, including short stories (particularly for less-able readers), biographies, autobiographies, magazines, and poetry.

To help them make these choices, you can talk with students individually about their prior reading experiences or favorite authors. You then help them clarify their own interests by narrowing down or eliminating genres or authors they do not enjoy to consider those genres or authors they do enjoy. Students can enter in information into Web sites that serve to link their interests with particular texts. Rather than recommending or advising them to select a particular text, it is preferable for you to have them consider some optional texts based on your own suggestions. By providing students with a lot of options, they are learning how to make their own choices based on some emerging sense of their particular interests and preferences.

The primary focus of an individualized reading program is simply to provide students with time to read during class. Students could read similar texts and share responses to those texts in small groups. You can ask students to share their evaluations or recommendations of texts with each other. Students could post brief reviews and ratings on 3 × 5 cards or on class Web pages. They could also nominate certain books, authors, characters, or illustrators for class book awards, to be juried by a group of students.

You can evaluate students' reading by having them report on the number of pages or books they have completed, as well as journal responses to their books. However, the primary focus of the evaluation should be on the amount of reading, as opposed to their responses.

How Will I Get There?: Selecting Interpretive Strategies and Critical Lenses.   In planning activities, you select those interpretive strategies and critical lenses that will best address your learning objectives based on the particular group of students with which you are working. For example, you may want to help students learn to construct the cultural world of the 1920s in America as portrayed in *The Great Gatsby* (Fitzgerald, 1991). To do so, you may first want to unpack your own interpretation of the world of the novel by reflecting on your own processes of constructing that world—an instance of how reflecting intersects with selecting and sequencing. You may reflect on how you use other, related interpretive strategies—inferring patterns in characters' practices or defining intertextual connections which suggest that certain cultural norms are operating in the world of the novel—the fact that there are differences between the world of the old, inherited wealth of Tom and Daisy and the world of the new, recently acquired wealth of Gatsby. You may also note the disparities between the upper middle class and the working-class worlds of Myrtle. And, you may also infer the larger cultural world of the "roaring 20s," a world of economic growth that would eventually lead to the 1928 stock market crash.

In reflecting on your own processes involved in employing this particular interpretive strategy, you may also consider the critical approaches informing your use of these strategies. You may note that in focusing on the class differences in the novel, you are adopting a class-analysis approach that highlights the influence of economic forces on characters. And, in considering your use of certain approaches, you select those strategies that will assist students in applying those approaches.

You then select tasks as well as drama, talk, writing, or computer tools (described in the next chapter) that help students employ those interpretive strategies or critical approaches you've selected. In Chapter 1, Tanya selected drama, and talk tools that helped her students construct a cultural world of *The Great Gatsby* (Fitzgerald, 1991). In formulating your tasks, you would then select those tools that would best assist students in completing these tasks. For example, to help students define patterns, you may select the writing tool of "listing" characters' actions, followed by "mapping" similar patterns in those actions, and then "freewriting" about the meaning of those similarities in terms of how these patterns reflect certain cultural norms. A student may then infer a pattern in Gatsby's practices of consistently displaying his wealth and status, a pattern that reflects his allegiance to the upper class world of new wealth.

In devising tasks, you select talk, writing, or computer tools that are best suited for completing a task. Rather than limit yourself to one tool, you may consider the use of different tools. For example, if students are writing up an investigatory news report about a character, they may first engage in some mock oral interviews with different characters. They may then put their news report on a Web page.

Selecting Discussion Tools. You are also selecting certain specific ways to organize classroom discussions around small groups, literature circles, book clubs, or conversational discussion groups that serve to foster a classroom community (Raphael & McMahon, 1997; see Chapter 5 on discussion tools). Whatever their name, these groups are student-centered, heterogeneous in makeup, and revolve around a literature selection chosen by the students. Several studies have lauded these book-discussion groups for providing an effective and enjoyable learning context for students to talk about literature (Frank, Dixon, & Brandts, 2001).

Paired Reading. Some students work more productively in smaller instructional pairing than in groups. Paired reading encourages students to help each other, and provides excellent opportunities for Vygotskian peer-mediated instruction. Short stories, poems, and short passages from longer works are ideal texts for paired reading. Paired readings are also ideal learning structures for strategic reading lessons such as scaffolded reading experiences, guided reading, and specific comprehension exercises.

Reading Workshop or Independent Reading.   Since the first publication of Nancy Atwell's (1998) *In the Middle*, workshop approaches have been successfully used for both reading and writing. Although the classroom management challenges of such an approach can be significant, there are many benefits as well, especially if the workshops alternate with some structured literature instruction. Reading workshops enable students to read books they are motivated to read and helps them learn the habits of effective independent readers.

Split Group Reading.   Occasionally, one might have two texts related by theme, author, topic, or style and choose to assign each to half the class. This method provides more teacher direction than literature circles or independent reading but also helps create smaller discussion opportunities, especially in a larger class. Teachers might also use a variety of jigsaw discussion techniques and conduct discussions across texts, thus providing opportunities for the kinds of intertextual connections that are often difficult in a single text serial approach to teaching literature.

Whole Class Reading.   For a multitude of reasons, both pragmatic and pedagogical, one class using one text is still the most frequently employed mode of literary instruction. One text is certainly easier to manage for the teacher, but it is particularly important to consider issues of pacing, variety, and providing multiple entry points for students through writing and discussion.

Once you've selected your activities and your talk, writing, or computer tools, you then need to organize the tasks so that each task builds on the next; how, for example, prereading activities lead to activities during reading that lead to postreading activities. In sequencing your tasks, you are continually reflecting on whether students have the background preparation or knowledge necessary for successful completion of that task. This requires you to think in terms of "first things first"—what tasks do students need to complete first to complete subsequent tasks? For example, you could start a classroom with a large-group discussion of a story. However, you may find that many students do not contribute to the discussion or have little to say about the story. Adopting an alternative "first-things-first" approach, you back up and consider those tasks that would better prepare students for a large-group discussion. That might include an initial freewrite about their responses to the story followed by sharing their freewrites with each other in small groups. Through this writing and discussion, students are articulating and extending their responses. Then, when they are in the large-group discussion, they can draw on their writing or discussion, resulting in the greater likelihood that they may contribute to the discussion.

Creating Contexts.   You also need to recognize that you are doing more than simply formulating tasks to achieve your learning objectives. You are also creating contexts or simulated worlds in which students engage with or create texts. These contexts themselves serve to motivate students to participate in activities because they become caught up in the activity itself. For example, in studying the medieval world, students created their own castle museum in which they assumed a variety of different roles associated with mounting and operating such a museum—the roles of historians, archeologists, artists, curators, docents, and so forth (Wilhelm & Edmiston, 1998). This context itself involved the students in actively producing a social world that served to involve them in a display of competence, as well as fostering learning about castles in the medieval world.

IMMERSING AND FACILITATING: HOW WILL I GET THERE?

In immersing and facilitating, you are involving students in activities so that they become engaged in the activities through how you facilitate their participation in the activities. This means that you want to select those activities that are most likely to engage students in some sustained manner. It is often preferable to begin with having students share or recount their experiences as a lead-in to a discussion about a critical approach. If you are doing a unit on gender roles and media, you may begin with having students describe their own experiences with gender-role stereotyping in their own experiences or in the media. By beginning with students' own experiences or interests, you are working in a "bottom-up," inductive way to link their lives to the classroom. You can then provide them with concepts, critical lenses, or frameworks in a more deductive manner that serves to help illuminate those experiences.

Having students produce texts through drama, oral activities, writing, or video and hypermedia production provides them with opportunities to display competence to peers. One study of high school students' engagement in various school activities found that students were most likely to be engaged with things such as art, music, sports, or drama productions in which they could physically display their competence to peers (Csikszentmihalyi & Larson, 1986). In contrast, students reported relatively low levels of engagement in many of their classes, particularly classes in which they had little opportunity for active participation. In participating in these events, students derive a sense of purpose and audience from the need to display competence to their peers or adults, something that contributes to developing their social status and self-worth. For example, students may construct and perform their own skits based on their everyday experiences or on fictional characters. Performing these skits for others gives them the opportunity to display competence. As illustrated by the castle museum project, students become engaged in activities that involve their active involvement in constructing their own versions of texts and social worlds.

In facilitating activities, you are providing directions on how to complete certain tasks. In giving directions, it is important that you state the purpose for doing a certain task based on the interpretive strategies or critical approaches associated with that task. Knowing the purpose for why they are doing something provides students with a road map or sense of direction so that they can determine not only when they have achieved that purpose, but also criteria for self-assessing their performance on a task. For example, in applying a poststructuralist approach, you want students to identify the binary oppositions related to gender (male versus female) and class (upper middle versus working class). To do so, you ask them to list characters' practices associated with these different categories and then reflect on how these practices reflect the influence of binary oppositions in the world of the text—the fact that upper middle class men are perceived as having all of the power, particularly in contrast to working-class women). Therefore, in giving students the directions for listing and reflecting, you provide them with a purpose—that they are making this list so that they can determine how binary, either-or categories influence characters' practices.

You need to provide students with an overview of what they are expected to produce—the outcome or product. Knowing that, for example, they need to create a poetry anthology along with articulated reasons for including each poem as the final product in a poetry unit shapes students' attention as they move through the unit.

In formulating your expectations, you are returning to your larger goals for an activity or unit. Providing students with a clear statement of what you want your students to learn from participating in an activity or unit helps them understand the value of an activity or unit. For example, in introducing the poetry unit involving creation of a poetry anthology, you may tell students that you hope they learn how to select poems based on both their articulated engagement and their aesthetic judgments.

MODELING AND SCAFFOLDING: HOW WILL I SHOW THEM WHERE TO GO?

In modeling and scaffolding, you are demonstrating how to employ certain interpretive strategies, critical lenses, and tools, particularly in terms of building connections to their own cultural backgrounds. Modeling involves showing students how to engage in certain tasks, or employing certain interpretive strategies or critical approaches, as opposed to telling them what constitutes appropriate responses. By modeling your own uses of strategies or approaches, you are providing students with assistance in how to employ new, unfamiliar ways of thinking or responding. You are building on students' familiar knowledge to help them understand the unfamiliar. In so doing, you are providing students with what Carol Lee (2001) describes as "cultural modeling" of connections between the students' cultural background and what they are learning. In working with African American students, Lee builds on their background knowledge of the use of symbolic language in hip-hop culture to help them interpret symbolic language in literary texts. This suggests that you not only need to be aware of your students' cultural background, but you also need to devise methods of making links between that background and the material in a unit.

To determine the level of your modeling or scaffolding, you need to consider your students' ZPD within which students will be able to understand your modeling without undue struggling on their part. You want to provide them with modeling that pushes them beyond their current or familiar level to acquire new or unfamiliar ways of responding within their ZPD. At the same time, if your modeling is too sophisticated, that is, is beyond or outside the upper level of their ZPD, they will then not be able to understand your modeling or will become frustrated in attempting something that is too sophisticated, or is "outside" or "beyond" their ZPD.

For example, if you are modeling a critical approach to analyzing stereotypical gender role portrayals in literature to a group of seventh graders, you consider your students' current knowledge and ability to examine stereotypical gender role portrayals in literature, recognizing that they may be more familiar with stereotyping in advertising than in literature. And, you recognize that a relatively sophisticated analysis of gender will be "over their heads," that is, beyond their ZPD. You then decide to begin with students' current level of development, starting with analysis of advertising, and then move to activities that build on students' familiarity with advertising.

You also need to recognize individual differences in students' ZPDs within a classroom. Some students may still be struggling with certain activities, whereas others may have had extensive experience with an activity. To accommodate for this variation, you can only approximate a composite ZPD for a group of students that takes into account individual differences in experiences and ability levels.

Another important aspect of the ZPD theory of learning is the idea of the opportunity to demonstrate ability to do an activity without assistance. Having modeled an activity, you are providing students an opportunity to try out an activity on their own. In many cases, the students may initially struggle, but they need to be able to try out an activity to gain confidence in their ability to participate in that activity.

ORIENTING AND SOCIALIZING: HOW WILL I SHOW THEM WHERE TO GO?

Orienting techniques include how you are introducing students to what it means to be an active participant in and member of your classroom community. In so doing, you are not attempting to create an exclusive or a controlling, rule-bound community. Rather, you are assuming the role of "tour guide" (Edelsky, Smith, & Wolfe, 2002) who supports students so that they perceive themselves as contributing something of value to a community, as well as respecting each other as community members.

You can most effectively orient students as much through how you operate in the classroom as through direct, deliberate modeling. How you respond to students' challenges to your role as teacher, student conflicts, classroom crises, or school and community events, as well as the everyday operation of the classroom, indirectly conveys powerful messages to students about your own identity as a teacher and as a person. In his discussion of teaching as a "moral activity," David Hansen (2001) quotes John Dewey (1974), who noted that " 'It is not too much to say that the most important thing for the teacher to consider, as regards his present relations to his pupils, is the attitudes and habits which his own modes of being, saying, and doing are fostering or discouraging in others' (p. 326)" (p. 847).

Hansen (2001) identifies three important elements of teachers' classroom actions in a classroom: manner, style, and tact. Manner has to do with how you conduct yourself in working with students, for example, the extent to which you are open-minded, flexible, tolerant, or civil in your relationships with students. Style has to do with particular, consistent, typical ways of interacting with students that reflect your beliefs and attitudes. Tact has to do with how you react to immediate, specific classroom situations. Knowing how to react on-the-spot requires a certain thoughtful, sensitive "mindfulness" to the particular aspects of a situation.

You are also orienting by demonstrating your own passion or interest in literature through how you talk about certain texts—the fact that you have certain strong preferences for certain authors or texts. As in teaching any subject, exuding your own passion or interest in the classroom may do more than anything to foster student interest in literature. Although your students may not all share your own enthusiasm, they may appreciate the fact that you have an enthusiasm for what you are doing.

Stances and Positions.   You are also orienting students to adopt certain stances or positions as readers of texts, stances, or positions associated with being critical readers. In helping students become participants in a literary community, you are continually orienting students to adopt a "point-driven" stance (Hunt & Vipond, 1992) in which they learn to read a text for its larger symbolic or thematic meanings. In so doing, you are encouraging them to move away from reading simply for information (an "information-driven" stance) or for participating in a story (a "story-driven" stance) to read as a reader attuned to how language implies larger meanings. Helping students to adopt a "point-driven" stance— learning how to read for the symbolic or thematic meanings—takes a considerable period of time as students practice interpreting texts. To help students adopt this stance, you are continually modeling your own interpretations of texts. You are also creating activities that help students learn to perceive patterns in characters' actions and dialogue that imply symbolic meanings. And, you are providing them with critical approaches that assist them in inferring thematic meanings.

REFLECTING: HOW WILL I KNOW I HAVE ARRIVED?

A final and underlying teaching technique is reflecting. As you engage in immersing, orienting, facilitating, and modeling, you are continually reflecting on your teaching to anticipate subsequent teaching activities and changes in your plans. You are reflecting on three
basic aspects of your instruction:

- What went well with students' learning?
- What did not go well with students' learning?
- What things do you need to work on to address what did not go well?

Such reflection is essential for your growth and development as a teacher. By identifying specific aspects of your teaching in which you need work, you can then focus your attention on improving those aspects. Reflecting on your teaching requires that you go beyond self-examination to continually attend to how your students are reacting to your
instruction. In observing your students, you note certain patterns which suggest aspects
that need more work. For example, you note that students are having difficulty or are confused what how to participate in your activities—confusion evidenced by the fact that they
are asking a lot of questions about your directions or expectations. Based on your observations, you then infer that your directions may not be clear or that you may need to provide
more modeling or scaffolding. Then, the next time you teach, you make a deliberate effort
to provide explicit directions or to model or scaffold your activities. You then note the degree to which students are able to complete an activity—the students are readily able to begin an activity and are no longer confused. In some cases, changes in your teaching will require long-term efforts as you continually observe changes and adjust your instruction.

As part of your methods course, you may engage in microteaching sessions in which
you teach your peers in a relatively safe, although somewhat artificial context—your peers
could be "themselves" or they could adopt the roles of secondary students. By taping your
microteaching, you can then reflect on the following in your journal:

1. Reflect on your own outcomes in terms of what you wanted your peers to learn and
   reasons why your methods will fulfill those outcomes.
2. Write a narrative about what happened.
3. Reflect on your teaching using each of the following criteria:
   - Clarity of purpose (did they understand what they were supposed to do and
     why?).
   - Interest in or engagement with the activity (were the peers involved?).
   - Degree to which your learning outcomes were fulfilled (did they accomplish
     what you wanted?).
   - Your own role as "teacher," facilitator, or organizer (what did you do to foster
     or facilitate involvement vs. dominate or control the activity?).
   - Other aspects of your teaching.

Writing about your teaching in a narrative form in a journal or teacher portfolio entry
encourages you to describe particular events in a manner that itself fosters awareness of
how students are responding to your teaching.

During your student teaching, you may ask your students to provide you with anonymous feedback as to specific aspects of your teaching—providing directions, formulating assignments, facilitating discussions, interacting with students, and so forth. You could ask them to focus on those areas in which you may have some concern so that you can then take steps to make improvements. You can then compare your students' feedback with your cooperating teacher and supervisor's feedback. If they all agree on the same aspects, you then know that you need to focus on those aspects. At the end of your class, you can also ask students to freewrite about what they learned in your class. You can then review the students' writing to discern what they learned as well as the variation in student learning.

DESIGNING UNITS

Now that we have described the planning model, we apply that model to designing units. In designing units, you are going beyond planning for individual activities to organize your activities according to some coherent, overall topic, theme, issue, genre, archetypes, historical or literary period, or production. During your student teaching, you may be employing a number of different units lasting from a couple of days to several weeks. It is important to prepare these units in advance of student teaching when you have the time to conduct research and pull together relevant resources. You can also discuss your units with your cooperating teachers in terms of how they are integrated into that teacher's curriculum.

Different Organizational Structures for Units. You first need to define a central focus around which you organize your specific daily activities in terms of a topic, theme, issue, genre, production or writing, archetype, or literary period. As summarized in Table 3.1, there are advantages and disadvantages to these optional structures to consider in selecting your central focus. In many cases, units combine different aspects of these alternatives; there is no pure prototypical example for each of these different approaches.

Topics. Organizing your unit around a topic such as power, evil, suburbia, the family, and so forth, means that you are finding texts that portray these different topics. For example, you may select a series of texts that portray mother–daughter relationships, as in *The Bean Trees* or *A Yellow Raft in Blue Water*. Students may then compare or contrast the different portrayals of the same topic across different texts.

It is important to select topics about which students have some familiarity or interest, or that may engage them. You may also want to have students study how certain topics are represented in literature or the media. For example, students may examine how the family is represented in 19th century literature compared to 20th century representations. Or, how rural, small-town social worlds are represented in 20th century American literature.

One advantage of a topics approach is that topics do not imply the kind of value or cultural orientation associated with a thematic or issue unit. Students may construct their own value stance related to a topic, for example, defining different attitudes toward the topic of mother–daughter relationships. However, without that additional value orientation, students may lack motivation to be engaged in a topic.

Themes. You may also organize your unit around certain themes portrayed in texts. A frequently used theme is that of individualism or conformity to society—the extent to which characters must conform to or resist societal norms. As we just noted, one advantage

TABLE 3.1
Different Methods for Organizing Literature Instruction

Method	Focus	Advantages	Disadvantages
Chronological	How literature develops over time, different periods of literature	Easy to organize, many literature anthologies are organized this way, provides continuity and coherence	Difficult to fit in contemporary literature, more challenging to motivate student interest
Author Study	On individual authors' work and lives	Provides an opportunity to read several works from a single author, can focus on style	Privileges a sometimes limiting biographical reading
Thematic	On large concepts such as identity, dreams, challenges, innocence, and so forth	Offers maximum flexibility to teachers in terms of creating collections of texts that vary in chronology, style, genre, and author	Can force an interpretation on texts; some themes are overdone and hard to keep fresh
Topical or issues	On the subject matter of texts or on current controversial issues	Provides immediate relevance and connections to students' experiences	Can lose the specific aesthetic focus that the study of literature can provide
Genre	On the structural aspects of literature	Helps students understand the structural and formal components of a particular genre	Students can easily tire of continuous study of one genre; can seem somewhat forced and artificial
Type of analysis (e.g., archetypal or by kinds of literary theory)	On particular methods of analysis	Offers students a range of interpretive strategies	Often focuses on strategies rather than the texts themselves

of thematic units is that students may become engaged with related attitudes or values associated with a theme. One disadvantage of thematic units is that they can readily become too didactic, in which you attempt to have students "learn" certain thematic lessons—the importance of not conforming to society or the need to be courageous.

This problem of didacticism relates to how you organize your unit. You can organize your unit in both a "top-down" deductive manner, providing students with theoretical perspectives or frames for them to apply in a deductive manner. You can also organize your unit in a "bottom-up" inductive manner, encouraging students to make their own connections and applications. To avoid the didactic tendency of thematic unit, you can move more to an inductive approach, allowing students to make their own interpretations and connections that may be different from any presupposed central thematic focus.

Issues. You also organize your units around issues, for example, the issue of gender and power—the degree to which women may have to assume subordinate roles in a culture. One advantage of an issue is that students may adopt different, competing perspectives about an issue, tensions that may create interest in that issue. One disadvantage of studying issues is that students may often bring rigidly defined stances on issues such as gun control or school vouchers, which may not allow for further development or consideration of alternative perspectives.

You may have students identify their own issues portrayed in a text. For example, students may identify the issue of social pressure from peers to adopt certain practices valued by the group, but perceived as problematic by certain group members. They could then explore this issue of social peer pressure in Robert Cormier's *The Chocolate War* or Muriel Spark's *The Prime of Miss Jean Brodie*.

Genres. You may also organize your unit around studying a particular genre—short story, novel, ballad, rap, drama, memoir, biography, poetry, film noir, or hybrid combinations or mixtures of genres evident in a multigenre approach to writing instruction (Romano, 2000). (For discussion of genres in film and television, see Chapter 12.) In studying a particular genre, students examine similar features of that genre in terms of prototypical settings, characters, story lines, and themes, as well as shared literary techniques.

One advantage of a genre approach is that students learn a larger literacy practice of making generalizations about similarities between different texts based on certain genre features. For example, having read a number of different autobiographical essays, students may then identify similar features common to those essays. One disadvantage of a genre approach is that it leads readily into pigeonholing or categorizing texts as representing certain genre features without critically analyzing those texts. Moreover, such reductionist genre approaches can also reify a formalist approach to English instruction—overemphasizing the study of formal structures without examining other aspects of texts. For example, it may be assumed that all short stories have "rising action," "conflict," and "resolution," when in fact there are many stories that do not follow that formal structure.

Production and Writing of Genres. You may also organize a unit around producing or writing certain genres, integrating reading and writing instruction. Students need to have opportunities to create their own genre texts based on their study of genre. For example, after studying the genre of rap, they create their own raps. In studying texts, students may then focus on techniques being employed with an eye toward producing such texts. In writing texts, they then draw on their genre knowledge in providing feedback to each other's texts.

Archetypes. You can also organize units around mythic or literacy archetypes, drawing on the critical approach of the archetypal approach discussed in Chapter 7. For example, you may organize a unit around the archetype of the Romance quest narrative pattern evident in epic and medieval texts, as well as contemporary journey or travel quests or the *Star Wars* and *Fellowship of the Rings* series. As part of this unit, you may focus on the initial initiation of the hero in preparation for the quest, linking the hero's initiation to adolescents' own experiences of initiation in their own lives.

One advantage of archetypal approaches is that students may enjoy studying what are larger mythic aspects underlying a range of different texts associated with their own lives, if, for example, they understand that initiation rites as portrayed in literature also pervade their own experiences. One disadvantage of archetypal units is that they may lead to the same pigeonholing as with genre units. Moreover, unless students are familiar with a lot of literature, they may not be able to make generalizations about certain archetypical patterns in that literature.

Literary Periods. You may also create units based on certain literary periods, for example, the Romantic or Victorian period in British literature or the Harlem Renaissance in American literature. In studying these periods, you can incorporate background historical events or cultural attitudes shaping texts, as well as similarities between literature, art, music, and popular media. For example, Coleridge's and Byron's art work reflect much of the spiritual and political romantic perspectives found in their poetry. One advantage of such units is that you can study writers' work as shaped by their historical and cultural contexts. One disadvantage is that it may simply become a matter of covering a lot of historical information or facts about features of the period without fostering critical response to the literature itself.

Historical, Regional, and Cultural Worlds. You may also organize units around certain historical, regional, or cultural worlds, for example, the short story literature of the American South—stories by William Faulkner, Eudora Welty, Carson McCullers, Flannery O'Connor, Tennessee Williams, Truman Capote, Reynolds Price, Bobbie Joe Mason, and others whose stories portrayed the world of the "Old South" and "New South." Or, you could organize a unit around the historical period of Puritan America based on Nathaniel Hawthorne's stories and *The Crucible.*

Initial Interest Rousers. In designing units, you need to begin with an interest rouser activity that hooks students into the topic, issue, theme, genre, and so forth. By initially engaging them with texts, material, or phenomena you will be studying, you are providing them with an experience that enhances their interest and leads them to perceive the value or worth of the unit. For example, in doing a poetry unit, rather than beginning with a discussion of "what is poetry," students may begin by bringing in and sharing favorite poems.

Providing Variety and Choice. In planning your unit, you also want to include a variety of different types of experiences to avoid redundancy and repetition. You can create variety by incorporating a range of different tools discussed in the next chapter: drama, videos and DVDs, different forms of discussion, art work, creative writing, hypermedia, and so forth. You may also build in choices between use of these different tools; again, students are more likely to be motivated to participate when they are given options. For example, rather than writing a final report, students may have the option of creating a hypermedia production.

Final Projects. You should also include a culminating final project that serves to draw together the different, disparate elements of the unit. This final project should provide students with an opportunity to extend approaches and ideas from the unit to create their own interpretations of texts. For example, in a unit on gender and power, students could analyze the portrayal or representations of gender roles in texts not read in the unit. Again, providing choices for different projects enhances motivation to complete their chosen project.

Activity: Analyzing Units

Go to the Web site and click on the "student units" file in the planning chapter to analyze units developed by preservice teachers. Select two of these units. What do you perceive to be strengths and limitations of these units? How would you revise these units to improve them?

CREATING UNITS OF INSTRUCTION: MELISSA'S NINTH-GRADE UNIT ON *THE HOUSE ON MANGO STREET*

Melissa is a preservice teacher who is just starting a 6-week placement in an urban high school. On her first visit to the school, she described it as "a humongous cardboard box sitting in the snow, brown brick with no windows immediately visible." That first day, she walked in the front door and was greeted by two "very friendly ladies" at a sign-in desk, flanked by a metal detector which, as one woman explained, is only used once in a while. The racial and ethnic breakdown of the school is primarily African American and White, with a small percentage of Native American, Latino–Latina, and Asian students. About 40% of the student body meets eligibility requirements for free or reduced lunch plans. Most of last year's graduating class continued their education at college or postsecondary school of some sort, whereas about 9% went directly to work after graduation.

After a few meetings with her host teacher, Melissa remarked as follows: "I was very surprised when Mrs. Mariani explained that our planning decisions were entirely up to us, slightly excited because there are so many options, yet a bit dismayed because I didn't know where to begin in selecting a topic for six weeks of teaching."

Melissa's mixed feelings about a wide array of choices are typical of beginning teachers. Fortunately, in time, she was able to take a deep breath and start thinking about the possibilities before her, beginning with the texts she might use. In the early stages of her planning, she wrote as follows:

> I feel most comfortable using a foundation novel (I'm most inspired by the possibilities of *Romeo and Juliet*, *West Side Story*, *Animal Farm*, and *The House on Mango Street*), and branching off with multiple texts, running theme exploration, critical lens interpretations, possible Webquest or Internet projects, and activities using language lenses.

Eventually, she settled on the *The House on Mango Street* by Sandra Cisneros, a text she had read and enjoyed in her "Adolescent Literature" course earlier that fall. Already, her anxiety was fading. In her words, "Fortunately, my concern for selecting a topic has moved on from the horror of not knowing where to begin, to a slightly less frightening task of narrowing down a ton of really inspired ideas and possibilities!" In the next section, we follow Melissa's journey through the planning process, presenting her story in terms of the five questions we posed earlier in this chapter: "Where am I going?" "Who am I going there with?" "How will I get there?" "How will I show them where to go?" and "How will I know I have arrived?"

Where Am I Going?

Melissa began by thinking about the class makeup and organization. She would be working in a ninth-grade advanced placement English class, consisting of 27 students—15 girls and 12 boys. Realistically, because this was only a 6-week placement, she planned to keep many of the structures her host teacher had already set up. Classes ran on a block scheduling arrangement of 80-min periods. Her host teacher's classroom was spread into an arc of desks with a smaller circle of desks in the center. In Melissa's words, "the students often seem to be comfortable enough to switch seating areas on occasion to talk to less-familiar peers."

Who Am I Going There With?

The class was comprised of both African American and White students in a 40:60 ratio. During her early observations, Melissa wrote the following in her teaching journal:

> They are an animated classroom, interact well with one another, and respond well to direction. During my observations, I noticed several students who appeared to take charge, some who quietly watched the rest of the class, and some who moved comfortably from group to group.

While none of the students have IEPs, there are several students who tend to fall behind the others and who can benefit from individualized organizational help. Interestingly enough, when I asked Mrs. Mariani how these students were placed in an AP class, she explained that should a parent simply request that his or her child be put in an advanced class, the child was automatically enrolled.

Melissa's teaching philosophy centered on a few basic principles. She explained the following in her journal:

> I believe it is very important for students to achieve a solid beginning to crafting and perfecting their writing. . . . The same goes for participation in class discussion, reading for comprehension, and grasp of literary devices in reading and writing. These aspects of the English Language Arts curriculum are going to help students obtain jobs after school, live a more fulfilling life, and get along better in social situations. . . . I think it's important to foster literacy for personal growth by allowing student choice and encouraging creative projects so individual students can choose a means of expressing their knowledge. Creating a safe classroom is imperative. Personal safety is a basis in Maslow's heirarchy of needs. How can children learn if they're uncomfortable or scared in the classroom? Literacy as a sociocultural practice is very important because it is the beginning of creating culturally aware, critical citizens. . . . These literacy issues will provide the basis of proud citizens, critical thinkers, and sensitive human beings, able to get along in the changing world.

More specifically, in terms of her ninth-grade students, she wanted to incorporate a mix of reading, writing, oral language, listening, viewing, and artistic representation in her lessons. She chose Cisneros's novel, not only because it was suggested as an option on the ninth-grade reading list, but also because, in her words, "it represents the diverse Chicano culture, provides multiple themes to build on and because of my personal desire to study the text." Her goals for reading it were to help students recognize "Cisneros's style+ of writing, culture, and character development." Her writing goals included "developing a final autobiography chapter book in order to practice creative writing for an outside audience, exploring autobiographical writing, and using a text to model common conventions of writing." Melissa planned to sponsor oral language activities for the purpose of helping students to "share ideas, aid in revision and drafting processes, and for students to gain an understanding of their classmates." Beyond these academic goals, Melissa wanted her students to explore aspects of their own personal identity, their neighborhood and community, and "their possibilities for the future."

How Will I Get There?

Melissa planned to focus on themes such as homes, families, neighborhoods, and city life in daily focused writing activities. Because the text is divided into short vignettes, she designed what she called a "creative autobiography writing project" as a culminating activity. "In my experience," she reflected, "most ninth-grade students have not written a lengthy project paper yet, and I feel that an autobiographical multiple chapter book will introduce them to the idea fairly easily." Because students would be writing about themselves, and because their writing would be chunked into fairly small sections over the course of the unit, Melissa felt that this assignment would be a good prelude to the longer papers they would be expected to write in their later high school years. Because some students come from families where space and time for homework are scarce or nonexistent, Melissa planned to allow class time for students to complete their informal and graded activities.

Considering the diverse needs and preferences of her students, she wanted to combine techniques such as read-alouds, silent independent reading, listening to the author on tape, and discussion in small and large groups. At times when students listened to the book on tape, Melissa made sure they had copies of the text as a way of fostering what she called "double sense accommodation, listening and seeing while following along in the book." She also planned to use a variety of print and nonprint texts such as music, film clips, newspaper articles, poetry, and short stories as a supplement to the main text. In all, she hoped to provide "something for everyone, varied activities in order to reach diverse student needs." Although her students were generally familiar with each other by the time she started her placement, another of Melissa's goals was to have students interact with each other in groups and pairs "in order to practice their collaboration and social skills."

Although *The House on Mango Street* is broken into fairly short vignettes, Melissa wanted to supplement her instruction with a variety of shorter texts. For example, on her second day of teaching, she read "My Name" from Mango Street while the students followed in their books, making notes about questions or comments on scrap paper. She then led a discussion about Esperanza's name, their own names, and the symbolic importance of names. She concluded the lesson by asking students to do a bit of research on their names, using a variety of reference books she had provided: *The Guiness Book of Names*, *A Dictionary of Names*, *Family Names*, and *Today's Best Baby Names*. For students who preferred computer research, she directed them to a Web site (http://www.beyondthename. com). The day before, she had planned too little, ending up with 30 of the 80-min period to fill. As a result of this unsettling experience, she planned some back-up activities. If the lesson ran short this time, students could construct a character chart of Esperanza's family on the overhead or watch the first 15 min of *Harriet the Spy* in which Harriet observes and appreciates the diverse inhabitants of her neighborhood. As it turned out, students needed the whole 80 min for the activities she had planned and Melissa didn't need these back-up activities. For homework, she asked the students to observe their own neighborhoods or talk to a neighbor, then write a 10-min reflection on what they saw or learned.

This variety of options was typical of Melissa's daily lessons. For example, in her eighth class, as shown in the following lesson plan, she related the lyrics of "The Rose that Grew from Concrete" by Tupac Shakur with Cisneros's vignette "Four Skinny Trees":

Lesson Number 8

Instructional Objectives

- Students will learn to extract information from specific lines of text and form their own opinions using text. (New York State Standards 1.1, 1.2)
- Students will listen and read along with a piece of American literature and relate it to their own lives. (NYSS 2.1, 2.2)

Materials

- *The House on Mango Street*
- *The House on Mango Street* (audio version)
- Cassette/CD player
- Writing prompt sheets on "Best Friends"
- Copies of "The Rose that Grew from Concrete" by Tupac Shakur

Procedures

- I will read "The Rose that Grew from Concrete" aloud to the class while they read along and highlight lines/phrases that stand out to them.
- The class will listen and read along to pages 74–89 in *The House on Mango Street*, thinking about how the Shakur poem relates to the vignette "Four Skinny Trees."
- Discussion about the poem and the vignette, comparing and contrasting the two and looking for overall themes in the novel that correlate to the poem. Reminder: ask the class about Esperanza's view of women.
- Students will write their next autobiography chapter on their best friends. Writing prompt sheets will be distributed to get them started.
- Time will be given to work on reading questions.
- Homework: Finish "best friend" chapter and illustrate it with photographs, a collage, or a drawing (materials will be provided to take home).

Assessment

Students will be assessed on their attentiveness during review and reading. Observations will be made as to whether students are on task when working on questions and writing project. There will be no formal assessment for this lesson; however, the reading questions will be due next week for a grade.

In all, during the 3-week unit, students wrote autobiographies, acrostic poems, and letters to friends. They responded to each other in peer writing groups, read companion literature by the likes of Gary Soto, listened to music from Ally McBeal and song lyrics by Tupac Shakur and Vonda Shepard. They created collages and other visual renderings, watched videos of "A Tree Grows in Brooklyn" and "Harriet the Spy," visited Web sites, researched in reference books, and interviewed parents and other adults. The biggest question still remaining for Melissa was how to grade and evaluate such a broad spectrum of activities and assignments.

How Will I Know I Have Arrived?

At the beginning of her unit, Melissa planned to use a mix of formal and informal evaluation techniques for her unit. Periodically, she planned to assign what she called "process points" for class participation and attentiveness, based on a simple "check, check-plus, and check-minus" system. In a nutshell, her overall grading and evaluation system was broken down into 15% for participation, with the remaining 85% to be divided among several aspects of the final autobiography project.

During the first few days of class, she handed out the following explanation to her students:

Grading

Your final project will be graded in the following manner. At the end of the unit, you will be asked to self evaluate your work by answering the "key consideration" questions.

Participation (15%)

In order to produce seven chapters of "grade A" writing, participation in listening, the revision process, and discussion are necessary. The participation grade is your way of reminding me that you are taking this project seriously. If you are staying on task with daily projects and activities, I will know that you are investing time and effort. Several of your writing drafts will be handed in for check, check+, or check– grades, to be considered when a participation grade is made. Key considerations:

- Were formative drafts turned in for a participation grade consistently?
- Was useful feedback given toward peers' work?
- Was participation in group and whole-class discussion evident?
- Were thoughtful listening skills employed during class read-alouds?

7 Chapters (10% each, 70% total)

These will make up the body of the autobiography project. A substantial amount of class time will be spent on the writing and drafing of each chapter. Key considerations:

- Are all seven chapters completed?
- Is writing inclusive, articulate, and organized?
- Is writing free of grammatical errors?
- Did the student participate in a revision process (evidenced by peer feedback forms and previous drafts)?
- Is the autobiography typed and legible?

Dedication (5%)

This is your opportunity to give thanks to the most important people in your lives, to those who inspire you. Key considerations:

- Is a dedication included at the beginning of the autobiography?
- Is a meaningful message included in the dedication?

Illustrations (5%)

Illustrations add color to the project. This is your chance to express your memories and ideas through a different medium. Key considerations:

- Were time and thought devoted to the illustrative process?
- Are illustrations placed in logical sequence within the final autobiography and relevant to the contents?

Cover/Title Page (5%)

Every book needs a title! Use your title and cover page to draw your readers in to make them excited about reading your work. Key considerations:

- Has a "catchy" or appropriate title been give to the autobiography?
- Is the cover neat, organized, and decorated attractively?

As you can see by this handout, Melissa not only clarified how much particular activities would count in the overall unit grade, but provided simple rubrics to help students in creating the various graded components. Even with this thoughtfully planned and articulated grading system, Melissa was still disappointed when it came time to assign unit grades. She wrote the following in her teaching journal:

> Students received their grades today. What a mess. I thought I was being more than fair with grades, rounding up rather than down and giving *plenty* of time for make-up work and time in class. Several students who received zeros came running up to complain, grovel, argue, etc. I don't understand why they are so cross w/ me when I so clearly made instruction understandable to them. I would be concerned that I've done something wrong, but the great majority did just fine—very well, in fact. There were only a few complaints. It certainly isn't as though I enjoy giving someone a zero—I hate it and it disappoints me, especially when it's given to someone I know can do better.

Melissa's comments illustrate something that all of us must reckon with countless times in the course of our careers: the recognition that even our "best laid plans" often fail to bring the unmitigated success we all hope for and cherish when it comes our way.

Gradually, Melissa was able to put her triumphs and struggles as a teacher into perspective. In a message to the class Listserv, she wrote the following:

> I feel like I'm learning, or making up, ways to deal with various new situations each day. I already have that feeling that once I finally get the hang of things the six weeks will be at an end. My students are great. I love seeing the diversity in each of their individual personalities. . . . Oh, and my host teacher rocks! She's really helpful and very supportive, readily answering any questions I might have. Even though this week has been kind of scary, it's been incredibly valuable in my learning. Now that I know I can generally deal with this teaching stuff, I'm aiming to actually enjoy my planning and lessons, instead of worrying so much. I can't wait to see all of you soon! Hope things are going well for each of you!

> Best, Melissa

Melissa's plans for *The House on Mango Street* demonstrate the multifaceted nature of planning literature instruction. Your goals for teaching literature and your plans for instruction must connect and inform each other. As your plans begin to take shape, revisit your goals and revise those plans accordingly. As Melissa, Molly, and Janet discovered, the triangulation of students, texts, and contexts will ensure that your planning changes every time you enter your classroom. Purposeful plans will help you and your students focus on the reasons why you wanted to teach literature. Those goals will come alive in your classroom.

Portfolio Addition: How Curriculum Reflects Beliefs and Practices Valued in a School

For your portfolio, collect and insert representative items or artifacts related to the contexts of community, school, curriculum, classrooms, and students: a community or school Web site, the school's mission or code of conduct, a school or department curriculum guide, your teachers' curriculum or units, or students' writing about literature. Then, reflect on how these items or artifacts reflect the beliefs and practices operating in their respective contexts and how these beliefs and practices will shape your development and planning of units you may use in your student teaching.

Review back over the planning activities in this chapter, considering your ability to effectively engage effective planning, and what evidence you would include in your portfolio to demonstrate your ability to performance this activity.

Online Additional Activities, Links, and Further Reading

Go to the textbook Web site, Chapter 3, for additional activities, links, and further reading.

4

Using Drama to Foster Interpretation:
How Can I Help Students
Read Better?

Chapter Overview

- Case Narrative: How enactment teaches reading strategies.
- Responding to literature as enactment.
- The power and flexibility of drama.
- Implementing drama activities.
- Role-play activities.
- Using think-alouds and enactment to teach inferencing with a short story.
- The power of enactment in fostering reading improvement.

A lot of your students may have difficulty understanding what they are reading, understanding necessary for them to engage in formulating interpretations of texts (O'Brien, 2003). This raises the key question addressed in this chapter: How can I help kids read more effectively? To answer this question, it's important that you first find out something about your students.

CASE NARRATIVE: HOW ENACTMENT
TEACHES READING STRATEGIES

A couple of years ago, one of us, Jeff, was working with one of his preservice teaching students, Seth Mitchell, during his student teaching experience.

Seth was working with 11th-grade literature students. "They have trouble with inferences," he explained, "particularly with seeing complex implied relationships. I'm at a loss of how to help them."

"That's a tough strategy to teach," Jeff empathized. "But a necessary one, otherwise they can't read and understand highly nuanced texts, figure out the thematic meaning, or justify that meaning with evidence from the text."

"In other words," Seth rejoined, "they might be able to read the literal level of a text, but they won't deeply understand it. And they won't be able to think about what they read, or think with it!"

We laughed.

"Well, what teaching strategies do you have that could assist your kids to see complex implied relationships in a text, and help them to apply these relationships to an understanding of the text?"

Seth thought for a moment, casting about.

"This is in their zone of proximal development so you are going to have to help them. What tools in your teaching repertoire," Jeff prompted, "would make seeing these kinds of relationships more accessible, more concrete, closer to home, more visible and available to them?"

Seth snapped his fingers. "I've got it," he laughed. "Drama!"

RESPONDING TO LITERATURE AS ENACTMENT

Expert readers use a common general repertoire of strategies when they read and we can apprentice our students into the reading fraternity by sharing these expert stances with them. Likewise, very specific communities of practice use particular reading strategies when reading the texts required of them, for example, lawyers when reading legal documents, historians reading artifacts, software designers reading code. (See Wilhelm, 2001; and Wilhelm, Baker, & Dube, 2001, for full discussions of task-specific reading strategies.) Furthermore, such experts bring specific content knowledge and content strategies to bear when dealing with the substance of such texts.

In this volume, we concentrate mostly on inducting students into the community of reading practice by focusing on strategies not actively taught in schools. Louise Rosenblatt, the most influential of reader response theorists, argues that reading is a transaction that requires a reader to converse with the meaning of a text. The result of this "transaction" is the "poem" which is the result of the meeting of personal meaning and purposes with the codes of a text. In *The Reader, the Text, the Poem*, she invokes the metaphor of enactment as she argues that "We accept the fact that the actor infuses his [sic] own voice, his own body, his own gestures—in short his own interpretation—into the words of the text. Is he not simply carrying to its ultimate manifestation what each of us as readers of the text must do?" (Rosenblatt, 1978, p. 13) (see Fig. 4.1).

Research conducted by Ross and Roe (1977) led them to maintain that enactment requires the exact same skills as those necessary to reading comprehension. They particularly cited how enactment develops the ability to identify key details; plot sequence; character and character motivation; various relations of details, ideas, and events; and the ability to discern mood, tone, and other constructs.

In *You Gotta BE the Book* (Wilhelm, 1997), Jeff used a robust database to formulate a theory of reading engagement. Jeff used data from that study to specifically argue that reading is more complex than has often been assumed, and that much more significant assistance is required by readers as they engage with more sophisticated texts. As an example, one feature of the texts older students are asked to read is its relatively high inference load—the requirement that students bring meaning to a text and construct meaning with a text that is not explicitly stated. The reader's first jobs are to articulate a purpose for reading and to build background that will create a context for meaning. After that, the reader must be very active, inferring, elaborating, and reflecting, as he or she constructs meaning with the text. To emphasize this point, the literary theorist Roland Barthes (1974) has ar-

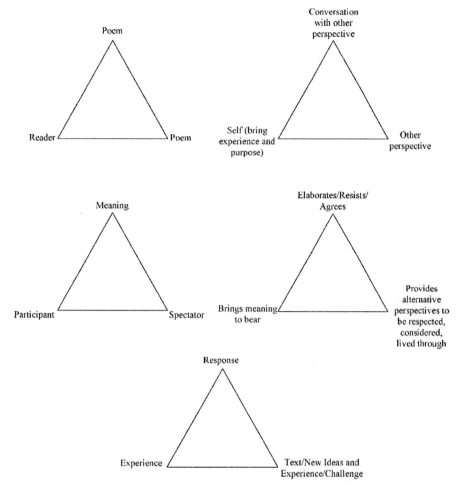

FIG. 4.1.   The responding and enactment transaction.

gued that the reader does not decode but overcodes. He further argues that elaboration is the surest sign of engagement in reading.

The studies Jeff conducted for the writing of *You Gotta BE the Book* and *Imagining to Learn* showed that enactment strategies are a particularly powerful way of assisting students to bring and create meaning with text. And that will be the emphasis here: on the readerly activity that is stimulated by the text, and how readers can use the created experience as an object and tool for thinking.

THE POWER AND FLEXIBILITY OF DRAMA

In fact, drama, also known as enactment or action strategies, helps students to evoke, experience, interpret, and reflect on all kinds of texts. They are assistive in developing the ability to use sophisticated strategies of reading visible and available to students in powerful ways that help them to internalize these strategies.

In addition to drama, you can also use a range of other tools to help bolster students' confidence and engagement in their reading.

Jeff has been working regularly with teachers and schools in the Chicago Public School system for several years now. He works through the Chicago Teachers Center, an amazing group of educators who work in various ways to improve the learning environments and achievement of students through the system. One of their missions, among many others, is to incorporate the arts as a learning tool across the curriculum. One of his particular functions is to help teachers use enactment strategies to facilitate improvement in reading with many students, including many who are second language learners or considered to be at risk for various reasons.

During his latest visit to Chicago, Jeff visited several schools where teachers are using various forms of enactment as strategies to support reading comprehension, engagement, and interpretation at particular places in a single text and in an extended form to create a designed knowledge artifact to reflect on and represent what had been learned through a unit of study. Jeff works with schools on probation for low test scores in reading achievement and all had been rapidly improving in this regard (as well as in several other ways cited by teachers, like sense of community, interest, and attendance). He was mightily impressed and gratified by what he saw.

Several of the schools were engaged in a unit studying the rainforest. Several teachers, representing each school, had gone on an expedition to the Amazon, had communicated with students back in Chicago through e-mail and Internet postings, and had brought back numerous artifacts and video footage for students to study. In the Audubon School near Wrigley Field, the first thing Jeff noticed was that all the teachers and most of the students were dressed as favorite literary characters. This was a special celebration during which all students would speak to their classes in character as they provided a dress-up book report and made a case for reading their books. A parade through the neighborhood was to take place later in the afternoon.

As the school day began, the students' sixth-grade teacher was using enactment to review important rainforest concepts that they would now use as they engaged in a social action project. Students from different groups then combined to perform short skits showing the relation among these ideas. The teacher then asked students to do "character walks" showing the life experiences of indigenous people and various species of flora and fauna due to recent changes wrought in the rainforest environment. She then asked them to walk into the future to imagine what might happen next under various scenarios.

The students used these ideas and experiences to brainstorm social action projects that could affect the various outcomes they foresaw. A design workshop had been set up as students created woodcut cards of various scenes and animals from the rainforest. These were beautifully printed in organic black ink on recycled cream paper. The students planned to use these cards to write letters to the superintendent of schools and various political figures as they outlined environmental issues (implicating the schools and local community as they did so!) and proposed solutions to these problems. One group, for example, had found in their research that Boise Cascade, the prime supplier of paper products to the district, harvested old growth forests. The students recommended that a public statement be made, and that business instead be turned over to companies that harvested only new growth forests. Other students argued for the gradual elimination of paper from the school system as students could use electronic technologies notably absent in the school. Returning to a neighborhood school concept to eliminate bussing and many other ideas of environmental import were offered. The energy was uncommonly high, and all the students Jeff spoke with were entirely engaged with their work; the sense of school community was astonishing.

Jeff traveled next to Otis School in an old building near the downtown area comprised entirely of Latino students, most of whom spoke English as a second language. The fifth-grade class had turned an entire classroom into a rainforest museum exhibit that represented what they had learned. Students played various roles in this museum. He was escorted by two museum guides who took him first into the upper canopy, which had been created with great artistic dexterity. Both real and artificial exhibits of plants, insects, and animals were accompanied by informational placards and essays. Some students role-played the parts of particular flora and fauna with whom he could talk. He not only elicited specific information from them, but also their feelings about the changes in their environment. He then proceeded to the middle and lower canopy, and finally into the Amazon River itself where he met pink dolphins (papier-mâché) and piranhas (taxidermical) and a variety of other aquatic life (role-played by students). As he continued back to shore, he felt himself getting wet. As Jeff looked up, he noticed students behind a facade misting the people in the forest! Talk about virtual reality.

As Jeff left this exhibit, he entered one about "indigenous people" (these were the words used by his fifth-grade guide!). The students playing these parts were preparing food with malioc and nuts and other native staples. They carefully explained to him how the malioc must be prepared to avoid poisoning oneself. Being a trusting kind, he accepted their explanation and ate a malioc pancake. He spoke with them at length about their life, religion, beliefs, and lifestyle. From there he went to a storytelling center where he heard native stories, and then to the final exhibit which was staffed by students role-playing environmentalists. He spoke to these students about ecosystems, symbiosis, chemical degradations, and deforestation and was astonished at their profound understandings. His tour guides told him about several real-world opportunities to sign petitions, lend his support to various environmental organizations to help purchase tracts of rainforest for a preserve, and gave him a check sheet of things he could do in his own home to protect the rainforests and the general environment. They said they hoped to add an exhibit about protecting the environment before it was opened to the general public and other schools. The museum had been such a success that community members and other teachers in the network wanted their students to experience it, too. Enactment had been used to create a real living knowledge document that did the real work of representing what students had learned and helped others to learn it, too.

One of the teachers told Jeff, "This whole project has really helped the students to seize!"

He thought her comment odd and assumed she meant "engage" as in "seize the idea or seize the day." He agreed with her and readily offered that the students seemed very excited and deeply immersed in the subject.

"Well, yes," she agreed, "but that's not what I meant."

"Oh," he said, "you meant it helps them to SEE in a new way! I couldn't agree more! They clearly have taken on the lens of other perspectives—the indigenous people, even the insects—and most profoundly they see from the future. It certainly has transformed their vision and their ability to see."

The teacher was patient as she explained that this too was true, but she had been using S.E.E.S. as an acronym. She meant that the enactment work used to construct the museum had helped the students to Support each other's learning and construct understandings together, to Experience the rainforest almost as if they had been there, to Embody new ways of knowing and being in the world, and to Share what they had learned with others. The drama work had helped them create knowledge and had made their knowledge visible and accountable to each other, their teachers, and now the community.

Jeff liked the S.E.E.S. acronym and agreed once again wholeheartedly. His research into drama and enactment, reading and learning, has demonstrated that these are some of the central things dramatic enactments help students to do as readers and learners, although this is not the full extent of enactment's potential by any means!

As gratified and as impressed as Jeff was with the students' work in these two schools, these were not singular experiences. He sees this kind of excitement, devotion to reading for the purpose of making and sharing things together, and the satisfaction that comes from a significant achievement, over and over again in his work with schools. These benefits accrue when using enactment for 2 min to explore a character's decision-making process or the meaning of vocabulary, and they accrue when students engage in more extended kinds of enactments like living history museums or the rainforest exhibit described here.

Enactment is a powerful tool for both teaching and learning because students actively create meaning together, listen to each other, explore implications, and enjoy themselves. The rest of this chapter provides you with some strategies and the work you can do to assist readers.

Although the focus here is on supporting and assisting students to grow in their interpretive facility while reading literature, and on learning from reading, enactment has many other powerful benefits that relate to reading. It can help students to learn difficult concepts from a variety of subject areas, it can provide a situation and context for learning, and it can support and guide the pursuit of various kinds of inquiry. Enactment supports students to ethically explore and engage with issues, and as we saw here, to work together in a democratic community. My own research studies with my colleague Brian Edmiston have demonstrated how all of these things can happen through the use of enactment strategies (Wilhelm & Edmiston, 1998). This research also demonstrates how enactment strategies work to help teachers integrate content area instruction, infuse all of the arts into their teaching, coresearch both learning and content topics with students and each other, and to generally revitalize their teaching through the use of drama.

Drama and Values. In interpreting literature, students are continually drawing on their values in explaining or judging characters' actions, for example, whether Nora's leaving her husband in *The Doll's House* is justified. Their ability to interpret texts therefore depends on their ability to define and draw on their values in interpreting texts.

Similarly, in using drama or simulation activities, you are placing students in situations in which they say certain things or adopt certain actions that reflect certain moral or ethical stances in "safe" contexts. Then, in postdrama reflections, they are learning to reflect on the attitudes and values shaping decisions they make in portraying certain roles. As Peter Singer (1991) argues, "We cannot avoid involvement in ethics, for what we do—and what we don't do—is always a possible subject of ethical evaluation. Anyone who thinks about what he or she ought to do is, consciously or unconsciously, involved in ethics" (p. v).

Because drama activities often revolve around addressing issues, problems, or conflicts, for example, how to create a new school policy on addressing issues of sexual harassment, students are learning to reflect on ethical and moral aspects of issues and then deciding on how to act on the basis of those ethical or moral stances.

In taking ethical or moral stances, students are learning how to connect their own identities to others through social relationships, connections defined through using language and discourse. As Bakhtin (1984) notes, "To live means to participate in dialogue: to ask questions, to heed, to respond, to agree and so forth. In this dialogue a person participates wholly and throughout this whole life . . . he invests his entire self in discourse, and this discourse enters into a dialogic fabric of human life, into the world symposium" (p. 293). In engaging in these dialogues with others in drama, students are confronted with other, alternative perspectives that serve to challenge their own perspectives. And, in committing themselves to act in a certain way, they must accept responsibility for the consequences of adopting certain actions or of not selecting other actions, choices which involve constructing their identities based on confirming their ethical stances.

In participating in drama activities over time, students face the consequences of their actions and decisions, which challenges their status quo beliefs and attitudes. For example, a group of students are engaged in a Space Traders drama activity in which they are having to decide on whether and how to trade certain groups of people. In the beginning of the drama, one student, Anthony, explained his decision to "trade" people on welfare to the aliens by stating the following: "It doesn't matter if they die, they're worthless anyway." During the drama, other students challenged Anthony's belief that the people on welfare were "worthless." And, after he lost his own job and had to go to the alien universe himself, he began to realize that he was actually passing judgment on people like himself. So, on the fifth day of the drama, he noted, "I've changed my mind. You can't decide for other people. Even if we need the money we can't make them go—they're people too."

And, through her experience of the drama, another student, Jenny, reflected on her initial decision to ban the welfare people:

> At first, I thought that the aliens could take our prisoners or the welfare people because we didn't need them. Then after I thought about it I kind of changed my mind. You can't put a price on a person's life. It was very prejudiced for me to do that. Maybe it was a mistake and they regret it and then it would be too late for them. Maybe they couldn't help not getting a job. We were all too selfish and to quick to decide.

Drama and Prior Knowledge. Students are also continually drawing on their prior knowledge to interpret literature. Rather than perceive "knowledge" simply as a set of facts or information, we define knowledge more broadly to include their ideas, beliefs, attitudes, and understandings about the world, which they are continually constructing through their life experiences. Through participating in drama activities, students are drawing on their ideas, beliefs, attitudes, and understandings to employ dialogue, define their roles, make decisions, adopt certain stances, or recognize the consequences of their actions. They need to activate relevant schema and relate their personal experiences to create and sustain a drama world.

Here, for example, is Michelle, a seventh-grade student, describing her experience in a drama about welfare:

> When we started I didn't understand how all the people were so poor. I just thought they were lazy or something and that they should have tried harder to get a job, or should have moved where the jobs were. So then we tried it out in the drama and I couldn't get a job. Then I got one from somebody with less pay, and then only meals, but I had a family so I couldn't do that. And I moved, but I couldn't find work there either and in the end I lived in a cardboard box and I was really frustrated and angry. Then the people [health inspectors] came and kicked us out . . . It really made me understand . . . I just didn't get it when I read about it.

In engaging in drama, students are also learning to infuse their knowledge with feelings—that facts, ideas, beliefs, and understandings are shaped by the emotions of love, hate, envy, desire, anger, grief, resentment, sadness, loss, happiness, or jealousy shaping actions. As Mark, a seventh grader, notes, "School is about facts—mostly boring facts—drama is about making facts exciting because you add the feelings . . . Drama takes facts and asks how they might have been different or how the facts might affect you or someone else and how all that would feel. That's why I like drama."

Drama and Cultural Understanding.   In reading literature, students need to be able to interpret characters' actions within their social and cultural contexts, for example, understanding the characters in Hawthorne within the world of the Puritans' values. In participating in drama, students are transported into and experiencing different social and cultural worlds. For example, in creating a drama activity based on a Hawthorne short story, students are experiencing how the Puritan characters based their decisions on religious beliefs about good and evil.

Drama is therefore an ethnographic research tool for learning to observe and experience distant cultures and historical eras as distinct from our own cultural or historical context. Learning how to act "like a Puritan" requires students to understand what the Puritans valued and how those values differ from their own values, for example, the fact that they assumed that people are easily susceptible to evil.

It is also a phenomenological research tool. Phenomenology posits the value of learning to attend to one's own and others' experiences through bracketing out forces shaping perceptions of that experience. In drama, students are adopting the insider perspectives and thoughts of others, a means for understanding how others perceive and experience the world in ways that differ from their own ways of perceiving and experiencing. In learning to think "like a Puritan," they are learning to perceive the world through a different, less familiar prism.

And, drama is also an action-research tool in that based on their drama experience, students can take action, reflect and evaluate the effectiveness of the action and how it changed the context through their reseeing that context. Drama, as reflected in the "theater of the oppressed" movement, can lead to social or community change related to a social justice agenda by having students address issues of homelessness, poverty, racial and ethic conflict, unemployment, inadequate health care, and so forth (Boal, 1985, 2002; Rohd, 1998).

IMPLEMENTING DRAMA ACTIVITIES

In implementing drama activities, it is important to begin with a series of warm-up activities that serve to help students become comfortable in participating in drama activities. You could begin with some nonverbal communication activities in which students must convey meaning through physical gestures. For example, students could pair up and create body sculptures of each other and the entire class must guess as to what is being conveyed. Or, they could form a circle and then walk through the middle point in the room, first as if they were walking down a busy city street and then walking down a small-town main street. In the first context, there may be little or no eye contact and an impersonal facial expression, whereas in the latter, there may be a lot of friendly nonverbal interaction. Then, you can add language, creating improvisations in which students must convey alternative roles and attitudes through varying speech. For example, in one scene, a mother is waiting up for her daughter to return home from a date past the time she was expected home. In the first scene, the daughter assumes an aggressive, assertive stance and the mother is passive and forgiving, whereas in the second scene, the mother is aggressive and assertive and the daughter is highly apologetic.

In her student teaching, Sarah McArdell employed the following activities designed to create "safe spaces" for her middle school students:

Circle Dash.   Students stand in a circle around one person. Two people in the circle silently signal each other to switch places. The person in the middle tries to get to an open spot before the switchers. The person left takes the spot in the middle.

Minefield.   Students stand in a circle and toss into the center any object they can find that isn't sharp or breakable. They then spread the objects around so that the whole center is evenly covered. A volunteer closes his or her eyes. The rest of the group, using only their voices, tries to direct the volunteer to the space directly across from them in the circle without hitting any of the objects in the "minefield."

Values Clarification.   Students sit in one part of the room facing the largest open space. They have their writing portfolios with them. In the open space are signs that say "Agree," "Disagree," and "Unsure." The teacher reads a statement and students move to the sign that expresses their view. Statements are written by the teacher to be appropriate for the age group and community. After everyone has chosen, students are given 2 min to write in their portfolios why they made their choice. After all the statements have been read, students will gather into a circle and discuss each statement and their beliefs. After this discussion, students are given 10 min of writing time to revise or reinforce their choices in the portfolio (examples follow):

- I am worried that I or someone I love will get AIDS.
- Sometimes violence is the only option.
- I am comfortable with my body.
- It's OK to drink to get drunk.
- I see discrimination in our community.

The activities are based on the work of Augusto Boal (1979, 2002) and Michael Rohd (1998).

ROLE-PLAY ACTIVITIES

Once students are comfortable with using nonverbal and verbal communication to express their roles, they can then begin to participate in role-play or skit activities. These role-play activities could be based on a scene from a story or novel or a situation in their own life. In choosing scenes or situations, it is often helpful to focus on a key conflict, tension, or decision that is dividing characters or people, but is difficult to resolve. You may also provide students with specific descriptions of traits, attitudes, beliefs, agendas, or goals—on slips of paper so that they do not know the different roles, or have them all know about the traits, attitudes, beliefs, agendas, or goals.

CONSIDERATIONS IN PLANNING ROLE PLAY

- Choose content—"What do I want my students to learn about?" This can be declarative knowledge, like learning about civil rights or harassment, or procedural knowledge, like learning the reading strategy of inferring character.

- Choose context—"What set of circumstances from the story (stated or implied) will motivate and require learning?" Tensions and turning points provide rich places for role play.
- Choose roles—"Who will the students be? What new perspectives or information will be opened up from these perspectives?"
- Choose your possible roles—"Who will I be and how can I assist and complicate student learning from these positions? From what positions can I add knowledge to the enactment?"
- Choose a motivating purpose and action—"What will this role play be about? What will students have to do? What clear achievable goal can students be given that will serve our larger purposes? How does this connect to student concerns?"

Shadows. Here, for example, is a role play based on a short story by M. E. Kerr (1984), "Do You Want My Opinion?" To begin the role play, Jeff usually asks a student to read each character's part, focusing on instances in which the characters misunderstand each other. Jeff has students read the first exchange between John and his father. Each character has two shadows. The first is an interpreter and explains what John and his dad really mean to say each other. When these shadows are done, the other shadows, playing the role of connector, explains what teenagers today should get from the story. After this, the shadows can converse or debate their conclusions with the characters, with each other, or with the class who could be playing the role of a forum. The next dialogue in this story is between John and Edna O'Leary, then between Mr. Porter and Lauren. The final dialogue is between John and Lauren at the story's end. The shadows can exchange places, can change the function of their role, or new shadows can take their place. In this way, students get to interpret and infer the subtext but also get to work at expressing theme. There are obviously many possible permutations of this technique.

Radio Show. Radio show is a kind of discussion drama during which students take on any role they want to comment on a particular issue by "calling in." Students, in role, can respond to each other providing "uptake" as they create meaning together. Jeff tells the students that there is a big issue to discuss: whether a new kind of love potion should be made available under certain conditions, for example, to marriage counselors. Clearly, this parallels many current cultural debates about legalizing marijuana or other drugs under certain circumstances.

Jeff then gives students 2 to 3 min to confer with a neighbor who might have strong opinions about this issue, and to brainstorm what they might have to say about it. They can call in as themselves, as characters from the story, as literary characters they have studied like Odysseus and Penelope, or political figures like George W. Bush, popular culture commentators like Dr. Phil or Dr. Laura, divorce lawyers, or anyone at all who might have something to say on the issue. He then asks students to write down who they might be, where they are from, and a few notes about their feelings on the issue.

Of course, they are free to change roles as they respond to each other.

Discussion during a radio show or other discussion dramas is always energetic. Jeff plays the talk-show radio host and so he merely comments on contributions and highlights major ideas to provoke further response. Students enjoy the playfulness, and more points of views are solicited because students do not have to speak as themselves. They enjoy parodying popular culture figures and viewpoints. They also feel safer in expressing provocative opinions because they are speaking in role, not as themselves.

USING THINK-ALOUDS AND ENACTMENT TO TEACH INFERENCING WITH "THE CHASER"

After Seth and Jeff had their discussion in Seth's classroom, Seth put together a lesson plan to teach inferencing using John Collier's (1943) story, "The Chaser." Seth also created several lessons to reinforce the same strategies.

Seth knew that enactments comprise a repertoire of strategies that are extremely powerful for all readers, learners, and teachers. They assist readers to do many things that they cannot do without support. The reading strategies for which enactments provide the most support are those that the National Assessment for Education Progress reading test results show that American students most lack: the ability to see complex implied relationships, make inferences, elaborate, see from multiple perspectives, discern subtexts, identify an author's generalizations, understand how text structure contributes to text meaning, and express opinions and justify them with textual and life evidence. The repertoire of enactment also helps learners in all knowledge domains, assisting them to use the language, strategies, stances, and concepts of experts as they are given practice and apprenticed into an expert community of practice (Wagner, 1999).

Jeff's Story Drama. In this section, Jeff presents a story drama for use in a unit around the following inquiry theme: "What makes a good relationship?" He considers the topic to be personally relevant and socially significant and one that cuts across many texts, both popular and canonical, and knowledge domains, as we look at the history of dating and courting rituals, the biochemistry and psychology of love, and many other topics.

He uses a variety of enactment strategies in this story to help students see complex implied relationships, read the subtext, and arrive at the author's implied meaning so that they can discuss this, consider it, reject, adapt, or embrace it for us in their life.

He uses this story early in the unit and in many ways it prepares students for the final project which is to create a documentary about some aspect of love or relationships that has piqued their interest during the unit.

"The Chaser" Lesson Plan (Thanks to Michael Smith of Temple University for his ideas about this lesson plan.)

Goals:

Personal: To help students bring their personal experience to a productive meaning-making experience with a complex text with a high inference load.

Conceptual: To explore our unit theme of "What makes a good relationship?"

Procedural: To help students see complex implied relationships in a story, and assist them to work on inferencing in service of making meaning with this story.

FRONTLOADING OR MACROFRAME

Mantle of the Expert Strategy. Jeff has students count off to form groups of four or five. He informs the students that he is going to ask each group to be crack teams of undercover CNN reporters. They are going to be going into schools and clubs to find out about the latest date drug, a kind of love potion that seems to have extraordinary powers. He tells them that he will be the head of CNN and he will brief them on their assignment. Then he asks if they are ready to enter the enactment.

As the students enter the enactment, Jeff tells them that he has very sketchy details about the story because it is not yet public. In fact, he wants them to get the scoop so that they can break the story. All we know is that one man and one woman are in the hospital, stark raving mad with love for someone their friends have told police they have never even liked. The police suspect foul play in the form of a love drug. Both victims attend the same school and went to the same club over the weekend. He then asks if there are questions.

There are usually a plethora of questions from the students in their roles as reporters. Some things he can tell them because he has read the story; he tries to keep his responses consistent with the story. For instance, he tells them that the love drug seems to be afford-able to young people. He makes up other things about their roles as reporters (reporters are not in the story, just a role from which he wants them to engage with the story). He also tells them that they will receive combat pay because this assignment is so dangerous—we are sending them in teams because we don't know if they are in danger of being affected. They will have high-tech undercover cameras and recording gear, and so forth. If they re-fuse the assignment, it will not be held against them, and so forth. Many other things he claims not to know, for example, whether the drug is natural or synthetic, where the kids are getting it, what are its exact effects, and so forth. He tells them that is what they have to find out.

He then concludes by wishing them good luck and asking them "to be careful out there."

After this scene, he tells them that they will engage in a few other enactments playing other roles. But all of the subsequent enactments and our reading of the story will be data they can use at the end of the story when they prepare their final news report to break the story on CNN.

GETTING STARTED

Group Role Play and Costs and Benefits.   We then proceed to another prereading en-actment activity. This time he tells the students they will be students in the school cafeteria. He will run in and offer them some of this drug and they will have only a minute to ask him questions before the teacher returns and he runs out. They are then to discuss at their tables about whether they should buy some. What are the potential costs and benefits of using the drug on their upcoming date with someone they really like but who isn't returning their af-fection? He asks if they are ready to enter the enactment.

He runs in and yells "Hey, hey, the teacher is gone. I have some of that stuff. You know what I am talking about. And you know you could use it! We are selling 25 pops, first come first serve. 25 dollars. Cash on the barrelhead. You can get it in perfume or pill form. Any questions?"

He fields a few questions and then runs out as an imaginary teacher returns, yelling, "Decide whether you can afford to pass this opportunity up!" The first questions usually revolve around whether he will take credit cards (no), will the drug work on men and women, or on a person of the same sex (yes, be careful how you use it), will it work on more than one person at a time (don't know), how many times can they use a pop (just once), where did he get the stuff (none of their business), has he tried it (don't happen to need it—this usually gets a laugh).

They talk for a while and he stalks around the lunchroom in role, secretly mixing it up with different groups to stimulate or complicate their discussions. After a few minutes, or when he senses the topic has been covered, he yells out, "The teacher is gone again. And the bell is about to ring. Tommy and I will be selling the stuff at the car!" At this point he fields a few more questions and then leaves the drama world.

Teacher Think-Aloud of "The Chaser."   Next he reads the story aloud to the students, completing a think-aloud that concentrates on complex implied relationships. He points out the importance of the title and Alan's name. He calls attention to incongruities, wondering why the old man doesn't have a name, why he seems so educated and polite yet lives in a rundown apartment. He focuses particularly on how the old man seems to anticipate Alan's every question, but won't answer them. Instead he tells Alan about the poison he has.

Jeff then makes inferences about why Alan is here and what must have happened to him right before the story. He continues to wonder aloud why the old man goes on and on about the "spot remover." He pays careful attention to the repetition in the description of the love potion and the poison, citing "rules of notice" (Rabinowitz & Smith, 1998), cues that tell him the author wants him to notice something: titles, the first few lines, character introductions, repetitions, undue attentions, weird behaviors, surprises, and so forth.

Frozen Moment.   He stops after Alan says "That is love!" He tells the students that the meaning of this story is subtextual and must be inferred by them as it is not directly stated. To help them, the students are going to freeze this moment in the story and examine what might be going on in Alan's mind so we can see the various ways this action he is taking might be thought about, and the different consequences to which it might lead.

Good Angel–Bad Angel.   He then assigns each group of students to be a council of bad angels or good angels, with half the class playing each. He tells them that Alan is at a moment of crisis and the good angels from each group must send a representative to save him. They must use any argument that is justified by the story to convince him not to buy and use the love potion! He turns to the bad angels and says that the "goody two shoes" good angels are on the case. It is their job to get down to earth and convince Alan to go ahead with his plan. They can use any argument justified by the story to make their case.

They have 3 min to brainstorm and choose a representative to visit Alan (in smaller classes, he allows for two representatives or everyone to visit Alan in role). When this is done, he asks for a volunteer to play Alan.

When the angels come up, they are to line up on opposite sides of Alan. One good angel speaks to him and flies off, then a bad angel, and so on. If other students feel compelled to jump in and join the lines because they have something that needs to be said, they are free to do so (and this often happens!).

He tells Alan that he is free to listen or to engage any angel he wishes in conversation. Then the enactment begins.

This usually has hilarious results, with good angels making logical or ethical comments like "do you really want her to love you because of a drug and not because of who you are?" "Alan, don't do it. Why do you think it is so cheap? He is tricking you into having to buy the poison from him!" Occasionally a good angel comes up with something like "Did you ever see Fatal Attraction, Alan? Watch out, this is going to be bad news!" But generally the sneaky and emotional and immediate gratification arguments belong to the bad angels who say things like, "Alan, you are a loser. This is your only chance to have a great girlfriend. And you'll never have it again!" "Alan, everything you ever wanted. Go for it!" And so on.

After that good angel–bad angel, we keep Alan in the hotseat and ask him how it felt. Whereas kids find hearing only the good angel comforting, they sometimes find hearing both angels confusing and disconcerting. He always asks whose arguments were most convincing. Interestingly, kids almost always find the bad angels most convincing (adults tend to go about 50–50). This gives us a chance to do some "imaginative rehearsal for living" to freeze time and examine what has happened. Why are the emotional, immediate arguments more convincing then the logical, far-sighted ones? What does this tell us about our immediate reactions to dilemmas and how we should deal with them?

Not being totally naive, he knows that his kids are faced with drugs, and he knows they are confronted with many confusing issues regarding relationships. He thinks that it is very important to rehearse imaginatively what they might do in analogous real-life situations and to examine their natural responses, their options, and potential consequences closely.

Many of the enactments he does with students revolve around edgy topics like child abuse, drugs, family problems, and the like. He would never address these issues directly, although he knows that many of his students suffer from them or know people who do. But in an enactment, it is safe to explore the issues, because it is not about you and your experience, it is imaginary.

When he deals with the topic of drugs in a drama, he includes information about the dangers of drug abuse and how to get help; he also includes this information within the drama. When he deals with child abuse, he tells students, in his role, that it is the law that one must report even the slightest suspicion of child abuse to an authority; he makes sure through the drama that they know who these authorities are. Kids often ask questions in role that they would not ask as themselves, but they really are asking for themselves or someone they know. When people question this tactic, he tells them that just because he ignores a problem doesn't mean it goes away. He wants to help students deal with real issues, and he wants them to see that literature and other texts are a powerful way to do so.

Group Think-Alouds.   Now that the subtext of the story has been articulated by the angels, and the various eventualities implied by the story facts have been highlighted, he asks the students to read the rest of the story in their groups. He has them underline any textual cues that express implications about future action, or any clues that imply something about a character and what he or she is like or will become. Then on the lines next to the story, he has them explain why they noticed this (was it a surprise, a repetition, did it get undue attention, was it the ending) and what they inferred from this.

After everyone is done with the reading, he asks the students to share what cues they underlined, why they knew to notice them, and what they inferred from them. Having practiced identifying cues for seeing complex implied relationships, and having reviewed in several ways what will probably happen after the story (an inference that is absolutely essential to understanding the author's meaning), he returns them to their roles as undercover reporters.

CNN Special Report Tableaux and Video Clips.   He then tells the students that they will return to the CNN enactment. He tells them that the story of Alan and Diana will be the centerpiece of their news story that is going to break tomorrow, and that they have the scoop!

One or two groups have footage of what happened to Alan before the story that caused him to go to the old man. They will show this as a still or as a short video clip. Everyone must be involved, and they may include a voiceover or CNN reporter commenting on the action. Another group or two have video of what happened between Diana and Alan the night he received the potion. They will show a still or clip of that.

The next groups will show Alan and Diana 6 weeks after the administration of the potion, and the final groups will do the ultimate end of the story after the story—the reason we must break the story now. Depending on the number of groups, a final group could provide a thematic analysis and commentary on the story after the story.

All of these tableaux presentations require students to use textual evidence to see and infer complex implied relationships, something that few American students have been shown to do. But the enactment strategies actively assist them to do it.

After giving students a few minutes to prepare, they reenter the CNN drama. He tells them that they are about to break the story, but that they now have the chance in the screening room to see the information obtained by the other groups of reporters and how the whole story will come together. He asks the first group to cue up their video and they get going.

Jeff has done this drama many times and students have always achieved a justifiable reading of the story, that is, that the chaser is the drink after the drink, the poison that must follow the potion because Diana will be driving Alan crazy. As one boy put it in his think-aloud, "it sounds like she'll become another mom! Who needs another mom?" A couple of groups found ways to bring Alan down with Diana, by having her insist that they drink together to their love or some such thing. But if a group did come up with an inconsistent conclusion, the enactment allows us to explore what they missed, and how this could be corrected. And because enactments are always exploratory and can be revised, students can rewind the tape and try it again.

He sometimes uses interviews with the Old Man and his Alter Ego as a follow-up to the story. What questions would reporters want to ask him? How would he answer? What would he really be thinking? What are such people really like and how can you tell who they are?

Correspondence and Choral Montage. Another technique he uses, for example, at the end of "The Chaser," is called *correspondence and choral montage.* He asks half of the class to become Diana, and to write a diary entry 6 weeks after the end of the story. He tells them they can start the diary entry with "I don't know what has happened to me. . . ."

The other half of the class becomes Alan, and he asks them to write a letter to the old man, that can start with "This isn't what I expected. . . ."

After they are done, students exchange the notes and circle a phrase that is especially poignant and powerful to them. He asks them to avoid phrases like "I love him" or those that might be considered trite in favor of something more substantive. Once they have chosen the best lines, they now need to put them in the best order. As Coleridge (1990) once maintained, poetry is the best words in the best order.

Group Poem or Choral Montage. Groups of students use their circled phrases to create a group poem, or choral montage. Students put themselves in a physical row, placing themselves where their phrase should go in the poem. Lines may be revised or tweaked. Some may be deleted and another line added. Sometimes a line might work well as a choral echo or ostinato that is repeated throughout the poem. Students can try their poem several ways, moving themselves and their lines to different places so they can see the effect of different orders and structures. This activity is a physical version of mystery pot, a technique in which a short poem or text is cut up into separate sentences and phrases. Students then reorder the text in various ways to see the different ways in which a text could be structured and the different effects. It is the revision process made visible and physical.

Large-Group Role Play.   You can also create large-group role-play activities in which different students adopt roles associated with a trial, hearing, election, town meeting, and so forth, in which a decision needs to be made and different opposing parties are attempting to influence that decision. For example, using a novel your students are reading, you could have a censorship hearing about a text you are reading. A parent lodges an objection to certain aspects of the text you are reading. You then employ the entire class in a school board meeting. Different students assume the roles of school board members, parents, students, teachers, school administrators, townspeople, religious leaders, newspaper literary critic, and so forth. The school board then calls up students who have adopted these different roles and asks them questions about their responses to the text and reasons they believe the text should be censored or not. After hearing testimony from students, school board members then vote on whether the book should or should not be censored. (Large-group role-play activities can also be conducted online in which students post messages to each other representing their perspectives.)

Students could also create museum and art exhibits, businesses, companies, schools, government agencies, media production units, and so forth, in which students assume certain roles and responsibilities (Wilhelm & Edmiston, 1998). For example, based on writing about their local town, they could then create a town museum in which they assume the roles of historians, anthropologists, archeologists, artists, photographers, exhibit designers, curators, publicists, educators, and so forth. Or, if a text portrays an issue such as racial or class conflict, poverty or unemployment, or homelessness, students could create a government agency or company designed to address this issue as portrayed in the text and then develop roles and strategies to address this issue.

REFLECTION ON PARTICIPATION IN ROLE-PLAY ACTIVITIES

One of the most important components of a role-play activity occurs after the completion of the role play when students step outside of their role to reflect on their experience in their roles. Students could discuss the degree to which they felt comfortable or awkward, strong or weak, active or passive, or connected or alone. They could also describe which roles assumed the most versus least power and reasons for power differences.

They could also reflect on any decisions reached in the role play in terms of whether such decisions would also occur in similar "real-world" contexts. For example, if the school board decided to censor a book in the censorship role play, students could discuss whether such a decision would be made by their actual school board. Reflecting on the verisimilitude of their role play leads students to consider whether they captured the complexities of real-world contexts.

And, students could reflect on what they learned about the issue, conflict, problem, or phenomena addressed in the role play and possible solutions they could develop in real-world contexts.

THE POWER OF ENACTMENT IN FOSTERING READING IMPROVEMENT

Think of all the things that were achieved to assist readers during this short set of enactments with "The Chaser."

Before reading, enactments help students to do the following:

- Activate their prior knowledge and relevant background experiences.
- Connect a text to related texts, either in terms of content, text structure, or both.
- Build the schematic knowledge or content background necessary to comprehend the text.
- Set purposes for reading.
- Build motivation to read.
- Prepare emotionally and cognitively for the reading experience.

During reading, enactments help students to do the following:

- Evoke the textual world.
- Build and sustain their belief in the textual world.
- Use appropriate reading strategies.
- Enliven their reading; be motivated to continue reading.
- Intensely visualize places, situations, actions, and people.
- Enter into varying perspectives; help students "become" characters, ideas, forces acting on the characters.
- Infer—to see and make meaning of simple and complex implied relationships.
- Connect the text to their lives and larger issues of social significance; to elaborate on the textual world.
- Engage their ethical imagination, helping them to ask "What if?" "What do we believe?" "What should we do as a result?"
- Assist others' reading performance through modeling, sharing, and collaborative work.

After reading, enactments help students to do the following:

- Negotiate and reflect on meaning.
- Discern, discuss, and evaluate author's vision, that is, an author's generalizations, themes, and main ideas.
- Reflect on text structure and how this affects meaning.
- Consider alternatives and elaborations, going beyond what is directly stated to other possibilities—pursue inquiry into questions raised by the text.
- Consider how to apply what has been learned from the text to their lives.

Enactments help students to know and do things that they cannot yet do on their own, because they provide teacher, peer, and environmental assistance that allows us to deal with strategies and concepts in human contexts and in concrete forms. We physicalize our reading and use the body, our voices, our feelings, and our whole being as an instrument of communication and understanding. Enactment allows us to deal with complexity starting with concrete particulars.

Enactments also allow us to bridge from students' funds of knowledge and the literacies they bring to school. They work by connecting intimately with the identity, family, and human connections to more formal and conventional forms of literacy.

Enactments allow us to teach at the point of need, to respond to opportunity, to provide kids a chance to actively construct and play with meanings, to experiment with their own voice, to coconstruct curriculum and meaning instead of being the bored recipients of pre-planned lessons unconnected to their current needs and concerns.

It is no wonder that enactments are so powerful for teaching given the immediacy, the use of all learning modalities, and all the language arts that allows us to address individual differences in a group project and to transform the way students learn and read, the connection of thought and feeling, the rooting of text reading in a human context that allows us to imaginatively rehearse for real living. Enactments provide us with a way to share expertise, and achieve action, agency, and choice that can be exported to the world.

Drama, as Jonathan Neelands eloquently tells us (2000), is a space of possibles, in which we can work for personal and social transformation, as readers, learners, and people. Enactments help us to overcome "habitus," the accepted way of looking at the world that we see as natural, and to see in new ways—to see that the world is changeable and so are we. To explore these possibilities of what we may become as readers, learners, and people, we need a space to imagine "what if," and that space is provided by enactment.

CONCLUSION

When Jeff spent his sabbatical in Australia, his daughter Fiona hugely enjoyed school there. This was a great relief to him as she had been so miserable in her American school, and seemed to be learning so little, that they had pulled her out and home schooled her for the year prior to this one. This was a very difficult decision because he and his wife have dedicated their professional careers to public schooling. And how fraught with irony, to find that public school was not working in any way for their own daughter.

In one heart-rending conversation, he told her, "Honey, you should excel in school. You are smart. You work hard. You are creative, you try things and you can make and perform things." Her reply was as follows: "You don't get it, Pappy. I don't go to a school for creative people who make and perform things." He was stunned. Everything that he thought would make her a model student, a dream for a teacher, had been ignored or even discounted by the school.

Why the sudden change in her attitude, enjoyment, and engagement, now that they are in Australia? It is largely due, Jeff believes, to the fact that her Australian teacher values the ways in which Fiona learns, and celebrates those things. One way in which Fiona learns is by being active, and her favorite class each day is drama and movement (a class that is required through many Australian schools). Before in America, they had to prod her to talk about school, and these conversations often ended in tears. Now every night they hear what she has done and learned in class and they get glowing reports about her work. This in turn makes her glow.

Her Australian school privileges multiple ways of knowing and this allows her to be successful and to be assisted into new ways of knowing in which she is less expert. However, Jeff does not think this is chance or an isolated incident. His own experience as a teacher and several of his research studies (Smith & Wilhelm, 2002; Wilhelm, 1999; Wilhelm & Edmiston, 1998) lead him to argue that other teachers will find enactments a way to enjoy their students, to teach them more powerfully, and to engage even those who may be resistant and reluctant. The documented possibilities of adding enactment to our repertoires is enormous.

His teaching in Australia covered the time during and following the terrorist attacks on the World Trade Center in New York. During this time, he was working with some high school students using enactments. On the day after the attacks, he and his students spent most of their time talking through these events; he was heartened by his students' responses. Many of them made the moves they had learned from enactment in their initial responses. They searched to understand the perspective of the people who engaged in and supported the attack. They wondered aloud why these others thought what they did of Western civilization, and whether our thinking about them was equally opaque or distorted. They formed their own four corners drama (a discussion drama in which students stand in different parts of the room that reflect different views on an issue or different levels of agreement or disagreement to various statements), without his prompting to explore what should be the responses to the terrorist attacks. When most of them favored a military response, another student asked what could be done to move them out of that corner, reminding them of an enactment we had done that had moved people from their original position.

The next day, a student brought in the following quote: "Peace is not the absence of strife; it is the willingness to fully and honestly face the inevitable conflicts." He asked if we were willing to fully and honestly face the conflict facing us through terrorism, its causes as well as its effects. He needed to do nothing more to guide the discussion that followed for the rest of the class.

Jeff was proud of them. They had internalized the strategies of enactment to think through issues, see multiple perspectives, and to look for alternatives. They independently used the strategies he had taught them to engage in their own reading and learning around a compelling issue. This is the kind of internalization we want when we teach, and these are the kinds of mature and democratic reading responses we want from our students. So much depends on it. And enactments can help it be achieved.

Action Research: Studying Students' Engagement in Drama Activities

Describe the different drama or enactment activities you have participated in or have conducted with students. For each activity, note the degree or level of engagement with the activity and reasons for high versus low engagement. Describe the kinds of interpretive strategies students were employing in engaging in these activities, for example, how they learned to adopt characters' perspectives or critique the values portrayed in a text. Then, describe the participants' reflection on their experience, and what they learned from that reflection.

Online Additional Activities, Links, and Further Reading

Go to the textbook Web site, Chapter 4, and the generic links for "drama/speech" for additional activities, links, and further reading.

5

Leading Classroom Discussions
of Literature: How Do I Get Students to
Talk About Literature?

Chapter Overview

- Leading classroom discussions.
- Teacher roles in facilitating classroom discussions.
- Online discussion tools.
- Small-group discussions and book clubs.
- Rachel's use of book clubs.

CASE NARRATIVE: JESSICA'S REFLECTION ON HER STUDENTS' DISCUSSION OF "THE BEAR"

The following is Jessica Breed's reflection on leading a discussion of the William Faulkner (1966) short story, "The Bear," in her student teaching. As you read it over, think about ways in which she was successful in leading the discussion and things she might have done differently to improve the discussion:

I guess another easy one we talked about was "The Bear" which is a short story by William Faulkner. I had them do a guided reading on their own; they were answering questions while they were reading it. It was all homework. And so the questions they answered were pretty much following the plot line. Who is the main character? What is Ian concerned about, just so that they could read for detail and get the basic story out of it and then ending with a more thoughtful question like, "Do you agree with the father's reaction to this, and why or why not." So you're taking a position trying to figure out what the philosophies behind the literature were.

Then when we came to class we went through the questions, and tried to flesh out what the story was all about and talked in a little more detail about symbolism. In particular there was a small mongrel dog that has an important part of the story. And we talked about what that might symbolize and why its mongrel and why that was important to the story and why it's important that its small. We read passages aloud and we talked about just bears in general and why was the bear such an important focus in this story and I showed a clip from a documentary. In the beginning, it shows this guy who's building this suit so that he can face a grizzly bear and his recollection of meeting a grizzly and the awe and respect he feels, and you know that the bear can kill you at any moment, that hunting feeling. We talked about how it's similar to the story and how its different, and went from there, and then finally I had them do a little piece of writing saying if you were going to tell this story again, how would you tell it? The purpose behind that on my part was to figure out what the tone of the story was.

There were definitely rough parts. It was one of the first texts I taught, so a lot of my questions were very pointed, and I had particular answers in mind, and it was a very much a teacher-led discussion, which I wasn't comfortable doing at first, you know, letting students go off to discuss on their own. But I think it would have been more interesting and more productive for them than if I'd let them go a little bit more on their own way, rather than doing it so formally, you know, question by question. Some people really liked the story and some people didn't like the story at all. That got me more interested in what is it in the story that makes people react in these strong ways?

I was just getting them to go back to the text to find reasons to justify their positions, to figure out whether or not they agreed or disagreed with this character, whether or not you understood why you know this boy acted the way he did, and then trying to find textural support for that. So that was the aim of the discussion. In terms of the handout, there were definitely very identifiable answers and a couple of them were more open-ended, but it was very easy to score because it was more objective, factually based, but at the same time it didn't get people to really analyze the text. And then the final one, I was just looking for a thoughtful response to how they would use it and what kind of tone they think the text has. How they might adapt that tone for their own use if they were to retell the story.

Um, I think it was difficult because I didn't model it, so some people weren't exactly sure what to do with it. But over all I was really impressed with the range of answers that I got, and just the amount of time I saw people reflecting on it and writing about it.

In response to Jessica's reflection on this discussion, what do you think she did effectively in the discussion and what do you think was problematic? What may have been some things that you would have done in this situation to enhance the discussion? To consider what constitutes effective use of talk, recall a time when you had a really good conversation or talk with one or more people. What were the ingredients that contributed to making this a thoughtful or meaningful conversation? What does it mean to be "caught up" in an absorbing conversation? What are some things that happened in this conversation or talk that you could draw on in leading discussions in a classroom?

LEADING LITERATURE DISCUSSIONS

Much of what you do in the literature classroom revolves around leading student discussions of literary texts. Your job is to provide students practice in learning to formulate, develop, and extend their responses. You are also helping students learn how to interact with their peers in a collaborative manner so that they are learning to mutually develop their responses, a process of shared thinking. When students share their individual private responses with peers, they can then combine each others' responses to create composite interpretations.

Unfortunately, teachers often limit the extent to which students can develop their responses. They control discussions in a ritual-like manner through the use of the IRE (initiate, respond, evaluate) genre (Mehan, 1979): the teacher initiates ("Mark, what's the setting of the story?"), the student responds ("Paris."), and the teacher evaluates ("Very good, Mark"). Teachers often use these recitation questions to control or dictate classroom interaction in which students are simply answering teacher questions with brief, unelaborated answers. As a result, there is no authentic, extended discussion between students.

Sharing Alternative Perspectives.   The alternative to these teacher-controlled discussions are discussions in which students share alternative perspectives. When students are bringing in a range of different voices and perspectives, they are more likely to disagree with each other, leading to a more lively exchange of ideas than if they all shared the same perspectives. And, you are more likely to foster alternative cultural perspectives. Barbara Davis (1993) recommends fostering alternative viewpoints, valuing all students' comments, involving all students in the discussion, and recognizing that some students may be reluctant to adopt critical stances.

TEACHER ROLES IN FACILITATING DISCUSSION

Teachers adopt a number of different roles in facilitating discussions through how they set up and guide those discussions. One teacher who believes strongly in the value of engaging students' in dynamic large-group discussions is Sharon Eddleston, a teacher at Armstrong High School, New Hope, Minnesota (Beach, Eddleston, & Philippot, 2003; Eddleston & Philippot, 2002).

Adopting an Inquiry Stance.   Sharon believed that effective discussions derive from students adopting an inquiry stance in which they perceive the need and value of formulating and exploring their own questions—what they did not understand about a text, as opposed to simply rehashing what the teacher already knows about a text. To help her students in her 11th- and 12th-grade contemporary American literature classes adopt an inquiry stance, Sharon modeled ways of posing questions about concerns, dilemmas, and issues associated with a text or generating hypotheses to explain or interpret characters' and students' concerns, dilemmas, or issues. To create a context in which students respected each other, she explicitly taught students the discussion skills of turn taking, agreeing and disagreeing, and acknowledging diverse responses.

In modeling question-asking, she used what are genuine, "authentic questions" (Nystrand, 1997)—which have no predetermined answers or that involve some follow-up to the student's answer. Because there is no assumed "correct answer," they foster teachers and students mutually negotiating meaning for a shared social purpose. Unfortunately, these genuine questions are rare in class discussion. In an analysis of 100 middle and high school classes, Nystrand (1999) found that only about 15% of the discussions involved use of "authentic questions."

Participant.   Sharon also assumed the role of participant in the discussion by contributing her own responses, a shift designed to de-emphasize her role as discussion leader. In reflecting on this shift in roles, Sharon noted the difficulty of sharing responses to a text she had read many times whereas her students were responding to the text for the first time. Because teachers are often responding on the basis of multiple rereadings of a text, they tend to emphasize retrospective interpretations of overall thematic patterns, responding according to what Peter Rabinowitz (1998) defines as "rules of coherence." In contrast, students who are reading the text for the first time are often concerned with what Rabinowitz (1998) described as "rules of configuration," readings having to do with understanding events or predicting outcomes. Sharon therefore attempted to assume the stance of a first-time reader, who is concerned with understanding or interpreting events.

Facilitator.   As discussion facilitator, Sharon was continually inviting students to participate by encouraging nonparticipants to join the conversation. She also pushed students to further elaborate on their responses with prompts such as the following: "tell me more about that" or "what are some reasons that you think that?" She avoided praising or evaluating students' responses, moves that only serve to reify the teacher's role as dictating the direction of the discussion. And, she reminded students about discussion norms regarding monopolizing the discussion, put downs, and interrupting.

Sharon believed that students are more likely to extend or develop discussions when they disagree with each other or express divergent, alternative perspectives. She therefore perceived her role as promoting diverse perspectives through encouraging a range of different interpretations. For example, in responding to August Wilson's play, *Fences*, students were asked to place the main character, Troy, on a scale from 1 to 10 representing their approval or disapproval of the character's actions as a relatively controlling father and husband. Some students were sympathetic toward Troy given his previous experience with racism in his work and on the baseball field, his support for his family, and the fact that he overcame an abusive childhood. Other students judged him in a more negative light, objecting to his drinking, his jail sentence for manslaughter, his treatment of his wife, and his affair with another woman. In sharing these alternative perspectives of Troy, the students challenged each other's beliefs, requiring them to further explore their interpretations of his actions.

Sharon also developed a few provocative questions designed to trigger a lot of different, alternative opinions about an issue, which themselves lead to further discussion, questions such as "Who is the most powerful or most important character in a text?" Rather the relying on long lists of questions about specific information, it is often useful to craft a few key questions that address key themes or ideas. In reflecting on teaching *Catcher in the Rye* in his student teaching, Chris Johnson distinguished between "basic questions" focused on surface details and "deeper questions" that dealt with central aspects of Holden's character motivation:

> On the surface we've got Holden and he's going through New York City and avoiding going home and he's coming up with all these fantasies of running away and doing these different things, and then he's got this fantasy of being the catcher in the rye and catching kids before they fall off the cliff. So on a deeper level, what does this mean, what is Holden so afraid of? What is Holden struggling with? And so finally to get down to come around to the idea that well he's afraid to grow up and he's afraid of facing sexuality and he's afraid of facing change in his life.

To foster debate between students, Sharon encouraged students to frame the discussion in terms of tentative hypotheses, hunches, or "passing theories" (Kent, 1993) about characters' actions or perspectives. Rather than boldly state a definitive explanation for characters' actions or perspectives, students adopted a more tentative, "I'm-not-so-sure-about-this" stance. Adopting this tentative stance invited others to test out the interpretations, leading to agreements or disagreements from their peers based on analysis of texts. In discussing *The Great Gatsby* in Sharon's class, one student, Berke, framed the discussion by reading aloud a freewrite about the narrator, Nick (Beach & Myers, 2001, p. 73):

> *Berke:* I think that this Nick guy is the most perfect guy in this book because he has no, I don't know, he respects everybody to a certain extent. I thought, in this chapter, to describe what kind of guy he is, like in the end, he goes home. He supposedly sees Gatsby like fifty yards in his yard, away. And he's like, should I go talk to him? He's like, no, no. He just lets the guy be alone with his thoughts, you know. He doesn't want to bother him. I mean, that's just a respectable gentleman. I know if I see somebody, and nobody lives around me really, you know, and there's somebody in my yard, I'm going to approach him late at night, you know, what are you doing? This guy, I don't know, he's just . . . yeah, he's just the kind of guy anybody could talk to and he keeps his own opinions in his head and his actions so far haven't shown much to what he really is. I think he's just a perfect gentleman. That's what I feel.

In initiating this topic, Berke adopts a somewhat tentative, exploratory stance as evident by the repetition of "I don't know." He also seeks to verify his belief about Nick as "perfect" by citing an example of his actions of not intruding on Gatsby. He assumes a "dialogic," "double-voiced" (Bakhtin, 1981) stance by mimicking his version of Nick's own voice: "should I go talk to him? He's like, no, no."

Framing the topic in a tentative, exploratory manner invites other students to respond with disagreements to Berke's contention that Nick is a "perfect gentleman" because "he keeps his own opinions in his head." Tom counters with the position, "I don't think keeping your opinions to yourself is a good quality at all." And then Sarah argues that, "It's not necessarily a good quality . . . it's true to Nick's character, though." Matt then supports Berke's original contention, noting, "I think that being able to keep things to yourself is a virtue . . . it's something very few people can do. People who tend not to keep finding themselves in situations that they shouldn't be in; I mean when someone opens their mouth at the wrong time in the wrong place." Tom counters with, "Yeah, but see, if people who didn't state their opinions are going to stay in the position that they are in, I mean, if no one were ever to state their opinion about slavery, there would still be slavery." Kyle then evokes further discussion by asking, "Do you agree with what he says that life is much more successfully looked at from a single window, after all? Instead of like trying to achieve some well-rounded objective? What do you guys think?" When asked to answer his own question, he notes the following:

> I've met like a lot of extraordinary people in the last year that tend to be less well-rounded but more, I guess, you could say, closed-minded, but I don't know if that's the right word. They're specialists, I guess you could say that, and I think I've learned a lot from those people and that obviously has some negative connotations, I mean because you're blind to a lot of stuff. But it might be a better way to live. (Beach & Myers, 2001, p. 75)

In this exchange, the students disagree about the value of asserting opinions, as well as the fact that issues are often framed by "closed-minded" "specialists" who may not perceive the larger moral implications of their acts. What kept this discussion going was the students' willingness to disagree with each other in a productive, exploratory manner. Some students argue that asserting opinions has negative social consequences whereas others argue that people have moral obligations to assert their own beliefs. These disagreements lead to a larger, composite interpretation of Nick's role as narrator based on the shared interpretations that unfolded in the discussion.

Concern With Low-Level Participants.   Sharon was also concerned about the need to engage low-level participants who are reluctant to express their own opinions. These students may assume that unless they can share definitive interpretations, they should not contribute to the discussion, or that unless their responses are highly original, they will be perceived as redundant to those of other students (Beach, Eddleston, & Philippot, 2003). Or, they may simply prefer to remain on the sidelines as observers, particularly when they feel excluded by what they perceive as a few students dominating the discussion.

Some of these low-level participants are unaccustomed to responding to high-level, open-ended questions because they have had little opportunity to engage in sustained discussions about ideas. Stanley Pogrow (2004) notes the following:

> The stare means: "I do not know what you mean when you ask me to think, or what you want me to do. Please tell me what to do so I can answer your question." Thinking is a cultural way of representing things, just like language. Every culture does it differently. Therefore, when a teacher asks a complex question that requires thought it is equivalent to speaking to them in a strange foreign language. No wonder the students stare blankly. (p. 6)

Pogrow (2004) notes that helping students learn to grapple with ideas requires a long-term effort of engaging them in programs such as a Socratic conversation. He notes that by engaging students in such conversations for 40 min a day in groups of 10 to 12 students working with a teacher trained in Socratic conversation can result in changes in understanding in 1½ to 2 years. He notes that "the critical need is for students to create and articulate ideas, and then articulate rationales, justifications, and strategies, over and over and over, and over again—with virtually no overt direction or hints from teachers" (p. 8).

To encourage low-level participants to become more engaged in discussions, Sharon worked with them on an individual basis regarding their perceptions of their roles in discussions, particularly in terms of their assumptions about the value and perceived redundancy of their responses. She assured these students that their contributions are of value, attempting to enhance their self-confidence. She also asked them to share their initial freewrites or to respond to peers' interpretations. And, she would begin with or interrupt the discussion with some paired or small-group discussions in which low-level participants may feel more comfortable participating.

Paired Think-Alouds.   Another approach to helping low-level participants build student confidence is the use of paired think-alouds. In doing think-alouds, working in pairs, one member of the pair makes explicit his or her thoughts as he or she is reading a short text or text excerpt on a line-by-line basis, what Peter Elbow (1973) describes as "movies of your mind" (p. 85). Students simply describe what they are thinking about in a spontaneous, stream-of-consciousness mode as they are reading a text, as opposed to reflecting on or analyzing their processes or reasons for responding (Pressley & Afflerbach, 1995). The other member simply encourages the student doing the think-aloud with verbal (e.g., "that's interesting," "uh huh," "tell me more," "any further thoughts?") and nonverbal encouragement (e.g., nodding, positive eye contact).

You may also provide students with think-aloud prompts (Langer, 1995, p. 22) such as the following, particularly if they have not done think-alouds or need more structure:

- I am thinking that . . . .
- I don't understand . . . .

- This word means . . . .
- This reminds me of . . . .

For more prompts, see the Web site.

For middle school students who are reluctant to express their responses, you may use images, graphics, maps, or cut-out figures representing characters, objects, settings, symbols, themes, or themselves that then serve as prompts or icons for talking about their responses. In a study of early adolescent girls, Pat Ensico (1998) used cut-out images to foster talk about identifications with "good" and "bad" characters in romance novels. Using a method described as a "symbolic representation interview," she asked the girls to describe their responses to a specific scene in the novel. They then make one or more cut outs out of colored construction paper that represent different characters or ways of responses to the text—"recalling other stories," "predicting," "becoming a character," and so forth. Then, as the girls moved through the story, they referred to the different cut outs to describe their responses to the text, particularly their positions and value stances in relationships to the characters.

Using Writing as Discussion Starters. Sharon also used informal writing as discussion starters in which students would volunteer to read aloud their writing to the group. For example, prior to a discussion of the last act of *The Crucible*, students were asked to "explain the difficult decision John Proctor makes at the end of this play. Explain why he makes this decision and where you think he made the right decision." The students then shared quite different opinions about Proctor's decision to die at the end of the play, leading to a lively debate about the value of standing up for one's principles.

Students also wrote "inquiry papers" in which they formulated questions or hypotheses about a particular text and then address those questions and hypotheses. Sharon would then write these questions on the board, questions that served as the basis for discussion. For example, in discussing Frank Chin's *Donald Duk*, students asked questions such as the following: Why does Donald burn his model plane early in the story? Why is he able to dream historical dreams about events he knows nothing about? Why does the author include so many references to food in the story? Why does the book end so abruptly?

Students also composed "oral essays" in which groups of students led by a student moderator made presentations to the class based on topics selected from a fish bowl the day prior to the discussion. For example, in discussing two August Wilson plays, group members discussed topics of the characters' development, racism, music, the use of the supernatural, symbols, and gender issues.

Fostering Self-Assessment of Discussion Participation. Sharon also encouraged students to assess their own discussion participation. For six discussions during a semester course, she had them complete a self-assessment rubric based on the degree of student participation, formulation and development of response, attention to other students' responses, facilitation of mutual exploration of responses with other students, and nonverbal aspects of participation. On the rubric form, students highlighted those statements that reflected their own roles in discussions. They then commented on their discussion abilities and noted those discussion skills in which they needed more work. Prior to the next discussion, Sharon then displayed transparencies of frequent students' comments, and the students discussed approaches to improving their discussions. The information on the transparencies provided students with feedback on changes in their individual and group participation.

CASE NARRATIVE: DARYL'S USE OF DISCUSSION TECHNIQUES

Another teacher, Daryl Parks, employed a number of similar strategies in working with a 12th-grade multicultural literature class in an urban St. Paul, Minnesota, high school (Beach, Thein, & Parks, in press).

Facilitator.   To break the traditional IRE genre of teacher-dominated discussion, Daryl would regularly encourage students to share their thoughts with each other. At one point in a large group discussion, he noted to the students after no one spoke, "I'm getting scared right now, cuz I'm afraid this is going to turn into twenty-six individual discussions between me and one student. (silence) See what I mean? I don't want that to happen."

He also encouraged students to avoid personal attacks by differentiating ideas expressed by students from the students who expressed the ideas. He explains one approach that he uses when the students are sitting in the circle, and one speaks as follows:

> I ask the students if they can see the idea sitting there. They say yes they can. So I say, "when you respond, you have to respond to that idea, you cannot respond to the source of the idea." So, we begin separating ideas from individuals, which they do not have a lot of experience with. So, then, literally, the students will say, "I do not see student A's idea as that different from student Bs idea" and they point to the middle of the room rather than the students. So, there is something there. I don't know what it is but it seems to be working.

To help students distinguish between individual persons and the positions they adopt as reflecting certain stances, he employed the strategy of noting instances in which "some people might say" to refer to statements of people's opinion that reflect these stances:

> I've encouraged students not to use the "I" if talking about a difficult topic, but instead to present the "some people might say" So, practically, in today's discussion, when some students say "Whites have the easiest life." And the white students are sitting there thinking "no." Then I heard the white students doing it, echoing me, saying "some people might say that because they are white that they have to pay for their own college. So that means that their life is harder." And the students distancing or being equipped with the skills to begin to talk about these things that they've never had the chance to talk about before.

Rather than direct students to certain text passages, Daryl encouraged students to select their own passages that served to illustrate their interpretations. He then refrained from voicing a clear perspective on these issues, preferring students to experience disequilibrium in relation to questions. In fact, as is discussed later, some 10 weeks into the class, students would ask him in individual meetings if he would please explain where he was on all of "this stuff;" "you never tell us what you think," explained one.

Using Writing as Discussion Starters.   As did Sharon, Daryl frequently employed writing to prepare students for discussions. He would shift through journal entries and provide students with a list of quoted statements as a means of sparking discussions. For example, in discussing the film "Smoke Signals," he asked students to circle the three quotes they perceived to be the most controversial, for example, "White people as a group enjoy an easier life than anybody else in the country." Starting with these controversial quotes fostered a debate between students about the moral responsibility for White Americans' treatment of Native Americans.

He also employed a "round robin" technique of going around the discussion circle and each student sharing some initial response to a text, for example, a one-word description of the previous night's reading with no explication. He would also have students pass their journal entries around the circle so that they could read each other's journal reactions as a means of starting a discussion.

Encouraging Minority Perspectives.   Students are often reluctant to express minority, alternative perspectives that challenge majority opinions (Pace, 2003). Daryl supported students who were resisting the shared, majority consensus emerging in the classroom, for example, that Whites should not be held accountable for past historical actions. He noted that one student, Devin, was expressing a minority perspective "that white culture and the white system is at fault in this country and he's starting to take up the offensive against others who don't see it." As Devin and others expressed these perspectives, he began voicing resistant students' ideas to give those voices a sense of legitimacy.

Performing Texts.   Daryl also engaged students in performing character monologues. In these monologues, students adopted a character's first-person perspective revealing information about themselves. To frame the idea of making revelations, he asked students to first describe the character's behavior, then proclaim, "You think you know me, but you don't," after which they launch into a monologue. He describes an instance of one student who adopted the role of the character, Tenorio, in Bless Me Ultima: "We all loved her little taped-on moustache and beard. She basically told us everything we knew about Tenorio. I loved when she threw the bird up in the air and said, 'whew I killed Ultima's spirit guide!' and she spun in a circle with glee."

Or, in reading Their Eyes Were Watching God, different groups of students assumed the roles of Janie, Janie's grandmother, and her multiple husbands and would meet with a "counselor" who interrogated them about their motivations.

These activities of performing texts through monologues, role play, oral interpretation, poetry slams, or readers' theater involve students in adopting characters' language and perspectives. In preparing for these performances, students should first determine the interpretive meaning they wish to convey to their audience and then practice performing their texts in a manner that conveys that interpretation. If, in performing the poem, "My Papa's Waltz," about a father who swings his son—the poem's speaker—around the room, a student may want to emphasize the idea of the son's experience of his father's love, as opposed to the possibility of his father's drunkenness.

Poetry slams allow opportunities for students to display their oral interpretation skills. You can create your own classroom poetry slam by having students perform as team members and then having students evaluate those performances based on their own criteria for evaluating the quality of oral interpreta-

tions. You can provide students with examples of poetry slams through use of clips from the documentary, Poetic License (see the Web site).

ONLINE DISCUSSION TOOLS

One of the important recent developments in classroom discussions has been the use of on-line discussions, either during class, or, more frequently, as part of homework. They can also be used for peer feedback sessions, online conferencing or advising with students, or discussions with guest speakers or outside experts with whom students could chat online. With the increased use of video-camera communication of speakers' faces, these online discussions are moving toward replicating face-to-face interactions.

There are several advantages of online discussions. Students who may not participate in face-to-face classroom discussions for various reasons, particularly nonverbal intimidation, may feel more comfortable participating online. In some cases, in having to write out their thoughts, students may formulate more thoughtful comments than if they were contributing verbal comments in a discussion. And, students can participate in discussions at any time of the day or night—organizing, for example, a discussion during the evening hours.

Another advantage of computer exchanges is that students can exchange with different audiences in other schools. For example, students in the classrooms of Melissa Borgman of North High School in Minneapolis, and Joy Hanson of Eastview High School in Apple Valley, Minnesota, were both studying *Their Eyes Were Watching God*. Because the students in these schools were from very different worlds—the students at North High School were largely urban African American students and the students from Apple Valley were largely suburban White students, these two teachers wanted their students to mutually wrestle with issues of racism portrayed in the novel. Students initially shared background information about themselves—their interests, hobbies, extracurricular activities, family, friends, and so forth. They then exchanged responses to the novel, specifying the topic in the subject line. Students were instructed on ways of replying to responses, perhaps one of the most important elements of fostering exchanges. They were told to first greet their partners and then to respond to specific lines in their partner's message that they cut and pasted into their own message. They were also asked to note whether they agreed or disagreed with their partners' responses and to give reasons for their agreements or disagreements.

On the other hand, there are limitations to online discussions. Just as with f-t-f discussions, they can be superficial, particularly in real-time chat rooms. Without some careful facilitation or structure, they can also lose direction, and, in some cases, result in instances of "flaming" or put-downs.

There are a range of different types of online discussion tools that can be organized into three larger categories: real-time, synchronous chat sites; asynchronous, threaded discussion sites; and e-mail and listserve sites.

Synchronous Chat Sites. There are also instant message and America Online buddy chat sites, which are used frequently by students for their own chats, and, increasingly by teachers for classroom discussions. One issue with these sites is whether students perceive them as relevant or appropriate for academic discussions, as opposed to their own social networking.

There are also free educational chat sites such as tappedin.org, nicenet.org, or moodle .org that can be used for large- and small-group discussions. One major advantage of tappedin.org and moodle.org is that that you can receive transcripts of students' discussions via e-mail for your analysis and evaluation. In these discussions, participants can also share URLs or PowerPoint™ presentations using the whiteboards located in these rooms. As a teacher, you can also join various professional groups' discussions or professional development events that are scheduled for various times during any given month.

MOOs or Blogs.   Another important technology tool involves the use of MOOs, or blogging sites for online discussions. MOO stands for Multiuser (many participants) and Object-Oriented—the type of program employed. To some degree, tappedin.org can be considered a MOO because it involves participation in different virtual "classrooms" or "offices" for discussions. In MOOs, students can also adopt different roles associated with characters in a text. MOOs also contain creations of simulated worlds such as the settings for certain texts. For example, one MOO site, Diversity U, contains simulations of Dante's *Inferno, A Midsummer Night's Dream,* and *Anne of Green Gables.* Students can also construct their own roles, settings, and languages in these sites. For example, in studying *Brave New World,* students assumed roles similar to those of the characters in the novel and created settings based on the novel. In a MOO, they then carried on conversations mimicking the language of the novel about issues faced by characters in the novel (Rozema, 2003).

Another tool involves the use of blogs, particularly for discussions with other classes or participants on issue-oriented blogs. Teachers note that Weblogs provide a greater sense of a shared community with people from outside the classroom, providing students with an audience larger than simply the classroom. Two popular blogs for adolescents that function as online book clubs for teens are *Book Diva* and *Teenreads.* (For links to these sites and other blog sites, go to the Web site).

For holding "academic" synchronous online discussions on blogs or free sites such as tapped.in.org, nicenet.org, or moodle.org, we offer the following suggestions:

1. As in giving journal prompt assignments, develop a clear sense of purpose for the discussion, as well as a relatively specific task or prompt, that is, develop some different explanations for why a character did what he or she did, and determine which of these explanations is the most valid.

2. Use small groups of three to four students; larger groups, as in actual classroom discussions, often do not allow enough students time to participate in any depth.

3. Continually remind students of rules of "netiquette": avoid put-downs or "flaming," respect others' opinions although one disagrees with those opinions, and avoid dominating the discussion.

4. Formulate some criteria by which you can evaluate transcripts of students' discussions and review those criteria with students (many of these sites provide you with transcripts; you may not want to evaluate all of the students' discussions).

Summary: Leading Large-Group Discussions.   Fostering effective large-group discussions involves the following:

- Posing "authentic," provocative questions that foster expression of diverse perspectives.
- Explicitly teaching students discussion skills of turn taking, agreeing and disagreeing, and acknowledging diverse responses.

- Framing discussion topics in terms of tentative, hypothetical hunches that need further verification.
- Using informal writing techniques to help low-level participants formulate their ideas in writing prior to discussions.
- Enhancing low-level participants' discussion contributions through working with them individually, using writing activities to prepare them for discussions, or using paired or small-group discussions prior to large-group discussions.
- Employing Web-based chat rooms to reduce intimidation of low-level participants due to nonverbal factors operating in classrooms.

SMALL-GROUP DISCUSSIONS AND BOOK CLUBS

Students rarely have an opportunity to practice and develop communication strategies in a 30-min discussion with 30 students in a class. Small groups, literature circles (Daniels, 2001, 2002; Daniels & Steineke, 2004), or book clubs (Alvermann, Young, & Green, 1997; Marshall, Smith, & Smagorinsky, 1995; McMahon, Raphael, Goatley, & Pardo, 1997) provide students with intimate settings in which they have more opportunity to participate than in large-group discussions (Almasi, 1995). By working in small groups of three to five, students have much more time to talk than in large groups.

In setting up groups, you may want to do the following:

- Assign students to groups to insure that there is a range of different talents or ability levels represented in your different groups, as well as a mixture of gender and race.
- Avoid having all of the students of a certain type in their own segregated groups.
- Ask students to assume different roles, such as the following:

  - Facilitator who poses questions, asks for reactions to members' statements, summarizes members' positions, encourages all members to participate, and restates others' perspectives.
  - Leader who initiates and concludes discussions.
  - "Scribe" who takes notes to report on the group's discussion to the large group.
  - "Devil's advocate" who challenges the group with alternative perspectives or positions.

Book Clubs. In classroom book clubs, students choose the texts they will read, set their reading agenda, and prepare their own topics for discussion. They then meet regularly with a small group of their peers several times for discussion (Alvermann et al., 1997; McMahon et al., 1997). In giving students autonomy to engage in discussions, you also need to recognize that students may have little understanding of how to engage in a thoughtful discussion. They may therefore fall back on familiar notions of their teachers' IRE/ "T/S" models in which they themselves then dominate discussions or exclude students (McMahon et al., 1997). In some cases, boys may assume that they have more power and attempt to dominate discussions (Lewis, 2001).

Rather than just send students off into groups without prior preparation, you need to assume an active role in developing and facilitating small-group discussion, roles assumed by Rachel.

RACHEL'S USE OF BOOK CLUBS

In her 12th-grade literature class at Champlin Park High School, Champlin, Minnesota, Rachel Malchow (2004) uses book clubs to foster discussion. She describes the ways in which she set up the book clubs for her class of 27 students (go the Web site for her Appendixes A, B, and E), and preparation for four book club discussions (Appendix C), self and group assessments of discussions (Appendix D), and their final group project (Appendix E).

She first administered an inventory to determine her students' reading habits and interests (Appendix A). Her nine boys reported that reading for personal pleasure was about 15 min per day, largely newspapers or magazines, with only one boy reporting being a "frequent" reader of novels. In contrast, the boys reported an average of 265 min per day engaged with some form of media (film, television, music, computers, or gaming). Her 17 girls averaged 18.8 min per day of reading for pleasure and 184 min per day devoted to media texts, with only one girl reporting being a "frequent" reader of novels. When asked to report the best book they had ever read for school, students cited *Of Mice and Men*, *To Kill a Mockingbird*, and *The Great Gatsby*; contemporary and young adult titles also only appeared twice on their lists.

A key element of the book club format is that students are given a choice over what they read in their groups. Predictably, that choice carries certain limitations, particularly the titles and numbers of books available to her 12th-grade team. Given that the regular English 12 course had contained a choice component in its curriculum for years, she did have a reasonable variety of books from which to choose. Her team decided to offer 10 choices each term, and tried to balance the list with a mixture of authors by gender and ethnicity each term. Most of the books are modern or contemporary books geared for the college-bound or adult reader (Appendix B).

Approximately 2 weeks before the first book club meeting each term, Rachel provides students with a choice of 10 books (Appendix B). Students then list their top three choices in order, and turn in their selections. She then creates assigned groups of three to five students based on student book requests and gender balance. (She finds that students often select books with protagonists that closely resemble themselves in terms of both gender and ethnicity, although girls are more willing in both terms to read about male protagonists.) The groups then meet once a week for 4 weeks for a duration of approximately 30 min to discuss their reading, and then meet twice to complete their final project, an introduction to the book for future students (Appendix E).

She modifies Daniels's (2002b) literature circle roles to add three key roles: discussion-director, cool-quote finder, and multiple-perspective-taker for each meeting. She also monitors the group discussions to identify instances in which students are having difficulty assuming different roles. For example, she found that students adopting the summarizing role were waiting until late in the discussion to summarize the text.

In analyzing transcripts of some of the book club discussions, Rachel found that some groups were more engaged in discussions than others. A key factor was selecting a text that evoked discussions about issues that were relevant to their own lives. A group that selected *The Bean Trees* and *The Secret Life of Bees* became engaged in a discussion of the tension between independence and motherhood. Another group that selected *The Things They Carried* focused on the harsh realities of becoming a soldier. She also found that students had difficulty adopting their roles in ways that limited discussions. For example, although the discussion director's role involves asking questions, it may be more useful to have all students posing questions. And, she found that in some groups, certain students assumed dominate positions of power in ways that excluded other students' participation, often in terms of differences in gender or race. In a group of three White girls and one African American boy, the boy was largely excluded from the discussion.

She also found instances of analysis of double-voicing in discussions of *Kindred*—a novel about Dana, a young African American woman living in the 1970s who is married to a White man, Kevin. The couple finds themselves traveling through time to the antebellum South to save the life of a White slave owner, Rufus, who is one of Dana's ancestors. Students used double-voicing of the characters' offensive opinions about women and African-Americans that reflected a critique of the discourses of slavery.

Portfolio Addition: Reflecting on Small-Group and Book-Club Discussions

For your portfolio reflection on materials related to uses of talk and write tools to fulfill your learning objectives and goals, you could include the following items:

- Transcripts of a small- or large-group classroom discussion (including online chat discussions) you facilitated, with a focus on your own highlighted strategies for facilitating discussion—the questions, uptake reactions, contributions, modeling, and so forth, that you employed. You may then reflect on the nature and types of questions you employed and the degree to which students were developing and extending their responses, as well as conversing between themselves. You may also reflect on difficulties or limitations of the discussion, for example, the fact that many students were not participating in a large-group discussion, and reasons for their lack of participation.
- Sample audio or video clips of students employing talk-tools, for example, clips of students engaged in think-alouds, author's chair or hotseat, debate, panel, or small-group discussion. You could then reflect on the quality and nature of the students' participation in these activities.

In your methods course or your practicum setting, you may have the opportunity to participate or set up some small-group or book-club discussions. In a study of preservice English Education teachers from Colorado State University, Cindy O'Donnell-Allen and Bud Hunt (2001) examined what the preservice teachers learned from conducting teacher research projects with young-adult literature book clubs in a local elementary and junior high school. The preservice teachers kept field notes journals and then shared their perceptions in teacher-research inquiry groups. In these groups, they generated inquiry questions that framed their analysis of the book clubs, focusing on some of the following issues.

Lack of Time to Read. One of the issues they confronted in working with a sixth-grade book club was that with all of their extracurricular obligations, the students simply did not have the time to read their books or to complete writing assignments. One of the preservice teachers therefore changed the assignment so that the students completed the freewriting about their books in the beginning of the book-club meeting.

Gendered Reading Choices. Two preservice teachers found that their mixed-gender elementary book-club students were selecting books based on gender, with boys, for example, picking a book with a sea monster on a blue cover, and girls choosing a book with a girl in a frilly dress on a pink cover. The teachers also discovered that the group could not agree on a book that would please both the boys and the girls. In studying this issue, the teachers recognized that gender can play a major role in book selections.

Categories for Defining Literature.   Another issue that emerged was how to categorize various book-club choices—as "young-adult" or "adult" literature. Students were selecting texts that cut across all of these categories. Based on her analysis of the utility of these categories, one preservice teacher argued that "young-adult" literature should be defined not in terms of text characteristics, but in terms of what adolescents like to read.

Online Additional Activities, Links, and Further Reading

Go to the textbook Web site, Chapter 5, for additional activities, links, and further reading.

6

Writing About Literature:
How Do I Get Students
to Write About Literature?

Chapter Overview

- Limitations of "list and gist" writing about literature.
- Building audiences into writing assignments.
- Using a reading and writing workshop approach.
- Informal writing tools.
- Integrating uses of informal writing tools in designing assignments.
- Rewriting texts for fostering perspective-taking.
- Formal writing about literature.
- Understanding texts through writing texts.

CASE NARRATIVE: DIFFERENT KINDS
OF WRITING ABOUT LITERATURE

Kathy contrasts her experiences between high school and college writing:

In high school, I'm really remembering a lot of more formal writing, not free writing, or informal kind of rough writing. Usually the writing that I was taught in high school needed to be polished; it was always grammar and usage and all that kind of stuff was always graded. College was much more, I want to say relaxed, but varied. There was no work-sheet writing. We didn't talk about plot, characterization, or setting so much, but we might spend an hour and a half talking about why a certain character made the decision that he did.

Recall your own experiences with writing about literature in your previous high school and college literature courses. What kinds of writing were typically assigned? What were the different purposes for this writing? What were some assignments that you found to be valuable and why?

LIMITATIONS OF "LIST AND GIST" CLASSROOM WRITING ABOUT LITERATURE

Much of writing about literature occurs solely as worksheets consisting of identification of information about a text, book reports that simply summarize a story, or five-paragraph essays focused on "proving" a single point with little development of thinking. This writing functions in an information-transmission classroom to simply inform the teacher that the student knows the "right answers," can retell a story, or "prove" his or her point.

From a constructivist learning perspective, there are several limitations to this "list and gist" writing as a learning tool. These limitations point to the need for the use of extended writing activities that foster constructivist thinking.

The Lack of Argument for an Interpretation. In an information-transmission classroom, students' use their writing to display "right answers." In constructivist classroom discussions, students are continually formulating arguments for certain interpretations or applications of critical lenses, often taking into account other students' counterpositions. They can then use their writing to extend their arguments in a more systematic, formal manner in which they formulate their claims and explore counterclaims. For example, in a classroom discussion about *The Crucible*, Jill is arguing that the hysteria in the town about witchcraft parallels similar moments in history in which politicians stir up fear to serve their own political agendas, as was the case of a fear of anti-Communism during the McCarthy era. Other students challenge this idea by noting that these fears of potential danger cannot be dismissed as simply serving political agendas. With this debate in mind, Jill writes an essay in which she explores the difference, drawing on examples from the play, of concocted fears that are designed to serve certain agendas versus authentic fears that are based on actual fears. Through her writing, Jill can explore her ideas and examine alternative claims related to the differences between concocted and authentic fears.

The Lack of Tentative, Exploratory Thinking About a Text. Another limitation of "list and gist" writing is that it does not foster exploratory thinking about a text, reflecting a "failure to be tentative" (McCormick, 1999, p. 203). If students are concerned about "getting the right answer" or "making the correct interpretation," they are reluctant to explore different aspects or complexities of their experience with a text. They assume that they need to be definitive and authoritative versus exploratory and tentative.

The Lack of Purpose for Writing. Another limitation of a lot of writing about literature is that the students perceive little purpose or value in writing about literature, other than to complete an assignment for a grade. Even if you use various informal writing tools to prepare students for writing, the result is writing that is often uninspired, pedantic, artificial, or, in some cases, contains borrowed material from the Internet. You may be left with 80 essays to read that you have little interest in reading, just as students have little interest in writing these essays.

In an inquiry-based, constructivist classroom, students select specific issues, concerns, or questions related to their reading about which they are engaged. For example, as someone who was interested in local politics, Jill was highly concerned about the ways in which some politicians were using fear of increased diversity as a "wedge" issue in a local campaign. She was able to draw on examples from this campaign to define parallel connections with *The Crucible*.

The Lack of Alternative Audiences. Another limitation of many literature-writing as-signments is that students are writing simply for the teacher for the purpose of being evalu-ated. If students are writing for their peers, parents, or other audiences outside of the school through dialogue journals, class Web sites or newsletters, or published essays, they then have some social purpose for wanting to write and write well. In her student teaching, Heidi Murphy created an extra-credit brochure-writing assignment: "They had to write a brochure for next year's sophomores telling what skills they'd need to survive and letting them know that what they'll read and what they'll be doing in class: I got quite a few bro-chures." In a college drama course, Russell Hunt (2002) had students create programs of "playgoers' guides" that were actually distributed to audiences in local theaters. In the syl-labus, Hunt formulated the value of these writing activities for students:

> First, I believe that people learn far more effectively when they're actively trying to find things out and explain and demonstrate them to others than when they sit and listen to them. Second, I believe that there is no one authority on questions like these—certainly neither me nor any textbook has the final word. In fact, there is no final word—as you'll have a chance to discover, people are continuously coming to new understandings and discovering new things about these matters. Thus it's at least as important to know *how* to learn about such a subject as it is to be aware of what others think they already know. This course, then, is organized to pro-mote (indeed, to require) the active and continuing engagement of each member of the class in the process of investigation.

(For the course syllabus, with examples of the students' playgoers' guides, go to the Web site.)

By sharing their written responses in dialogue journals or online discussion sites with oth-ers, as in discussions, students are continually thinking about how others may react to their interpretations, what Bakhtin (1981) described as "answerability"—how an audience's po-tential reaction or "uptake" influences one's ideas or positions—anticipating that others may respond influences students' thinking. Knowing that their audiences may react in certain ways, students rehearse others' reactions and then use those reactions to expand on or revise their thinking. For example, Molly is writing in her dialogue journal about what she per-ceives to be the sexist attitudes in some of Hemingway's short stories. In thinking about how her male journal partner, Sam, may react to her entry based on his previous reactions, she an-ticipates that he may adopt a defensive stance and argue that Hemingway was just portraying the cultural attitudes of the time. This leads Molly to add some material on the cultural time period of the story as also shaping both Hemingway and his portrayals of characters. Thinking about Sam's potential reactions led her to elaborate on her interpretations.

BUILDING AUDIENCES INTO WRITING ASSIGNMENTS

All of this suggests the need to build in audiences other than yourself—actual and fic-tional—into your writing assignments. You can have students adopt certain roles as audi-ences who would respond in dialogue journal exchanges, letter writing, essay drafts, or on-line chat based on those roles. See Table 6.1 for audience alternative roles.

USING A READING AND WRITING WORKSHOP APPROACH

Underlying the idea of having students write for and to each other about texts is what is called a reading and writing workshop approach (Atwell, 1998; Kirby & Kuykendall, 1991; Olson, 2003). In the reading and writing workshop, students are given a high degree

TABLE 6.1
Building Audience Roles Into Assignments

Audience Roles	Audience Reactions According to
Characters in a text	how students' writing captures their identities
Authors	how student's writing is consistent with intentions
Advice columnist	how to cope with characters' problems identified by students
Critics adopting a particular lens	differences between the critic's lens and the student's lens
Editors of a class newspaper or online journal	whether student's writing would be published in the newspaper or online according to the editors' criteria
Museum curator of exhibits about certain literacy periods, cultures, or places	how the students' writing about literacy periods, culture, or place would contribute to the exhibit
Web master of a Web site about certain authors, genres, or types of writers (e.g., *Voices from the Gaps*) devoted to women writers of color	how the writing contributes to the Web site

of ownership in terms of their choices for selecting certain texts from a well-stocked classroom library or writing activities. Students are continually collaborating with each other on their work and reacting to each other's work, as is often the case in an art classroom. There is a lot of reading aloud by teachers and students from texts, use of drama activities, display of work, and small-group projects. And, students continually collect their work for inclusion in a portfolio.

Although this may imply a lack of structure, there is still a considerable degree of teacher structuring of expectations, rules, deadlines, and criteria for evaluating work, particularly in terms of creating a safe, supportive environment. Teachers give minilessons in which they demonstrate the use of specific interpretive or inquiry strategies, as well as modeling their own work. They also carefully structure activities according to variations in students ZPDs by continually interacting with students to monitor their work. To encourage students to express alternative, deviant voices, you can share some of your own writing in which you entertain a range of alternative perspectives and voices.

Issues With Idealized Notions of the Classroom Writing Community. Workshop approaches are often described in terms of idealized notions of a "community" in which students will all be equally motivated by the idea of writing to and for their peers. The reality is that any classroom community is rife with potential challenges, competition, tensions and conflicts between students as well as between students and the school. To foster, rather than suppress, these challenges, conflicts, and tensions, you may think of your classroom in terms of what Tim Lensmire (2002), drawing on John Dewey, defines as creating a sense of democracy. By democracy, he means a certain way of living based on developing students' capacities for thought, feeling, and action through sharing of stories that foster "transgression"—oral and written stories that "direct students to cross boundary lines that divide them from other people, stories that imagine others as possible sources of learning, meaning, value, friendship, and love" (p. 110). These stories engage students in deliberative reflection about the perspectives of others, leading them to understand the value of participating in a classroom "way of life" that builds relationships through literacy.

He also proposes that teachers capitalize on certain "opposing moments" in the classroom to foster students' reflections of status-quo notions of themselves and the world in ways that lead them to entertain alternative perspectives. And, in responding to and creating narratives, he has students focus on ways in which these narratives often do not always turn out positively due to the social forces shaping characters' and students' lives. And, he encourages students to adopt subversive, unofficial stances that challenge the often officially-sanctioned practices operating in classrooms, for example, sanctions against writing about violence. In all of this, students are performing and exploring a range of different, competing voices as part of both being and becoming, explorations that "help them transform these struggles into occasions for becoming" (Lensmire, 2002, p. 84). Although you may be uneasy about enacting Lensmire's (2002) vision of a classroom community that invites conflicts and subversion, you are also more likely to help students acquire certain ways of living consistent with Dewey's notion of democracy.

To foster expression of multiple voices, Lensmire (2002) proposes that teachers support students' reflections on their writing by capitalizing on certain "opposing moments" in the classroom. He has students focus on ways in which things do not always turn out positively by taking a realistic perspective on social forces shaping characters' and students' lives. Students then explore a range of different, competing voices that reflect the tensions portrayed in a text.

INFORMAL WRITING TOOLS

Informal writing differs from more formal essay writing in that it is spontaneous, exploratory, tentative, subjective, expressive, and even contradictory (Anson & Beach, 1995). In writing informally about a text, students are using writing to create a record of their thoughts as they are responding to the text through freewriting, notes, lists, journal entries, maps, or diagrams. And, informal writing is spontaneous and tentative, as opposed to predetermined and definitive.

The following are some specific types of informal writing tools (Anson & Beach, 1995; Burke, 2002). In modeling the uses of these different tools, it is important that you make explicit reasons for use of these tools related to uses of interpretive strategies and critical approaches. As informal writing, you want to avoid evaluating this writing in ways that undermine student spontaneity and lack of concern about audience, while prompting them to use these tools in specific ways, for example, by telling them to "try to list as many items as possible."

Freewriting.   In using freewriting, students write in a nonstop, spontaneous manner for 5 or 10 min without premature concern for editing. Essential to freewriting is avoiding the propensity to edit, censor, block, or revise initial reactions to texts. Students can be asked to simply freewrite about a text or specific part of a text. Or, in a "focused" freewrite, they can be asked to freewrite about a specific topic, theme, issue, or question related to a text or unit, for example, "gender and power." Or, in what Peter Elbow (1973) describes as a "looping" freewrite, students freewrite for 5 min. They then pick out one or two key terms or ideas, and freewrite for 5 more min about those one or two key terms or ideas, using the freewriting itself to generate and focus in on specific further topics by loping back through previous freewrites.

Students may also dictate their thoughts to a peer, into a tape recorder, or to a computer using voice-recognition software. For students with learning disabilities who may have difficulty with writing, this use of dictating or oral sharing can serve as a useful, alternative accommodation for writing; these students could even pull together their oral materials to create final oral essays.

Freewrites can also be used to help focus students' thinking on a specific topic or idea in the beginning of class as well as prepare them for verbally sharing responses. For students who are reluctant to verbally share their responses, having something to read can bolster their confidence. As a discussion unfolds, students could take time out to write their thoughts about or reflections on the discussion topic(s). By writing during the discussion, students can recharge their thinking to interject some new ideas into the discussion or push the discussion in new directions. Then, at the end of the discussion, students could write about what they learned from the discussion by synthesizing their perceptions of the discussion. By studying these reflective "learning entries," teachers may determine differences in how students are perceiving their classroom experience.

Note-Taking and Jotting.   In note-taking or jotting, students are recording their reactions and interpretations to texts, presentations, or lectures. Central to effective note-taking and jotting is the ability to summarize one's perceptions of a text or lecture in one's own words, as well as adding one's reflective interpretations. Some students may need instruction on writing summaries that go beyond simply quoting verbatim from the original texts to formulating your interpretations of texts. You could model this process by sharing your own notes about a text on the whiteboard, overhead, or computer.

You can initially simply restate or summarize the characters' actions or story events, asking students to add their own restatement and summaries. You can then ask students to reflect on certain ways of organizing the notes in terms of categories or patterns. You then show how you use these categories or patterns to formulate new summaries or interpretations.

In teaching *The Great Gatsby* in his student teaching, Dan Gough began by asking students to write in their journals in response to the following prompts (in reality, this sheet would be spaced out over two or three pages to allow room for notes):

Characters in The Great Gatsby

This sheet is designed as a place for you to keep notes regarding the characters from the novel as you meet them and as they evolve through the story. Beneath each character you should keep track of events, things they say and things that are said about them as the novel progresses. Make sure to use direct quotes from the novel, referenced with page numbers. It may also be a good idea to differentiate between traits that you feel are positive or negative within a character (+/–)

Gatsby

Nick

Tom

Daisy

Minor Characters (Myrtle, Wilson, Jordan, Owl Eyes, etc.)

Listing.   Students can list different aspects or elements of a character, setting, or story event. For example, you might ask students to list a character's attributes, a set of questions they have about a topic, some problems they wish to investigate, or people they can contact to discuss an issue or topic. In asking students to list, you want them to go beyond just one or two items and list as many items as possible.

To encourage students to think further about the idea of the American dream in his Gatsby unit, Dan asked them to respond to the Langston Hughes (1994) poem, "I, Too sing America," and list the following:

What is the poem saying? (Write at least 3 different answers)

What emotions are expressed in the poem? (Write at least 3 answers)

What are the three key words in the poem? (Come up with 10 words and narrow your list down as a group. Each member must be able to justify the final selection)

You can also ask students to list questions based on the text, questions you could then list on the whiteboard. You could then collapse, combine, or reorganize the questions and use them as the basis for a discussion. After a discussion, students could also submit to the teacher a list of "unanswered questions" which can be used to plan future discussions.

Journal Writing.   Students may also use a journal or reading log in which they react to texts (Anson & Beach, 1995). You may help students distinguish between formal essay writing and informal journal writing by sharing examples of journal entries representing more spontaneous, open-ended, exploratory, subjective responses than formal essay writing. You may also want to distinguish between the idea of a journal used in a writing class designed to foster expressive fluency—in which students write about their daily experiences or thoughts—and a "literature" or "reading-log" journal that focuses more on interpreting texts, although the distinction between the two may be somewhat arbitrary.

In some cases, you may ask students to use their entries to describe their reactions to a text, but generally students need more direction in the form of specific open-ended prompts related to responding to certain aspects of a text.

In teaching *The Diary of Anne Frank/The Play*, by Frances Goodrich and Albert Hackett (1998), to her eighth-grade students, Naomi Remple had students keep a diary in a manner that paralleled Anne Frank's own process of keeping a diary. To prepare students for diary writing, Naomi asked them to write down personal details that Anne included in her initial diary entry. To emphasize the value of details in diary writing, she asked them to discuss the importance of details, how those details help the reader, and what those details reveal about Anne. She then provided each student with blank journals with a quote taken from Anne's diary on each cover: "I hope I shall be able to confide in you completely, as I have never been able to do in anyone before, and I hope that you will be a great support and comfort to me."

Students may also use "dual-entry" journals in which they write down their perceptions or reactions on one side of a page and then reflect on these perceptions or reactions on the other side of the page. The perceptions on one side of the page trigger reflections on the other side, which, in turn, trigger further perceptions. Ideally, in moving back and forth between the two sides of the page, students enter into a dialectical inner dialogue. In a similar activity, to encourage students to expand or elaborate on their diary entries, Naomi asked them to create two columns on a sheet of paper, the first column titled, "Statement," and the second, "Prompt." In the statement column, students wrote various statements such as "I like cheese. I went to the mall yesterday. I want to go to Africa." The students then drew an arrow to the right column and wrote a question or a prompt to find out more about that first statement: "Why? What do you mean by that? What else?" After they wrote the prompt, they then drew an arrow back to the other side and wrote a new statement answering the prompt until they wrote at least six links to their "chain" of statement or prompt connections.

For writing in their diaries, Naomi provided the following prompts:

"I dream that one day . . ."

"If I had to hide in an attic like Anne did I would . . ." 5 minutes.

"What would be your first wish, if you were free from hiding?"

"Write about a memory or person that made you angry or hurt. Have you forgiven this person?" "Choose one of the characters in Scene II to write an interior monologue or diary entry for that character, Peter, Dussel, Margot, or Anne."

In response to Raymond Carver's poem, "Fear," write a list poem, each line beginning with, "Fear of . . ."

"List times you were either a victim or a perpetrator of injustice or when you witnessed injustice."

Dialogue-Journal Exchanges.   Students can also exchange entries with each other in paper form or on the computer. Or, they can share written responses on online chat sites, such as those described in Chapter 5 (see also the Web site).

These dialogue journals serve to bolster students' social exchange of talk and writing. In writing to and for their peers, students mutually construct a shared stance that transcends each of their own individual perspectives. In so doing, they experience disagreements, misunderstandings, conflicts, resistances, and divergent understandings that create dialogic tensions between their own and others' stances. They also begin to anticipate others' reactions to the point that they could predict how they will respond to certain of their positions—the fact that their partner will probably disagree with their position. This reflects Bakhtin's notion of "answerability"—that all utterances anticipate some potential reaction from another person. In anticipating potential reactions, they extend their responses or pose questions of their partner—"I didn't understand what's happening—what do you think?"—questions that invite their partners to reciprocate. These "outer" or "public" questions then form the basis of an "inner" set of questions for further thinking about a text.

Exchanging entries between peers has certain advantages to teacher–student exchanges. If students perceive teachers as superiors, they may be less likely to share feelings, doubts, and concerns than with peers. As is the case with online chat, although it lacks the immediacy of oral conversation, the peer-dialogue journal also has advantages over oral conversation. Participating in face-to-face nonverbal conversation can be intimidating for some students, particularly those that are reluctant to assert themselves. The anonymity inherent in written exchanges may reduce students' fear of asserting themselves in conversation.

At the same time, as Nancie Atwell (1998) does in teacher–student exchanges, in responding to student entries, you can pose questions that model certain ways of thinking or interpretive strategies or critical approaches to help students extend or elaborate on their thinking with each students' particular ZPD. These include questions as simple as "I wondered why the character did that?" to more complex questions such as "How were the characters trapped within their own narrow notions of gender differences?" Over time, as students internalize these questions, they begin to apply them to writing entries on their own, ideally resulting in more elaborated interpretations. Consistent with an apprenticeship model, by demonstrating this question-asking, you are socializing students into a community of practice associated with being critical readers. As students appropriate the use of increasingly higher order questions, they are more likely to become successful members of that community.

As a variation on dialogue-journal writing, for his student teaching unit on the novel *Holes*, Bryan Legrand had students write letters to their peers:

1. Read a letter home from Barf Bag (the previous camper at Green Lake whose place Stanley took). In this letter, Barf Bag will tell his parents that if they don't get him out of there, he

will intentionally step on a rattlesnake so that he'll have to be sent to the hospital. Ask the students, if a camper might do that. Why or why not?

2. Write a letter home from Camp Green Lake. Students will be given an envelope to put their letter in. I will select letters at random, open the envelope and read them aloud. Framing questions to use as a discussion when reading the letters: Why did Stanley lie in his letter? Why is Stanley called Caveman? If you tried to explain to your parents that the conditions at Camp Green Lake were horrible would they believe you? How could you convince someone in your letter that you weren't lying about Camp Green Lake?

And, in teaching about the portrayal of war in *The Things They Carried*, in her student teaching, Bridget Hoolihan read some letters to her students from her brother who was fighting (in 2004) in Iraq. She then had her students write letters back to her brother in which they introduced themselves in the letter and posed at least three questions relating to the situation in Iraq, letters she then sent to her brother.

Self-Assessing Journals.   Jane Smith (2000) asks students to keep a reading journal of one page of 250 words per work assigned. They can "1) explore feelings about the work, 2) discuss characterization or other literary elements, or 3) compare the work to something else they have read" (p. 129). She collects entries at the beginning of each class and often uses those journals to assess what students need most from her during a particular class period. In the middle of the term, students evaluate the work they have done in their journals by answering questions provided by the instructor:

1. How would you evaluate your writing at this point? What are your strengths? Did you have any problems I can help you with?
2. Describe what you see in your journal writing. What kinds of responses to the literature have you experimented with?
3. In what ways do you hope to improve your journal over the rest of the term? (Smith, 2000, p. 130)

At the end of the term, students revisit these questions as well as answer the following items:

1. Describe the kinds of writing you did in your journal at the beginning of the term; then, describe the kinds of writing you did at the end. What changes do you notice, if any?
2. Why do you think these changes (if any) occurred? If none did, why not? What did you feel you did well in your journal? What would you have liked to improve?
3. Do you feel that keeping a journal in this class was worthwhile? Why or why not? If you felt that this was a worthwhile experience, what particular value(s) did the journal have for you?
4. Is there anything that could be done to make the journal assignment more effective and useful for the students? (Smith, 2000, p. 130)

Mapping and Diagramming.   Students can use maps or diagrams to chart out and define the relations between the different aspects of a text. These drawings or diagrams help students perceive their thoughts in visual form, something particularly appealing for those with a high "visual and spatial" intelligence (Gardner, 1993; 2000). Learning to use these visual tools is part of learning how signs and images are used to represent larger meanings.

Students can use circle maps to portray the different characters' circles and then, with spokes emanating from each circle, describe traits, beliefs, and goals associated with each character. They can also use circle maps to define the different subworlds in a text and how characters' practices may vary across those subworlds. To help his students define the different subworlds of *The Great Gatsby*, Dan had his students create maps representing the novel's different settings:

> Movement and location are very important in *The Great Gatsby*. That characters and action move around from place to place and locations themselves can tell us a story. For extra credit you are invited to create a map of the novel. To get full credit your map should be accurately based on the novel, contain all the important areas and landmarks mentioned in the novel and be imaginatively and artistically created. The map should document what happens in the various locations. Some of the locations that your map must contain are: East Egg, Buchanan's house, West Egg, Gatsby's house, Nick's house, Valley of Ashes, T. J. Eckleberg billboard, railroad tracks and motor road, Wilson's garage/house, New York.

Students could also draw maps that represent how they believe characters conceptualize or define their worlds—creating a graphic version of characters' cultural models of the world—with some practices and beliefs being on the top of the map that they value as "higher," or more important, than other practices or beliefs. For example, they may create a map for Holden Caufield in which certain experiences in his life—his relationships with other characters—are more important to him than his schooling or certain status markers.

Art Work.   Students can also create art work that reflects their experiences with texts. In some cases, they may portray their perceptions of characters or setting, whereas in other cases, they may depict thematic or archetypal interpretations. In response to novels, Linda Reif's (1992) eighth-grade students, working in teams, created their own paintings and wall murals containing images that represented their experience with these novels. As they worked on the paintings, they discussed their responses, often revising their perceptions through the process of having to visually convey their experience. The result was three large abstract paintings that were placed on a hallway wall of Reif's middle school. Students may also use art work in creating book covers that convey summary images portraying their interpretations of a text in the same manner as illustrations in children's literature. Or, they may create covers for anthologies of collections of poetry that include prefaces and discussions of the poems included (Scimone, 1999).

Students can also create body biographies, life-size drawings of characters with descriptions of different aspects of each character (see the Web site for directions). For his student teaching unit on *Holes*, Bryan Legrand had students create criminal "rap sheets" based on characters they create who might be sent to camp such as the one in the novel. The students give themselves new names (their real first name, with a last name that is simply their first name spelled backwards like Stanley Yelnats, the protagonist of *Holes*), and the crime of which they are accused (it will be humorous, like feeding Ex-Lax to their neighbor's dog, who then proceeded to ruin their neighbor's carpet). Students had to reflect on whether they were guilty or innocent, what happened in their "crime," and whether they were caught.

They then draw a picture of their character or find a photo that looks like their character and paste it on the back of their sheet. Also on the back, they write answers to the following prompts: Describe what your character looks like. Where does your character live? Who does your character live with? What does your character like to do? If your character had another chance to speak with the judge before being sent to Camp Cooper, what would your character say?

INTEGRATING USES OF INFORMAL WRITING TOOLS IN DESIGNING ASSIGNMENTS

In planning your classroom activities, you are considering how these different tools can be used to support each other. Just as freewriting, note-taking or jotting, or listing are used to develop material for mapping and diagramming and art work, so mapping and diagramming and art work can lead to freewriting, note-taking or jotting, or listing. By having to first write down their ideas, students are developing and rehearsing their thoughts to then share in discussions. Because they have previously formulated responses to a text, they are then more likely to participate in the discussion.

Sequencing "First Things First."   This means that you need to consider how you sequence uses of these tools so that some tools prepare students for use of other tools—"first things first." One key question to ask yourself in sequencing activities is the following: Can students complete activity A without some using some prior activity B that prepares them for that activity A? For example, you are considering whether to begin a lesson with a short story with a mapping or a freewrite activity. You then ask yourself, will they be able to first do a mapping or freewrite activity? Students are more likely to have difficulty doing a mapping activity than a freewrite, so you may then decide to use the freewrite to prepare students for the mapping activity.

Specifying Purposes for Activities.   It is also important that students know the purposes for each activity—how that activity will serve to prepare them for the next activity. For example, in giving them the freewrite assignment, you may tell the students, "You will be using this freewrite to develop character traits, beliefs, and goals to construct a map about the story's characters." Knowing why they are doing the freewrite activity to prepare them for mapping provides them with some direction for focusing their freewrite on character traits, beliefs, and goals.

Providing Criteria for Self-Assessment.   And, in assigning the use of tools, you may also provide students with criteria for reflecting on their use of certain tools, criteria such as sufficiency ("Do you have enough material?"), specificity ("Have you cited specific examples?"), and relevancy ("Does what you wrote address the topic or prepare you for the next activity?").

By self-assessing their writing, students may learn the value of specifying their responses in some detail. In one study of eighth-graders' mapping of short stories, students were asked to create maps for the character traits, beliefs, and goals in the F. Scott Fitzgerald story, "Bernice Bobs Her Hair," a story about one female seeking revenge of her cousin who betrayed her. They first did a freewrite about their interpretation of the characters, which prepared them for their mapping story. They then had to think of another similar text, freewrite about that text, and draw a map of characters in that text. They then had to draw lines between their maps indicating similarities between stories, and write a final interpretation of the Fitzgerald story. Analysis of the final interpretation found that the more detailed the mapping of character traits, beliefs, and goals, the higher the quality of students' final written interpretations (Beach, Appleman, & Dorsey, 1990).

Activity: Developing Informal Writing Tools to Explore Responses

Devise some classroom activities in which you use a range of different informal writing tools to foster development of responses in a microteaching session with your peers or pupils:

1. Select a poem or short story.
2. Reflect on how each tool serves to support uses of other tools. Formulate prompts that specify the purposes for using these tools.

REWRITING TEXTS: A WRITING ACTIVITY FOR FOSTERING PERSPECTIVE-TAKING

Another informal set of writing activities that can also be used to foster perspective taking is the use of rewriting of texts. Robert Pope (1995) describes rewriting the text as a way to " 'recenter' it, thereby deflecting and re-directing its dominant 'ways of saying' and its preferred 'ways of seeing' " (p. 4). "Deliberately put [the text] 'off balance' and alter its emphasis . . . do not be afraid to try it out in—and against—difference styles, discourses and co(n)texts" (p. 11). After rewriting a text, students then discuss reasons for the interventions or changes in terms of the preferred or intended meanings. They "consider what light these changes throw on the structures, meanings, values, and functions of the base text" (p. 11). In rewriting original texts, students entertain an alternative, hypothetical "what if" perspective and create an alternative text that reflects a different perspective or meaning (Pope, 1995). This may include the following:

- Translating the text into simpler or different language—For example, rewriting a section of a Shakespeare play or sonnet into contemporary English, Spanish, or French.
- Parodying the text—In which students mimic or alter the text to ridicule the style or themes. Students could study contemporary examples of parody, for example, *The Onion*, a newspaper parody of current news events.
- Rewriting the text or a section of a text in a different genre—A diary entry, letter, memo, e-mail message, poem, memoir, newspaper report, and so forth, for example, creating a story or play out of a newspaper report, or having a character write diary entries or letters to other characters.
- Creating a multigenre text—In which students write other short texts that are linked to certain aspects of the text; they then insert these linked texts into the text (Romano, 2000).
- Creating a hypertext version of the text—In which students use an electronic version of a text to insert links to related Web sites (by inserting URLs); background historical information about settings, characters, authors, events; and links to other related texts (using the multigenre material). Students could use computer software such as Hyperstudio™ or Storyspace™ to create their own hypertext versions of texts.

- Inserting dialogue into texts—In which students add dialogue as interior monologues to show what characters are really thinking about each other or their reflections about events in the story.

- Switching the point of view or perspective—For example, telling the story from a different or another character's perspective or switching a third person omniscient narrator point of view to a first person point of view to illuminate a main character's own perspectives on events. In shifting the perspective, minor characters, as in *Rosencrantz and Guildenstern Are Dead*, may assume a major role in providing their own versions of events.

- Switching the character or reader audience—In which, a character may address an alternative character in a different way or the text itself may adopt a different stance toward the audience. Students could consider which audiences an author is not addressing and then address an alternative version of the text to those audiences (Pope, 1995).

- Adding characters or expanding minor characters—In which students insert characters—characters from other texts, historical figures, celebrities, ghosts of deceased characters, narrators, authors, etc., who assume a role in the story. Students could read novels such as *Ragtime* that include historical figures from the same historical period. Students could discuss other historical events or famous people of the same time period that are excluded from the text, and include those events or people in the text (Pope, 1995).

- Inserting alternative events or story lines—Based on the "Choose Your Adventure" genre and the more current hypertext fiction or computer games, students could insert alternative events or story line pathways or endings.

- Creating a different setting, period, culture, or time for a text—In which the characters are transported into a different setting, historical period, or culture. Students could read *Kindred* in which contemporary African American characters are transported back in time to the period of slavery.

Creating Alternative Representations.   Texts represent certain phenomena or worlds in certain ways that reflect certain beliefs, attitudes, or ideological orientations. For example, advertising often represents gender roles in sexist, essentialist ways, portraying women as valuing physical or sexual attraction related to relationships and men as valuing athletic and physical activities. Or, corporations attempt to represent themselves in ways that place them in a positive public-relations light: for example, oil corporation ads portray themselves concerned about ecology or as supporters of education. Having defined these representations, students could also create alternative, more complex, accurate representations that parody the original simplistic, misleading representations. For example, they may represent gender roles in ways that portray men and women crossing traditional gender boundaries or corporations as engaged in questionable practices.

Storyboard or Comic Books.   Students could create storyboard or comic book versions of texts, after studying examples of comic-book or graphic-novel styles such as Art Spiegelman's (1993) novel, *Maus*. Students select certain key scenes or part of a text and imagine what it would be like to create their own video or film of those scenes or parts through the use of different types of camera shots (establishing or long, close-ups, midshot, long-shots), camera angles (down shots, up shots, point-of-view shots, reverse angle shots), length of each shot, and background dialogue or music. Using open-box panels, they then fill in with drawings, caption boxes, and dialogue balloons (Morrison, Bryan, & Chilcoat, 2002).

Revising One's Own or Others' Response. Students may reflect on the perspective, stances, or lenses they adopt in their own or others' written responses and then revise or rewrite those responses adopting a totally different perspective, stance, or lens. They may have initially responded in a manner consistent with how the text was positioning them to respond. In responding to the Cinderella story, they may have been pleased that everything works out for Cinderella at the end of the story because she has "found her man." In reflecting on the question, "How is this text positioning me?" (Ellsworth, 1997), they may recognize that the text wants them to respond in this manner consistent with a patriarchic value stance. They may adopt an alternative, feminist stance and write about the difficulties associated with establishing a relationship based on one supposedly magical night at the ball.

Or, students may find others responses, for example, online book reviews on Amazon.com, and, based on analysis of the stances adopted in those responses, rewrite them in terms of a totally different stance.

USING REWRITING TO CRITICALLY INTERROGATE TEXTS

Through rewriting texts, students can challenge certain implied dominant value stances, discourses, or positioning of how they should respond. By identifying how they should respond, students could then define their own alternative responses. They then use those alternative responses to invent alternative versions of a text.

We recommend beginning with a simple text such as an ad, children's story, fable, or fairy tale, with a defined or obvious ideological message or theme for students to interrogate. For example, as noted earlier, the Cinderella story represents a traditional gender role portrayal that presupposes that a woman's primary concern is with attracting a future marriage partner. Students could then look at examples of rewritings of these texts, such as Anne Sexton's poem, and discuss the ways in which these rewritings functioned to challenge the dominant implied meanings. For example, parodies of cigarette or alcohol ads challenge the glamorization of smoking or drinking by presenting a realistic version of the adverse effects of smoking—showing, for example, the Marlboro Man coughing or the shape of a liquor bottle as a coffin. Students could also read parodies of children's stories such as the "Three Little Pigs" or "Little Red Riding Hood" and discuss the how these different versions reflect different perspectives and value stances.

Students could then rewrite these texts in ways that challenge the dominant implied stance. For example, with the Cinderella story, they could rewrite the story in ways that portray Cinderella as a more complex character who is interested in a career, her education, political matters, and so forth. They could also rewrite school texts, for example, creating a different set of questions for their literature text that are more consistent with their own interests or agendas.

FORMAL WRITING ABOUT LITERATURE

In contrast to more informal writing, students are also writing more formal essays about literature. In more formal essay writing, students are pulling together material developed from informal writing to formulate an essay that reflects sustained, systematic analysis or interpretation.

Formulating Writing Assignments.   Central to the success of formal writing about literature is a well-formulated assignment. One limitation of many assignments is that students are simply provided with a topic—"Is Willy Loman in *Death of a Salesman* a tragic hero? 500 words"—without providing students with any sense of purpose, interpretive strategies, audience, and criteria for success. Students need to understand your expectations related to the purpose for writing an essay, the interpretive strategies involved in writing the essay, and criteria for how you will be evaluating their writing.

The following are some specific components to include in an assignment:

- Purpose—In stating the purposes for writing, you are defining the reasons students are writing their essays; for example, in teaching a unit on the portrayal of small-town worlds in short stories. The final essay for the unit is as follows: "Describe the ways in which the small town is represented in one of the short stories." However, to write that essay, students need some sense of the purpose for writing the essay—how it fits into the larger unit. The purpose for the essay is to "demonstrate what you learned in this unit about characters' relationships with small-town life by showing how a short story portray characters' feelings of attachment with or detachment from their small-town community as statements about the value or limitations of small-town life."

- Interpretive strategies—It is also useful to specify the kinds of interpretative strategies students will use to fulfill the purpose of the assignment—in this case, how the short story characters' positive or negative relationship with small towns reflects the positive or negative aspects of small-town life. These strategies would include the following:

  - Identify several characters' thoughts or statements about their small town in the story that reflect their feelings toward or attitudes about their small town.
  - Interpret the types of feelings or attitudes in characters' thoughts or statements as positive or negative.
  - Provide reasons for why these feelings or attitudes are positive or negative.
  - Compare and contrast the different characters' feelings or attitudes.
  - Interpret what you believe to be the story's stance toward the value or limitation of small-town life.

You can create your own terms for helping students talk about writing strategies. Here are some typical terms: backgrounding, setting the scene, stating opinions, posing questions, defining problems, explaining, giving reasons, hypothesizing, giving supporting evidence, comparing, contrasting, connecting, summarizing, restating, refuting, criticizing, contradicting, listing, requesting, demanding, charging, praising, announcing, concluding, gaining sympathy, ordering, and challenging.

You may also describe how students, as writers, use certain cues to signal to readers that they are employing certain strategies or speech acts. "For example" signals a supporting strategy; "on the other hand," a comparing strategy; "in conclusion," a concluding strategy; "first," "second," "third," a listing strategy; and so forth. To help students identify these cues, have them underline the strategies, and circle the cues used to signal the strategies.

Students also need to be able to define the relations between strategies, for example, the fact that in stating opinions, you typically provide supporting examples or evidence. In giving reader-based feedback, you may make explicit your own expectations shaping your responses—the fact that, as a reader, when someone expresses an opinion, that person needs to provide supporting evidence.

• Criteria—It is also useful to provide students with specific criteria by which their writing will be judged. Students can then use these criteria to assess and revise their drafts. (In Chapter 12, on evaluating students, we discuss in more detail criteria for evaluating students' interpretations.)

Employing Multigenre Writing Assignments.   In formulating essay assignments, you may also want to invite students to adopt a multigenre or multimedia approach to include a range of different genres—quotes, poems, letters, diaries, stories, advertisements, field notes, photos, drawings, and so forth (Romano, 2000). Collecting a range of different related texts associated with the primary text encourages students to entertain intertextual links between these texts, links that serve to illustrate certain themes or ideas portrayed in texts. These could include texts about or by the author; texts portraying a similar or related theme, topic, issue, region, literary period, archetype, setting, character type, story line, or use of symbols; or texts of the same genre. For example, the small-town writing assignment could be expanded to include quotes from other texts about small-town life, photos and images, or travel promotional materials.

Students could study examples of hypertext literature such as *The Collected Works of Billy the Kid* (Ondaatje, 1996), which contain poems, stories, actual newspaper articles, and pictures about Billy the Kid. They could also study the scrapbooks kept by Mark Twain that contained souvenirs, pictures, illustrations, clippings, and articles about his books (for online interactive examples of his scrapbooks for nine of his books, go to the Web site). Students could also study the hypertext sites such as George Landow's Victorian literature site, as well as the Eastgate Web site, for examples of uses of Storyspace™ to create hypertext links and fiction (see the Web site and Chapter 12).

Students could then create their own multigenre essay on paper or as a PowerPoint™ presentation or as a Web site. For example, to represent their analysis of the 1950s world associated with reading Jack Kerouac's (1991) autobiographical novel, *On the Road*, they could find song lyrics, film reviews, newspaper accounts, poems, speeches, protest signs, art work, historical documents, short stories, biographical information, material on the Beat Movement, and so forth, that reflected the cultural values of that era, and then link those to specific aspects of the book. They then define the nature of the links between these texts and how these links contribute to their interpretation of the original texts. Students can also use this material to create hypermedia modes of response, as discussed in Chapter 11.

Students could also create what Kathleen Yancey (2004) describes as "pop-up" writing, based on the "Pop-Up Video" show on VH1 in which music videos are continually interrupted by visual pop-up bubbles that contain interpretations, background contexts, or critiques of the music video. Yancey notes that use of these pop-ups applied to a text invites connections across different texts:

> Collectively, pop-ups on or in a single text can create a random metatext, and it is equally possible that collectively pop-ups can create a series of parallel texts, or, perhaps, multiple stories prompted by, but not necessarily limited to, a "primary" text . . . [they] allow both composer and consumer to engage in intellectual *interplay* of both visual and verbal varieties. (p. 65)

In teaching the novel, *The Octopus: A Story of California*, by Frank Norris (1994), Yancey has groups of students choose at least two of eight contexts related to the novel: epic, romance, Gothic, Western, railroad history, California history, naturalism, and Norris and then create pop-up links to these contexts for group presentations as posters,

PowerPoint™ presentations, or Web sites. She then has students write individual essays in which they interpret three of the stories in the novel through use of related images, allusions, references, and other texts.

Summarizing Versus Analyzing Texts.   One problem with many student essays, particularly in writing in the "book report" format, is that students simply summarize the text, without formulating any interpretative analysis or arguing a position about the text. To help her first-year college students in an introductory theater course move beyond summary writing of the play, *Madame Butterfly*, Lisa Peschel (2002) of the University of Minnesota employed the following activities:

> In past years, some students have summarized the plot instead of analyzing the play. A few weeks before the text analysis paper was due, I give them a short take-home writing assignment: bring in a summary of the plot. This assignment serves as a springboard for discussion during the next session, and it also gets the "plot summary" out of their system so that they can then turn to analysis.
>
> A few weeks before they start the M. Butterfly paper, I ask students to write one page about any performance they have seen, including performative events that are not normally considered "theatrical" (weddings, lectures, concerts, etc.). I make extensive comments on these assignments, then meet with the students individually to discuss the comments and how they might apply them to the M. Butterfly paper.
>
> To prepare for the text analysis, I have my students write a practice paper based on model thesis statements I provide. Their assignment is to choose one of these statements and take a position agreeing with it, disagreeing with it, or complicating it, then to write a 1.5–2 page paper defining their position and supporting it with two passages from the play. In past sections, students have indicated that the biggest challenge was formulating the thesis statement itself. By giving them thesis statements to choose from, I moved the focus of the assignment to the process of taking a stand and defending it. This assignment gives them confidence in their ability to do that, and thus help prepare them to formulate and defending their own thesis statements for the M. Butterfly paper.

Lisa was therefore demonstrating ways of shifting from a summary retelling to an argument structure in which students had to develop that argument.

Distinguishing Between Summary, Supporting Evidence, and Analysis.   Secondary students may need even more assistance in moving beyond summary to adopt an interpretive stance or to formulate an argument. You may need to help students learn to distinguish between summarizing the story and providing supporting evidence or analysis by giving them illustrative examples (Olson, 2003; Schaffer, 1995):

> Summary: In "The Lottery," the townspeople conduct an annual lottery in a ritual-like manner.
>
> Supporting evidence: The townspeople engage in this ritual because they do not stop to reflect on what they are doing or the consequences of their actions.
>
> Analysis: People participate in group rituals without thinking about what they are doing because these rituals give them a sense of reassurance.

Students could also read sample essays written by previous students and color-code examples of summary, supporting evidence, and analysis using yellow for summary, blue for supporting evidence, and green for analysis (Olson, 2003; Schaffer, 1995).

Formulating a Thesis.   Students also need to learn how to inductively formulate a thesis, position, or argument based on their informal writing material. You can model the process of identifying patterns and formulating positions, for example, by reviewing your freewriting on an overhead about the townspeople's behavior in Shirley Jackson's (1988) story, "The Lottery." You note a pattern of the townspeople consistently failing to challenge or question what they are doing as they ritualistically proceed with the annual lottery. You can then apply that inferred pattern back to the text, noting the few exceptions—the fact that it is noted that a nearby town has abandoned the lottery and that Tessy—the ultimate victim, challenges the fairness of how the lottery was managed. This may then lead to some further analysis of why these challenges are ignored or marginalized—the fact that they can do little to derail the power of community ritual.

Entertaining Counterarguments and Evidence.   Even if students do formulate a thesis, they often prematurely adopt this interpretation as their thesis, provide some limited support for their thesis, and then end the essay without developing adequate supporting evidence. Because they prematurely assume that their thesis is valid and does not really need much support, they do not perceive the need to argue the case for the validity of their thesis.

All of this reflects "monologic," absolutist thinking—that what I believe must be true, as opposed to a more "dialogic" (Bakhtin, 1981) exploration of alternative perspectives. Students therefore need to learn to interrogate the limitations of their thesis or argument by entertaining challenges to their thesis or counterarguments as "rival hypotheses" (Flower, Long, & Higgins, 2000). For example, in writing her paper on "The Lottery," Laura argues that the ritual-like nature of the lottery squelched any attempt by the townspeople to challenge the lottery. In a peer-feedback conference, Laura might consider alternative or conflicting explanations—that the townspeople did not perceive it as a ritual, but as an expression of their community coherence or as an attempt to encourage crop growth. As Old Man Warner chants, "Lottery in June, corn early soon." By explicitly entertaining these counterarguments in the essay itself, students can then refute them in their essays, bolstering the validity of their own thesis. Teachers can encourage entertaining of alternative arguments by frequently using the words, "Some people think . . ." to evoke the existence of alternative perspectives.

Students also need to learn to be open to counterevidence that challenges their thesis or arguments. For example, Laura entertains the idea that the townspeople's ritual-like behavior is associated with life in a small town in which people readily fall into familiar habits and routines associated with small-town life. However, in a peer conference, other students note that these familiar habits and routines are not unique to small towns, challenging Laura's supporting evidence, and leading her to discount her idea that the characters' ritual-like behavior was a function of living in a small town.

UNDERSTANDING TEXTS THROUGH WRITING TEXTS

Students learn much about different literary genres such as short stories through writing stories or short autobiographical narratives. Students could write one of any number of different types of stories: character sketches, problem–solution stories, fables, parables, children's stories, parodies, detective stories, or adolescent fiction. In doing so, they are learning to employ various literary techniques they can then recognize in reading narratives. And, in revising their stories, they adopt the role of what Donald Murray (1968) describes as their "own best reader" to reflect on whether their use of techniques achieves their intended effects on an audience, for example, whether their use of dialogue serves to portray conflict between two characters.

Working in groups, students could write their own skits or one-act plays based on lived-world issues, experiences, or conflicts (Hart, 2004). They then practice their skits or plays within their group, making further revisions. They then perform their skit or play for the entire class or school. For example, a group of students at Central High School in St. Paul, Minnesota, created a play entitled "Barriers to Entry" on the process of applying to college (Shah, 2005). The play, which included poetry, song, and comedy, revolved around a bright student who is caught between his friends who have little interest in college and his own desire to go to college. In one scene in the play, a student who is grappling with how to write a 750-word essay about herself declares, "I'm not a 750 word essay" (Shah, 2005, p. B4).

Students could also write stories based on formulaic genre fiction—mystery, romance, or adventure (Hubert, 2000). Or, they could also draw on their knowledge of popular cultural material to create "fan fiction" (see the Web site for fan fiction or "slash" sites). Students could create "fan fiction" by drawing on and revising characters, story lines, dialogue, images, and themes from computer games, television programs, films, magazines, and so forth, to create their own narrative versions that reflect values quite different from the original. Two adolescent girls' fan fictions reflected heavy use of Japanese Anime material, fantasy, science fiction, romance, and "teen-buddy" genres to create multigenre narratives (Chandler-Olcott & Mahar, 2003).

Creating Characters.   In creating characters for their stories, students need to know how to portray characters through their actions or dialogue, as opposed to providing abstract descriptions about a character. To help them define specific actions or dialogue, students could list the various traits they want to portray about a character—the fact that a character is angry, defiant, and moody. For each of these traits, they could then list specific behaviors or bits of dialogue that would serve to convey these traits.

Creating Problems and Conflicts.   Students could create problems and conflicts facing characters by posing questions about characters' actions and motives in ways that lead them to further develop story events. If a teacher character and a student character are not getting along and experience a conflict, this raises the following question: Why aren't they getting along? This question may revolve around characters' failure to fulfill certain goals or expectations. If a character is having difficulty establishing a long-term relationship with another character, a question that arises is, why is he or she having difficulties? Addressing these kinds of questions leads students to formulate some characters' behaviors to add to their stories.

Developing Dialogue.   Dialogue functions to not only move forward the story events, but to also portray character traits and relationships. It is often difficult to write dialogue that rings true—that captures people's talk as they actually talk. This requires attention to use of specific dialect features, current lingo, pauses, interaction styles (interruptions, talking-over), inflections, emphasis, and so forth. Students may analyze examples of dialogue in literature, particularly drama texts, to note how dialogue is used to develop character and story lines. They may also listen to or overhear people calling on cell phones or engaging in conversations in restaurants or shopping malls, attending to the particular aspects of their conversations. Or, they could use role play to improvise dialogue appropriate for these situations.

Portraying Setting.   In creating setting, students create a context that evokes a reader's spatial or temporal schema as to the physical layout of the setting and what characters are sitting or standing in what location. This may include providing readers with a "grand tour" sequence of, for example, a house in which the reader is led by the hand through the living room into the kitchen and then out onto a deck where the protagonists are conversing. However, students also need to go beyond these physical aspects to portray the social, cultural, and historical aspects of setting. This involves creating a social world that provides readers with details about the historical period through descriptions of dress, language use, architecture, leisure time activities, music, or art unique to that period. And, students also may portray the social and cultural attitudes prevalent during a certain period. For example, in setting a story in the late 1960s, students may use descriptions of the "hippie" dress, talk, and social practices to portray the anti-establishment and anti-Vietnam War attitudes prevalent during that time.

Writing Poetry.   Learning to interpret poetry, as described in Chapter 7, is often linked to writing poetry. Simply the process of reading a lot of poems may transfer over to writing poetry. And, as students are writing poetry, they adopt the perspective of a writer who begins to notice the use of certain techniques, word choices, use of white space, and use of meter or rhythm patterns.

Students are often intimidated by the idea of being able to write out a poem in one sitting. This suggests the need to use initial freewriting or listing, out of which students pull key words or vivid images, and, using a looping technique, they do more freewriting and listing. For example, Linda Christensen (2000) has students write "Where I'm from" poems by first listing items associated with their home, yard, family, favorite foods, places, neighborhood, or town or region. Students then read aloud their lists, adopting the language or dialect of the students' homes, families, or neighborhoods. They then use their lists to link to the idea of how these specific items reflect their home, family, or neighborhood cultures based on the idea of "Where I'm from." Students then read aloud these poems and receive feedback from peers that leads to revision. Here are some lines from some of the poems students wrote: (a) "I'm from clothespins,/from Cloraox and carbontetrachloride, /I'm from the dirt under the back porch" (p. 18); (b) "I am from get-togethers/and Bar-B-ques/K-Mart special with matching shoes" (p. 19); and (c) "I am from poke, brie cheese, mango, /and raspberries,/from Marguritte/and Aunty Nani" (p. 21).

Another basic approach is to use ideas or material from other poems or texts as "poetry ideas" (Koch, 1973, 1980) to stimulate ideas or materials for students' own poems. For example, students may develop "found poems" or "clippings poems" based on combinations of words or texts from ads, newspaper stories, flyers, letters, and Web sites (Somers, 1999). Or, they can create "clippings poems" by taking clips of words from ads, Web sites, and short poems and combine those clips in creative ways to create new poems.

Students can also employ different forms of writing poems: haiku (traditional Japanese three-line poems; Higginson, 1992), ballads, lyric, or raps. As noted in Chapter 7, students can write rap lyrics to be performed in classroom or community poetry slams. And, students can write poems based on different visual shapes in which the appearance of lines on the page reflects the subject of the poem—for example, a poem about loss shaped like a tear.

Publishing Stories and Poems.   Students are often motivated to write stories or poems if they can be published in classroom newsletters, anthologies, school literary journals, or some of the many print and online publishing outlets for student writing (see the Web site for a list of publishers and online sites). Knowing that a large audience may be reading their stories or poems, students are more likely to carefully edit their writing.

Portfolio Addition: Reflection on Your Uses of Talk and Write Tools

For your portfolio reflection on materials related to uses of talk and write tools to fulfill your learning objectives and goals, you could include the following items:

- Sample writing assignments that illustrate the use of a range of informal writing tools, as well as information about the purpose, audience, tasks, and evaluation criteria employed. You may then include sample student writings to these assignments, noting the ways in which the assignments served to foster certain uses of interpretive strategies or critical approaches in the students' writing.

- Samples of student uses of various informal and formal writing tools, with reflection on differences in students' abilities to use these tools, as well as analysis of how developing material through the informal tools served to prepare students for more formal writing.

- Transcripts of drafting conferences with students that illustrate your own or peers' use of reader-based feedback, along with examples of students' revisions and self-assessing precipitated by this feedback. You may reflect on how your instruction in peer conferencing may have led to student success in providing peer feedback.

- Samples of students' use of alternative writing formats, such as multigenre writing, and reflection on how these alternative formats fostered use of certain interpretive strategies such as defining intertextual links.

- Samples of students' narrative or autobiographical writing, with reflections on students' uses of certain narrative development techniques related to your instruction.

- Case-study profiles of a range of individual differences in students' uses of talk and write tools, as well as changes in students' responses in the beginning and end of your instruction. You may explain differences in students' uses of talk and write tools in terms of variation in learning styles, needs, attitudes, knowledge, interest, as well as factors related to race, class, and gender.

Online Additional Activities, Links, and Further Reading

Go to the textbook Web site, Chapter 6, for additional activities, links, and further reading.

7

Using Narratives in the Classroom
for Both Teaching and Learning
Literature: What's the Use of Story?

Chapter Overview

- Uses of narratives.
- Sharing and analyzing oral narratives.
- Using narratives to construct identity.
- Interpreting narratives.
- Studying narrative genres.
- Applying different critical lenses to narratives.

CASE NARRATIVE: MIKE'S STORY

In listening to a group of adolescents talking in the hallways, one hears a lot of stories told for social purposes—to make impressions, maintain friendships, gossip, or flirt. Understanding the meaning of these stories requires some sense of the social roles and motives of the tellers, as well as the social context. For example, Mike says the following to Gail: "I was just sitting, as usual, on the bench. Then, all of sudden the coach puts me in as an end. And, on the next play, the quarterback throws me a long pass and I caught the ball on the three-yard line. I couldn't believe it." The meaning of this story derives from more than the words or even the use of various storytelling techniques. It evolves out of Mike's relationship with Gail as constituted by his goals—his desire to impress her with his "benchwarmer makes good" story—as well as Mike's beliefs about Gail and Gail's beliefs about Mike.

In studying stories as social acts, students focus on social purposes or motives for telling a story—motives that imply the point of the story. This involves determining what a teller or writer is really up to—what point he or she is trying to make in telling a story. For example, a new member of a soccer team may tell a joke in the locker room not only to entertain the other team members but to also establish the fact that she is "one of the girls."

To explore the social functions of stories, recall some stories you recently shared with your peers or family members; tell those stories to others in your class. Reflect on the underlying social purposes for sharing your stories, what you were trying to convey through telling a story. What was the underlying point of your story? What ideas, beliefs, or attitudes were you trying to convey?

Using Stories to Make a Point.   Schank and Morson (1995) posit that a primary purpose for telling stories is to illustrate ideas, beliefs, attitudes about life—that stories are case studies that try to make some statement about life. For example, in discussing effective teaching, someone may share a story about a highly enthusiastic teacher to illustrate the idea that teaching requires a high level of enthusiasm. If we subscribe to the belief that a high level of enthusiasm is essential to effective teaching, then we cite stories about enthusiastic teachers which confirm that belief. As Bruner (2002) notes, "we come to conceive of a 'real world' in a manner that fits the stories we tell about it" (p. 103).

In literature classes, students study narratives in the form of short stories or novels, examining the ways in which authors develop story lines, plots, conflicts, settings, characters, and themes. However, they are also continually using narratives as oral anecdotes as social acts to share everyday experiences with peers or to define their identities to others. And, they may use narratives as a means of reflecting on their experiences, for example, recalling a series of events from a mountain climbing trip to reflect on the value of going mountain climbing. So, in addition to studying about narratives as a literary genre, you can also use narratives as a learning tool for helping students interpret and reflect on their experiences. Through activities involving sharing and reflecting on narratives, you are helping students learn to begin to recognize the different aspects of narratives, an experience they can use to interpret literary narratives—short stories or novels.

In this chapter, we also consider your own uses of narrative as a tool for sharing and reflecting on your challenges and breakdowns in your teaching experiences, particularly when your expectations didn't pan out in reality. By sharing or writing of narratives about your teaching, for example, about a confrontation with an angry student, you are grappling with your beliefs and values about what constitutes good teaching and learning (Florio-Ruane, 2000; Ritchie & Wilson, 2000). For example, Jim is reflecting on his student teaching experience of teaching Catcher in the Rye to a group of 10th-grade students in an urban, working-class high school.

Who's read a novel? Not many hands went up and they, I guess most of them had read one or one of those adolescent novels, but I don't think any of them, well some of them, I'm sure had read, in fact I know one in particular that is a reader of paperbacks, and she read quite a few but a lot of them hadn't really read any "adult" novels before, and only a few adolescent or teen novels.

I went real slow because the chapters in Catcher in the Rye are about 5 or 6 or 10 pages. We did maybe two or three chapters a day. I had study questions for each chapter that I made sure they had to answer and they could really skim through every chapter to answer the questions. I didn't make the questions too challenging because I didn't want them to get hung up on questions, have that interrupt the reading. What I did to settle the questions and I tried to direct them towards specific things in the novel that I just wanted to make sure they noted. Not necessarily what the meaning of them was but to note the detail and had to write the detail down and then talk in class about those details. Why they were in there. What did they represent? So when we went into discussion they already had the details down. Like for instance, I'd ask something like what was Holden asking the cab driver about? The ducks in Central Park. I didn't ask what do you think the ducks in Central Park might represent. I just said, what's he asking about? They would answer, yeah, he's asking about ducks in Central Park. So they've already got that in their minds. What are the ducks all about? So that's the way I structured it and it worked really well.

I tried to make it a mix of mostly just basic questions and a few that are called deeper questions, I guess what I mean by that are questions where they have to um, do some interpretation of the text. On the surface we've got Holden and he's going through New York City and avoiding going home and he's coming up with all these fantasies of running away and doing these different things, and then he's got this fantasy of being the catcher in the rye and catching kids before they fall off the cliff. So on a deeper level, what does this mean, what is Holden so afraid of? What is Holden struggling with? And so finally to get down to come around to the idea that well he's afraid to grow up and he's afraid of facing sexuality and he's afraid of facing change in his life. He seems to admire things like mummies and kids that die before they reach maturity and so what's going on with that, why does he fetishize the state of stasis?

Well, after we had finished reading the book, well first of all, I had been discussing things I noticed throughout the whole book in the way I interpret the book basically. So I wanted them to focus on Holden and his struggle of growing up and struggles with having sexuality, struggles with the death of his brother, basically all the issues he had gone through, but I had a lot of discussions in class about that and as we finished the book, I did a group activity where I gave them a list of 5 essay questions and they had to pick one of them to put on the test, and I broke them up into groups of about 4 or 5 kids in each group, and each group had to take an essay question, and had to discuss it and they each had a role. One person was the recorder, one person was the leader and so each group had to discuss the essay questions and come up with a way that they would answer the question on a test and to present their findings to the class. I was a little nervous about it, because they were in-depth questions. I mean, they were college-level questions. And I thought, oh boy they're really going to bang their heads against these ones, but I was really pleasantly surprised that they all, all the groups came up with real solid answers and I was going around as they were working on them and helping out here and there, but I really didn't have to do as much as I thought I would do, I just had to nudge them along. That really showed me that they had been listening and paying attention and it wasn't just two or three kids that did a lot of participation in the discussions who understood what was going on but they really most of them you know had been listening to what we're talking about. I was real happy with that.

Jim uses his narrative recollections to reflect on his strategies and beliefs about teaching—that he wasn't prepared for the fact that his students had read so few novels, leading him to "go slow." And, he reflects on the value of using a range of different kinds of questions and small-group work in which students had a choice of essay questions. He also uses the narrative to reflect on his beliefs and role as a teacher who wants to encourage students to learn to interpret texts:

I guess I try to get the students to be interested in something that goes beyond what happens next in the plot, and try to get them to see that there's a little bit more going on and what I've found is that if you take the time, if you have the patience to sort of almost harass them into looking deeper into the text, to keep asking the same questions over and over again until somebody gives you an answer, and then you challenge that answer and just dig deeper and deeper, they actually do get interested and they are really surprised to find out that there are more levels to the text than they thought there would be and then they get curious about it. I've had students ask me, how do you learn to read like that? How did you figure out how to do that? So that was good to hear. If they have to make an imaginative world that's different from their own, I think I'd just try to help them do that and not worry too much about making everything a direct hit.

Jim's reflections demonstrate that narrative recollection can serve to foster further thinking about your teaching (Anderson, 1997; Britzman, 1991; Clandinin & Connelly, 1999; Johnson & Golombok, 2002; Lyons & Laboskey, 2002). Narratives lend themselves well to reflection on teaching because they revolve around the relations between your actions, plans, and goals, and how your actions and plans do not always achieve the goals you want to achieve. Jim wanted to foster his students' interpretations, so he developed a plan to achieve that goal.

How is narrative related to your own teaching? How can you use narrative in teaching literature? We address these questions in this chapter by examining how narratives help you not only reflect on your teaching, but also share experiences, build relationships, and define identities. All of this can be used in teaching students to respond to and create their own narratives.

Using Narrative to Reflect on Your Teaching.   You can use narratives to recapture the particular aspects of your own teaching, creating a record that can serve as the basis for your reflection on your teaching. Recall a recent experience you have had in your work with students or in a microteaching session with your peers. Write a narrative about that experience in which you describe particular behaviors, dialogue, and feelings as if you were writing a short story.

Then, reflect back over your narrative about your teaching episode.

Goal-Plan Relations.   What were you trying to accomplish and did your plan achieve that goal? In the story, "The Tortoise and the Hare," the tortoise's plan is to methodically persist in the race, knowing that the hare will be overconfident. The storyteller dramatizes the expectation that the tortoise's plan will fulfill the goal, conveying the belief that persistence pays off in the long run.

Expectations.   What may have gone wrong or how were your expectations not fulfilled—what was the difference between what you wanted your students to do and what they actually did?

Previous Experience.   Did this experience remind you of any previous experiences involving a similar problem—in what ways was this experience different or similar to your previous experience(s)?

Context and Setting.   How did this particular context or setting shape the experience?

Your Own Role as Teacher.   How did you portray yourself in the narrative: what role(s) did you assume in your narrative? Did you portray yourself as having agency and power or as limited by the classroom or schooling as a system?

Share your reflections with your peers in small groups, noting what you learned about your teaching through your narrative reflection. Then, discuss what it was about the narratives themselves that served to foster reflection on your teaching. Note how your portrayals of goal-plan relations, expectations, previous experiences, context and setting, students, and your role helped you learn more about your teaching.

USES OF NARRATIVES

Your use of narrative to reflect on your teaching is only one of many uses for narratives. We use narratives to construct our personal history, instruct and entertain others, illustrate arguments, and record history. Telling brief stories about events is one of the first things children learn to do with language (Applebee, 1978). As adults we continue to use stories as a way of testing and refining the abstract propositions contained in more logical, argumentative discourse. As Jerome Bruner (1986, 1990, 2002) has argued, narrative provides a way of organizing experience; it is thus a way of knowing. Rather than stating opinions, generalizations, or "truths" in a search for "what is," narratives directly portray settings, characters, and events in a search for "what it is like" to pass through a particular experience. In Hal Rosen's (1984) terms, "stories are a primary act of mind—we tell stories in order to think, and we think about the stories we tell" (p. 5).

In this chapter, we discuss practices involved in both understanding and producing narratives. Teaching narratives involves more than just teaching short stories. Narratives pervade all forms of literature and everyday life. We are continually telling and hearing stories about everyday events, experiences we draw on in making sense of literary and nonliterary narrative texts.

It is useful to distinguish between three different ways to talk about narrative suggested by Paul Cobley (2001). He distinguishes between story, plot, and narrative. Story "consists of all the events which are to be depicted" (p. 5). Plot "is the chain of causation which dictates that these events are somehow linked and that they are therefore to be depicted in relation to each other" (p. 5). For example, a story may consist of the events of a father being killed and a son seeking revenge for that killing. The plot based on these story events involves the son seeking revenge for the killing because he discovers that the murderer was his mother's new husband (*Hamlet*). Understanding the plot involves understanding the causal relation between the event of the son, Hamlet, seeking revenge, and the fact that his father was murdered by his mother's new husband.

Narrative consists of "the showing or the telling of these events and the mode selected for that to take place" (Cobley, 2001, p. 6). Different versions of the same story or plot may emphasize different events to evoke different meanings. Different productions of *Hamlet* may select certain events of the play in different ways to represent particular meanings. Some narrative representations may emphasize Hamlet's indecision in deciding to seek revenge whereas other narrative representations may emphasize his tenacity in seeking revenge.

Narratives reflect tensions between the ideal that challenges status-quo norms, and the real that is locked within status-quo norms. In his theory of narrative, Jerome Bruner (1986, 1990, 2002) posits that narratives play off the tension between the ordinary and the exceptional. He argues that people use narratives to make sense of the exceptional—deviations from expected norms: "narratives mediate between the canonical world of culture and the more idiosyncratic world of beliefs, dreams, and hopes" (Bruner, 1990, p. 52). For example, as a teacher, you may tell or hear stories about teaching that challenges status quo practices. These stories dramatize the tensions between new, alternative ways of teaching that differ from the familiar, traditional ways of teaching. Narrative therefore functions as a way of knowing. Stories of innovative teaching may serve to inspire you to entertain new ways of thinking about teaching.

SHARING AND ANALYZING ORAL NARRATIVES

In addition to using your own stories to reflect on your teaching, you can also use students' everyday oral anecdotes as the basis for discussions and story writing. In working with inner-city students in an alternative school context, Julie Landsman (1993) noticed that her students would share rich oral narratives, but were reluctant to write to stories. She therefore asked students to dictate their stories to her. She would write down the bare bones events of their stories and then add details to create a short story version complete with dialogue, setting, and character development. She would then share these stories with her students. As she became known as the "story lady" in the school, other students would volunteer to share their stories with her. These stories were then used as the basis for discussion and as a model for the students' own story writing. These oral anecdotes can serve as a rich resource for reading and writing.

You could certainly adopt a similar role by asking students to share their stories with you and then create your own versions of those stories. You could also ask students to dictate stories to each other, and have them write their own stories.

What Makes Stories Effective?   In studying students' oral anecdotes, you can discuss what makes certain stories more effective or engaging than other stories. According to William Labov's (1972) theory of narrative, a story is worth telling if it's about an unusual, extraordinary event, endowing the story with what Labov calls "tellability." A student who simply reports that she drove to school is relating something that may not be worth telling. In contrast, a student who reports that she witnessed an accident while driving to school is likely to get our attention, particularly if she dramatizes the nature of the accident with a lot of gory details. In Labov's theory, effective narratives dramatize unusual, extraordinary events by emphasizing violations of the norm—the fact that the event was out of the ordinary. In telling a story about a student who threw a chair out of a classroom window, a storyteller dramatizes the fact that such events don't take place everyday in the normally "small, quiet, rural high school."

Storytellers use particular techniques to dramatize violations of the norm. You could provide students with a list of the following techniques and have them identify the use of these techniques as they listen to a Garrison Keillor monologue on "Prairie Home Companion."

- Abstract—Describing the type or genre of story; providing an overview of the story's content: "Let me tell you about an accident I had."
- Orientation or setting the scene—"It had just started to sleet and the roads were getting very slippery. So I was driving very, very slowly." In the beginning of a story, a storyteller sets the scene by announcing the topic ("This is a story about my crazy grand-

mother." "Let me tell you bout my own fraternity initiation.") or by describing the physical setting or place ("I was canoeing slowly down the Connecticut River. . . ."). By setting the scene or announcing the topic, tellers or writers establish the fact that certain norms are operating in the story world, norms that will be violated. Or, storytellers forecast the symbolic importance or significance of certain information, by, for example, the use of titles to highlight or abstract key aspects of a story. Eudora Welty uses the title, "Why I Live at the P.O.," to encourage readers to look for answers to that question. Or, Gina Berriault uses the title, "The Stone Boy," to signal the main character's plight—having accidentally killed his brother he has emotionally turned to "stone." Audiences or readers attend to certain information in a story using what Peter Rabinowitz (1998) describes as "rules of notice" to attend to certain text features—titles, first and last sentences, opening scenes, and so forth.

• Complicating action—"Then, all of a sudden, I hit an ice patch and started to slide towards the side of the road. I steered the car towards a snow bank and thud—I went right into the bank."

• Use of evaluative cues—Labov (1972) uses the term *evaluation* to define cues that serve to signal the story's tellability or point—the fact that something unusual or extraordinary has occurred. As a storyteller, you need to dramatize the fact that the story has tellability—that the events are unusual or extraordinary enough to make them worth telling. So, you use cues to emphasize the unusual nature of the event. In this story, the use of pluperfect verb tenses serves to set the scene. The fact that the "roads were getting very slippery. So I was driving very, very slowly" creates a sense of time passing, but that something is going to happen. Similarly, when someone begins a story with, "I just sitting there minding my own business," an audience knows that they are being set up for that fact that the norm associated with "minding my own business" is about to be violated. And, the repetition of words, as in "driving very, very slowly," or the use of asides—"all of a sudden," serve to dramatize the unusual nature of the event.

• Building suspense or fostering predictions—Effective storytellers also build up suspense through the withholding and revelation of information about the final outcome or resolution of the story (Brooks, 1992; Cobley, 2001). This keeps audiences wanting to know what happens at the end, involving them in an active guessing game of predicting possible outcomes. Stories draw us in by creating and then resolving anticipations for what's going to happen next.

• Resolution or coda—"That snow bank saved the day; it just stopped the car and kept me from going over the edge of the side of the road. I was just really lucky."

The Social Meaning of Stories.   In having students analyze these textual techniques, they also need to recognize that the meaning of a story depends on the social context in which the story is being told—the relationships between the teller and audience. For example, a story's tellability—what makes it worth telling—is that it's "point" is not "in" the story, but is socially constructed by the teller and the audience in the storytelling event (Hunt & Vipond, 1992).

Students therefore need to examine the social contexts in which stories are told to determine the meaning of those stories. For example, narratives are often used to socialize new members to adopt the beliefs and attitudes operating in an organization or social world. Staton Wortham (2001) gives the example of a veteran Alcoholics Anonymous (AA) member who provides testimonial narratives to novice members about their experience of "hitting bottom" and then, through following the AA regimen, restoring their sense of self-worth (Cain, 1991). The meaning of his narrative is best understood in the context of a veteran convincing the novice of the value of sticking diligently to the AA regimen to define one's identity as an AA member. In these situations, the context influences what and how a story is told—the veteran AA member emphasizes what he or she learned from being in AA. And, the story creates the context by positioning the teller and audience to adopt certain roles. The AA member is positioned as the expert and the new members, as novices.

Studying How Narratives Create and Position Audiences in Social Contexts. To have students study the relations between stories and social contexts, have them share stories to each other about recent experiences in their lives. Audiotape or videotape these stories and then, as the class reviews the stories, have students reflect on reasons they chose to tell (or not tell) certain stories given the types of events portrayed and their perceptions of their peers as an audience. For example, students may not want to tell stories that portray them in a negative manner in front of their peers. Have them also reflect on reasons they selected certain specific aspects within their stories based on their perceptions of their audience's prior knowledge, attitudes, or interests. For example, in telling a story about visiting a swamp, students may recognize the need to describe specific aspects of the setting knowing that their audience knows little about swamps.

Then, have students tell different versions of the same original story that serve to convey a different social meaning. Although the original version of a story about a small fire that started in a chemistry lab positioned the teller as an active agent who "took charge" was designed to impress the audience, the revised version portrays the teller as a passive victim of events over which she had no control. Or, although the original version played up the potential danger of the fire to build suspense and impress the audience with the potential danger of the fire, the revised version may portray the fire as not at all dangerous. Students could then compare how the different versions positioned them in different ways as audiences. Students could then examine how narratives told by characters to each other in stories or novels serve to define their identities or build social relationships with other characters.

The Cultural Meaning of Stories. The ways in which stories are told also vary according to cultural differences. The same myth or fairy tale may differ markedly across different cultures (Zipes, 2000). These cultural differences may be evident in differences in your students' oral or written narratives given their cultural, ethnic, or class backgrounds. In a comparison of written stories based on a picture of two adolescents crossing a creek, written by 49 7th-grade students in a school consisting largely of Plateau Indian and Latino students in the state of Washington, Barbara Monroe (2004) found that Latino students wrote stories that focused primarily on reporting events in relatively literal, nonelaborated modes. The Plateau Indian and White students provided a lot of dialogue and more detailed descriptions of characters' actions. Although being careful not to essentialize the cultural differences between these groups, Monroe attributes the differences in the degree of elaboration to the students' language socialization and interactions in the home related to class differences. Drawing on the work of Shirley Brice Heath (1986) on bedtime stories told to middle-class versus working-class students, she notes that middle-class students at an early age engage in turn-taking and "why" questions that serve to foster elaborated verbal interactions, along with recontextualizing events from different perspectives. In contrast, children in working-class homes focus more on accurate representations of immediate events associated with "what" questions, with less opportunity for "why" questions and shifting of perspectives.

Monroe (2004) notes that working-class students bring a rich background knowledge of popular culture and television to the classroom, which serves as the basis for constructing stories based on familiar television, film, or game genres, while using their own versions of these genres to critique those genres.

On the other hand, working-class adolescents are more likely to employ and value narratives. A comparison of working-class versus upper middle class adolescent girls' language use in interviews about their lives (Gee, Allen, & Clinton, 2001) found that working-class adolescents frequently employed narratives to construct identities grounded in the everyday world of social interaction and relationships. In contrast, the upper-middle-class girls used more abstract, analytic language in ways that aligned themselves with institutional norms and trajectories associated with achievement. This suggests the value of sharing narratives in the classroom, particularly as a means of involving working-class students (Christopher, 1999).

USING NARRATIVES TO CONSTRUCT IDENTITY

Narratives also serve to define one's identity associated with what it means to be a certain kind of person with certain kinds of values. As Rymes (2001) notes, "Through telling [stories], people are not creating a merely random identity, rather, they are actively narrating themselves relative to a moral ideal of what it is to be a good person" (p. 498).

Storytellers also use narratives to convey their sense of self to an audience or reader. As Harold Rosen (1984) notes, "We are our stories." The "male hero's" boastful stories convey a masculine self-image of the heroic man who can triumph over anything. Someone who is a "good storyteller" may be perceived as "the life of the party" or as "outgoing."

Jerome Bruner (1986, 1990, 2002) has argued that narratives function as ways of making sense out of randomly organized events, making sense that is linked to one's beliefs about his or her world and one's identity. As Bruner (2002) notes, we impose a certain narrative logic onto events as "self-making" narratives: "We constantly construct and reconstruct our selves to meet the needs of the situations we encounter. And we do so with the guidance of our memories of the past and our hopes and fears for the future. Telling oneself about oneself is like making up a story about who and what we are, what's happened, and why we're doing what we're doing" (p. 64).

Bruner (2002) argues that these "self-making" narratives reflect cultural beliefs and attitudes associated with what it means to be a "good self," narratives that can influence actions in both positive and negative ways. He cites the example of 23-year-old Christopher McCandless, whose dead body was found in a deserted bus in Alaska, along with some autobiographical writings. McCandless believes that he could survive in the Alaska wilds totally on his own:

> They tell the story of a "radically autonomous identity gone wrong." "Dealing with things on his own" was his ideal, and he understood Thoreau's injunction "simplify, simplify" to mean that he should depend on nobody, strive for unfettered autonomy. His self-narratives fit this formula to the end of this days, he was living in remote Alaska, eating only edible plants, and after three months he died of starvation. (Bruner, 2002, p. 79)

In a study of Los Angeles Latino high school students' dropout narratives, Betsy Rymes (2001) documents how the students used narratives to project their "moral selves" in a positive light. The students' descriptions of why they dropped out of school often reflected their negative response to threats, violence, mistreatment, or boredom in a school. Through foregrounding aspects of the setting as leading to their reactions, the students define a causal relation between the negative contexts and their actions in ways that portray themselves in a positive light as a necessary or justifiable response to violent, threatening situations. She cites the example of one student, Rosa, who described the event of a teacher chasing her down a school hallway and then holding her:

> Me and her started getting in a fight, and when I—when when when we—when we stopped fighting, they said a teacher's coming a teacher's coming so I ran you know. I was trying to get away eh—and he was chasing me. An' then, and so he wouldn't let go of my hand and I was telling him let go let go and he goes no your going with me an I was go get her, she—she started it and he wouldn't let me go—he wouldn't let me go so, heh heh, I don't know I got mad and I just hit him. That was why I didn't go to school cause I knew he was looking for me. (p. 31)

From her experience in conducting this study, she recommends that teachers listen to students' narratives to understand the difficulties and complexities of students' lives. She also recommends that students tell stories in groups so that they can build on each other's stories. Rosa's story dramatizes her identity as someone with the agency to resist authority.

INTERPRETING NARRATIVES

Students' sharing and analysis of oral narratives provides them with a basis for interpreting narrative elements found in short stories or novels. They then recognize a link between their uses of everyday oral anecdotes and the techniques employed in published narratives.

Characters' Actions.   One of the most basic elements in interpreting narratives is the need to explain characters' actions based on and motives for characters' actions. The meaning of actions can only be understood within the social context in which they occur. In explaining characters' actions in response to questions such as why did Scout in *To Kill a Mockingbird* continue to defend her father, students need to provide reasons associated with constructing a larger social context. Robert McMahon (2002) proposes examining five basic components for analyzing characters' actions—action, situation, agent, purpose, and attitude—based on questions for each (p. 3):

> Act: "What does the character do?"
> Situation: "How does the character understand the situation in which he acts?"
> Agent: What is the character's moral character?" "How does the character understand himself as the agent in this act?"
> Purpose: "What does the character intend—aim to gain or accomplish—by this act?"
> Attitude: "With what attitude or feeling does the character perform this act?"

One teacher (Rekrut, 2003), who adopted these questions for her 10th-graders studying the actions of Abigail Williams in *The Crucible*, noted the following:

> We examined Abigail's Moral Character—the students decided that she was a selfish liar—and we readily recognized that Abigail's Self-Understanding indicated she knew what she was doing, even though she might not be ready for the consequences. The class suggested that Abigail had two purposes—to get John Proctor back and to keep the spotlight on herself—and that his Attitude was negative, even cynical (although they didn't use that word), because she focused only on what she wanted. (p. 532)

Dialogue.   Students interpret characters' dialogue as certain types of speech acts: requesting, promising, inviting, asserting, praising, apologizing, challenging, and so forth (Austin, 1975). To infer these acts, students need to construct a social context so that they can infer characters' beliefs about their own and their audience's status or power, their intended meaning and actual effect, their ability to perform the act, their sincerity, and the context in which the act occurs. For example, two people, Bill and Molly, husband and wife, are talking at the dinner table:

Bill: "There's a new restaurant opening up this Thursday down the street."
Molly: "That's nice."
Bill: "I heard that it's going to be mostly Cajun food."
Molly: "I don't really like Cajun and besides, I'm busy this Thursday."

In this exchange, Bill and Molly infer the meaning of each other's utterances by inferring the type of speech act being performed and the intended effect of those acts, or "uptake" (Austin, 1975). "Uptake" refers to whether an audience follows through on a speech act's intended force. In making a request for assistance, a speaker believes that his or her audience will follow through on that request. However, an audience may not believe that a speaker has the power or right to make a request, and therefore not follow through on the request. Molly may interpret Bill's initial utterance, "there's a new restaurant opening up this Thursday down the street," as simply an announcement about or description of the restaurant or as an invitation to go to the restaurant. Bill may then interpret Molly's reply, "That's nice" as either a confirmation of his description or as a rejection of his invitation. Molly may then interpret his next statement, "I heard that it's going to be mostly Cajun food," as a further description of the restaurant or as a reiteration or clarification of the invitation. Her own statement suggests that she reads the uptake of his statement as an invitation, which she rejects.

Readers impute Bill's and Molly's beliefs and knowledge about each others' status, power, rights, responsibilities, and roles within the discourse community of their martial relationship. They may infer that if Bill believes that Molly does or should simply defer to him as being in a position of power, then he may assume that his description would be read as an order—that they were going to go to the restaurant. Or, they may infer that if Molly believes that she and Bill are on an equal power level and therefore mutually negotiate all decisions, then she will interpret Bill's actions as attempts to discuss the possibility of going to the restaurant.

Another perspective on speech acts has to do with whether the actions confirm or violate norms operating in a conversation. H. P. Grice (1989) defined these norms as "conversational maxims" having to do with relevancy—is the talk relevant to the shared conversational topic, sufficiency—does the speaker provide enough information, validity—is the speaker telling the truth, and sincerity—is the speaker sincere? A speaker who begins talking about something that has nothing to with the topic at hand violates the relevancy maxim. A speaker who blathers on needlessly violates the sufficiency maxim. A speaker who lies violates the validity maxim. And, the speaker who is just adopting a pose violates the sincerity maxim.

In some cases, speakers deliberately violate, call attention to, or flout a maxim to indirectly imply certain meanings. For example, you ask someone whether they liked a restaurant, and they respond, "The water was good." This speaker is calling attention to the fact that they are maxim by saying no more than is necessary to imply that the restaurant wasn't very good.

Students could analyze transcripts of recorded conversations with each other to discuss how they make inferences about each other based on dialogue using their knowledge of speech acts and conversational maxims. Then, they could apply the same analysis to discussing how they make inferences about characters' traits, beliefs, status, agency, and goals, as well as narrative conflicts, in response to dialogue in a story or novel. For example, in the short story, "Raymond's Run," by Toni Bambara (1999), the main character or narrator, Hazel, an African American early-adolescent girl, is continually responsible for taking care of her younger brother, Raymond, who is mentally challenged and needs constant attention. Hazel perceives herself as a track star, who is now about to be challenged by Gretchen, a newcomer to the neighborhood; two of Hazel's former friends, Mary Louise and Rosie, are now Gretchen's friends. In the following scene (with just the dialogue included), Hazel and Raymond meet up with Gretchen, Mary Louise, and Rosie on the street:

> "You signing up for the May Day races?"smiles Mary Louise, only it's not a smile at all . . .
>
> "I always win cause I'm the best," I say straight at Gretchen . . .
>
> "What grade you in now, Raymond?" [Mary Louise]
>
> "You got anything to say to my brother, you say it to me, Mary Louise Williams of Raggedy Town, Baltimore."
>
> "What are you, his mother?" sasses Rosie.
>
> "That's right, Fatso. And the next word out of anybody and I'll be *their* mother too." (pp. 24–25)

In this exchange, Hazel and Mary Louise and Rosie are sparring with each to establish status that is similar to the oral genre, "playing the dozens," in which participants taunt each other. Mary Louise begins by putting down Hazel with the implication that she may lose to Gretchen. Hazel's retort to the challenge is to assert that she will still beat Gretchen. Mary Louise then poses a question to Raymond, which is really flouting question-asking to further taunt Hazel. Again, Hazel challenges Mary Louise by implying that she has her own limitation as a resident of "Raggedy Town." Rosie then challenges Hazel by reverting to taunts frequently found in "playing the dozens," making references to one's mother. However, again Hazel retorts with her own challenge to the three girls that ends the conversation. These series of speech acts of taunts and retorts functions to not only develop character relationships, but it also sets up potential narrative conflict with the now expected May Day race between Hazel and Gretchen.

Analyzing Conflict. Students are also analyzing the conflicts between characters due to differences in their beliefs and values. In the young-adult novel, *Catherine Called Birdy* (Cushman, 1994), Catherine, an adolescent girl living in medieval times, is opposed to her father's attempt to marry her off to an older suitor whom she despises. In studying Catherine's conflict with her father, middle school students examined how that conflict stemmed from the family's sense of purpose, the roles family members assign to each other, the rules governing decision making in the family, or beliefs about power and privilege in the family (Galda & Beach, 2001).

In other cases, narrative conflict revolves around characters' different versions of the same event. Characters formulate competing versions of the same event. The governess in "The Turn of the Screw" believes that the ghosts she observes are real, whereas others do not. As a reader, you proffer your own version of the conflict that may differ from others' versions, versions that themselves draw on narrative perspectives (Abbott, 2002). If you adopt a ghost-story narrative, you may believe that the ghosts are real. If you adopt a psychological narrative of repressed sexuality, you may believe that the ghosts are only sexual fantasies.

Activity: Different Versions of Conflict

To examine different versions of a story event, go to the online story, "A Jury of Her Peers," by Susan Glaspell (2004), first published in 1927 (http://www.learner.org/exhibits/literature/story/fulltext.html). This story portrays the murder of a husband who is found to be dead by his wife, Martha Hale, in a rural farmhouse. The wife, Minnie Wright, claims not to know who killed him. However, she is charged with the murder and is awaiting trial. When two other women go to the house to gather clothing for Mrs. Hale, they note signs of her husband's violent abuse. The conflict in the story revolves around different perspectives on whether Minnie Wright killed her husband, and, if she did so, any motives for her action. The men in the story apply one perspective to her actions, whereas the two women begin to formulate quite a different perspective. Determine your own version of what happened and note how certain narrative prototypes shaped the construction of your version. Because this story also serves as the basis for the play, *Trifles* (Glaspell, 1987), students could compare the narrative structure of the original story and the play.

Making Predictions. Readers make predictions by drawing on their narrative knowledge of master plots or typical story lines. They know, for example, that comedies typically have a happy ending or that tragedies end with the hero's suffering and death. When their predictions are violated by story events, they then revise their predictions and formulate new predictions. What is important is that students learn to revise their predictions as well as knowing reasons why their predictions may or may not be working. It is also important that they recognize that there are no "correct" or "right" predictions. Students also need to learn how to draw on previous events in a narrative or their own knowledge to make predictions. Having students articulate reasons for their predictions helps them recognize how they draw on their knowledge of making predictions.

Constructing Settings or Social Worlds. As they enter into the world of the text, students construct social worlds or cultures operating in the text world constituted by certain purposes, roles, rules, beliefs, traditions, or history (Beach & Myers, 2001). This involves far more than simply inferring the physical setting. It involves defining the social, cultural, and historical contexts shaping characters' social practices. Understanding, for example, Elizabeth Bennett's social practices as a female in the early 19th-century world of *Pride and Prejudice* requires some understanding of how social behaviors were perceived as appropriate for certain social classes—the aristocracy, the landed gentry, the mercantile middle class, the military, and the working class.

Studying these social worlds or cultures requires an understanding of historical events shaping these worlds (Galt, 2000; McCormick, 1999). In studying *To Kill a Mockingbird*, students could study the history of the civil rights movement in the South through videos such as "Eyes on the Prize." Or, in studying *The Crucible*, students could study the McCarthy anti-Communist campaign that served as the basis for Arthur Miller's portrayal of witch hunts in the play.

In studying a text's historical context, students examine the influence of prevailing cultural values or discourses on characters' perceptions of authority, power, status, and resources. In Hawthorne's *The Scarlet Letter* and Miller's *The Crucible*, the notion of strict government control based on Puritan morality conflicts with the democratic ideas of individual civil liberties. In interpreting the world of *The Crucible*, students examine how Puritan religious beliefs led townspeople to believe that their peers were agents of the devil and should be hung. In *The Great Gatsby*, Gatsby's "rags-to-riches" individualistic model of achieving power through competing with others conflicts with Nick's more "Midwestern" conception of the need for community support. In *To Kill a Mockingbird*, the townspeople were accustomed to a separate, but equal, segregated world. Atticus's principled defense of Tom Robinson poses based on the vision of a new world of integration challenges the practices of a familiar segregated world. And, in adopting a postcolonial approach, it is important to examine the values and discourses of European imperialism and capitalistic control of much of the world. In his study of "Orientalism," Edward Said (1978) demonstrated how "Orientalism" was a racist and sexist cultural model for a superior European perception of the Orient as exotic, mysterious, erotic, different, and non-White or "other." These narratives themselves served to define and justify historical events through representing Europeans as civilized, advanced investors who were saving savage, primitive, uncivilized "other" people in Africa and the Mideast (Achebe, 2001; Cobley, 2001). Similarly, American narratives of the "conquering of the West" reflected the belief in "manifest destiny" of White settlers to "civilize" the "Wild West" and the "savage" Native Americans.

Inferring Rules or Norms. Readers also interpret characters' actions in terms of whether those actions are appropriate or inappropriate given rules or norms operating in a social world. In studying characters' or people's rules or norms constituting what are considered to be appropriate, significant, or valid practices within a social world, students may ask the following: "What is considered to be appropriate versus inappropriate behavior? What rules does this suggest? Who do you see as following versus not following these rules? What do these rules suggest about the type of world the characters inhabit?"

In the story, "the Lottery," by Shirley Jackson (1988), the citizens of a small town conduct an annual lottery that results in the stoning of one citizen. The townspeople blindly adhere to community traditions regardless of their destructiveness; when some townspeople begin to question this practice, noting that a nearby town discontinued the lottery, an older man comments, "We've always had a lottery," reflecting blind adherence to status quo community norms.

Students could examine the reasons for this blind adherence to institutional traditions.

Thematic Meanings. Learning to interpret these different story elements should help students infer stories' thematic meanings. Understanding how the insular world of the town in "The Lottery" perpetuates the townspeople's ritual-like adherence to the lottery with no opportunity for debate or questioning leads students to examine such related adherence to examples in their school, family, community, and nation. Students then infer larger thematic applications of the story to analyzing actions that occur without adequate debate or questioning.

Central to inferring thematic meanings is perceiving characters such as those in "The Lottery" as shaped by larger institutional forces. Characters learn to challenge those forces when they begin to perceive themselves as limited or constrained by those forces. In writing about adult development, Robert Kegan (1994) describes this as a shift between perceiving oneself as a "subject"—being "subject to" others' thinking and feeling, to "object"—having one's own thoughts and feelings. Kegan (2000) cites the example of Nora in Ibsen's play, *A Doll's House*. Nora announces to her husband, Torvald, that she is leaving. He implores her to recall her "sacred duties . . . toward your husband, and your children." She replies, "I'm no longer prepared to accept what people say and what's written in books. I must think things out for myself, and try to find my own answer." This is not just about Nora "changing her mind," Kegan points out; Nora has come to, "a new set of ideas about her ideas, about where they even come from, about who authorizes them or makes them true" (p. 56). In this sense, she is no longer subject to others' definitions of "sacred duties." Her emerging "way of knowing" holds these as object, available for critical reflection. These changes involve more than simply adopting a different way of knowing. They involve being someone different—the Nora at the end of *A Doll's House* who has the temerity to call her "sacred duties" into question. In shifting to perceive themselves as "object," characters recognize the ways in which they are positioned by institutional forces, often a central theme of literature.

PROTOTYPICAL NARRATIVES: STUDYING NARRATIVE GENRES

Another important aspect of narrative is the study of familiar text genres found in both literature and popular media (Berger, 1997; Lacey, 2000; Mittell, 2004). These genres include mystery, romance, science fiction, horror, comedy, adventure, and so forth. These genres each contain their own prototypical settings, roles, story lines, themes, and value stances or assumptions. For example, in the typical mystery story, a detective and often sidekick sort through various clues to solve a murder or crime. Or, in the comedy genre, characters become confused about who's who or experience conflicts with others only to eventually resolve these problems, celebrated by a happy ending. (For examples of specific text genres, particularly in film, go to the Web site.)

In her study of 33 adolescent girls' reading preferences, Holly Blackford (2004) found that her female readers did not necessarily identify with female characters similar to themselves, but based their preferences for mystery, fantasy, Gothic, and science fiction novels on ways in which they are engaged by suspenseful participation in fictional worlds. For example, participants cited "out of body experiences" in reading the Harry Potter books, noting, for example, "I just think I'm in the story, like floating above them." Through experiencing the different perspectives and voices portrayed in these alternative versions of reality, the girls learned to recognize their own reality as only one version of reality, leading to challenge absolutist versions of reality.

There are a number of different approaches to use in analyzing text genres.

Formalist and Structuralist. A formalist and structuralist approach focuses on the perspective of the "semantic" components of a particular genre. A *syntactic* approach examines the particular arrangements between these building blocks—the ways in which a filmmaker has structured a genre text (Altman, 1999). Altman (1999) cites the example of semantic components of the Western as consisting of the open, natural setting; the cowboy or sheriff and the values of the "Wild West." A syntactic perspective focuses more on the relations between the elements of culture versus nature, frontier versus civilization, community versus individual, and future versus past:

- oles—Roles of hero, heroine, sidekick, alien, monster, criminal, cowboy, mentor, detective, femme fatale, villain, talk show host, and so forth.
- Settings—The prototypical setting or world associated with a genre, for example, see the following:

  - Western—Wide open vistas of the Western plains or desert; the small town.
  - Gangster—Dark, urban, back-street settings.

- Soap opera—Indoor, upper middle class setting.
- Spy-thriller—Exotic, often urban international setting.
- Science fiction—Futuristic worlds.

- Imagery—Certain prototypical, archetypal images (black = evil vs. white = good) or symbols (the sheriff's badge, water as initiation) associated with a setting or world.
- Plot or storyline—Predictable narrative sequences of events often revolving around familiar problems and how those problems are solved. For example, in a crime or detective story line, the problem or solution structure is often as follows:

  - What is the typical problem?—crime.
  - Who solves the problem?—the tough cop.
  - With what means?—violence.

  Or, in a comedy, the problem or solution structure is often as follows:

  - What is the typical problem?—mixed identities: someone is confused with someone else.
  - Who solves the problem?—the characters eventually sort out the confusion.
  - With what means?—characters discover the true person by exposing deceit or clarifying the confusion.

- Themes or value assumptions reflected in the text—Underlying each of these storyline phases are certain value assumptions that reflect larger thematic meanings. Students can infer these value assumptions by asking, what beliefs or values are inherent in the portrayal of the problem, who or how does one solve the problem, and toward what end? For example, in studying crime or detective story lines

  - What's the problem?—We live in a crime-ridden-world.
  - Who solves the problem?—Cops, who need to be tough.
  - By what means or tools do they solve the problem?—"Eye for an eye, tooth for a tooth."
  - Toward what end; what values are reflected in the solution?—Show that crime doesn't pay.

Historical. An *historical* approach focuses on the evolution of a genre over time. Genres develop because of changes in the culture or historical period in which the genre is being produced.

Audience-Based. An audience-based approach focuses on how the meaning of a genre text is constructed by audiences' application of their knowledge of specific genre conventions. Rather than assuming that a text must be a certain type, this approach posits that a text is a certain type depending on the particular conventions audiences apply to a text. Given their background knowledge and attitudes, one set of audience members may perceive a movie as an action or adventure film, whereas another set of audience members may perceive it as a horror film.

Critical and Ideological. A critical and ideological approach examines how genres reflect values constituting status quo and dominant institutional forces. Many critics argue that traditional genres reflect the standardization of literature, film, or television in ways that simply perpetuate status quo values. For example, the large number of Hollywood action films such as "Patriot Games" serve to glorify America as a technological and military global power player.

This suggests the need to study how genres position audiences in ways that are associated with the interests and agendas of dominant institutional forces creating genre texts. For example, using the problem or solution structure (discussed earlier), analysis of the law-and-order urban police detective can demonstrate that audiences are often positioned to believe that crime is best solved by violent control as a deterrent, as opposed to alternative approaches—reducing poverty, providing jobs, instituting drug prevention programs, or enhancing education. Moreover, such shows often invite audiences to position people of color as the "urban criminal" who needs to be controlled.

Similarly, narratives in books such as Mary Pipher's (1995) *Reviving Ophelia* portray female adolescents as at-risk and vulnerable to the consumer cultural messages that focus on appearance and romance. Janice Radway (2002) argues that these narratives position female adolescents as passive and defenseless, as well as isolated from peers, school, and relationships with others: "Girls are depicted in these at-risk narratives as incapable of a selective, critical response to narrative structures, that, theoretically at least, could be subjected to scrutiny, dismantled and decomposed in a miscellany of parts, gleaned for usable images, ideas, and concepts, that is, for materials applicable to the process of self-fashioning" (p. 185). She finds counterexamples to these narratives in instances of girls creating their own "zine" versions of their lives that adopt, reuse, and exploit popular cultural images to assert their own values.

Archetypal Approaches.   Archetypal critics identify a range of different narrative patterns such as the Romance quest or journey of epic and medieval literature, the antiquest of contemporary literature, comedy, and tragedy, as well as numerous recurring patterns found in of myths, fairy tales, or fables (Campbell, 1988; Frye, 1957). In working with students on interpreting these patterns, it is essential that you carefully balance a deductive and inductive approach. One problem with much of the instruction based on archetypes is that it can be overly deductive. Students acquire a lot of concepts, but do not have the background literary experiences to know how to apply those concepts. On the other hand, when examining disparate texts representing the same pattern, students need concepts to make inductive inferences about the similarities between texts.

In the Romance quest (Frye, 1957), the hero engages in a quest or journey to destroy an evil force and often to rescue or save a person or valuable treasure. The Tolkien *Lord of the Rings* trilogy popularized by the "Lord of the Rings" films portrays the quest of the Hobbit. Frodo Baggins, a Hobbit, makes a perilous journey through Middle-Earth to the Crack of Doom to attempt to destroy the One Ring which is controlled by the Dark Lord, who wants to use the ring for evil purposes. Similarly, in Tolkien's *The Hobbit*, Bilbo Baggins goes on a quest to rescue a fortune from the evil dragon and save the home of the dwarves. In the Greek myth, Jason and his Argonauts go on a quest to find the golden fleece of a ram guarded by a dragon. In Thomas Malory's *Morte d'Arthur*, Arthur and medieval knights go on quests for the Holy Grail, assumed to be the cup from the Last Supper and kept on a castle guarded by the Fisher King (Edwards, 2001). And, in "Star Wars," Luke Skywalker goes on a journey to find and destroy Darth Vader.

Joseph Campbell (1988) argues that in the quest myth, the hero's journey is a metaphor for not only the triumph of good over evil, but also the search for the self—the attempt to define one's identity through recognizing one's own inner strengths. For Campbell, the quest involves the "killing of the infantile ego and bringing forth an adult" (p. 138). In "Star Wars," Luke Skywalker discovers that is it his father beneath the mask of Darth Vader. Vader is only an impersonal "robot," "a bureaucratic, living not in terms of himself but in terms of an imposed system" (p. 144), a foil to Luke's discovery of his own humanity.

Prior to going on the quest, the hero undergoes an initiation or trial to determine his or her ability to succeed on the quest. This initiation is not unlike those adolescents experience in many cultures in which they are left to survive on their own. The initiation represents the novice person's ability to prove oneself worthy of going on the quest. New members initiated into groups and organizations through gate-keeping rituals involves a demonstration of one's willingness to be a member of a group. For example, in the Sylvia Plath (1999) short story, "Initiation," a college student going through sorority rush recognizes that when the sorority rejects one of her friends because she was "different," she then decides that she also does not want to join the sorority. In making that decision, she recognizes that her friendship was more important to her than subscribing to the sorority's exclusive values.

Frye noted that the opposite of the Romance quest is Irony in which the antihero, a more contemporary figure who lacks the heroic qualities of the Romance hero, can only fail given his or her weakness and the destructive nature of contemporary society. The world of Romance represents the world of the romance hero engaged in a triumphal quest or journey that occurs in the summer, as contrasted to the world of Irony, in which the antihero suffers a series of setbacks in the contemporary, urban world of Winter—death and destruction. This opposition is portrayed in the John Cheever (2000) story, "The Swimmer," in which the hero, a successful suburban man, begins his quest by swimming from pool to pool. In the beginning of his quest, he appears as a triumphal romance hero in the midst of summer. As he moves from pool to pool, he is rebuffed by his ex-mistress and former friends. At the end of the story, as a storm moves in, he returns to find his home dark and empty, representing his failure as a hero.

Antiheroes abound in contemporary literature and film, characters who are trapped by institutions and society. Ralph Ellison's (1995) *Invisible Man* features an African American hero who is constricted by the racism of contemporary American society. Joseph Heller's (1996) *Catch-22* portrays the frustrations of Yossarian, who must cope with the madness and inanities of a corrupt military system filled with "Catch-22" contradictions. In the road-movie film, *Thelma and Louise*, two women challenging a sexist system are doomed from the outset of their journey.

Frye (1957) identified two other opposing narrative patterns: tragedy and comedy. A key characteristic of tragedy is that the tragic hero, like the antihero, challenges the system, but, in contrast to the antihero, the proud tragic hero suffers in a noble manner that could be characterized as tragic. For example, Oedipus and King Lear were too proud to perceive their limitations until it was too late. Hamlet must revenge his father's murder, leading to his death. Joan of Arc, in George Bernard Shaw's *St. Joan*, sacrifices her life for her principles.

In contrast to the focus on the tragic hero's challenge to the system, comedy celebrates the renewal of the system, the fact that institutions, even when they seem to be falling apart, can be renewed and restored in the end. The characters in comedy are more prototypical than unique. They often experience mix-ups in identities and breakdowns in relationships. However, at the end, these mix-ups and breakdowns are sorted out and resolved, often with a final celebration or wedding. In studying tragedy and comedy, students could inductively extract certain patterns common to examples of each narrative pattern, for example, comparing different tragic heroes or comic resolutions.

Teaching the Romance or Romantic Comedy.   We illustrate the application of genre or archetypal analysis to studying the romance novel or romantic comedy film, in particular, the novel, *Pride and Prejudice*, by Jane Austen (1983), which also draws on genre conventions of parody and satire (for links or resources, go to the Web site).

In teaching the novel, you are not only providing students with background knowledge about the historical period of the early 19th century, but you may also want to connect the novel to their own lives through discussing the idea of the "figured world" of romance shaping the romance or romantic comedy. Based on a study of college students' romantic relationships, Holland and Eisenstat (1990) defined what they describe as a "cultural model" of romance constituting the "figured world" of romance. In that world, female value attracting males is a high priority, in some cases, higher than their academic pursuits. They learn certain strategies and tactics for building successful relationships from veterans who provide them with advice and tips. They develop a set of categories for defining certain types of men and women based on their appearance, social skills, and commitment to romance. Although "cultural models" of romance may have changed since the study, students may discuss their own notions of romance and what strategies and practices are involved in romantic relationships.

Students could then discuss the genre conventions of the romance novel or story. The romance heroine of the popular romance novels of the 1950s to the 1980s was based on the role of the woman in society as one whose primary mission is to nurture others in the role of lover or wife within the context of a patriarchal value system. Janice Radway (1984) noted that the romance novel story typically begins with the cold, impersonal male hero initially rejecting or being rejected by the nurturing female protagonist. However, over time, the female protagonist brings out the more subjective, nurturing, romantic side of the man, transforming him by the end of the story into a more caring partner, resulting in a love relationship often leading to marriage. Heroines in more recent romance novels are more likely to assume professional roles consistent with economic opportunities for women in the workplace, a shift away from simply assuming the nurturing role.

Students could then examine the story line and roles in *Pride and Prejudice*. In this novel, there are clearly defined rules constituting appropriate dating behavior, rules very much related to class distinctions and gender. None of the Bennett daughters could themselves initiate contact with members of the opposite sex. The reclusive Mr. Bennett had to make all contacts, and was reticent to do so with aristocrats such as D'Arcy. Women also needed to marry to achieve some financial or social status beyond remaining dependent on their own family for support. Unless they could attract a man who himself had money, they were doomed, a theme that Jane Austen was continually playing with in her novels. Elizabeth's sisters, Charlotte and Lydia, are desperate to be married, entering into marriages Elizabeth perceives to be less than desirable.

Students could study the ways in which D'Arcy fits the role of the cold, impersonal man who is slowly transformed through his relationship with Elizabeth, who fosters his ability to express his emotions. Students could study other similar characters in films such as "Dirty Dancing," in which the tough, working-class hero is transformed through his relationship with his dancing student.

Students could also study Austen's use of language designed to parody the assumed norms shaping male–female relationships. For example, Mrs. Bennett often blathers on about her concerns with her daughters' relationships, representing Austen's deliberate exaggeration of Mrs. Bennett's beliefs in the need to marry off her daughters.

Students could also study the related genre of the romantic comedy in the plays—*Comedy of Errors, A Midsummer Night's Dream, As You Like It, Pericles, The Tempest, and*

The Winter's Tale, Twelfth Night, The Importance of Being Ernest, and films—*My Best Friend's Wedding, French Kiss, When Harry Met Sally, Sleepless in Seattle, The Princess Bride, While You Were Sleeping, Sixteen Candles, Moonstruck, Clueless, Shrek*—which involves the use of comic elements associated with the genre of comedy: mixed identities and confusion associated with social class differences; a series of improbable adventures; the discovery of "true love" after doubts, challenges, and breakups; and a happy ending that celebrates the restoration of social institutions (Frye, 1957). Students could also critique some of the value assumptions underlying this genre: that family and love are important and desirable institutions, that being single is not fulfilling, that being in a heterosexual relationship completes one's development, that popularity is competitive, and that love overcomes all adversities, citing counterexamples from their own experiences. Students could then examine Elizabeth's development during the novel in terms of her growing recognition of D'Arcy's positive attributes—the fact that his early warnings about Wickam were valid, and how her development reflects larger assumptions about what it meant to be a strong woman in the early 1800s and whether such assumptions would apply to contemporary notions of being a strong woman.

Poststructuralist Approaches.   Narratives also revolve conflict between competing perspectives about the meaning of characters' actions. In Alice Walker's (1994) story, "Everyday Use," Dee, a graduate student who has developed a strong interest in African American history and culture, and her boyfriend, come for a brief visit to her mother's home. In contrast to the assertive, worldly, college-educated Dee, the mother's other daughter, Maggie, still lives at home and subscribes to her mother's values. While they are visiting, Dee asks the mother if she could have an old butter churn and a quilt, items she considers to a valuable part of her heritage. Her mother is reluctant to give up the quilt, which she wants to give to Maggie for her own "everyday use." Dee is applying a more academic perspective of the outsider anthropologist-ethnographer who would treat butter churn and quilts as cultural artifacts rather then items for "everyday use" by the mother and Maggie.

A poststructuralist approach focuses on the oppositions between different categories operating in a text world, and the ways in which binary oppositions can often shape characters' actions. By first identifying and listing the various oppositions operating in a text world, students can then interrogate those oppositions and how they influence characters' actions. They could then note alignments between these oppositions, for example, that male versus female is equated with control versus resistance, and which of the two opposing forces seemed to be preferred by the characters or implied author—the fact that reason seems to be preferred over passion (Pope, 1998).

Good Versus Evil.   Narratives often revolve around binary oppositions between good versus evil, in which evil seems to be triumphing over good, only to have good win out in the end. The specific events or episodes in stories are defined in terms of how they function to develop the story structure. Understanding these oppositions helps audiences define the meaning of signs and images in texts. For example, the meaning of the "road" imagery in "Lord of the Rings: The Fellowship of the Ring" reflects the code of the open-ended journey in which the hero(es) confront multiple challenges within what archetypal critics define as the "Romance" quest narrative.

Male Versus Female.   Another set of oppositions has to do with differences between "masculine" versus "feminine" as mediated by the cultural meanings they assign to these categories. The largely "female" world of soap opera is often set in the private world of the home and family with a focus on inwardness, emotion, and personal relationships as opposed to the "male" world of the public, the street, work, action, outwardness, reason, and business relationships (Lacey, 2000).

One useful application of poststructuralism to studying narratives is the NCTE Chalkface Series, textbooks designed for use by high school students: Mellor and Patterson (2001), *Investigating Texts: Analyzing Fiction and Nonfiction in High School*; Mellor, Patterson, and O'Neil (2000a), *Reading Fictions: Applying Literary Theory to Short Stories*; Mellor (1999), *Reading Hamlet*; Moon (2000), *Studying Literature: New Approaches to Poetry and Fiction*; Mellor, O'Neil, and Patterson (2000b), *Reading Stories: Activities and Texts for Critical Readings*; Martino and Mellor (2000), *Gendered Fictions*; Moon (2001b), *Studying Poetry: Activities, Resources, and Texts*. For example, in *Gendered Fictions*, students are asked to identify the gender category oppositions in fairy tales and poems, as well as respond to critics with opposing perspectives. All of this serves to help students understand how language categories themselves define how they perceive the world.

EVALUATING STUDENTS' RESPONSE TO NARRATIVE
AND NARRATIVE PRODUCTION

The following are some criteria for evaluating students' responses to narratives. You may evaluate them in terms of the following:

• Elaboration of retelling—Students' degree of elaboration in their recounting or retelling of narrative events or in connections to other texts or autobiographical experiences. The fact that students elaborate narrative events in some detail as opposed to a superficial gloss may mean that they begin to explore their beliefs or attitudes about those events.

• Application of rules of notice—Students' ability to note cues, titles, beginnings, endings, complications in characters' plans, or conflicts that imply larger thematic meanings.

• Uses of intertextual links—Students' ability to link the current text to other texts in terms of similar genres, settings, character types, narrative patterns, themes, or stances.

• Perspective-taking—Students' ability to consider alternative perspectives operating in the text. This includes the ability to discern the difference between a narrator's and other characters' perspectives. As we noted in conjunction with a poststructuralist approach, this also includes the ability to recognize characters' conflicting category conceptions of events and actions. This also includes their ability to use conflicting perspectives to judge which perspective represents a more realistic or valid conception within the context of the story world. For example, students may recognize that, in *The Great Gatsby*, Nick's perceptions were ultimately less deluded than Gatsby's perceptions.

• Range of explanations of events—Students' ability to explain characters' actions in terms of a range of different characteristics—characters' traits, knowledge, beliefs, plans, and goals. Students who base their explanation on only one minor characteristic may not develop as valid an explanation as a student who cites a range of different characteristics.

• Range of competing hypotheses—Students' ability to entertain alternative hypotheses for explaining events or characters' actions. Entertaining alternative hypotheses means that students may be more open to questioning their own, sometimes faulty, initial hypothesis by weighing it against other hypotheses. Experienced students of literature are often more likely not to settle for their initial hypothesis, and devote more time to entertaining contradictory hypotheses (Earthman, 1992).

• Constructing of a story world—Students' ability to construct a text's story world in terms of the particular cultural or historical norms and conventions operating in that world, as opposed to imposing their own lived-world assumptions onto the story world.

Portfolio Addition: Narrative Materials About Yourself

For your portfolio, include some of the following narrative material:

• Autobiographical events reflecting your identity development—Write about some specific events in your life that reflect key moments in your development (Eakin, 1999; Olney, 1998; Quigley, 2000). In doing so, attempt to portray past events from the past point of view so that you capture the details of that event through the perspective of your past identities. Reflect on how those past events shaped your past and current identity development.

• A family history study—Collect narratives or autobiographical recollections from previous generations in your family of their experiences with you. Reflect on how those events and others' perceptions of you influenced your identity development. Consider ways in which differences in historical period, class, gender, education, and so forth, influenced family members' development, self-concept, attitudes and values, aspirations, success, and so forth.

• Teaching narratives—Write about some specific teaching experiences in working with adolescents. Reflect on how those events shaped your perceptions of yourself as a teacher.

Online Additional Activities, Links, and Further Reading

Go to the textbook Web site, Chapter 7, and to "story response/writing" for additional activities, links, and further reading.

8

Teaching Text- and Task-Specific
Strategies: How Does the Shape
of a Text Change the Shape
of My Teaching?

Chapter Overview

- Teaching different kinds of texts.
- Working with "struggling" readers.
- Teaching task-specific ways of interpreting specific kinds of texts: poetry, stories, myths and fables, drama, expository texts.
- Assessing students' use of reading processes.

CASE NARRATIVE: JAMIE TEACHING SHAKESPEARE— SEEING POSSIBILITIES IN EVERYTHING

Jamie Heans is an extraordinary teacher. He works in the Professional Development School site in Maine where Jeff worked for several years. He is particularly adept at reaching kids who are considered reluctant or resistant.

One wintry night, Jeff had taken Jamie out to dinner in downtown Bangor. They were walking back to Jamie's house crunching through the snow that filled the empty streets. The next day was one of those special pick-up days when you could leave out pretty much anything for the garbage men to cart away—furniture, stereo equipment, appliances, and so forth.

It was cold and Jeff thought he would freeze to death because Jamie kept stopping to paw through piles of people's castoff belongings. "This speaker could be fixed!" he'd tell Jeff. "You just need some new wiring!" Or "this chair could be cool if you would just recover it." Sometimes he would think of wild new uses for something: "You could take the shelves out of this bookcase and it would probably make a good sandbox!"

Jeff had a flash of insight. This was why Jamie was such a great teacher. He saw the possibilities in everything! He saw the potential of every student and what he or she could become. He sometimes referred to kids as "rough diamonds," as if he knew with the right care they could become something special. He expected to have to tinker and to work carefully and attentively with his students as individuals. A cookie-cutter approach to teaching was not something that worked for Jamie or his students.

Later that spring, Jamie had a problem. He was teaching Romeo and Juliet to his basic and average English classes, as required by the curriculum. The kids were not into it. They didn't get why they were reading this text. Some complained that it was "in a foreign language!" Yes, Jamie replied, that would be late-middle English. But what seemed particularly troublesome for them was that they didn't know how to read dramatic scripts. "It's just people talking to each other!" one boy complained. "You have to go back after every page and figure out who said what to who! And even then you don't know enough to know what the heck is going on!"

Jamie is not the kind of guy to push on mindlessly when things are not working. He likes to figure out with the kids what they could do differently.

"Ok, guys," he told his class, "we have to read this play. What can we do to make it easier and better and more fun?"

They came up with a lot of excellent ideas. To give their reading a purpose close to their hearts, they framed their reading of the play around the following inquiry question: what makes a good relationship? To help them with translating and understanding the language, different groups of kids took on the mantle of the expert to become video documentary makers. Each group was assigned a scene, and their job was to take an assigned literary term, re-enact a part of the scene in which this device was used, explain the scene and the use of the device in modern language, and explain how the device contributed to the meaning of the scene. The kids took to their roles of video designers with relish and panache, and did exciting and creative work which they could not wait to show their classmates.

TEACHING DIFFERENT KINDS OF TEXTS

In this chapter, we ask the question of how we need to change our instruction to meet the demands of unique kinds of texts. Jamie knew he had to help his students understand the conventions of scripts, so that they could be helped to both read *Romeo and Juliet* (and all other dramatic scripts) and to write the scripts for their videos.

Dramatists rely entirely on dialogue and extratextual directions because they cannot take advantage of the same textual features used by novelists or other writers. This is because scripts are intended to be performed. Therefore, students are confronted with textual conventions they may not have seen before. If students don't pay attention to these conventions, they will be missing a major part of dramatic work, and will miss much of the meaning.

Jamie found out that the drama theorist Esslin (1987) identifies 22 basic elements used in dramatic scripts that no other kind of text uses. Esslin divides these 22 elements into five basic categories: framing systems, systems at the actor's disposal, visual systems, the text, and aural systems. David Anderson (1988) has adapted these systems for viewing drama to make them useful to reading drama. These conventions require what could be called "text specific" reading strategies, because the demands of scripts require readers to make very particular meaning-making moves that are specific to this text type or genre.

Anderson's categories are prereading, descriptions of settings, technical stage directions, the character's words, and stage directions and character descriptions.

Prereading strategies help students to build background that will guide them in reconstructing and visualizing the action in their mind. They need to know what kind of script it is and how it is intended to be performed (radio, television, proscenium stage, etc.). They will need to look at the title, the genre (tragedy, comedy), lists of characters, names and titles, stage directions, and character descriptions.

As they read, students will need to know how to ascertain important information and make inferences from descriptions of settings, which imply tone and mood, reveal character as well as social and historical perspective. They also need to know how to read dialogue, understand speaker designation, and understand that in scripts dialogue will be expected to convey mood, tone, symbolism, setting, and clues for story and character development. And, students need to learn to visualize stage directions describing sounds, lighting and properties, and the movement of characters and properties. Finally, students need to learn how characters are represented through the dialogue—their own and others—and how characters are represented through stage directions and descriptions.

Most textbooks and resources on reading only identify "general" reading strategies, that is, those strategies that all good readers use any time they read anything at all. General process strategies include activating schematic background; setting a purpose for reading; decoding words; visualizing settings, scenes, characters, events and ideas; summarizing and bringing meaning forward throughout a reading; predicting; and asking questions.

Finding Out About Your Students' Perspectives on Reading. In the beginning of the school year, it is often helpful to find out about your students' perspectives on reading—how they define reading and what they like or dislike about reading—by conducting brief interviews with them or asking them the following questions:

1. What do you think reading is—explain what you do when you read?
2. *Why* do you read?
3. What sorts of things do you *like* to read (interest, choice)? Why do you like those texts (this includes reading inside and outside of school)?
4. What kinds of things do you read that your friends are also reading?
5. What reading assigned in school do you like? Why? Explain.
6. If you could pick topics to read in school, what would you pick? Why? Explain. If you could pick topics in this class to read about, what would you pick?
7. How do you read difficult texts? How do you read texts in this class, particularly ones that you think are difficult?
8. How do you know if you are reading well? How do you know if you are having problems with reading? How do you know if you are having problems reading texts in this class?

Answers to these questions provides you with an awareness of individual differences in students' notions of reading. In some cases, they may perceive reading as simply decoding words, whereas others may perceive it as understanding larger meanings. Some may express few if any things or topics, suggesting that they lack an interest in reading or using reading to learn about new things or topics. Some may also have difficulty knowing how to address difficult texts, for example, by applying context cues to understand unfamiliar words. Knowing about these individual differences can then help you build your curriculum around redefining notions of reading as meaning-constructing, providing types of reading and topics that interest students, and modeling ways of addressing reading difficulties.

Think-Alouds. Another way of finding out more about your students is through think-alouds. In doing a think-aloud, you are asking students to verbally report on what they are attending to as they are reading. They do not describe or explain what they are doing when they are reading; they simply report what they are attending to as they are reading through a short text or section of a longer text (O'Brien, 2004). You can work with students individually or have them work in pairs with the other students simply providing encouragement to the students doing the think-alouds. Here are some sample instructions you might use:

> As you read today, I am interested in what you say to yourself as you read. So I can know what you are thinking and saying to yourself, I want you to actually talk aloud. I want you to say out loud, everything that you say to yourself silently. Just act as if you are alone in a room speaking to yourself. If you are silent for too long, I will remind you to keep talking.

Because think-alouds can seem artificial, it is important that you allow students practice doing think-alouds, helping them to learn to focus on reporting their thinking rather than attempting to describe or explain their thinking. Students will want to summarize what they are reading rather than thinking aloud or reflect and interpret rather than just talk aloud. By modeling your own use of think-alouds with a different text, you can demonstrate what you mean by reporting thoughts.

You can also use think-alouds to focus on certain reading processes (O'Brien, 2004).

Think-Aloud Before Reading. For example, what do students think the selection is about by looking at the title, headings, and skimming through the text?

1. Tell me what you think this is about.
2. Talk about what you expect to learn from this.
3. Talk about why you think it might be useful to read this.
4. Tell me how you think using this might be useful in the class project.

Think-Aloud During Reading (Online Comprehension). What is the student understanding from the text; what is difficult about the text (comprehension or problems with words, vocabulary); what is he or she doing to make sense of the text; and what strategies can he or she use? What parts of the text are particularly important or relevant to his or her purpose for reading?

1. Talk aloud about what you are thinking as you read the text.
2. Talk about what you think is most interesting as you read.
3. Tell me what you are thinking about difficulty—what is hard or what is easy about the text.
4. Talk about what you are doing to try to understand it—what are you doing to figure out the difficult parts?

Think-Aloud While Monitoring. What is the student aware of as he or she reads: is the person aware of whether he or she is understanding the text? Does it connect to his or her prior experiences and is that helpful as he or she reads? If the person is having problems reading (words or understanding), does he or she know what the problems are?

1. As you are reading, tell me what you are thinking about your understanding.
2. In the beginning, you talked about what you expected this to be about and what you expected to learn—talk about whether this text seems to be what you expected it to be.
3. As you are reading, talk about what this text reminds you of (like things you know, interests, other things you have read).
4. Now that you are actually reading this, tell me about how you think it will help you in your work on an assignment or project.

Using Think-Aloud Data.   Listening to the students' think-alouds should provide you with an understanding of their ability to construct meaning from texts, information that may be consistent with their answers to the questions about reading. In some cases, the students' reports may reflect a focus on attempting to comprehend the words without attempting to infer larger meanings or ideas. These students may need help in learning to infer larger meanings or ideas.

MONITORING COMPREHENSION AND USING SELF-CORRECTION STRATEGIES

Reading strategies are used in all reading tasks. If students do not use these strategies, they need to be taught and assisted how to do so. Teaching students these general process strategies has huge transfer value because they will use these strategies any time they read.

However necessary these strategies are, they are insufficient to engage in expert reading. Your students could use all of these strategies expertly and still be stymied by almost every text with which they are faced in middle and high school. That's because there are sets of strategic demands called "task-specific" demands, that is, strategies that are required by certain conventional codings like symbolism or irony that run across different types of text or genre conventions specific to argument, extended definition, satires and parodies, classifications, ironic monologues, fables, lyric poetry, and the like (Smagorinsky & Smith, 1992). For example, in interpreting the meaning of an argument formulated in a newspaper editorial, a reader applies his or her knowledge of how writers make effective arguments—the fact that a writer objectively reformulates the position he or she is opposing and then critiques that position with counterarguments or evidence. This interpretation process differs markedly from interpreting a parody in which readers apply their knowledge of language and style to adopt a seemingly serious pose to ridicule some phenomenon. Reading these two different genres requires applying their "knowing-how" ability to apply different conventional ways of understanding acquired through practice in reading those genres. Someone without experience of reading parodies may believe that the parody is based on actual events. All of this suggests that, contrary to labels applied based on high stakes standardized reading tests, there is no such thing as a "poor" or "good" reader—readers' ability varies with what they are reading, given differences in their knowing-how capacity.

WORKING WITH "STRUGGLING" READERS

In working with students who seem to be "struggling" or "poor" readers, you may assume that if they are having difficulty with decoding vocabulary, then they will not be able to understand the texts you assign them (VanDeWeghe, 2004). If someone is stumbling in reading aloud a story, you may assume that he or she will not be able to make any thematic interpretations of that story. In a study of English teachers' perceptions of students' reading, Fred Hamel (2003) found that teachers may underestimate students' capacity to interpret texts based on narrow measures of "reading ability," and thereby have low expectations for their potential success. At the same time, he also found that literature teachers need to recognize that students will need help with reading comprehension as something that's not distinct from literary interpretation. Helping students with reading comprehension means more than just assisting them with decoding; it means having students engage in think-aloud activities as they are reading a text to determine the ways in which they can make interpretations as well as difficulties they are encountering. (As we previously noted, student simply describe their thoughts in a spontaneous mode as they are reading a text, as opposed to reflecting on or interpreting those thoughts.) You also need to place yourself in the mind-set of a student reading a text for the first time, bracketing out the fact that you may have read it many times and that you're bringing years of experience as a literary reader to your experience of the text.

Although students acquire these conventional ways of reading largely through reading, you can certainly model or scaffold their experience in encountering new text genres by making explicit the strategies you employ with these texts. For example, when the class is reading a Jonathan Swift parody, you can describe how you identity his use of language and a mock-serious tone as signals that he's engaging in parody.

Readers' understanding of texts varies not only by differences in knowing how to apply genre conventions, but also their prior knowledge about certain content or subject matter. A student who knows a lot about playing video games may breeze through directions to a game, whereas another student who knows little about playing video games may spend a lot more time trying to understand the directions. This means that you need to consider what your students may know about certain topics, concepts, ideas, or disciplinary knowledge related to understanding a certain text. This is particularly the case with links to other texts with similar story lines, character types, themes, topics, issues, or perspectives. Encouraging students to draw on intertextual links from their previous reading helps them inductively define similarities constituting genre knowledge. In reading a story such as "The Turn of the Screw" with a narrator whose perspective they begin to challenge as unreliable, they may recall other texts with unreliable narrators.

And, readers' understanding varies according to the purpose for reading a text within the context of a larger activity (Duffy, 2003). Having a clear sense of purpose—what they want to learn from reading a text—means that readers know what kind of information or ideas they want to extract from a text. The video-game player who's not sure about a certain rule peruses through the game directions knowing just what to look for to play the game more effectively. Helping students clarify their sense of purpose for reading helps them know what aspects of a text to attend to that address what they want to learn from a text.

Readers' sense of purpose often influences their engagement with what they are reading as well as the larger activity surrounding that reading influences their understanding (Guthrie, 2004). The video-game player is highly engaged with winning the game, which means that he or she is engaged with learning from the directions what's needed to win.

Finally, readers' understanding of language or vocabulary is certainly a factor shaping their understanding. A key element in understanding word meaning is understanding how that word is being used in a certain context. When a female character, Jill, utters to a male suitor after a first date, "That was a nice dinner," these words could mean any number of different things depending on the larger context. Jill could be meaning that although the dinner was "nice," the date itself was less so. Or, she could be meaning that she actually enjoyed the date. Sorting out these competing meanings requires an understanding of characters' beliefs about each other, motives, agendas, and goals.

All of this means that trying to teach reading in a vacuum—teaching reading skills or strategies in isolation for their own sake—won't be as successful as teaching reading within the context of a unit, project, or activity in which reading is used as a tool to accomplish some larger purpose driving student engagement. For example, a group of middle school students had to write a letter to their school board arguing their case to not shut down their school (Sheehy, 2003). They conducted surveys of their peers' attitudes about the school and then interpreted the survey data to create multiple drafts to build their case for why they wanted to stay in their school. In this activity, they were engaged with achieving a larger purpose—convincing the school board of the value of their school—that shaped their understanding of survey data and their drafts. When they lacked knowledge on how to craft a convincing argument, their teacher provided them with assistance about genre conventions of argument.

The teaching of reading often breaks down when students lack knowledge of genre conventions, prior knowledge of subject matter, purpose, and engagement with the activity. Many researchers (see, e.g., Wilhelm, Baker, & Dube, 2001) argue that this is the reason for the well-known fourth-grade slump. Students have been reading narrative and learning general strategies for several years. Suddenly they are faced with new task- and text-specific demands which they never learned to acquire, and which teachers seem to assume they will learn on their own. In fifth grade, students are starting to focus much more on specific subject matter texts in science, social studies, or math, texts that require specific disciplinary ways of thinking, for example, how to conduct an experiment. If students are not provided with these discipline-specific ways of thinking and prior knowledge as part of larger units or projects, they struggle. In their study on boys and literacy, Smith and Wilhelm (2002) found that many boys said they used to be good readers, and then they, as one boy put it, "got dumber." This assuredly did not happen. They weren't necessarily "poor readers." They were "poor readers" of a certain kind of text requiring certain kinds of genre or disciplinary knowledge they never acquired from their teachers. Some of the boys recognized this and complained that "teachers give you really hard stuff to read, and no helps you know how to read it."

So What's a Teacher to Do? Making Explicit Your Ways of Reading.   What this means is that in addition to embedding reading instruction within an engaging, purposeful unit or project, you need to make explicit your ways of reading or interpreting texts by describing the genre conventions and prior knowledge you apply to those texts. This means that for advanced reading of texts for your units or projects, you need to identity differences between your own reading processes as an experienced reader and the processes your students will bring to the texts. In planning his activities, Jamie knew that he first had to understand the demands placed on readers by dramatic scripts. Then he had to find a way to assist his students to learn how to recognize and deal with these demands so that they could meaningfully comprehend and interpret the text they were being asked to read. Jamie identified the most important of those demands as setting directions, stage directions, and character directions.

You then need to determine how to provide your students with the genre conventions for understanding specific kinds of texts. To help his kids understand how these directions needed to be used to create a visual image in the mind, Jamie brought in several cartoon strips that dealt with the topic of romantic love in a way that helped address the following question: What is a good relationship? He told his students that they needed to translate the cartoon into a script.

The students brainstormed what kinds of information were encoded in a cartoon that could not be encoded in a straight textual presentation. The students identified how characters looked, what they wore, facial expressions, where they stood, how they interacted, how they moved, how they said things, how things changed from panel to panel, and so forth.

Jamie informed his students that scripts used particular kinds of "codes" to communicate this kind of information so that a reader or play director would know how to visualize and stage the scene in her mind.

Students spent a couple of days practicing translating cartoons into scripts and identifying the kinds of script conventions they had to use. They were now much better prepared to write their own scripts and to read *Romeo and Juliet*.

Student teacher Andrew Porter was faced with the same problem when introducing the play, *The Diary of Anne Frank*, to his eighth graders. He chose another method for introducing his students to the conventions and importance of dramatic script.

Andrew went to the Internet and downloaded the scripts for famous scenes from popular shows like "The Simpsons" and "Seinfeld," like the scene where Homer teaches Bart how to fight, and the scene where Kramer drops a mint into a patient during surgery.

He split the class into groups and allowed them to choose the scene they wanted to reenact. He gave them time to review the scripts and to rehearse. The kids then enacted their scenes and talked about what made an enactment powerful. They then talked about where they received the clues for how to enact a scene. Although a few students had seen and remembered these scenes from their television viewing, most of them relied somewhat on the stage, setting, and character directions. Andrew identified these conventions of scripts and the class had a discussion about how to read these directions and how to use them to visualize a scene and "reenact it in your mind."

Short frontloading activities like these helped both Jamie's and Andrew's students induce and master the use of these conventions and greatly assisted their reading of the plays they were subsequently asked to read. Moreover, because the students had some larger purpose for reading the texts—to prepare for a drama production in which they could display competence in front of their peers—they were engaged with wanting to understand their texts. Jamie and Andrew were not teaching "reading" in a vacuum. They were helping their students acquire certain ways of reading of certain kinds of texts within larger, engaging contexts.

Frontloading Activities.   Jamie and Andrew also knew that they needed to frontload activities in ways that served to engage students so that they had some purpose for wanting to understand the texts they were reading. In frontloading activities, try to do the following:

1. Frame the frontloading work as fun, interesting, relevant and usable—immediately, in terms of the unit work, and in the future. Make sure the connection to usability is made!

2a. Design an activity (or short series of activities) that will show the procedure in action and give students some introductory practice using the procedure.

2b. Make sure that this activity (or sequence of activities) provides you with pre-assessment feedback about what the students can and cannot do with the procedure.

3. Use the activity (or activities) to articulate and highlight the textual tip-offs that one must activate in this procedure and the steps to use the procedure.

4. Plan to continue following up on this introductory frontloading until all students have mastered the basics of the procedure.

5. Make sure students know how the procedures will be used in their culminating project or final student composition.

TEACHING TASK-SPECIFIC WAYS OF INTERPRETING SPECIFIC KINDS OF TEXTS

In Chapter 3 on planning, we discussed ways of creating units or projects that provide students with prior knowledge, purpose, and ideally, a sense of engagement. In this chapter, we discuss teaching specific ways of interpreting certain, specific kinds of texts within the larger forms of poetry, narrative, drama, and argumentative texts. One of the major problems with formalist genre instruction or units on teaching poetry, short story, drama, fantasy and mystery, or the essay is that these genre categories are so broad as that they provide little guidance for reading certain kinds of texts. For example, in teaching poetry, Peter Rabinowitz and Michael Smith (1998) argue that students need to be taught more finely sliced kinds of poetry such as lyric poetry, ironic monologues, sonnets, or narrative poetry that each share quite different genre features that are useful for interpreting and writing these different types of poems. Or, in reading and writing stories, students encounter fables, parables, myths, tall tales, anecdotes, jokes, character sketches, unreliable narrator stories, comic book stories, and a range of different types of genre stories: mystery, ghost, horror, romance, comedy, or adventure stories. Applying generic strategies such as predicting story outcomes or endings is of little use because making predictions varies so much across these different types of stories in how they end or are resolved.

Poetry

There are several basic processes involved in reading poetry.

Rereading Poems. One of the most basic processes in reading most poems (aside from Hallmark card poems) is that you need to reread poems several times, noting changes in the meaning of the poems across each rereading. Students need to appreciate the fact that poetry is difficult and that one rarely interprets complex meanings of a poem on a single reading (Blau, 2003). In rereading poems, students may notice how a twist or revelation at the end of a poem leads to what John Ciardi (1975, p. 65) describes as "movement across the fulcrum," leading to changing one's interpretation of the first part of the poem. For example, in reading Gwendolyn Brooks's (1999) poem, "We Real Cool," describing a group of pool players "real cool/We left school. We/ lurk late/," the last line, "We die soon," introduces a dark undertone to the poem that challenges the celebratory first part of the poem (p. 73).

Students could pair up and share think-aloud responses to each rereading—with one student functioning as an audience who simply encourages the other to continue their think-alouds. Students could then reflect on how the meaning changed across different rereadings.

Interpreting the Meaning of the Title. Another essential process is noting the symbolic, thematic meaning of the title. The title represents a summary of the poem's focus. In reading poems with students, have students compare the differences between reading a poem with and without the title, asking them to discuss how knowing the title shaped their interpretations.

Figurative Language.   Students also need to be able to infer the meaning of figurative language—how metaphors, similes, or personification are being used to convey meanings. Rather than having students memorize the different types of figurative language and then identify examples of these types in poems, what's more important is that they understand how figurative language can be employed to engage readers in the poetic experience. One of the basic notions of comprehension proposed by Frank Smith (1997) is that comprehension is the reduction of uncertainty. Readers bring familiar semantic categories of their prior knowledge to a text and then use those categories to infer meanings and reduce uncertainty. They are therefore moving from their familiar prior knowledge to understanding new, unfamiliar text. Metaphors or similes help readers move from the familiar to the unfamiliar by providing them with a familiar concept to infer a certain meaning. Metaphors or similes often consist of familiar physical, concrete entities that are used to portray conceptual meanings or serve as ways of knowing (Pugh, Hicks, & Davis, 1997). Lakoff and Johnson (1980) describe the use of "cultural metaphors" such as a journey used to describe a life experience, madness used to describe being in love, or war used to describe sports The life is a journey metaphor is evident in notions of being "off track," on a "long, bumpy road," or "at a crossroads" in one's life. To convey her conception of death in the poem "Because I could not stop for Death," Emily Dickinson (1990, p. 36) uses the metaphor of a carriage moving through time to describe the experience of death:

Because I could not stop for Death—
He kindly stopped for me—
The Carriage held but just Ourselves—
And Immortality.

We slowly drove—He knew no haste
And I had put away
My labor and my leisure too,
For His Civility—

We passed the School, where Children strove
At Recess—in the Ring—
We passed the Fields of Gazing Grain—
We passed the Setting Sun—

Or rather—He passed us—
The Dews drew quivering and chill—
For only Gossamer, my Gown—
My Tippet—only Tulle—

We paused before a House that seemed
A Swelling of the Ground—
The Roof was scarcely visible—
The Cornice—in the Ground—

Since then—'tis Centuries—and yet
Feels shorter than the Day
I first surmised the Horses' Heads
Were toward Eternity—

Students could also discuss the originality or creativity of the use of figurative language. They could start with some of the cliché uses of figurative language frequently found in advertising slogans, similes such as "Miller: The Champagne of Bottle Beers" or "Breakfast without orange juice is like a day without sunshine" or cliché metaphors such as "Sherwin-Williams covers the earth." They could then create their own more original metaphors or similes for use in their poetry writing by observing or finding physical objects, artifacts, images, or colors that can be used to describe certain experiences, concepts, or emotions. For example, the emotion of anger can be associated with red ("seeing red"), an explosion ("blew up"), water ("reach a slow boil"), a furnace ("blew a gasket"), madness ("had a fit," "went berserk"), and so forth. These meanings also depend a lot on cultural differences. For example, Yu Ren Dong (2004) asked his English Language Learners students to iden-tity how the word *bread* can be used in different contexts to be certain things, resulting in examples such as the following: "Give us this day our daily bread. My landlord wants his bread now. Man cannot live by bread alone. His curve ball is his bread-and-butter pitch. This is the bread of life. He knows which side his bread's buttered on. Cast your bread upon the water" (p. 29). These different examples reflect differences in how the meaning of bread as a symbol of power and agency varies among different cultural contexts.

Inferring Binary Oppositions.   Applying a deconstructionist lens, students can identify the binary oppositions or categories operating in a poem by listing the different oppositions and then inferring the thematic meaning of these oppositions (Moon, 2001). Some of these oppositions reflect basic cultural tensions: male–female, rich–poor, strong–weak, pub-lic–private, old–new, and so forth. In the Dickinson poem (1990), there's a tension between time as slowly and inevitably passing as the carriage heads toward eternity, representing the aging process, and time as a reoccurring cycle of life—the children at recess, the grains growing in the field, the setting sun, that represent the renewal of life in opposition to death.

Making Intertextual Connections.   Students also need to make intertextual connec-tions between the words, images, metaphors, topics, styles, or techniques and others texts, for example, between the images of love in Shakespeare's love sonnets and in contempo-rary song lyrics. To facilitate making these links, students could create hypermedia pro-ductions of poems using Hyperstudio™ or iMovie™ that employ images, songs, and other texts connected to the original poem's topics or themes.

Different Reading Processes for Different Poetry Genres.   At the same time, students learn to apply different reading processes for different poetry genres, recognizing that read-ing of texts needs to be combined with oral performances or reading aloud of poems. (For an anthology of poems that lends itself to performance, see *Poetry Out Loud*, Rubin, 1995.) In working on oral interpretation as a form of reading, students need to first study the poem to determine the meanings they want to convey through their performance by marking words for emphasis, noting flows from one line to the next, or places for pauses. You can model oral interpreting strategies by having students view performances of online clips from the PBS "Poets Read: Fooling With Words" (http://www.pbs.org/wnet/foolingwithwords/main_video.html) or "Poetic License" (http://www.itvs.org/poeticlicense/).

They then practice their performance, focusing on pausing, emphasis, sounds, and alter-nating voices. They could also employ alternative readings of the same poem, or stereo or quadrophonic performances with students in different corners of the classroom, or readers' theater productions with a chorus voicing the refrains.

Sonnets or Ballads.   Central to reading sonnets or ballads is an appreciation of rhyth-mic patterns, meter, and pauses. Students could study the ways in which meter is established through identifying which words to accent and how meter adds to reading (Powell & Halperin, 2004).

Lyrics. Reading lyrics, particularly lyrics of popular songs, involves understanding the role of repetition of words or refrains as part of interpreting poets' larger rhetorical purpose. For example, in blues, lyrics usually contain the repetition of a lament about a loss or problem in one's life and the difficulty of a possible solution, so that the repetition of the lament reflects the challenge of having to deal with something that is a continuous burden. (For examples of studying song lyrics, see Lloyd, 2003.)

Rap. In reading rap, as contained in collections such as *Rap: The Lyrics* (Stanley, 1992) or *Hip-Hop and Rap: Complete Lyrics for 175 Songs* (Spence, 2003), students could study the evolution of rap lyrics as reflecting changes in the Hip Hop culture from the 1970s in the Bronx, when local neighborhood artists began to play records on record players in new, original ways, to the gangsta rap and political commentary of rap of Public Enemy, KRS-One and Queen Latifah in the 1980s to the increasing commercialization of rap in the 1990s and first 5 years of this century (Chang, 2003; Jones, 1994). To understand the connections between classical poems and rap to their historical context, students could compare poems and raps, for example, "Kubla Khan"/"If I Ruled the Coleridge World," Nas; "Love Song of J. Alfred Prufrock"/"The Message," Eliot Grand Master Flash; "O Me! O Life!,"/"Don't Believe the Whitman Hype," Public Enemy; "Immigrants in Our Own Land," Baca/"The World is a Ghetto," Geto Boys; "Sonnet 29," Shakespeard/"Affirmative Action," Nas; "The Canonization," Donne/"Manifest," Refugee Camp (Morrell & Duncan-Andrade, 2002, p. 91). In comparing Grand Master Flash and T. S. Eliot, students examined the similar portrayals of a wasteland of death and decay.

Students are also reading for creative instances of rhyme in raps, noting the range of different words that rhyme (for an online resource for rhyming words, see http://www .rockstargames.com/rhymerator/).

Narratives

In reading fictional narratives—short stories, novels, epics, and so forth—students are learning a range of specific reading processes, some of which were described in Chapter 7.

Predicting Story Outcomes. Given the idea of comprehension as the reduction of uncertainty, readers are continually predicting story outcomes based on their knowledge of text genre conventions or story development, as well as inferences about patterns in characters' actions. In asking students to make these predictions, it is therefore useful to have them formulate reasons for their predictions based on perceived patterns or on knowledge of genre or story conventions. Take for example, the Shirley Jackson (1999) story, "Louise, Please Come Home," about a young girl, Louise, who runs away from home only to return years later after her family conducts a nationwide search. When she does return home as a young woman, Louise is then accused of being an impostor by her family. Students who predicted that her family may have welcomed her with open arms are challenged by this ending, causing them to examine reasons for her family's rejection.

Identifying Different Voices. As noted in Chapter 7, one general reading process involves identifying the different voices operating in a narrative—based on the question, "Who is speaking here?" in which the "who" represents different stances or worlds of romance, business, legal regulations, the military, politics, and so forth—in ways that create conflicts between competing ideological versions of events. For example, in the novel, *Catch-22* (Heller, 1996), many of the characters voice a military or business bureaucratic perspective in opposition to perspectives of spirituality, madness, and romance. Contrasting these competing voices prepares students to interpret conflicts between these different perspectives. M. Scott Momaday's (1977) *The Way to Rainy Mountain* contains three distinct voices—his father's voice, the more impersonal voice of historical records, and his own autobiographical recollections.

Differences in points of view—first person versus third person—also reflect differences in voices—between first-person narrator's subjective perspectives on experiences versus the use of a third-person point of view to describe characters' perspectives. Students also need to consider from whose point of view they are experiencing events in a story. For example, in the story, "A Jury of Her Peers,"described in Chapter 7, the local sheriff investigating the murder of a husband by his wife fails to note certain clues in the murder scene that the sheriff's wife notices—signs of abuse of the wife.

Gaps or Silences.   In reading stories, students may identify certain gaps or silences which are themselves meaningful—the fact that key information about characters' motives or events is missing (Moon, 2001). Students therefore engage in "gap-filling" (Iser, 1980), processes of filling in the missing information by drawing on their prior knowledge or experience. They could ask themselves, "What's missing from this text or picture," and then speculate as to why this information has been excluded.

Fables or Myths.   In reading fables or myths, students are transported into different worlds that portray or represent larger universal themes related to the meaning of life (Buxton, 2004; Campbell, 1988, 1993; Hamilton, 1999). Fables or myths often functioned in cultures or societies to explain certain phenomena—the creation of the earth, the meaning of birth and death, the seasons of the year, natural disasters, and so forth, consistent with the values of a certain culture. Understanding fables and myths therefore requires some understanding of the culture or society that produced these fables and myths. For example, in the Greek creation myth, the children of the marriage between Earth and Heaven battle for control of the universe with Zeus emerging as the winner. Zeus then assigns his family members responsibility for the different parts of the world, including Prometheus to create humans, but because Prometheus gives humans fire, he is punished by Zeus. In the Norse creation myth, three gods—Odin, Ve, and Vili—kill a wicked giant, Ymir, and from Ymir's body create the earth. Odin then creates a huge ash tree and two chips from the tree become man and woman—Ve gives them speech and hearing, and Vili, thoughts and emotions. In a Native American creation myth, a holy man, Wenebojo, is assisted by a wolf to help him hunt. However, an enemy tribe, the Manido, kill the wolf, so Wenebojo kills the Manido king. The Manido, who control the waters, try to drown Wenebojo, who climbs a tree and asks another tribe, the Otto, to bring him to earth. This earth becomes an island and eventually the world.

These myths share a similar pattern of gods creating earth, but differ in terms of the values of the different myths' cultures. In the Greek myth, the cultural values of military power and control are reflected in Zeus's authority. In the Norse myth, the emphasis on nature reflects that culture's nomadic cultural values. And, the Native American myth depicting animals as playing a key role reflects the ecological values of that culture.

It is also important to study the ways in which current literature and films draw on myths or fables; how, for example, "Star Wars," "The Lord of the Rings," "The Last Unicorn," "The Earthsea Trilogy," and "The Dark is Rising" incorporate the archetypal narrative pattern of the quest discussed in Chapter 9, in which the hero not only conquers evil, but also searches for the larger meaning of life. For Joseph Campbell (1988), the hero's quest represents the "killing of the infantile ego and bringing forth an adult" (p. 138). On the quest, the hero attempts to discover and conquer the dark side of the ego, which, in "The Earthsea Trilogy," is the hero's shadow. Dale Allender (2002) describes his teaching of Beatriz Rivera's short story, "Shango's Rest," based on the myth of Shango, a Yoruba god of thunder who committed suicide as an act of both shame and sacrifice. In the contemporary story, the mother protagonist saves her son from dying from stab wounds through ritual sacrifices based on the example of Shango. Allender recommends having students read other stories involving ritual activities related to holidays.

Fantasy, Science Fiction, or Mystery. In her study of adolescent girls' responses to literature, Holly Blackford (2004) finds that rather than identifying with female characters similar to themselves, they respond positively to fantasy, science fiction, and mystery novels through being engaged by being in different, alternative fictional worlds that differ from their own lived-world experiences. Rather than simply being a form of escape, entering into these alternative worlds affords them with an awareness of different ways of perceiving their lived-world experiences.

One of the most basic reading processes in responding to fantasy, science fiction, and mystery novels is the ability to suspend one's disbelief and adopt the worldviews operating in the worlds of the text. J. R. R. Tolkien (2005), author of *The Lord of the Rings*, describes how readers begin to believe that this alternative world is " 'true'; it accords with the laws of that world. You therefore believe it, while you are, as it were, inside. The moment disbelief arises, the spell is broken; the magic, or rather art, has failed" (p. 37). This requires the ability to define the norms operating in these worlds—noticing cues which suggest that certain norms are operating in that world constituting good versus evil.

In responding to mysteries, students also need to be able to employ their own problem-solving abilities to vicariously work through the different clues, false leads, and red herrings by attempting to discern, with the detective, who's telling the truth and who is lying.

Reading any of these genres also requires interpreting the symbolic meaning of characters and their actions. Students could use The Inquiry Square to make inferences about fables (see Table 8.1).

TABLE 8.1
The Inquiry Square

	Declarative	*Procedural*
Form	Features of the fable, including animals as symbols, and so forth.	How to generate the substance of the proposed fable in an appropriate form. Explore foibles that irritate you. Think about how people with this foible act. What animals have that foible as a trait? Choose a big one that causes problems for self and others. Choose a foible that is correctable.
Substance	Human qualities that are evil or immoral or irritating in some way to the writer, foibles, and so forth. Knowledge of content in fables.	How to produce the substance of fables, brainstorming for qualities that are immoral or irritating. Generating foibles and their concomitant actions, and so forth.

CASE NARRATIVE: RYAN TEACHES SYMBOLISM

Ryan Mahan was teaching his eighth graders *Number the Stars* by Lois Lowry (1998). He noticed that his students did not notice, and therefore did not meaningfully interpret, the symbols that Lowry uses throughout the text.

Ryan's class was pursuing the following inquiry question: What are civil rights and how can we best protect them? *Number the Stars* is an excellent text for pursuing this question, and understanding the symbolism will help students more fully understand and appreciate Lowry's answer to this question—that we must pull together and depend on family and friends when civil rights are under assault.

Being an excellent teacher, Ryan did not want to identify the symbols and their meanings for his students. He wanted to help them learn the tip-offs that something was a symbol, and to go through the steps of connecting the symbol to a cultural meaning and then reinserting that meaning back into the text in a way that made sense. Following are steps for understanding symbolism:

1. Recognize the tip-offs that an object could be symbolic.
   - Obvious symbolic meaning of the object—flag symbolizes national values, Star of David symbolizes Jewishness.
   - Less obvious tip-offs: action or object is described in detail or with a striking metaphor, relates to title, a character associates the object or event with something important, is repeated, appears at important point, refers to a color, shape, animal, or natural element.
2. Entertain ideas about the object's or action's symbolic meaning by connecting it to a cultural meaning.
   - For example, in Western culture, the color white implies purity or life, but in Australian Aboriginal cultures, white refers to death. So the symbol must be connected to the culture that expresses or uses it. In Western culture, the owl is a reference to Athena, the goddess of wisdom; in Native cultures the owl can be a symbol of impending problems.
3. Infer the symbolic meaning and insert that meaning into the text in a way that makes sense.

Ryan then decided to plan a follow-up lesson on reading symbols.

Drama

In reading drama texts—ideally coupled with viewing live or filmed productions—students must rely solely on dialogue to construct characters' traits, beliefs, goals, and relationships with other characters. As we noted in Chapter 7 on narratives, making inferences about dialogue involves inferring the kinds of speech acts that are being performed—requesting, informing, questioning, charging, inviting, ordering, and so forth. To successfully perform these acts, characters need to have certain traits, beliefs, goals, and relationships.

To construct these characters, students could employ "character profiles," listing aspects about a character or the nature of his or her conflicts with other characters; "value sorts" in which they identity virtues and vices of most versus least admirable characters; "turning points," in which they note when and why a character changes; "inexplicable acts" of characters in which students explore motives for actions; "temperature charts" in which students describe the nature of the relationships between characters—from "hot"—

vilify, condemn, or hate to "cool"—tolerate or ignore; "major or minor," in which students explore the ways in which minor characters are used to reveal certain aspects of major characters; and "unspoken words," in which students imagine characters' inner thoughts (Milner & Milner, 2003, pp. 237–239).

Expository Texts

One of the approaches typically employed in teaching reading of expository texts is to identify the text structures employed: thesis or support, cause and effect, comparison or contrast, problem or solution, and so forth. One problem with this approach is that all of the different kinds of expository texts employ a range of different kinds of structures, including narratives. Harvey Daniels (2002) identifies just a few of the many different kinds of texts: "standardized test passages, reference books, textbooks, manuals/instructions, contracts, news stories, feature stories, narrated nonfiction profiles, editorials, essays, biographies, memoirs, travelogues/adventure, historical accounts" (p. 8). He also argues that contrary to the often stale, dated expository texts found in high school essay anthologies, it's important to find expository texts that are "important or engaging" with "people we can care about; a narrative structure or chronological line; places we can visualize; danger, conflicts, risks, or choices; value, moral, ethical, or political dimensions; [and] some ideas that reasonable people can debate, dispute, or disagree about" (p. 9).

Learning to read essays involves applying a set of specific reading processes. Essays considered as literature are written in a manner that engage in what Charles Suhor (2002) described as "contemplative reading"—a reflective orientation about the world reflected in "emotional exploration; awareness of paradox; flashes of insight and discovery; aesthetic and intellectual highs, often sustained; a sense of wonderment; relaxation of the ego; glimpses of the transcendence; a tendency to incline the reader toward positive behaviors such as thoughts or acts of generosity; ineffability" (p. 29). He experiences these responses in reading the essays, letters, or speeches of Howard Cushnir; Annie Dillard; Frederick Douglass; Emmet Fox; Kahlil Gibran; Thich Nhat Hanh; Jane Hirschfield; Thomas Kelly; Martin Luther King, Jr.; Abraham Lincoln; W. A Mathieu; Thomas Merton; Thomas Moore; Stephen Nachmanovich; Rachel Remen; Sharon Salzberg; Marilyn Sewell; John Tarrant; Henry David Thoreau; and Christopher Titmuss.

We next discuss the reading of essays, which involves several specific processes.

Identifying the Writer's Persona or Voice.   Writers adopt a range of different persona or voices, even within an essay. In "A Modest Proposal," Jonathan Swift (1994) adopts the ironic, serious pose of a policymaker proposing an absurd remedy to the problem of poverty. In her descriptions of the commercial wastelands of southern California, Joan Didion (2003) adopts the voice of an ethnographic observer cataloguing the landscape in descriptive details. In their essays about the conditions of deteriorating urban schools, Jonathan Kozol (1991) and Mike Rose (1999) adopt the voices of despair over the influence of these schools on poor, urban students. Students could study how these writers' voices reflect certain beliefs and attitudes toward a topic or issue.

Identifying the Invited Audience.   In adopting certain personal stances or voices, writers are also attempting to create an invited audience stance or position with which they hope a reader will identify. To gain a reader's identification with their stance or position on a certain issue, writers describe people or experiences in a manner that gains a reader's sympathy.

Determining What a Writer Is Doing.   Writers are also using a set of rhetorical strategies that students could identify to examine the effectiveness of those strategies or to use in reflecting on their own essay writing.

Backgrounding or Setting the Scene.   Writers place an audience into some physical, cultural, or theoretical scene or context, filling in the background so that a reader understands where he or she is positioned in the essay's imagined world. In describing a physical scene, a writer may use visual or spatial schema to literally walk the audience from one part of the scene to another. In describing an issue, writers define the competing positions around an issue, for example, school shootings and gun control, to locate their own position within these different positions.

Defining Concepts.   Writers not only define unfamiliar concepts or key terms, but they may devote an essay to exploring the meaning of a certain concept—romantic love, work, patriotism, a just war, the value of education, and so forth.

Formulating an Argument.   Writers formulate their arguments by positing certain positions or claims which they then defend with supporting reasons or evidence. To examine these arguments, students could discuss the following question: Why do people bother to argue? They could then list three reasons why they've gotten into an argument recently, and then reflect on instances when they have lost and won arguments. They could also address questions such as the following: What makes a good argument? How do you win people over to your side? Why should you care about arguments? How can a good argument be powerful? How can a bad argument be powerful?

Providing Support for an Argument.   In formulating supporting reasons for their position, students need to recognize the relation between the claim being made and the reason in terms of the underlying assumptions or warrants. For example, if a writer is claiming that passing ordinances banning smoking in restaurants leads to loss of jobs for people working in those restaurants given a potential loss of customers, then the underlying assumption or warrant is that imposing a smoking ban on a restaurant will lead to a loss in customers and jobs. In examining assumptions or warrants, students can find evidence and counterevidence to support that assumption or warrant. For example, based on analysis of advertisements, students could argue for the need to purchase a certain product based on providing two supporting reasons and then connect each reason to the claim through a warrant. For example, the claim could be as follows: "You should really buy this empty CD case." The reason could be as follows: "The case is still very functional for holding CDs and keeping them safe." The warrant could be as follows: "If you buy the empty CD case, you'll have a spare the next time you find an unprotected CD. After all, a protected CD lasts longer, and you'll be able to enjoy it for years to come." They could then test out the validity of their warrants based on evidence supporting or challenging these warrants.

Examining the Validity of Explanations.   Students also need to be able to examine the validity of the explanations or reasons formulated for a thesis, testing those reasons against the evidence provided or omitted. To do so, they could list the reasons given, for example, to support the mandated use of school uniforms, and then provide evidence for those reasons.

Biography, Autobiography, or Memoir.   In reading biographies, autobiographies, or memoirs, students are constructing the writers' or other persons' identities based on portrayals of those writers' or other persons' experiences. In autobiographies, writers portray their past selves by adopting past points of view to portray how they are experiencing past events. For example, in *I Know Why the Caged Bird Sings*, Maya Angelou (1969) adopts the perspective of a child describing her experiences of a child growing up in a racist world of the South, while reflecting on those experiences from her present perspective as an accomplished poet, writer, and artist. Students therefore need to be able to distinguish between the person's past versus present points of view.

Web Sites.   Given the amount of time adolescents now spend on the World Wide Web, they have intuitively learned a new set of reading processes involved in reading Web sites, processes that are more complex than the left-to-right processing of print texts. They focus their attention on visual cues related to color, shape, font size, location on the page, configuration, and function to define a reading path related to where to go next. This requires that they have some sense of the importance of certain cues over others based on what is most relevant to achieving their purposes for reading (Kress, 2003).

REREADING TEXTS BASED ON INQUIRY-QUESTIONS

Another basic strategy for interpreting texts involves rereading texts based on a series of inquiry-questions that guide students' analysis of that text (Petrosky, 2005). These questions scaffold students' attention on different aspects of each rereading of a text—its arguments, difficulties, use of voice, perspective, and theme. As they write about and discuss each aspect on a different rereading, they formulate new, alternative interpretations that can be used to retroactively alter previous interpretations. After creating a paper trail of written responses on these different aspects of a text, students can then return to their initial responses to share with peers what they learned from rereading the text from the different perspectives about themselves as readers and learners. At the conclusion of their work with the text, they step back to reflect on what they've learned about the text, the inquiry process, and the teacher's moves and theirs that enabled their inquiry (Petrosky, 2005).

Anthony Petrosky (2005), building out from his work with David Bartholomae in *Ways of Reading* (2005), illustrates this inquiry-based rereading with difficult texts through a series of tasks for interpreting a chapter, "Tame the Wild Tongue," from *Borderlands = La Frontera: The New Mestiza*, by Gloria Anzaldua (1987). Petrosky, working with Stephanie McConachie at the Institute for Learning in the Learning Research Development Center's Disciplinary Literacy Project at the University of Pittsburgh, uses this work with difficult texts to apprentice teachers and teacher-coaches to inquiry projects that involve multiple texts in thematic units, so that they then design their own inquiry units using various architectures that enable inquiry across multiple texts. Anzaldua, in the reading selection for a Difficult Text unit, writes about her use of different voices and languages (English and Spanish) to portray her multiple identities in terms of race (Spanish, Indian, White) and gender (female, lesbian). This introductory unit scaffolds students through a series of rereadings for a single selection as a model for ways to make such texts accessible for inquiry with students unaccustomed to inquiry and difficult texts. The sequence looks like this:

1. After a first reading in which students note significant moments in the essay, they write about Anzaldua's arguments—what she says in the essay.

2. The first rereading focuses on ways in which they coped with Anzaldua's use of Spanish and English. They share that writing with peers in inquiry discussions to contrast peers' ways of coping with Anzaldua's polyglot style.

3. For a third rereading, they identify specific language or moments that represent shifts in Anzaldua's different voices. They share this writing with peers in inquiry discussions to open a study of how voice appears and shifts in written language.

4. Students then return to their first writing, and, based on responses to numbers 2 and 3, write a revision of their initial interpretation of what Anzuldua is trying to say. Then they compose a quick-write about how this revised interpretation reflected a change in interpreting the text.

5. They share this writing with peers, noting specific aspects from the text that reflect the changes in their interpretations. They formulate further inquiry-questions as to what aspects of the text are still difficult to understand and remain unexplored.

6. Finally, they step back from the sequence of work to study the different interpretive strategies they used and what the teacher did to influence their use of these strategies, so that they reflectively develop metacognitive understandings of the work and its discourse.

These rereading and reflection activities help students learn the value of rereading of and posing questions about texts to attend to different aspects of a text. And, through sharing alternative interpretive strategies with peers, students are learning how to reflect on themselves as inquiring readers who are continually formulating new questions leading to new ways of reading and rereading.

ACTION RESEARCH: ASSESSING STUDENTS' USE OF READING STRATEGIES

How do you know if students are learning these different reading strategies on their own? Although we address this question in more detail in Chapter 12, we want to emphasize the need of providing students with ample opportunity to practice using these processes in discussion and writing so that they gain confidence in their ability to use these processes. You then need to consider, given the students' grade level, reading ability, literary knowledge, or learning orientation and issues, what constitutes effective use of these processes. For example, in having your eighth-grade students make story predictions, what constitutes effective predictions? We would argue that the predictions themselves are far less important than the ability to provide valid reasons for those predictions based on perceived patterns in characters' actions which suggest that a character is or is not likely to behave in a certain consistent manner in the future. You then need to consider how you will determine their use of processes—through oral think-alouds, discussions, journal entries, essay writing, drama activities, and so forth. You then need to formulate some criteria to provide to students as to how you will evaluate effective predicting; for example, in evaluating their journals, you might say the following: "I will evaluate the predictions you make in your journals based on your ability to provide specific reasons based on observed patterns in characters' actions."

Action Research Study

To study differences in your students' ability to read and interpret different texts, you could first study individual differences in the types of texts they most versus least like to read and reasons for those preferences. For example, some students may prefer to read fantasy or mystery novels because they enjoy being transported into a world distinct from their own familiar world (Blackford, 2004). Other students may prefer realistic fiction because they can vicariously experience characters' coping with challenges they assume they will face later in their adolescence, for example, having a serious love relationship, going off to college, or facing competing allegiances to the peer group versus their own ethical beliefs. Other students may prefer nonfiction books or newspapers given a strong interest in current affairs.

Once you've determined their preferences and reasons for those preferences, you can then note the interpretive strategies or reading processes they employ in reading preferred versus less preferred types of texts. You could interview students, drawing on the questions in this chapter on students' notions of reading, asking them to describe those strategies and processes they employ in reading their most versus least preferred types of texts. You may find that their less preferred texts are those about which they lack confidence in using certain strategies or processes. This would then help you plan activities to bolster their use of those strategies and processes about which they lack confidence.

Online Additional Activities, Links, and Further Reading

Go to the textbook Web site, Chapter 8, and to "poetry," "story response/writing," "drama/speech," "mythology/science fiction/fantasy," and "nonfiction" for additional activities, links, and further reading.

9

Teaching the Classics: Do I Have
to Teach the Canon, and If So,
How Do I Do It?

Chapter Overview

- The value of the canon.
- Themes and big ideas.
- Considerations of language.
- Historicism and cultural considerations.
- Points of relevance.
- Approaches and strategies to teaching the classics.
- Lesson planning.

CASE NARRATIVE: TEACHING THE SCARLET LETTER
AS A CANONICAL TEXT

Marcia teaches at Jefferson Park High, a first-ring suburban school of a large metropolitan area in the Midwest. Her department has made the collective decision that all 11th-grade teachers will include Nathaniel Hawthorne's (1850/2004) The Scarlet Letter in their American Literature curriculum. No stipulations are made about how the book is to be presented or where it is to be included in the curriculum.

Jefferson Park has a fairly diverse student body: about 20% African American students; 12% students of East Asian descent, two thirds of whom are English language learners; and approximately 8% Hispanic Latino students. Nearly 20% of the school's population qualifies for free or reduced-price lunches. About half of the students who graduate continue on to college.

As she thinks about her curriculum and themes around which her course is structured, Marcia considers a variety of ways to approach The Scarlet Letter (Hawthorne, 1850/2004) with her students. Eventually, she decides that the book would be useful for eliciting conversation about a number of important themes: community and social norms, unintended pregnancy and nontraditional families, and the destructive nature of secrecy. She thinks, too, about the ways in which contemporary American society replicates the behavior of the Puritans: a pervasive belief in punishment for shaping public opinion and behavior, a focus on ethical and moral conflict, the efficacy of guilt, reverence for public proclamations of sin without attention to sinfulness itself, and the conscious exclusion of those who do not conform to community expectations. As Marcia thinks about the novel itself, she realizes that there will be several challenges in teaching it to high school juniors.

First of all, the language of the novel is difficult for less experienced readers. The sentences are long, with multiple coordinate clauses and frequent embedding of one sentence within another. The vocabulary, although not difficult, exhibits unfamiliar usages. Most importantly, there is a subtlety to the language that can be easily missed. Statements made by the narrator are frequently tentative, couched in language that more experienced readers will recognize as indeterminate, ambiguous, leading readers to doubt whether something—Dimmesdale's comet, for example—was actually present or merely imagined by a character. Marcia knows that her students will have to come to recognize this subtlety if they are going to be aware of the novel's interpretive possibilities.

Another potential challenge involves the narrative ambiguity of the novel. A hallmark of American Romanticism, this ambiguity works directly against the reader who attempts to closely determine what is and is not real in the telling of the story. It requires readers instead to consider events from the perspectives of the characters, then to weigh the plausibility of those perspectives. It also forces readers to acknowledge that the narrator's perspective may not be accurate. The great advantage of teaching the romance is that it compels readers to extend the range of their interpretive skills. The disadvantage is that it can be overwhelming to novice critics. Marcia, then, needs to decide how much help she can give without undoing the lesson by too closely circumscribing the interpretive possibilities of the novel.

Historical context, for example, will be something Marcia needs to consider as she prepares to teach The Scarlet Letter (Hawthorne, 1850/2004). It would greatly help her students to know the history and cultural mindset of the people about whom the book was written. If understood literally, however, this history might overwhelm Hawthorne's (1850/2004) characters and inhibit the readers' interpretive sensibilities. A potential confusion of Hester Prynne with the antinomian Anne Hutchinson, for example, could entirely derail the lesson. Marcia needs to consider, then, how much history to provide as background and how much to let the book stand on its own.

If Marcia decides to focus on close reading rather than historicism in scaffolding the students' reading of the novel, she will certainly want to focus on romance as a fictional genre. This strategy, too, runs the risk of leading readers to find what they are supposed to be looking for in the text. For example, once acquainted with the rudiments of allegory and the knowledge that Hawthorne was a self-proclaimed "writer of allegories," Marcia's students might become preoccupied with the discovery of the novel's lesson. As a well-versed reader of Hawthorne, however, Marcia knows that Hawthorne's own words are no more to be trusted than those of his narrator's.

The classic novel also presents questions about the interpretation of symbols. Symbolism works because readers have a shared understanding of the meaning of symbols. These meanings, however, change with time. The comet (astrological event) that Dimmesdale witnessed would certainly have seemed more mysterious and significant to a 19th-century reader than to a 21st-century reader. As a symbol, then, it probably invites both more possibility and more literary scrutiny to readers of Hawthorne's day, and thus its cultural significance might be lost on a contemporary close reader. Marcia thus needs to decide what strategies she will ask her students to employ in interpreting this romance.

Contemporary culture might also mask some of the social significance of Hester's motherhood out of wedlock. Today, this circumstance is no longer viewed with the degree of shame that it entailed just a few decades ago. Given the decreased social stigma of unwed motherhood today, students might wonder how this book is relevant to their lives. The same is true for any discussion of adultery, a word now relegated to use in discussion of scripture. Students looking at the response of Salem's citizens to Hester's situation might decide that at least today we've gotten this right, and, thank God, this could never happen today. Marcia will need to find a way to make students feel sympathy for Hester and Dimmesdale.

One last problem that Marcia contemplates as she prepares to teach this novel is diversity of perspective. Although Hawthorne (1850/2004) clearly makes Hester the central figure of the novel, he does not admit a great variety of cultural viewpoints. The only non-White, non-Western people we encounter (and then only indirectly) are American Indians, who are distinctly seen as heathens and savages because of their non-Christian worldview. Although Marcia believes that great books speak to students about great ideas, she also understands that she might need to pair The Scarlet Letter (Hawthorne, 1850/2004) with a more contemporary text that speaks to the same ideas in different ways from a different cultural perspective. But what could she use? Reflect on some ways in which you could connect a canonical text such as The Scarlet Letter to more contemporary print or media texts based on similar issues, themes, topics, character types, or cultural contexts.

THE VALUE OF THE CANON

The canon is itself an argument. It purports to name the most significant literary works within a national literature or historical period. It is also an invitation to students to engage in this argument, and that invitation needs to be framed and extended by teachers of literature.

In the popular film "Mona Lisa Smile," an inexperienced teacher asks a group of art history students the following: "What is art?" Their collective answer is both predictable and facile: "It's what people say it is—the *right* people." These students had not yet been invited to answer the question in a meaningful way for themselves. Thus, one wonders what value the study of any canon might have.

A well-founded literature class should engage students with this question and allow them the latitude to pursue an authentic answer. This may be particularly difficult when the subject matter consists of canonical literary works, but the question may be even more important in this case. Study of canonical works is without value if students don't gain an understanding of the basis of canonization.

Preparation to Teach Canonical Works.   Before inviting students into an argument about the validity of the canon, teachers need to be well versed in the criteria that lead to canonization. They need to be able to explain that the very existence of the canon grows out of a desire to create a particular kind of cultural representation, one that shows a nation, its people, and its literature in the best possible light. If students are to understand what the canon is, teachers need to help students discover and question the criteria for canonization. In this way, they can get at the critical ideas that canonical works entail.

The first and most important thing to remember about text selection, then, is that we are not just teaching books. We are teaching ideas. The central question about teaching classic works of literature, then, is not "What book should I select?" but rather, "What book will lead to the most compelling and productive discussion of an idea my students need to confront?"

THEMES AND BIG IDEAS

If it is the case that great books speak to us about important ideas across the generations, then we might want to start thinking about a classic by looking at the ideas it contains. One approach to *The Scarlet Letter* (Hawthorne, 2004), for example, may begin with a series of questions like these: How does a society establish the norms that control human behavior, and, in the end, are these constraints good or bad? How effective are guilt and punishment within a social system? How does inclusion in a society inhibit individual moral choices? How does exclusion from a society enable a person to accomplish things that he or she would otherwise not be moved to undertake? To what extent is "sin" a human construct, and to what extent is it an expression of God's desires for human action and restraint? What basic human motivations does this book examine?

This set of big questions leads to a more specific list of questions for the interpretation of *The Scarlet Letter* (Hawthorne, 2004). As seen through the lens of Hawthorne's (2004) novel, what does Puritan society value among its members? According to Hawthorne, do these values work well to bind the community of Salem together? To what extent do the main characters of the book conform to Salem's expectations, and what are the results of their behaviors, both those that conform to social expectations and those that do not? In the end, we are likely to judge the society of Salem by its responses to the book's three main characters—Hester, Dimmesdale, and Chillingworth—and the extent to which these responses match our own. Where, then, do we sympathize with the people of Salem, and where do we take them to task?

These open-ended questions should lead to fruitful conversations about both *The Scarlet Letter* (Hawthorne, 2004) and the larger questions that it seeks to address. Teachers of classics will also find Mortimer Adler's (1992) six great ideas useful for framing questions about the works they are teaching. These ideas include truth, beauty, goodness, justice, liberty, and equality. It is a near certainty that more than one of these ideas will present itself in the discussion of any great work of literature.

NARRATIVE AMBIGUITY IN THE ROMANCE GENRE

Whereas literary realism tries to establish in the imaginations of its audience a stark sense of the world in which its stories take place, romance admits a range of possible interpretations about the story itself: what happens, what effect it has on its characters, and what might be the ultimate meaning of the story. Causality is far less clear in romance, if it is present at all. And so readers of a book like *The Scarlet Letter* (Hawthorne, 2004) must inevitably wrestle with questions about what happened and why.

The ambiguity that brings about this lack of certainty within romance is both troubling and exciting. For less confident readers, this narrative indeterminacy can lead either to false confidence or interpretive despair. Being overconfident, a reader may be easily misled by false information. Being in a state of despair, a reader imagines a seemingly myriad possibilities of the narrative that don't seem to lead anywhere, thus causing a reader to stop short of making meaning from the text.

Clearly, then, background concerning the genre of *The Scarlet Letter* (Hawthorne, 2004) will be essential to the students' successful reading of the book. Because genre shapes our expectations for any form of discourse—its purpose, its methods, its treatment of its subject—an identification of genre and its conventions provides an important piece of scaffolding for any interpretive reading.

At the same time, we don't want students to imagine that all works of the same genre are intended to do the same things or that they all function in the same ways. For this reason, it may be useful when teaching classics to provide an overview of the author's body of work: its recurring themes, its typical characters and their various oppositions, as well as some overview of what past critics have thought and how their ideas have evolved over time. Although, on the one hand, we want our students to have the freedom to impose their own ideas, on the other hand, we don't want them exploring dead ends. The background we provide, then, needs to balance guiding principles with freedom of interpretive motion.

CONSIDERATIONS OF LANGUAGE

A successful reading of any work of fiction requires the reader not only to decode the literal meaning of the work and to track its main ideas, but also to read the nuances of the narrative for hints about tone, mood, the subtleties of motivation, hints of judgment, or intimations of doubt. These nuances are like the subtle facial expressions that accompany a speaker's words. Sometimes they tell us more than the words themselves. For this reason, readers need to have a keen ear for style.

Each historical era has its own characteristic features of linguistic style. The literary style of the American renaissance—the era of Poe, Hawthorne, and Melville—for example, seems to favor long sentences, with multiple modifying phrases, and these are frequently embedded within other phrases and clauses (reflecting, somewhat, the style of this sentence). Coupled with uncharacteristic usage and occasional strange words, this syntax challenges readers to maintain attention to the immediate idea while piecing together the events of the narrative. This exercise has value of itself; the advanced placement Literature and Composition exam, for example, requires students to read and understand difficult passages from a variety of historical eras. Before students can begin to discuss the issues of a text like *The Scarlet Letter* (Hawthorne, 2004), however, they need to be able to decode the language of the narrative.

There are several strategies that teachers can use to prepare students to encounter a text from another historical period. One strategy is to introduce readers to the author's style by giving them a shorter work by the same author to habituate them to the language and style the author favors. This strategy will work particularly well for *The Scarlet Letter*, because Nathaniel Hawthorne (2004) was a prolific writer of short stories. Another strategy involves preteaching the vocabulary of the story so that students can read without interrupting their train of thought by going to the dictionary or otherwise stopping to puzzle out the meaning from context or other cues. Teachers can also preview the plot of the novel so that students don't need to spend as much time trying to work out the events of the narrative and discover what is happening. This preview could include showing students scenes from a film adaptation of the work.

In addition to these specific strategies, teachers can set up more expansive strategies by breaking students into groups or literature circles to attack the text from different angles. Within this familiar strategy, students can take any of a number of roles: travel tracers, whose job it is to follow the narrative from setting to setting; character experts, who keep track of who's who in the book; vocabulary specialists, who look up unfamiliar words or usages and explain their meanings; story predictors, who attempt to logically link the events of the story together to see where it might lead; plot summarizers, who keep track of the events as they transpire; and finally, question askers, whose job is both to locate uncertainties in the text and to ensure that everyone is focused on the salient features of the literary work.

HISTORICISM AND CULTURAL CONSIDERATIONS

An understanding of the historical context within which a story is set provides readers with a number of important interpretive advantages. First, if the story is part of a larger historical occurrence—for example, the colonization of North America, the migration of farmers from the Dust Bowl to California, or the Vietnam War—a historical overview serves as a backdrop for the story at hand. Students may recognize not only typical events of the era but also their historical and cultural significance. They will know whether a character's choices or actions are typical or atypical because they will know how real people from that historical period acted and thought, what they actually did, and how their choices turned out.

Second, understanding a cultural mindset like that of the Puritans, the Okies of *The Grapes of Wrath* (Steinbeck, 2004), or the soldiers of *The Red Badge of Courage* (Crane, 1990) allows readers to get a glimpse inside a character's head. If students can successfully adopt this perspective, they will know what is possible or impossible, acceptable or unacceptable, purposeful or futile within a character's scope of choice because they will comprehend the cultural constraints under which that character is operating.

Third, a historical framework supplies readers with a set of plausibility measures for possible interpretations. Knowing about the physical isolation and scarcity of resources among the Puritans, readers know better than to suggest, even to themselves, that Hester ought to leave Salem in favor of a more accepting community. Background in Calvinist theology would also explain the prevailing cultural outlook of 17th-century Salem, a community in which religious and social constraints were one in the same. The Puritans would have had a clear understanding of Dimmesdale's mysterious death, a death perhaps made less mysterious to us by our understanding of their abiding belief in God's providence. A historicist reading would also help our students understand Hester's social position as a Puritan woman or Tom Joad's social status as an itinerant farmhand. It might also give them more insight into both the cowardice and the courage of Henry Fleming when they realize—as the book does not tell us but historical scholarship has since revealed—that *The Red Badge of Courage* is set at the battle of Chancellorsville, a particularly difficult and gruesome battle.

Reading historical literary works without benefit of cultural background might lead to interesting, even productive interpretations. When we attempt close readings without historical context, however, we risk the imposition of contemporary cultural assumptions on circumstances quite different from our own. Although universal themes undoubtedly abide in "timeless" classics, we do well to remember that even timeless themes are colored by the times through which they have moved.

POINTS OF RELEVANCE

The key to active, involved reading of literature is engagement with a text. Reader-response critics sometimes like to say that experiencing no response to a text is, in fact, a response, although maybe not the one for which we had hoped.

Although the term has been overused in education, *relevance* is crucial to a student's ability not just to understand but to experience a text. Relevance is the source of engaged reading. Students want to know that the subject they are reading about is pertinent to their lives, their decisions, the shaping of their individual worldviews. They want to know that the lessons of human behavior related in works of literature can be applied in their own lives. Often, they want to read about people like themselves, people they can recognize. One critical task of the literature teacher, then, is to help students see this relevance where they might otherwise not.

One way of thinking about response is that it is a form of cognitive activation, causing existing neural connections to fire again, this time in concert with new associations. As teachers, we have neither direct access to our students' brains nor to the myriad potential points of association that reading a text might evoke. This is all the more reason to select and teach classic works of literature. It provides a kind of common literary ground for unpredictable responses.

One effective means for helping students to connect their own unique experiences to those of other students, other people, is to look for shared points of experience that share as well a sense of value. If we understand that each student's mind is a closed system, each shaped differently by a different set of life experiences, then we need to help them find meaningful points of connection to the experiences of other people, both real and fictional. The beauty of literature is that we read and respond to fiction as if it were real, at least to some degree.

When we read, we hold at arm's length our literal realities, and we enter into fictional worlds that, amazingly, we understand in concert or in contrast to those same literal realities, even as we acknowledge their fictional nature. It is a sense of common ground that allows us to do this, a sense that we know how and why fictional characters ought to react to fictional circumstances. Classic works of literature are classics because they allow us to locate this common ground.

It is precisely the timelessness of literary themes that makes reading classic texts important to our students, and so issues of diversity and history may well need to be balanced with issues of common ground. Part of our job as teachers is to know our students, to know the literary canon, and to know where these two might meet harmoniously.

APPROACHES AND STRATEGIES TO TEACHING THE CLASSICS

If we accept that teaching classic and canonical works of literature can lead to fruitful discussions of important, even universal ideas, then we need to start thinking about how to ensure the best possible conversation among our students. To do so, we need to think in terms of four stages for our own preparation: selection, context, focus, and method.

The first step is to select appropriate, interesting, and important works of literature. Our primary criteria here relate to the experience of our students: personally, academically, and in their communities. If we aim too high, we teach over their heads; if we aim too low, we waste our time and theirs. Once we have identified an appropriate literary work, our next step is to consider a secondary set of connections that students can make by reading related texts. A favorite way to do this is by pairing a classic with a more contemporary or more easily accessible text so that students can make triangulated comparisons among their own experiences and the worlds of two distinct but comparable texts. These paired texts are selected for their thematic congruity, the ways in which they treat similar ideas. And finally, teachers need to strategically select a critical method (or methods) for approaching these texts.

Accessibility.   As experienced readers of literature, we all have favorite literary works: pieces that seem to speak to us, telling us more each time we reread them. At times we might feel as we do when viewing a waterfall: the experience is richer if it is shared, and we imagine that our students might feel the same way. If we choose to share a work by a contemporary postmodern writer such as Thomas Pynchon, on the other hand, we may find that we have made an invitation to a train wreck rather than a waterfall.

It is not just the postmoderns, however, who provide problems to access. Even Shakespeare requires us to help students find a way in. This point of entry might be a synopsis or an introduction to the main character and a source of conflict. It might be a familiar theme, such as mistaken identity, lust for power, a consuming infatuation, or one of the deadly sins embodied within a character. It might be a question about one's role in life: the duties of a prince, loyalty to friends and kin, or submission to the will of a deity. Once inside the text, students will typically take up the exploration on their own. Granting admission to the text, then, is among our most important tasks.

For that reason, selecting accessible texts is a key to making our students successful. This is especially true early in each term or course. Again, language, cultural context, social convention, and literary technique—working singly and in concert—provide formidable barriers to less experienced readers. Good early text selections, then, will be marked by the presence of important but familiar ideas, recognizable language, well-known customs and social practices, and simplicity of narrative style and voice.

There are sometimes external factors that enter into the selection process, and there is some validity to these concerns. They continue to say something to students, and to all of us, despite the passage of time. Many teachers claim that they teach classics for resource reasons—the books are in the bookroom—and in school districts with tight resources, this may be a legitimate concern. Still, this should not be a deciding factor in the selection process.

Another reason for teaching classic and canonical texts is that they are more likely to be appropriate than more recent texts. Graphic sex and graphic language are more common in newer books, and so issues of parental and community approval are less likely to arise when teaching canonical works. Again, however, this should not be seen as a reason to teach classic texts; it is more a reason not to teach contemporary works. In the end, teachers should teach classic texts for what they offer, not for the problems they avoid.

The primary issue in text selection should be literary merit. Although all teachers will establish their own criteria for arguing this merit, several criteria seem universal: multidimensional characters, complex themes, narrative intricacy, and cultural importance.

Matching our selections to our students' backgrounds is also a successful strategy, at least early on in the course. *The Great Gatsby* (Fitzgerald, 1991), although it has something of a universal appeal, may speak more to people in an affluent suburb than in an urban school. At the same time, however, it is replete with significant ideas. It addresses the themes of identity construction, the appeal of wealth, social mobility, the desire to be loved, the compromise of personal integrity for external rewards, and so forth.

Pairing.   In the end, it's not why we teach classic texts but how we teach books that challenge kids. We want to present students with a variety of possible interpretations and a series of competing arguments for those interpretations. We want students to develop comfort with ambiguity by helping them recognize the sources of literary complexity, the subtlety of language, the origins of metaphor, and the intricacy of human motivation. For example, to help students see the relevance of literary works to their own lives and communities and by pairing classics with newer texts, we can demonstrate important themes more clearly, more fully, and in greater multiplicity.

If two books, one canonical and one contemporary, address the same theme or illustrate similar ideas, the best tactic may be to pair the two rather than to choose between them. The difference in the treatment of the central idea within the texts will, of itself, make the case of teaching the classic. Typically, the complexity of the classic will help a teacher illustrate the intricacies of the issue at hand. Assigning readings with thematic links also makes for greater ease of access.

Thematic Focus.   Teachers continue to assign time-honored books because they know what classics have to offer, year after year, class after class. Students continue to find fascination in the themes and situations that these books present. *The Adventures of Huckleberry Finn* (Twain, 1981) seems to speak to students about a childhood that kids long for but no longer get to have—they wish for both the freedom and responsibility that Huck experiences, and so they identify with Huck. Aldous Huxley's *Brave New World* (Huxley, 1998) asks students to consider the roles that they will be expected to play in their society and the ways in which they are prepared to play them. Joseph Conrad's *Heart of Darkness* (Conrad, 2000) has myriad reflections in our culture today, one of them metaphorically expressed by Willie Loman's brother Ben, who claims that he went into the jungle and came out rich.

The real motivation for selecting a classic text is the opportunity it provides to talk to students—and have students talk to each other—about an important issue or idea. Although we value the chance to acquaint students with canonical works, the lesson is ultimately about more than the book. For the students, the value of the book is in what it says to them. Our students don't care that the book is old. They just want the book to deliver something interesting, something that helps them understand the world in which they live.

One measure of the importance and timelessness of a book is the reflections we find of it in the world around us. With consistency, while we are teaching a classic, we find stories in the newspaper that reflect the idea of the book. It is not the case that contemporary or noncanonical texts are better aligned with popular culture than would be a classic. As one teacher put it, "You can tell that a book has made it if you see it on 'The Simpsons.' " Such allusions speak both to the status of the work and the importance of its central theme.

Finding interest in what students think about—finding a way to get to know the students, how they are going to respond to a well-known text—is part of the fun of teaching classic works of literature. When teachers make careful choices about the classics they teach, they don't wonder about whether their students will like the text, but rather what they will like about it. The excitement of teaching classics is in seeing what students in your school, in your class, bring to the book. We never just teach the book; we teach the ideas addressed in the book.

Critical Method.   Although new historicism is the most obvious method for approaching classics, there are at least three other lenses that offer productive analysis. Archetypal criticism, structuralism, and biographical criticism work well because they each address aspects of literary tradition. These methods can be used singly or in combination. (See Chapter 10 for a more extended discussion of the use of different critical lenses.)

Archetypal criticism focuses on recurring story structures, symbols, and character types. Certain recurring themes are prevalent enough to lead us to posit an underlying formula. Others seem to play off of prevailing modes of thought—what Jung would have called "primordial images," or what cognitive scientists today would attribute to kinesthetic image schemas: typical ways of seeing experience, such as a path to a goal (a quest), a cycle (such as the seasons of a year), or something that contains something else (whether a dungeon or a refuge). In the end, archetypical stories tend to be about quests and tests, journeys and struggles that lead to highly sought rewards.

Structuralism overlaps with archetypical criticism to the extent that it focuses on our expectations for a given kind or piece of literature. Like grammars, these expectations are part of our unconscious knowledge. We expect a typical narrative, for example, to revolve around a conflict involving the main character. This character struggles against a host of obstacles and antagonists until tension rises to a peak and the conflict is finally resolved. We imagine this structure as an arc—a Cartesian drawing representing the increase and decrease of tension over time. We learn these structures by repeated experience, without even knowing that we know them. Dreamworks Studio's "Shrek" (2001) includes running commentary by the characters about these expectations and our disappointment at seeing them subverted. Poetic meters, epic tropes, and genres of all forms lend themselves well to structuralist critique.

Biographical criticism is always a bit risky, because it suggests connections between the text and the author's life that might have little basis. At the same time, however, it is useful to know what experiences the author did have to better understand the perspective of the literary works that the author has left behind. The works of Ernest Hemingway provide a pertinent example of this principle. Although Hemingway's male characters are seen by many to reflect a long-outdated machismo, Malcolm Cowley's (1994) approach to Hemingway focuses on the author's physical wounds from World War I. His novels are about wounds that never heal, Cowley would say, and about how characters deal with pain that can never be abated. The novels of Thomas Wolfe also lend themselves well to biographical investigation, because they seem to mirror so closely the author's memories of his childhood in Asheville, NC. In the case of Nathaniel Hawthorne, on the other hand, the author's biography leads to little productive insight.

No matter which critical methods we choose, it is best to be explicit about our methodology. As Terry Eagleton reminds us, there is no such thing as an atheoretical reading of literature. The better we prepare students to understand and use critical methods, the better they will be able to focus on the task at hand and arrive at coherent critical conclusions.

LESSON PLANNING

Overview of the Lesson.   In lesson planning, we need to provide more support for students as they approach a classic text. We may need to assign more prereading to set up their investigation of the text. We may need to introduce them to the author, his or her prevailing themes, and the periods both in which the story was written and in which it takes place. We may need to provide historical and cultural context for the story. All the while, we will do well to remember that this preparation is motivated more by the complexity of the text than by its status as a classic.

If we return to our aforementioned case, we can imagine Marcia reviewing all the considerations we have named in this chapter and attempting to put them to work. *The Scarlet Letter* (Hawthorne, 2004) is a subtle and challenging text, one that will not be easily interpreted by high school juniors. Careful planning will be the key to Marcia's success. Let us speculate, then, about what she might do with this 19th-century American romance.

Who Are Marcia's Students?   Although most of the students in Marcia's class come from a majority cultural background, there are enough nonmajority students in the class to suggest that Marcia should include other cultural perspectives in the discussion that she hopes to have about *The Scarlet Letter* (Hawthorne, 2004). The students for whom this book will present the fewest cultural challenges are students from White Christian backgrounds. African American students will relate to a discussion of early American community experiences in very different ways from White students. East Asian and Hispanic Latino students may relate in a variety of ways to Salem's treatment of Hester and to her choice of isolation; these will be based on their own community's values concerning family, morality, romantic love, and responsibility to community. Marcia can anticipate, then, that her students will bring diverse responses to the dramatic situation around which *The Scarlet Letter* revolves, each representing a perspective about appropriate social responses to a member of the community who violates its social norms.

What Kinds of Literary Experiences Do They Need?   The decision that Marcia's department has made suggests a number of implicit values for literary experience. First, because 11th-grade English classes are devoted primarily to American literature, they presumably value literature as a means to explore national and historical perspectives. The specific choice of *The Scarlet Letter* (Hawthorne, 2004) suggests at least three values concerning the students' literary experiences: first, that they should reflect America's cultural heritage; second, that their reading should familiarize them with the conventional literary aesthetic that the canon represents; and third, that the ability to read a complex text marked by narrative ambiguity is an essential part of their literacy.

Given these three values, Marcia will want to ensure that her students' experience of *The Scarlet Letter* (Hawthorne, 2004) goes well beyond their familiarity with the story. Their reading of this book should allow them to answer three fundamental questions: To what extent is literature a valuable means for examining a nation's heritage? What is it that makes *The Scarlet Letter* a classic work of literature, and how does it embody beauty and importance? And finally, what is the value of romance, or any other complex genre, for understanding human motivation? If Marcia's students can successfully answer these questions, their experience of *The Scarlet Letter* should be a valuable one.

What Approaches Should Marcia Use to Accomplish Her Goals?   As the previous discussion of teaching the classics suggests, there are several literary lenses that Marcia can use to teach *The Scarlet Letter* (Hawthorne, 2004). The first among these will be new historicism, which will require the class to delve into the history of America in both the 17th and 19th centuries: the historical setting for the story and the author's reflections on it. Although the story will no doubt take center stage, it would be hard to develop a complete historical perspective for the novel without some understanding of the American Renaissance and the aesthetic to which it gave rise. To the extent that Marcia decides to introduce her students to the conventions of American romance, she will be able to make use of structuralism approaches as well in a discussion of the ways in which this genre creates expectations for its readers.

Should Marcia choose to address symbols and images within the text, she may find that archetypal criticism is valuable, as this approach will allow her students to interrogate the cultural and psychological bases of the story. Of less importance would be an investigation of Nathanial Hawthorne's life. Although much has been made of his Puritan roots, especially in interpretations of "Young Goodman Brown" (Hawthorne, 1999a), the author's connection to the place and people of *The Scarlet Letter* (Hawthorne, 2004) will lead to marginal results at best.

Marcia decides to create several activities to help her students connect to the characters and the themes of this canonical novel. She wants to balance close textual reading with relevant connections to contemporary issues. First, she creates a character log assignment that requires students to become experts on a particular character through the text (see Activity 1). In keeping with her goals of having students argue with a canonical text, rather than simply receive it, she creates a discussion-debate activity (see Activity 2). Finally, to give students the opportunity to construct an individual interpretation of the text, she designs an essay assignment (see Activity 3).

WHAT KINDS OF TEXTS WILL SUPPLEMENT THEIR READING OF *THE SCARLET LETTER*?

The subject of pregnancy out of wedlock is clearly an emotional and controversial one, and so any discussion of this topic in literature will require sensitivity and a good bit of preparation. Adding the perspectives of literary texts from other times and cultures, however, can be a valuable method for examining the issue. A few texts that look at this topic from differing cultural and historical perspectives on gender and class are Maxine Hong Kingston's (1989) *The Woman Warrior*, Gloria Naylor's (1983) *The Women of Brewster Place*, Dorothy Allison's (1993) *Bastard Out of Carolina*, and Chimamanda Ngozi Adichie's (2004) *Purple Hibiscus*. To familiarize students with both Hawthorne's prose style and with 17th-century Salem, Marcia could assign "Young Goodman Brown" (Hawthorne, 1999a) or "The Maypole of Marymount" (Hawthorne, 1999b).

Other texts can be used to not only make related thematic connections with a canonical text, but also to read against the canonical text by applying an alternative ideological, historical, or cultural perspective to the text. For example, in reading *The Women of Brewster Place* (Naylor, 1983), students first interpret the ways in which the female characters in the novel provide support for each other, a central feature of African American culture. They then use this interpretation to contrast this supportive cultural context with the cultural world of *The Scarlet Letter* (Hawthorne, 2004), in which female characters who do not conform to religious rules are marginalized and punished with little support from other women who are fearful of providing such support. Reading other texts against the canonical texts provides students with alternative perspectives on how historical and cultural contexts constitute characters' practices.

OBJECTIVES FOR TEACHING CANONICAL LITERATURE

There are four general outcomes that we want for students as outcomes of literacy education: cultural literacy, aesthetic appreciation of literary art, well-developed interpretive skills, and the ability to apply critical and theoretical perspectives.

Activity 1

Character Log

Background

Over the course of this unit, we will be reading *The Scarlet Letter* and preparing to write a literary analysis on it. One way to prepare for an analysis paper is to pay close attention to the text and stay focused on a particular aspect of it. For *The Scarlet Letter*, we're going to be focusing on characters. There are three main characters: Hester Prynne, Arthur Dimmesdale, and Roger Chillingworth (aka Roger Prynne). Each of you will be assigned to one of these three characters.

What to Do

You will keep a character log that records important information on the character you have been assigned. As you read, look for information about your character. Then, record the page number and write the information. In many cases, you will want to quote portions of the text directly. This will aid you greatly in using evidence for your analysis papers.

What Kind of Information

- Physical characteristics
- Personality traits
- Relationships with other characters
- Mannerism or other telling actions
- Symbols associated with the character
- Surprising revelations
- Puzzling actions
- Psychological traits/hang-ups
- Questions you have about the character

How Much to Write

At the very least you should be averaging five items a day. Of course, some days your character will hardly appear in the chapters. On other days, however, there will be a chapter focusing directly on your character. Thus, sometimes you'll have very little to write and other days you'll have a multitude of comments to make. Overall, it should be several pages of notes.

Reasons to Do Well

First, it's worth 25 points, easily enough to affect your grade. Second, it will help you on other assignments. Third, I'm having you do this instead of quizzes.

Grading

10 points for number of entries (if you want full credit, impress me)
10 points for quality of entries (same as above)
5 points for having it organized in a manner that makes it easy to understand

Activity 2

Scarlet Letter **Discussion/Debates**

In *The Scarlet Letter* there are many questions that seem like they have simple answers, but upon closer examination, they are more complex than they seem. Tomorrow (Wednesday) we will debate several of these questions. Each of you will be assigned a question and a side to argue.

What to Do:

Prepare a 1–1½ minute speech in which you argue your point. Another person will argue the other side of the question. Each of you will tell what stance you are representing and offer support for your argument (citing the text). After you have each argued your points, there will be a brief period for questions. You may have notes when you present but do not simply read off of a paper.

What to Turn In:

Turn in notes that tell what question you are answering, which side you argued, and what your main points are. Your notes should also include a summary of your position and the reasoning behind it. You should also have a list of textual evidence (at least three quotations with page numbers) that support your stance.

Points and Grading

You will receive up to five points for delivering a fluent argument in class. You will receive up to ten points for having a well-prepared, well-organized sheet of notes to turn in.

The Questions:

Hester

1. Is Hester Prynne a victim?
2. Is Hester Prynne ashamed or proud of her sin?
3. Is Hester a good mother for Pearl?
4. Does Hester deserve the punishment she received?

Dimmesdale

1. Would Dimmesdale be better off if he confessed to his "sin"?
2. Should a reader feel sympathy for Dimmesdale?
3. Is Dimmesdale a good clergyman?
4. Does Dimmesdale know (consciously or unconsciously) who Chillingworth really is?

Chillingworth

1. Is Roger Chillingworth an evil man?
2. Is Chillingworth justified in his deep examination of Dimmesdale?
3. If you were living in this town and you fell ill, would you go to Chillingworth to get better?
4. Is Roger Chillingworth a wise man or a fool?

Overflow Question

To what extent is your character responsible or blameworthy for the adultery?

Activity 3

Scarlet Letter **Final Paper**

This paper is a 2–3 page literary analysis. You will be allowed to choose your own topic, but your paper should focus on the character you have been assigned. Your paper should present an argument and be thesis driven. This means that you will be required to form an interpretation and support it using the text.

By Thursday, you should have a topic chosen for your paper. On a note card or sheet of paper, write what your preliminary thesis statement is. You may decide to change it later, but I want to ensure that you are thinking about your papers. This will be worth an all or nothing 5 points.

This paper will be due on Tuesday, November 9th.

Requirements:

A title distinct to your paper

- Thesis statement (A sentence in your introduction that summarizes your argument) 2–3 pages
- Double Spaced
- Parenthetical documentation (no works cited/bibliography required)

Sample Topic Questions:

- Each of these characters undergoes a change during the seven years between the beginning and end of the book. How has your character evolved over time?
- What has been the toll of the 7 years? Be specific (go beyond: Dimmesdale/Chillingworth gets worse).
- All of these characters have two distinct sides that seem to be at odds (ie. Hester's pride and shame). Identify two opposite sides of one character and argue which of them is dominant.
- Compare two chapters that deal with your character (ie. 'Hester at the Needle' and 'Another View of Hester' or 'The Interior of a Heart' and 'Minister in a Maze'). What does an examination of these chapters tell us about a character or the relationships between two characters?
- Choose a symbol that is closely associated with your character. Why is this symbol associated with the character and what does it tell us about him/her? Is the symbol constant or does it change over the course of the book?
- Are there any points with regard to your character that you and another person in your group disagree on? Write a paper that argues your side of the disagreement and have your friend write the opposite point of view.
- All three of the main characters have a conflict between their conscious and unconscious desires. Write a paper that identifies both of these desires and argue in favor of the one that ultimately controls them.
- Adapt one of the questions from the discussion/debate for a paper. You will need to narrow the topic and make it more specific.
- Choose a topic of your own and get it approved by Thursday at the end of class.

By cultural literacy we mean more than simply factual knowledge of authors and texts (Hirsch, 1988). We mean the broader ability to read the cultures portrayed in a text—the common beliefs, values, and ideas of a society that shape characters' actions. Classic literary texts allow us to do this because they represent, in significant part, a cultural heritage. They provide a perspective that spans history as they represent historical choices about literary subjects, moral decisions, personal characteristics, and social conflicts.

Classics also allow us to track the history of our aesthetic judgments. They show us how narrative structures change over time, how the limits of taste and social tolerance shift, and how standards of beauty change and cultural values change. The assignment of "classic" works of literature contributes directly to these outcomes.

Gauging our expectations for the reception of classic texts is a matter of knowing the students. It depends on the kind of place in which you are teaching, the experiences the kids in the school have had, and the expectations they have for themselves and their school. Students from more traditional schools or more affluent districts may accept canonical texts without question, simply thinking that these are among the things they are supposed to do. Students attending an affluent suburban high school might be more friendly toward a book like *The Great Gatsby* (Fitzgerald, 1991) than students at a less affluent urban school. The learning objectives that we plan around thus need to fit the settings in which we work.

For many experienced teachers, a book is a book. Classics add the advantage of predictability. Because they contain ideas with universal appeal, we know what students will respond to most powerfully. This predictability in some ways makes assessment of the students' work with classics a bit easier than assessment of contemporary works of literature.

For a book like *The Scarlet Letter* (Hawthorne, 2004), we might imagine a specific set of objectives like the following:

1. Understand and articulate the motivations of each of the main characters.
2. Recognize and explain instances of narrative ambiguity.
3. Understand and critique the novel as a reflection of American social norms.
4. Apply a variety of critical lenses to the novel to discover more than one interpretation of the text.

Portfolio Addition: Past and Present Ways of Teaching a Canonical Text

What classic texts did you read as a high school student? What memories do you have of how one of those classic texts were presented or taught to you. Recall, in as much detail as you can, how one of your literature teachers approached that text. Then, create your own lessons around that text, detailing what changes you would make and why and put that on your teaching portfolio.

Online Additional Activities, Links, and Further Reading

Go to the textbook Web site, Chapter 9, and to the generic links for "American literature," "British literature," and "Shakespeare," for additional activities, links, and further reading.

ADDITIONAL RESOURCES

You may find the following books helpful as you consider using classics in the classroom.

Abrams, M. H. (1999). *A glossary of literary terms* (7th ed.). Boston: Heinle & Heinle.

Appleman, D. (2000). *Critical encounters in high school English: Teaching literary theory to adolescents.* New York: Teachers College Press.

Blau, S. (2003). *The literature workshop: Teaching texts and their readers.* Portsmouth, NH: Heinemann.

Carey-Webb, A. (2001). *Literature and lives; a response-based, cultural-studies approach to teaching English.* Urbana, IL: National Council of Teachers of English.

Jago, C. (2004). *Classics in the classroom.* Portsmouth, NH: Heinemann.

Moon, B. (1999). *Literary terms.* Urbana, IL: National Council of Teachers of English.

Scholes, R. (2001). *The crafty reader.* New Haven, CT: Yale University Press.

10

Multiple Perspectives to Engage
Students With Literature: What
Are Different Ways of Seeing?

Chapter Overview

- Reading the world.
- Different critical lenses.
- Resources or tool box.
- Portfolio addition.

CASE NARRATIVES: TEACHING CRITICAL
LENSES IN THE CLASSROOM

For decades, To Kill a Mockingbird has been a staple of the high school curriculum. Its perma-bound status in bookshelves across the county attests to its enduring presence in literature classes. Like many school districts across the country, the Lake Woebegone school district, located in the suburban Midwest, includes To Kill a Mockingbird as a required part of its 10th-grade curriculum. The teachers love teaching it, and the students, well, if they didn't love it, they didn't complain about it, either.

In recent years, the Lake Woebegone district has experienced radical demographic changes. The largely White, blue color population has been diversified by many families of color, predominately African American and Latino. Until this year, the changing student population was not reflected by changes in either the content or approach of the high school literature curriculum.

Recently, however, several students of color have reported feeling uncomfortable in the classrooms where To Kill a Mockingbird is taught. They object to the use of the "n word," to teachers reading the text aloud, to feeling singled out as representatives of the "Black experience." An emergency meeting is held with the language arts department. All of the district's teachers are White, and most of them are unwilling to stop teaching the novel, because it has long been a centerpiece of their curriculum.

Harry, a veteran teacher who has recently been introduced to the idea of using multiple perspectives, has an idea. He doesn't want to stop teaching the novel, either, but he understands why some people might object to it, especially because it's the only novel that all 10th graders are required to read. He creates a set of exercises that uses both the feminist and social class lens to question and resist the portrayal of characters in To Kill a Mockingbird. Harry feels that by inviting students to read the text through different lenses, lenses that highlight ideology, he is addressing the concerns of those who object to the text and at the same time, preserving the role of the text in his curriculum.

Harry remarks as follows: "The lenses help us read the text in a richer way. We are no longer ignoring its problematic aspects; we are actually teaching them. Using the lenses helped me address the community's legitimate concerns about the text without abandoning it entirely. I guess there's more than one way to kill a mockingbird!"

Harry's handouts are presented on the Web site in Chapter 10, activities.

Walking down the halls of Southeast High School, an aging and traditional school at the edge of a large Midwestern city, I stop short at the door of a classroom. In front of the door is a mannequin, clothed in a pink sleeveless debutante dress. The dress is covered with feminist slogans: "the personal is political," "a woman needs a man like a fish needs a bicycle," "equal rights for humankind." The sign on the classroom door reads as follows: "Ms Crosby: IB Literature From A Feminist Perspective."

Ms. Crosby, a recent college graduate with 2 years of teaching experience, as follows:

> I just thought I'd go all out. My class isn't any more one-sided than the traditional IB curriculum; it's just that I approach it from the other side and that I'm honest about it. I teach to offer some balance in an ideologically unbalanced world. The kids are loving it. And I feel like we're doing something really important together. This approach works well for so many texts, both traditional and contemporary. They went crazy with Hamlet from a feminist perspective. I really think that using critical theory makes the literature seem more alive and more relevant.

Needless to say, Ms. Crosby's classroom threshold provides a dramatic visual reminder of some paradigmatic shifts in our approach to teaching literature. It is important to note that Ms. Crosby is not teaching a course called feminist literature; rather, she is integrating a very traditional canon through the use of critical lenses.

READING THE WORLD

What exactly are we trying to accomplish when we read texts with young people? If we think back to the goals that we discussed in Chapter 2, it is clear that we want to do more than simply transmit our literary cultural heritage. We want to help young people understand the social, political, and cultural contexts that shape their lives. We want to help students see that the literary texts we assign them to read are inscribed with issues of power and shaped by ideological influences as they are created and as they are read (Beach,

1997). Teachers like Harry and Ms. Crosby know that the world of their classrooms, bounded by texts and interpretive conventions, is shaped and influenced by larger forces. To teach *To Kill a Mockingbird* effectively, Harry needs to take into account the context of the changing nature of his community. To make the canon of International Baccalaureate relevant to her 21st-century postmodern students, Ms. Crosby wants her students to read and resist the ideology of traditional texts through the use of critical theory. Harry and Ms. Crosby do want their students to read texts. Bruce Pirie (1997) explains as follows: "It is not that we shouldn't care about individual students and texts. We should, and I do. We also recognize, however, that students and texts are embedded in huge, living, sometimes contradictory networks, and if we want students to understand the workings of textuality, then we have to think about those larger systems" (p. 96). Helping students think about those larger systems means helping them learn to read the world. Reading the world is a concept perhaps first most powerfully articulated by Paulo Freire (Freire & Macedo, 1987). Freire writes as follows:

> Reading the world always precedes reading the word, and reading the word implies continually reading the world. . . . [T]his movement from the word to the world is always present; even the spoken word flows from our reading of the world. In a way, however, we can go further and say that reading the word is not preceded merely by reading the world, but by a certain form of writing it or rewriting it, that is, of transforming it by means of conscious, practical work. For me, this dynamic movement is central to the literacy process. (Freire & Macedo, 1987, p. 25)

Post–September 11, 2001, literacy teachers need to be mindful of what is "central to the literacy process." We need to do more than help students master traditional interpretive skills of close reading. We need to help them read the world. In a video presentation, bell hooks (Jhally, 1997) claims that the primary purpose of literacy is to transform young people into "enlightened witnesses" to cultural assumptions and representations. In the video, hooks (Jhally, 1997) offers the following equation:

$$\text{Transformation} = \text{Critical Thinking} + \text{Literacy}.$$

Critical lenses offer students a way to read and think critically, to become "enlightened witnesses." Being an enlightened witness, possessing multiple ways of seeing, means understanding the nature of ideology. Bonnycastle (1996) provides a straightforward, adolescent-friendly definition of ideology:

> In essence an ideology is a system of thought or "world view" which an individual acquires (usually unconsciously) from the world around him. An ideology determines what you think is important in life, what categories you put people into, how you see male and female roles in life, and a host of other things. You can visualize your ideology as a grid, or a set of glasses, through which you can see the world. (p. 33)

Others emphasize a less benign conception of ideology. For example, Michael Ryan (1999) argues that ideology serves to perpetuate the social power structure. Norman Fairclough (1989) calls this preservation of social power "ideological common sense" (p. 2). It's what makes us surprised at female airline pilots, African American senators, or househusbands. Fairclough writes as follows:

Ideology is most effective when its workings are least visible. If one becomes aware that a particular aspect of common sense is sustaining power inequalities at one's own expense, it ceases to be common sense, and may cease to have the capacity to sustain power inequalities, i.e., to function ideologically. And invisibility is achieved when ideologies are brought to discourse not as explicit elements of the text, but as the background assumptions which, on the one hand, lead the text producer to textualize the world in a particular way, and on the other hand, lead the interpreter to interpret the text in a particular way. Texts do not spout ideology. They so position the interpreter through their cues that she brings ideologies to the interpretation of texts—and reproduces them in the process! (p. 85)

To see what Fairclough means, let's consider the poem, "The Road Not Taken" (Frost, 1916/1993):

The Road Not Taken
by Robert Frost

Two roads diverged in a yellow wood,
And sorry I could not travel both
And be one traveler, long I stood
And looked down one as far as I could
To where it bent in the undergrowth;

Then took the other, as just as fair,
And having perhaps the better claim,
Because it was grassy and wanted wear;
Though as for that the passing there
Had worn them really about the same,

And both that morning equally lay
In leaves no step had trodden black.
Oh, I kept the first for another day!
Yet knowing how way leads on to way,
I doubted if I should ever come back.

I shall be telling this with a sigh
Somewhere ages and ages hence:
Two roads diverged in a wood, and I—
I took the one less traveled by,
And that has made all the difference.

Most American students have encountered this well-known poem in their secondary education, most commonly as part of their 10th-grade American Literature curriculum. When asked, readers of this poem easily offer the theme or lesson embedded in the poem. "It's about individuality, about nonconformity, about walking to the beat of a different drummer." "Its about how America privileges the individual." "It's about refusing to succumb to peer pressure."

Or is it? All of these sentiments seem consistent with an Emersonian ideal of self-expression, a Whitman-like celebration of individuality. But can these interpretations really be supported by the text of the poem? Is it about which path the poem's speaker chose or the fact that he had to make a choice? According to Fairclough (1989), we let the text spout ideology because it fits into our notion of who we are, about what America is and what it might stand for. Yet this approach doesn't encourage students to resist any commonsense readings. Without reading the text from multiple perspectives, we are transmitting traditional cultural messages, not teaching students to read critically.

GETTING YOUR CLASS STARTED

We recommend that you begin by emphasizing the idea of multiple perspectives or multiple ways of seeing rather than beginning with the heady and sometimes overly academic concept of literary theory. One way to begin is to ask students to consider family stories and how each family member may have a different perspective on the same event. See the handout that follows:

A MATTER OF PERSPECTIVE

Most "post modern" fiction violates traditional narrative expectations by telling the story from the perspective of a variety of characters, rather than from the perspective of a single protagonist. Let's spend the remainder of the next hour exploring the notion of perspective.

1. Tell the story of "The Three Little Pigs."
2. Now, listen to the children's book *The True Story of the Three Little Pigs, As Told by A. Wolf*. What differences does that switch in perspective make?
3. Think of a family story, preferably one that is retold often, a part of your family mythology. In a paragraph or so, tell that story from your own perspective. Write your version below.
4. Now, think of another family member, and retell the story from his/her perspective. Write that version below.
   Family Member:

In groups of no more than four, share those stories and discuss the difference perspective makes. How can we know what is the "true" version of the story?

You can also stage an unusual event—a clown bursting into the classroom, a staged argument between two class members, an animal intrusion, a visit from the principal or a fellow teacher in costume. Then ask students to write down exactly what happened. Compare their versions, discuss the inevitable discrepancies, and the documented fallibility of eye witnesses. Then talk about the kinds of things—beliefs, attitudes, prior experiences and predispositions—that affect both our perceptions of contemporary events as well as our reading.

At this point, students are ready to expand their experience with multiple perspectives into explicit knowledge of particular literary theories. We also acknowledge that up to this point, your English Education may not have prepared you to feel comfortable teaching literary theory. Although we don't expect that you will feel prepared to write a textbook on deconstruction, you should have a solid grounding in the basic outline of the theories. There are many short glossaries available (Appleman, 2000; Moon, 2001) or the Web site for sample lessons; or, you can use the theory cards adapted from Lynn (2000; see Figs. 10.1, 10.2, 10.3, and 10.4). After you've given students a general working understanding of the theories, you can apply them together to films that lend themselves to a spectrum of readings from archetypal to poststructural. I currently favor using "Star Wars," any episode of "The Lord of the Rings Trilogy," or "Shrek" (see sample activities on the Web site).

Feminist Criticism

Assumptions

1. The work doesn't have an objective status, an autonomy; instead, any reading of it is influenced by the reader's own status, which includes gender, or attitudes toward gender.

2. Historically the production and reception of literature has been controlled largely by men; it is important now to insert a feminist viewpoint in order to bring to our attention neglected works as well as new approaches to old works.

3. Men and women are different: they write differently, read differently, and write about their reading differently. These differences should be valued.

Strategies

1. Consider the gender of the author, the characters: what role does gender or sexuality play in this work?

2. Specifically, observe how sexual stereotypes might be reinforced or undermined. Try to see how the work reflects, or distorts, or recuperates the place of women (and men) in society.

3. Imagine yourself as a woman reading the work.

Psychological Criticism

Assumptions

1. Creative writing (like dreaming) represents the (disguised) fulfillment of a (repressed) wish or fear.

2. Everyone's formative history is different in particulars, but there are basic recurrent patterns of development for most people. These patterns and particulars have lasting effects.

3. In reading literature, we can make educated guesses about what has been repressed and transformed.

Strategies

1. Attempt to apply a developmental concept to the work (Or the author or the characters). For example: the Oedipal complex, anal retentiveness, castration anxiety, gender confusion.

2. Relate the work to psychologically significant events in the author's life.

3. Consider how repressed material maybe expressed in the work's pattern of imagery or symbols.

FIG. 10.1.   Reprinted with permission of Stephen Lynn.

Biographical, Historical, New Historical Criticism	Deconstruction
Assumptions	*Assumptions*
1. Meaning is contextual.	1. Meaning is made by binary oppositions, *but* one item is unavoidably favored (or "privileged") over the other.
2. The context for a literary work includes information about the author; his or her historical moment; the systems of meaning available at the time of writing.	2. This hierarchy is arbitrary and can be exposed and reversed.
3. Interpretation of the work should be based on an understanding of its context.	3. Further, the text's oppositions and hierarchy can be called into question because texts contain within themselves unavoidable contradictions, gaps, spaces, absences that defeat closure and determinate meaning. All reading is misreading.
Strategies	*Strategies*
1. Research the author's life, and relate that information to the work.	1. Identify the oppositions in the text.
2. Research the author's time (the political history, intellectual history, economic history, etc.), and relate that information to the work.	2. Determine which member appears to be favored and look for evidence that contradicts that favoring.
3. Research the systems of meaning available to the author, and relate those systems to the work.	3. Expose the text's indeterminacy. Whereas New Criticism assumes that you should read a poem closely as if it made sense, deconstruction assumes the opposite: that if you read closely enough, the text will fail to make sense—or at least will contradict itself.

FIG. 10.2.   Reprinted with permission of Stephen Lynn.

Reader-Response Criticism

Assumptions

1. An author's intentions are not reliably available to readers; all they have is the text.

2. Out of the text, readers actively and personally make meaning.

3. Responding to a text is a process, and descriptions of that process are valuable.

Strategies

1. Move through the text in superslow motion, describing the response of an informed reader at various points.

2. Or describe your own response moving through the text.

3. React to the text as a whole, embracing and expressing the subjective and personal response it engenders.

New Criticism

Assumptions

1. The critic's interest ultimately should be focused on the work itself (not the author's intention, nor the reader's response).

2. The purpose of this attention is to expose the work's unity; every element should support its unifying theme.

3. The work should also have some sort of complexity; great literature unifies ambiguities, ironies, tensions.

Strategies

1. Determine what oppositions or tensions or ambiguities are present.

2. Read closely. You can assume that every aspect is carefully calculated to contribute to the work's unity—figures of speech, point of view, diction, recurrent ideas or events, everything

3. Say how the work is unified, how the various elements work to unify it.

FIG. 10.3.   Reprinted with permission of Stephen Lynn.

Marxist Literary Theory

Assumptions

1. The German Philosopher Karl Marx argued that the way people think and behave in any society is determined by basic economic factors.

2. In his view, those groups of people who owned and controlled major industries could exploit the rest of the population, through conditions of employment and by forcing their own values and beliefs onto other social groups.

3. Marxist criticism applies these arguments to the study of literary texts.

Strategies

1. Explore the way different groups of people are represented in texts. Evaluate the level of social realism in the text–how is society portrayed.

2. Determine the ideological stance of the text–what world view does the text represent.

3. Consider how the text itself is a commodity that reproduces certain social beliefs and practices. Analyze the social effect of the literary work.

Postcolonial Literary Theory

Assumptions

1. Colonialism is a powerful, destructive historical force that shapes not only the political futures of the countries involved, but also the identities of colonized and colonizing people.

2. Successful colonialism depends on a process of "othering" the people colonized. That is, the colonized people are seen as dramatically different from and lesser than the colonizers.

3. Because of this, literature written in colonizing cultures often distorts the experiences and realities of colonized people. Literature written by colonized people often includes attempts to articulate more empowered identities and reclaim cultures in the face of colonization.

Strategies

1. Search the text for references to colonization or current and formerly colonized people. In these references, how are the colonized people portrayed? How is the process of colonization portrayed?

2. Consider what images of "others" or processes of "othering" are present in the text. How are these "others" portrayed?

3. Analyze how the text deals with cultural conflicts between the colonizing culture and the colonized or traditional culture?

FIG. 10.4.   Reprinted with permission of Stephen Lynn.

LESSON PLANNING

To give you a clear sense of how using critical lenses might serve to help enrich your students' literary experience as well as address other instructional purposes, we offer a lesson created by Tim, a 3rd-year English teacher.

Like many teachers Tim felt that his male students were less engaged in reading literary texts than were his female students (Pirie, 2002; Smith & Wilhelm, 2002). He decided to combine two strands of current literacy research by trying to create lessons that would appeal to his male students and focus on engaging all students through lessons that integrated the use of critical lenses (Appleman, 2000).

Tim followed some of the basic considerations of lesson planning that we outlined in Chapter 3.

BASIC CONSIDERATIONS IN LITERATURE LESSON PLANNING

1. Who are my students?
2. What kind of literary experiences do they need?
3. Given that, what kinds of texts should I choose?
4. What approaches to those texts should I use?

Here's how Tim answered these questions.

Who Are My Students?   Tim's students are juniors and seniors (19 boys and 11 girls) in the second quarter of Contemporary Literature I. Although counselors won't publicly admit this, it is considered the "easier" alternative to American Literature for juniors. Students must take two semesters of a literature course to graduate, and their choices are enriched or regular American Literature, regular or advanced placement world literature, and contemporary literature. Many struggling readers and writers end up in contemporary literature because the other courses are perceived by counselors and others to be too difficult for them. Other students who might be looking for someplace to "hide" in a less rigorous literature class make up another section of the class. Still another section of the class is made up of perfectly capable and willing students who want an alternative to what they might consider the staid traditionalism of American Literature. The result is a hodgepodge of attitudes and literacy levels.

What Kind of Literary Experiences Do They Need?   Tim decided that the entire class needed a literary experience in which both male and female students would be equally engaged. Somehow, Tim thought that would be as important for the girls, to see their classmates enthusiastic and engaged, as it would be for the boys.

Tim also wanted to engage students in an inquiry approach to texts, as Smith and Wilhelm (2002) write

> Because students pursued their own arguments in their own ways, they had an element of control over their work that they didn't get in much of their schoolwork. Because the texts were not read as artifacts or objects of study for some future or opaque purpose, but as conversants in the ongoing debates, the purpose for reading them was both clear and immediate. (p. 87)

Finally, he wanted his students to be able to use a variety a critical perspectives to help give them authority, power, and flexibility over their own reading. Literary theory allows students to focus on the immediate experience because it can relate directly to their own lives, forcing them into the realm of the present instead of thinking of it as preparation for the future.

Given That, What Kinds of Texts Did He Choose?   Tim chose to use *Montana, 1948* by Larry Watson (1993). He thought that the genre of contemporary Westerns would be especially appealing to the male students. He also thought that this class seemed to be more interested in encountering a relatively recent text rather than a canonical one.

What Approaches to Those Texts Should Be Used?   Before the students began reading the book, Tim used an idea by Pirie (2002). Pirie notes the importance of allowing students to make connections in their reading to TV or movies they've seen to give them the chance to show knowledge and competence about the issue in question. In a slight variation on this, he showed the film "The Searchers" starring John Wayne and directed by John Ford so that the entire class had at least one common media connection to draw on when they started reading *Montana 1948*. They would be able to activate prior knowledge about the film, or discussions about, as Ebert (2001) writes, "the dying days of the classic Western, which faltered when Indians ceased to be typecast as savages" (p. 1). "The Searchers," says Ebert, is of two minds regarding treatment of Indians, which provides an excellent jumping off point for *Montana 1948* and its views of Indians. "I think Ford was trying, imperfectly, even nervously, to depict racism that justified genocide" (Ebert, 2001, p. 3).

Historical or Biographical Lens.   This film, then, along with providing common knowledge, also worked to introduce the historical or biographical lens when Tim introduced it during the reading. We discussed how, in the 1950s, before the civil rights movement, stereotypical treatment of Indians and other minorities wasn't as frowned on as it would be later. Nonetheless, Hollywood was beginning to come to terms with its harsh treatment of Indians in Westerns. Hence, the split personality of "The Searchers." He also showed clips from the Westerns "Stagecoach," "High Noon," "The Good, The Bad, and the Ugly," and "Unforgiven," discussing for each the influence the time period in which the film was made had on the content and themes. For data, groups of three students were asked to list three books or films they knew of that they believed were influenced by the specific historical context of the time in which they were made. They were also asked to expand on that historical information. They also discussed the activity as a class.

Reader-Response Lens.   To introduce the reader-response lens, Tim used the Sylvia Plath poem "Mushrooms" that Beach (1993) writes about (as cited in Appleman, 2000, p. 32), and discussed the transaction the reader has with the text. The data Tim collected was twofold: first, he collected students' responses to what they thought the subject of the poem "Mushrooms" was (they didn't know the title), along with evidence from the text and their personal experience; second, he asked them to do the same thing for *Montana 1948* on the same sheet of paper—a meaning they've gotten from the book due to textual evidence and their personal characteristics as readers. The students also discussed the activity as a class.

Marxist Lens.   Tim introduced the Marxist lens with a worksheet that combined a few exercises from Appleman (2000, pp. 163, 165–166). After explaining the concept and definition, they narrowed to a key focus: Who has the power and money in the text, and what happens as a result of it? For data collection, students were asked to plot the characters on a social latter according to their class, identify conflicts that pertained to class, plot themselves in a social structure diagram, examine whether they thought their own social class affected their reading of the text, and issues and questions they had about the world in general now that they've examined the text through the Marxist lens. They also discussed the activity as a class.

Feminist Lens. Tim started with a brief definition—that it was almost exactly the same as the Marxist lens, except you substitute gender for money and social status. In either case, it's about power and who has it. Then he used the concrete poem by Pedro Xisto found in Appleman (2000, p. 167) to give students a quick experience in looking at a text through the feminist lens. To tie the lens to the text and for important data collection, he asked students to reorganize their social ladders from the Marxist lens according to the feminist lens. They also had to choose characters about which to write both a traditional statement and a feminist statement, citing specific passages.

Final Project. For a culminating assessment, students (working alone or with a partner) designed a visual presentation that asked them to present an argument about how they understood the Western through one critical lens of their choosing. The project also required them to do some outside research. For data collection, they summarized their findings in an approximately one-page paper that they handed in at the time of their presentation.

ASSESSMENT OF STUDENTS' USES OF CRITICAL LENSES

In the unit outlined earlier, Tim's students designed a presentation that applied one critical lens to a class text. He also required a one-page paper. To assess student engagement, Tim also gave his students a survey to determine the overall effectiveness of the unit and the responses that students had to each lens. You can employ a variety of assessment strategies to determine if your students are able to comprehend, apply, synthesize, and evaluate the use of critical lenses as ways of reading literary texts.

You can use several handouts and group activities for informal assessment to gauge students' level of engagement. See, for example the activity on theory stations on the Web site and note that students are asked to reflect on their relative ability to apply several critical lenses to a text. They are also asked to compare which lenses seem to work best.

You can also use oral presentations as a form of assessment by dividing students into groups, making each group responsible for offering an interpretation of the classroom text they are reading through a particular lens. You then follow up with a written assessment where each individual student explicates the text through all the lenses that have been discussed through the group presentations.

You can also have students keep reading journals or logs to keep track of their individual responses to texts in their growing interpretative abilities. Assessing through journals or activities provides a formative rather than summative approach to assessment of students' interpretive abilities.

As a summative response, teachers can offer written examinations or paper assignments that ask students to view a text from several critical perspectives. This can be a culminating activity for a text that the entire class has read, or you can present students with a short text they have not previously read or discussed, such as a poem or a short story, and ask students to do a "cold" reading using at least two critical lenses. This is a particularly good way to assess whether students have internalized the basic premises of each lens and can offer autonomous and original interpretations, rather than interpretations that are reiterations of class discussions.

FINAL THOUGHTS AND A FINAL ACTIVITY: THE IMPORTANCE OF MULTIPLE PERSPECTIVES

We began this chapter with a discussion of the importance of helping students develop multiple ways of reading texts and reading the world. To close the chapter and to demonstrate the importance of encouraging students to "read the world" is a culminating activity that has worked well with students in grades 9 to 12 in virtually any classroom context. This activity asks students to identify and then read a variety of cultural texts, ranging from print ads to Web sites and music videos. We offer three examples here; there are other examples of student work on the Web site for Chapter 10.

Critical Encounters: Reading the World

The relationship between the text and the world is not simply a fascinating problem for textual theory. It is, above all others, the problem that makes textual theory necessary.
—Robert Scholes

1. Based on your reading as well as class discussions, briefly describe in your own words, the following literary theories. (Spend no more than a few minutes on this part of the exercise.)

   psychological criticism

   feminist literary theory

   Marxist literary theory

   reader-response theory

   other? (Choose one as a group)

2. Not all of the texts we encounter in everyday life are literary. "Cultural" texts can include music videos, television ads or programs, print ads, billboards, or films. Think of something you've read, heard, seen outside of class that particularly struck you as worth thinking about. Describe the example below.

3. What lens might you use to help you understand this cultural text? How might that lens affect or increase your understanding?

4. On the index card provided, please:

   a) Describe your popular cultural text (bring in a clip or copy of the original, if possible).

   · b) Analyze that text through a critical lens

   c) Conclude what the significance of the text is and why it is important to read it critically.

5. Can we use critical lenses to "read" the world? Explain.

Example 1: Famine and Earrings: The Marxist Lens. (Go to the Web site, Chapter 10, for the images from *The New York Times*)—Matt selected two different parts of the same page of *The New York Times* for his description. An article about famine in Ethiopia is juxtaposed with a Tiffany's ad for earrings that cost over $10,000 dollars. In his response to this ad, Matt demonstrates a growing sense of class inequity, which began with a Marxist reading of *Of Mice and Men*. Although some teachers, depending on the climate of their districts, may change the name of this lens to the "class" lens, it can provide a powerful tool for enabling students to understand the social conditions of both text and world and how they are implicated in it.

Example 2: Dodge Durango Ad—The Feminist Lens. (Go to the Web site, Chapter 10, for the images from *The New York Times*)—Jeremy and Ashton were delighted to discover that they chose the same ad for Dodge Durangos for this assignment. The ad separates the qualities of performance as being valued by men and qualities of refinement that are valued by women. This is a perfect example of Fairclough's (1989) ideological common sense. Both Jeremy and Ashton recognize that the ad serves to calcify gender stereotypes. Through their perceptive readings, Ashton and Jeremy animate the importance of teaching young men and young women to learn to resist the ideology of gender that limits and objectifies.

Example 3: fcuk Perfume Ad: "Scent To Bed." (Go to the Web site, Chapter 10, for the fcuk ad)—This provocative ad is for French connection United Kingdom perfume which is advertised as "fcuk." Although some of you might find the campaign unsettling, students find it in the pages of nearly any magazine they might open. The ad depicts a scantily clothed couple with the following headings: "Open her to try to fcuk her, and Open her to try to fcuk him." Then in larger letters, one reads the following: "Scent to bed."

Sarah makes a surprising interpretive move here. Although she might have chosen to read the ad through the feminist lens, she chose the reader response lens instead and demonstrated her understanding of the complex cognitive processes that underlie the act of reading. Sarah can easily transfer her metacognitive understanding of what readers bring to texts to other reading in her literature class. Sarah may also be less susceptible to manipulative media that counts on particular responses from unsuspecting readers.

As you can see from these examples, this activity encourages students to adopt the sensibilities that will encourage them to understand, and if necessary resist, the ideological common sense that calcifies the dominant hegemony of class, gender, and race. Using multiple perspectives will help your students develop the ability to inhabit a variety of perspectives, which, in turn, will help them develop the ability to understand the point of view and perspective of others. Your students will then be able to bring these awarenesses to text worlds that require them to understand and sympathize with characters whose situations are very different from their own. Remember, the point of using theory is not to make either you or your students certified literary theorists. The point is to use literary theory as a means to some larger educational ends. Using multiple perspectives helps students learn to read resistantly, whether it's textual or actual worlds. Reading with multiple perspectives encourages students to become the kind of "enlightened witnesses" that bell hooks (2003) describes. We hope that this chapter on the notions of ideology and reading the world have convinced you that helping students view literary texts through multiple critical lenses should be integrated into your approach to teaching literature.

Portfolio Addition

Consider how Harry, in our opening vignette, used critical lenses to save a text, *To Kill a Mockingbird*, that over time had become problematic. Reread both his story and the activities he created to help his students view the text from multiple perspectives and to reframe the text to acknowledge the challenges it may present in a contemporary classroom context.

Select a literary text that you might want to teach but is problematic or challenging for a variety of reasons. Perhaps it's anachronistic like *The Scarlet Letter* or *Catcher in the Rye*. Perhaps it's potentially politically tricky like *To Kill a Mockingbird* or *The Adventures of Huckleberry Finn*. Perhaps voices or perspective of women or people of color are largely absent from the text, such as in *A Separate Peace* or *The Great Gatsby*.

In your portfolio, describe the text, the challenges you might encounter in teaching it, and then design an approach to the text that incorporates at least two critical lenses. Include your handout in your portfolio.

Online Additional Activities, Links, and Further Reading

Go to the textbook Web site, Chapter 10, and "Critical Approaches" for additional activities, links, and further reading.

11

Teaching Media Literacy: What Else
Is a Text and How Do I Teach It?

Chapter Overview

- Integrating and justifying media instruction.
- Teaching use of film and video techniques.
- Using film adaptations of literature.
- Studying film and television genres.
- Studying media audiences' construction of media texts.
- Studying popular music.
- Studying news and documentary.
- Studying radio.
- Showing films and videos in the classroom.

CASE NARRATIVE: THE CHALLENGE OF INTEGRATING MEDIA LITERACY INTO THE ENGLISH CURRICULUM

Two language arts teachers, Jessica Dockter and Anne Holmgren, who teach in the Bloomington, MN, school district, face the challenge of developing a media literacy curriculum for their seventh- and eighth-grade language arts classes that are consistent with the state standards for media literacy (Minnesota Department of Education, 2003):

1. Evaluate the accuracy and credibility of information found on Internet sites.
2. Make informed evaluations about television, radio, film productions, newspapers and magazines with regard to quality of production, accuracy of information, bias, purpose, message and audience.
3. Evaluate the content and effect of persuasive techniques used in print and broadcast media.
4. Identify distinctions in how information is presented in print and non-print materials.

5. Critically analyze the messages and points of view employed in different media, including advertising, news programs, websites, and documentaries. (p. 9)

In attempting to address these standards, they identified several problems:

> The difficulty with these standards is that there is little distinction between them. Making informed evaluations about quality, accuracy, bias, purpose, message and audience is much the same as critically analyzing messages and points of view. These, in turn, are similar to evaluating persuasive techniques and credibility. At the same time, this lack of distinction offers freedom for teachers to meet the needs of their own students. Another problem with the standards at the state level is that they remain virtually the same at each grade. Our district, on the other hand, takes the standards a step further by breaking them down into what is "essential," "important," or "enhancement" for each grade level. The only difference, however, is that most of the media literacy standards are merely "enhancements" in 7th grade while they are identified as "important" in 8th grade. Enhancement implies that it is not necessary that the standard be met at that level; while important means that teachers incorporate the standard, but there is no district-wide assessment for it. We took this into consideration when thinking about our assessments and units in 7th and 8th grade, but we felt that media literacy needed more attention in 7th grade than just getting to it if time allows.

All of this raises difficult questions regarding priorities you give to teaching media literacy. It's often assumed that teaching media and digital texts is a distraction from or even irrelevant to teaching literature. It is further assumed that classroom time should not be devoted to viewing videos or DVDs when students are spending time viewing outside of class or when such viewing is perceived to be simple entertainment. At the same time, given the amount of time and levels of engagement with media and digital texts, you may often hear calls for the need for more critical analysis of what is assumed to be "mindless," "biased," "stereotyped," "consumerist" texts.

If you were in Anne and Jessica's situation, how would you justify the teaching of media literacy? How would you respond to the state standards? How would you integrate media literacy activities into the curriculum in the school in which you are working?

INTEGRATING AND JUSTIFYING MEDIA INSTRUCTION

Rather than make either-or distinctions between literature and media studies, we believe it is important to combine the two in highly interactive, constructivist ways that consider both as texts. Anne and Jessica recognized the need to integrate literature and media studies in ways that are consistent with the following trends in society.

Texts Are Being Redefined in Multimedia Formats.   Your students continually use e-mail, chats, blogs, games, cell phones, and Web sites as tools for communicating with others or building social relationships (Livingstone, 2002). In so doing, they draw on other media texts—digital images, music, video clips, texts, and so forth, in creating texts. For example, in creating a Web site, they are combining hypertext (texts linked together by multilinear nodes) and multimedia (photos, video, art, audio, text, etc.). This suggests the need to rethink traditional notions of traditional texts to thinking of texts as highly multimedia and interactive (Myers & Beach, 2001; Hammett & Barrell, 2002).

Understanding media now requires an understanding of how new digital media forms have transformed or "remediated" (Bolter & Grusin, 1998) traditional media forms of television, radio, music, and print texts. For example, http://www.cnn.com or http://www.msnbc.com provide continually updated news information along with multiple hypertext links to related bits of information, a digital form that has influenced CNN and MSNBC television news broadcasts, in which updated headlines stream across the bottom of the screen or references are made to the Web sites for more information.

Learning to effectively communicate involves the ability to combine print and media and digital texts in engaging ways. For example, creating a Web site involves combining print and digital images in ways that convey information and point users in certain directions. This suggests the need to incorporate learning new media and digital literacies (Kress, 2003) into the English curriculum. Having students produce their own media texts helps them understand the relation between purpose and their use of media and digital literacies. In creating their own ads, students assess the degree to which their intended message has been conveyed in their ad by judging the degree to which their intentions are fulfilled.

Media and Digital Texts Employ Visual Images to Communicate Meaning.   Visual images consist of signs whose meaning is based on a set of cultural codes (Scholes, 1983). The meaning of images of beauty as portrayed in romance novels, soap operas, romantic comedies, or song lyrics are constituted by what Linda Christian-Smith (1993) describes as "codes of beautification"—that being physically attractive contributes to building a love relationship with a man. Students need to learn how to critically analyze visual images in terms of their larger cultural meanings.

In a poetry activity that Anne developed, she integrated a study of figurative language with a study of media images. She showed students a series of photographs from the *National Geographic* magazine or Web site (http://www.nationalgeographic.com/photography/). Students would then choose the words that describe these images. They then took those words and made them into metaphoric statements. For example, an image of a misty landscape might become "a blanket of mist covered the land." Before writing poems employing these images, she asked students the following questions that Krueger and Christel (2001) employ for studying still images:

1. What is the first element of the image that you notice? What draws your attention to it?
2. Close your eyes and look at it again. What do you notice on second viewing? Why is your eye drawn to that aspect of the image?
3. Why are elements of the foreground, middle ground, or background the most dominant?
4. How does lighting and/or color draw your attention to specific aspects of the image? (p. 4)

Then, drawing again on Krueger and Christel (2001), she has students select a theme and tell a story illustrating that theme using digital images.

Media and Digital Texts Shape Perceptions of the World.   Media and digital texts play a central role in reflecting and shaping perceptions of the world (Freccero, 1999;

Lankshear & Knobel, 2003; Ogdon, 2001; Simon, 1999). For example, radio, television, and online news shapes people's understanding of events, understanding that influences their beliefs and actions. Films, television programs, and video games provide narrative versions of reality. Studying media representations of race, class, and gender roles involves studying stereotypical constructions of what it means to be certain kinds of persons in terms of race, class, or gender.

Critically analyzing media and digital texts' representations also involves understanding how texts position audiences to adopt certain desired responses consistent with certain stances (Ellsworth, 1997). For example, students may use online "zines" to challenge what they perceive to be status quo sexist and racist norms in the culture, often through parody, satire, and spoofs. Or, they could critically analyze Web sites in terms of accuracy of information, authenticity, viewpoints represented, use of visual images, ease of use, interactivity, and commercial appeals (Buckingham, 2003).

In devising units, you can include activities that continually involve students in making intertextual links between language, images, characters, topics, or themes. Students can create hypermedia productions in which they create intertextual or hypertextual links between language, images, video clips, or music as a means of interpreting a text (Beach & Myers, 2001). They can simply tack up magazine images onto poster boards for display in the classroom or create PowerPoint™ presentations or Web sites using HyperStudio™ or Flash™ that contain digital images, video clips, or music. Roberta Hammett (1999) describes the example of a group of preservice English teachers who created a hypermedia production on the themes of identity, representation, and spirituality. Their production includes a series of images of Native American women, starting with Disney animation portraits of Pocahontas followed by images of the "real" Pocahontas followed by Pocahontas in Elizabethan costumes followed by images of Native American children. The preservice teachers then linked these images to the following statement:

> Representations are often assigned to us by the media and long held belief systems. These representations are sometimes accurate; often they're not. Dominant, mainstream representations are believed to be accurate. We want to juxtapose these long-standing portrayals with more truthful representations and explore their effects on identity. (p. 216)

Then, based on discussions of spirituality as portrayed in the novel *Ceremony*, the students created a QuickTime™ video that included different religious images from different religions and cultures: images of a shaman, children praying, a Native American drum circle, an angel, and the Virgin Mary. In the background a song plays: "Someone told me long ago/There's a calm before the storm/I know—It's been coming for some time . . ." (p. 216). The students then showed images of an eagle, flute music, and a buffalo as used as stereotypical representations of Native American culture with the following statement:

> Movies such as "Dances with Wolfs" and "Pocahontas" developed a certain stereotypical Native American image. This culture is no longer a group with many individual personalities. It has become a group with spiritual and environmental connections, etc. It has been said that a Native American film can not be called thus unless it has flute music, buffalo, and an eagle. (p. 217)

As we noted in Chapter 8, through setting images, video clips, music, and text against each other in these hypermedia productions, students can adopt a critical stance toward media. In all of this, students are learning to adopt more critical stances toward different media.

In their unit, Anne and Jessica develop an activity for having students critically examine how the media represents issues of school censorship and control. They used Avi's (1993) *Nothing but the Truth* in which a student is suspended for his actions of whistling patriotic songs during homeroom. Based on the idea that this is a "documentary" novel based on letters, memos, interviews, and narratives, students, working in groups, create their own documentaries on issues facing their school.

Anne and Jessica also develop activities to help their students critically analyze media representations of adolescents. They first view video clips of portrayals of adolescents. Then, for homework, they view a television program with adolescent characters and analyze the typical problems facing these characters, how these problems are solved, whether these solutions are realistic, the degree of stereotyping, and positive versus negative portrayals. Students also analyze Web sites created for teenagers in terms of assumptions made or biases about teenagers as well as appeals employed to attract an adolescent audience. Students then analyze gender representations of male and female teenagers in teen magazines, creating poster presentations with images from the magazines to support their claims. They also write a response to the presentations answering the following questions: "What message about your gender do teen magazines give to readers of the opposite gender? Is this message accurate?" Finally, based on analysis of these representations, students write a proposal for an original teen sitcom or drama, depicting the characters, their typical dilemmas, and the intended audience, as well as some sample storyboards.

Media and Digital Texts Create Interactive Simulations Based on Narratives. In playing interactive, role-play video games, such as "Sims," students are participating in interactive storytelling that draws on traditional narrative forms (Lemke, 2003). Game characters interact with each other based on certain narrative scenarios. These games employ learning principles that may transfer to use in constructing game-like simulations and drama activities in the classroom (Gee, 2003; Wardrip-Fruin & Harrigan, 2004). For example, video games are designed in ways that support novice players in ways that serve to minimize taking risks or failing and in ways that reward success. Online games involve active chat room participation that create a supportive community of game players. This suggests the value of drawing on game design to create classroom simulations or activities that serve to foster students' sense of agency through their display of competence.

TEACHING USE OF FILM AND VIDEO TECHNIQUES

Another important component of media literacy is learning to identify and employ film and video production techniques. This involves identifying the use of different types of camera shots and angles (see the chapter Web site for a list of shots and angles). In so doing, it is essential that students understand the purposes for what the shots and angles are being used—for example, that a close-up of a baseball pitcher's grip on a ball is being used to call attention to the way in which he/she prepares for the pitch.

To help students analyze purposes for techniques, they could create a script and storyboard for a specific scene or for an advertisement. They first need to construct a script that outlines the key events or scenes in the film, specifying actions, dialogue, sound effects, and music. In creating a storyboard with scenes portrayed in boxes, they need to consider purposes for editing decisions regarding the length of shots and scenes, relations between shots and scenes, and linking sound and music to the action. For each box, students could list the number of seconds for a shot or scene, the type of shot or angle, the use of music or sound effects, and any special editing transitions between shots.

Editing. Students could also analyze the use of editing—how individual shots are combined in sequence to convey certain meanings. The relations between certain shots function to convey certain meanings. For example, a famous scene of Cary Grant in Hitchcock's "North by Northwest" being lured to an Illinois cornfield only to be attacked by a low-flying crop-duster plane (for a storyboard, see Giannetti, 2004) demonstrates the deliberate juxtaposition of shots of Grant's face and escape movements with shots of the plane as it makes another turn to swoop down on Grant.

One of the best ways to teach editing is to have students engaged in their own editing using iMovie™ or other editing software programs such as Adobe Premier™ and After Effects™, for both Macintosh and Windows, and Final Cut Pro™, for Macintosh. Once students have imported material into computers from their camcorders, they then select the material they want to use and import it into iMovie™. They then name or rename the different clips using the box below each small picture. They then can insert the clips into the horizontal bar on the bottom of the screen. They can then rearrange the clips, crop them, and add sound. They can also add fades, wipes, or dissolves between shots.

Students can then apply their knowledge of shots and editing to consider how they would create a film adaptation of short stories or scenes from a novel.

In her 11th-grade literature class, Jennifer Larson of Maple Grove High School has students study film technique in conjunction with formalist analysis of novels. She first provides students with analysis of still images—photos, art work, comics, magazine ads, and asks students to identify the use of various techniques (see Web site for a list of techniques). In having students study techniques, she believes that it is important to understand the underlying purposes for why filmmakers are using these different techniques. Rather than simply identifying the types of techniques, students need to describe the reasons for using those techniques, for example, why a long shot showing a character in the middle of a large, expansive field is used to portray that character as a relatively small, insignificant person, as well as how that shot positions the audience in relation to the character—as someone distant from the audience.

She shows clips from films such as "The Lord of the Rings: The Fellowship of the Rings," stopping frequently to discuss plot, character, and story development and asking students questions about the purpose for using film techniques:

1. How is the character being portrayed?
2. What is the mood in this part of the film?
3. What's happening with the plot? Why is this plot point important to the overall story?
4. Why is this setting important to the overall story?
5. How does the film technique communicate any of this—lighting, camera angle, camera movement, camera positioning, framing, color, sound, etc.?

She also uses freewrites to focus on specific aspects of the film clips. In so doing, she encourages students to focus on specific images and sounds using an "image-sound skim" in which they list specific images or sounds. Then, next to these images and sounds, they could describe the types of emotions or feelings evoked by these images or sounds. For example, if they list, "close-up of raised knife in killer's hand," they may then list "fear about what will happen." Students then share their lists and discuss some of the reasons for the associations between certain images and sounds and certain emotions, associations that are based on semiotic meanings.

Working together in pairs, students choose a 5-min clip of a film to analyze the techniques and what is being communicated about character, plot, setting, and theme. They then present their analysis of the clip to the class in a 10- to 15-min presentation. They must give a brief summary of the film, set up the context for the clip, point out the message being delivered and how the film technique delivers that message, and show the clip. She uses the following point system to evaluate the presentations:

1 point for each item checked off in numbers 1–6.

_____ 1. Summarizes the film

_____ 2. Sets up the context for the clip

_____ 3. Points out the message being delivered

_____ 4. Explains how the film technique delivers that message

_____ 5. Shows the clip

_____ 6. Meets the time limit (10–15 minutes)

_____ 7. Accuracy 2 3 4

_____ 8. Quality insight into how technique delivers message 2 3 4

_____ 9. Clear, accessible delivery 2 3 4

_____ 10. Succinct explanations 2 3 4

Total: _____/22 points

To help students learn to analyze the function of specific clips in a film, Adam Kinory (2002) had students examine the portrayal of five motifs in the film "Inherit the Wind," about the Scopes Monkey Trial, in which a teacher was put on trial for teaching Darwin's theory of evolution: "South versus North," "need for progress," "religion versus intellectualism," "limited perspective," and "questions." As students viewed the film, they recorded key moments in the film for each of these five motifs. Then, based on the students' recording of key moments, he identified 30 of the most noted clips and digitized those clips. After each clip, the students did more freewriting and discussion of those clips, particularly in terms of four types of textual connections (see Kinory example in Chapter 7):

1. Text to Text—This reminds me of something in another book, film, or media.
2. Inter-Text—This reminds me of something in this book, film, or media.
3. Text to Self—This reminds me of something in my own life.
4. Text to World—This reminds me of something in the world.

He then put the 30 clips into each student's iMac™ and asked them to select three clips that stood out in their mind based on some thematic or narrative connection, connections that served as the basis for an essay about the film.

Animation.   Students could also study technique through producing their own animation films, which are relatively easy to make by simply using paper cutouts, clay, art work, or computer graphics. To teach her students animation techniques, Ann Ayers of Coral Springs High School, in Broward County, Florida, had students, working in groups, create characters who would serve as the basis for clay or cutout animations based on a storyboard idea. Some group members then selected objects, worked on the clay figures, or created cut-outs to portray their characters. Others worked on the background settings using boxes, poster board, and other art materials. They then used digital cameras to take "frame-by-frame" shots of their characters as they were being moved. They then imported images into iPhoto™ for sorting, enhancing, cropping, or rotating images. Based on their storyboards, they then integrated the images to iMovie™ and added sound, voice-overs, and music. Their final products were then exported to QuickTime™ to burn CDs (http://ali.apple.com/ali_sites/deli/exhibits/1000678/The_Lesson.html).

Video Production of Documentaries.   In teaching video production at the Inter-district Crosswinds Middle School in Woodbury, MN, Norina Beck has students create their own documentary videos as a way of learning to analyze techniques used in documentaries. She begins by showing students a short film with several examples of camera shots, angles, and camera movements along with written worksheets to reinforce student understanding of important vocabulary. She then demonstrates proper handling of video equipment and set guidelines for acceptable use.

She has students work in groups in which students assume the roles of camera-person, director recorder, and production assistant—roles that are alternated every three shots; she also models each of these roles.

She then introduces different editing techniques—jump cuts, match cuts, cross cuts, montage, and how they are used in clips from different documentaries. She then has students develop a treatment script for creating a video portrait based on 2-min interviews of students in their group. Students practice asking interview questions and then begin shooting in groups. They then edit their material to create at least five different cover shots.

She demonstrates the need for the camera-person to pause between each question to employ a different angle or shot type, as well as use variety of extra cover shots to capture the context. She also coaches the production assistant to make sure the interview does not go on for more than 2 min and to notice potential problems—outside noise level, bad lighting, or interruptions.

She encourages students to consider adopting certain positions or perspectives in making a documentary about their school—advocate, observer, or poet. Students then choose shots and sequences that convey their position that are included in a treatment script and storyboard.

All of this serves to help students understand some of the larger issues of objectivity and bias associated with analysis of documentary. Based on their work in producing documentaries, Norina's students then analyze the ways in which certain shots, interview questions, or editing techniques serve to present a certain bias or perspective. If the interviewees only presented one side of an issue, her students then recognized the need to present alternate perspectives.

USING FILM ADAPTATIONS OF LITERATURE

In selecting film adaptations, it is important to use films that have high levels of cinematic value, as opposed to films that are simply reproductions of a staged version of the original text (Costanzo, 2004; Teasley & Wilder, 1997). In studying film adaptations, you could have students compare a text, theater, or film version of the same text, not in terms of whether one is "better" than the other, but more in terms of differences in how the different media present the same material (Corrigan, 1999; Stam & Raengo, 2004). Louis Giannetti

(2004) notes that time in film is highly flexible, whereas in theater, it is continuous. He notes that space in film depends on how and where the camera positions an audience, whereas in theater, audiences can select what they want to watch and how they focus their attention; space in film exploits "off-frame" action—the fact that we are aware of someone outside a frame, whereas in theater, once actors leave the stage, they are forgotten. Films can obviously employ a range of different settings, whereas the theater is limited to what can be done on a stage.

Giannetti (2004) contrasts three different types of adaptation, "the loose, the faithful, and the literal" (p. 406). In a loose adaptation, a director may only use the original situation, story idea, or characters to create a film that bears little resemblance to the original text. For example, the film "Clueless" was based on the story line and comic, ironic wit of Jane Austen's *Emma*, but is set in a contemporary world with quite different characters. Faithful adaptations attempt to recapture the original text as closely as possible, a careful translation of the original into film form that retains the characters, story lines, and most events, for example, *Emma, Henry V*, and *Much Ado About Nothing*. Literal adaptations are typically older video versions of play productions, with limited use of cinematic techniques.

In teaching film adaptations at Champlin Park High School, Champlin, MN, Rachel Malchow (2002) avoids the use of literal adaptations because they, as simply filmed stage dramas, lack cinematic quality. She is more likely to use faithful adaptations because they attempt to "re-create the tone of the literary work in filmic language" (p. 6).

> Franco Zeffirelli's 1968 "Romeo and Juliet" captures the passion and violence of 16th-century Verona best through its music and visual imagery. Kenneth Branagh's "Henry V" (1989) uses flashbacks from the "Henry IV" plays and gruesome slow-motion depictions of war to problematize the issues of leadership. Conversely, Branagh's "Much Ado About Nothing" (1993) manages to create a lusty, sunny comedy through its "giddy" panoramic shots of the Tuscan countryside and its musical score.

Rather than showing entire films, she shows clips and has students compare clips of films with the original texts.

She identifies five types of "loose" adaptations:

> ***Displaced.*** The "displaced" adaptation in which the setting is altered, but the text's language is retained, applies to texts such as the 1995 *Richard III*, set in Europe in the 1930s; the 1996 *Romeo + Juliet*, set in contemporary Los Angeles; or the 2000 *Hamlet* set in the contemporary corporate world of New York City.

> ***Acculturated.*** The acculturated film adaptation shifts both language and setting of the original text into a new context, as in Akira Kurosawa's "Throne of Blood" (1957, based on *Macbeth*) and "Ran" (1985, based on King Lear), placed in the midst of 16th-century Japan. "Clueless," a 1995 version of *Emma*, is set in a Beverly Hills high school, featuring adolescents using contemporary language.

> ***Politicized.*** A 1944 version of "Henry V" was commissioned by the British Ministry of Information during World War II as war-time propaganda. "Mansfield Park" (1998) portrays the often silent heroine, Fanny Price, as an outspoken feminist critiquing gender and class bias.

> ***Commercialized.*** The commercialized adaptation transforms the original story to make it palatable to a larger audience, limiting the original text's complexity, irony, and

ambiguity, and dramatizing the hero—often a Hollywood celebrity—in ways consistent with traditional American values. Franco Zeffirelli's "Hamlet" (1990) casts Mel Gibson and Glenn Close as Hamlet and Gertrude, eliminates the Fortinbras subplot, and thus any attention to the political themes in the play. Kenneth Branagh's 1996 version of "Hamlet" includes cameo appearances by numerous American and British actors, opulent sets, and scenes replete with special effects, sex, and swash-buckling action.

Radical. The radical adaptation creates an entirely new version of original material, for example, "Shakespeare in Love," based on how or why Shakespeare wrote *Romeo and Juliet*. Malchow notes the following:

This film is highly accessible for students: its narrative is linear, the tone both humorous and touching, and the art design vividly re-creates Elizabethan London. The main benefit for students might be the insight into the Elizabethan theater that the film provides: the rivalries, the hectic rehearsal pace, the lack of money and technology, as well as the laws against women performing on stage. The film's climax transports the audience to the premiere of the play, where we can imagine what it may have been like to see this now canonical text on opening night.

Some other adaptations appropriate for high school students (from Ayers & Crawford, 2004, pp. 199–200) include "The Lone Ranger and Tonto Fistfight in Heaven (Smoke Signals)," "A Clockwork Orange," "Two Years Before the Mast," "Do Android Dream of Electric Sheep?," "Like Water for Chocolate," "A Lesson before Dying," "The Tin Drum," "The Autobiography of Malcolm X," "Seabiscuit," "High Fidelity," "The World According to Garp," "Hoop Dreams," "One Flew Over the Cuckoo's Nest," "Being There," "Born on the Fourth of July," "To Kill a Mockingbird," "A River Runs Through It and Other Stories," "All the Pretty Horses," "Master and Commander," "East of Eden," "Grapes of Wrath," "The Joy Luck Club," "Zoot Suit," and "The Piano Lesson."

Online Film Resources. In working with films, there are a lot of useful online resources that provide students with online clips—largely in the form of trailers—as well as summaries of film reviews, and further information about individual films. One of the most important of these resources is The Internet Movie Base (http://www.imdb.com/), a database of 260,000 film and television productions, including information about directors, filming locations, awards, and trailers.

In teaching the adaptation of *The Grapes of Wrath* (Steinbeck, 2004) in her student teaching, Jennifer Viland had her students create five storyboards or drawings from various scenes throughout *The Grapes of Wrath* as if they were directing the movie version of this novel. Then, one student "director" positions students physically in a still-frame shot; the "director" then introduces each character and explains how this scene is effective.

Working in pairs, students then choose a theme from the book, and, using digital video cameras, attempt to capture footage that reflects the theme from *The Grapes of Wrath* (orIMBD clips). For example, students may choose the theme "family" and videotape several shots of families in their natural environment or surroundings. Students then write an essay about why they chose that theme, how easy or difficult it was to find people and settings which clearly and effectively illustrated that theme, what cinematic or editing techniques or strategies they chose which would further impact the viewer in experiencing each student's interpretation of that theme, and a personal reflection on the project as an expression of their understanding of the novel as a whole.

Comics and Graphic Novels.   The comic book and graphic novel genre has been consistently popular with certain loyal fans as a genre that draws on adventure, thriller, science fiction, horror, and other text genres, as well as animation, film, art, and digital forms (Crawford, 2003). Students can study the artistic aspects of comic book design by analyzing the use of technical aspects of blocking, shifting between blocks, visual display, lines, dialogue balloons, story summaries, and so forth, related to the development of story lines and characters. Probably the best known graphic novel is Art Spiegelman's (1993) *Maus: A Survivor's Tale: My Father Bleeds History/Here My Troubles Began*, which portrays the world of a Polish Jewish ghetto during World War II in a comic format that combines the visual material of comic books with the novel form; this tends to be written for more of an adolescent audience.

Teachers have increasingly incorporated the use of comic and graphic novel versions of literary texts, particularly in working with struggling readers. For example, Diane Roy, who taught ninth-grade English students who had failed the course the previous year, after having students read Spiegelman's (1993) novel, asked them to select a minimum of five graphic novels to read on their own (Méndez, 2004). She found that all of the students read twice that number.

Although some educators may be concerned that these texts will replace traditional literature, Philip Crawford (2003) argued that reading these comics and graphic novels often leads students to read other texts; for example, Wonder Woman comics may interest students in Greek mythology.

Critiquing Media Representations.   Media representations often essentialize, generalize, or categorize people or institutions based on essentialist notions or stereotypical generalizations. For example, teachers are represented in limited ways as "caretakers," "jailers," "saviors," "drillmasters," "keepers of wisdom," "facilitators or guides-on-the-side," "technicians," "agents of social change," or "underpaid unionists," or as totally dedicated, lone saviors of students, who fight against the often repressive school to help their students (Shannon & Crawford, 1998). Urban communities or neighborhoods are often portrayed, particularly in television news or crime shows, as crime-ridden or poverty-stricken, without providing additional contextual information about the causes of these phenomenon: high unemployment, lack of government support, or lack of affordable housing. In contrast, suburbia is often represented as an idealized, pastoral, tree-lined world, or as a vacant, sterile wasteland.

Students could also examine the ways in which film adaptations address certain issues of race, class, and gender. For example, the film "Smoke Signals" (Alexie, 1998), an adaptation of Sherman Alexie's (1994) stories, *The Lone Ranger and Tonto Fistfight in Heaven*, portrays the lives of two young Native Americans, Victor Joseph and Thomas Builds-the-Fire, who go to Arizona to collect the remains of Victor's alcoholic father who abandoned Victor when he was young. The film continually plays with the tensions between stereotypes about Indian life—alcoholism, rusting automobiles, absent fathers, and challenges to those stereotypes.

In teaching "Smoke Signals" to her eighth-grade students, Rachel Godlewski began with the familiar topic of media representations of gender by having students first list adjectives associated with different gender groups, she then had students find examples of gender representations from film, television, commercials, magazine articles and advertisements, newspapers, Web sites, books, songs and music videos, and cartoons. Students then made presentations in which they addressed the following questions: "What adjectives describe the men and women being portrayed in their examples? If there is a power dynamic between people, who has the power? Who solves the problems? How do they solve the problems? What activities are the people doing in the images? Are all forms of media providing the same range of representations of gender? Are some widely different? If so, which ones? How can you account for the differences? How do the audiences affect the representations offered? Where are certain representations most prevalent?

Students then turn to the less familiar topic of media representations of Native Americans. She started by having students list adjectives they would use to describe American Indian culture and people as a reflection of their preconceptions. Students then viewed "Images of Indians: How Hollywood Stereotyped the Native American" and "Hollywood's Indian: The Portrayal of the Native American in Film." Students then read the screenplay, "Smoke Signals," and wrote in their dialogue journals about the two characters' relationships with each other. Students then viewed the film, noting the use of techniques. They read "Sending Cinematic Smoke Signals, An Interview with Sherman Alexie" in *Cineaste* (West & West, 1998) for homework and discussed his selection of the title and his perceptions of the film, leading up to writing a final review of the film.

Critiquing Advertising.   Students could also critique television or magazine ads in terms of the marketing, merchandising, promotion, sponsorship, and branding strategies employed (Cook, 2001; Klein, 2000; Myers, 1999). In so doing, they need to examine larger issues of consumption associated with environmental impact as well as construction of values and identities in a consumer society. Advertisers have recently moved away from stand-alone, overt "ads" to embedding products or brands into Web sites, films, TV programs, video games, sports events, museums, shopping malls, and other contexts in which potential consumers are already being entertained so that they associate that entertainment with certain products or brands.

Students could analyze rhetorical appeals to audiences through attempting to gain audience identification with groups or causes. For example, Pepsi™ ads portray celebrities as members of the "Pepsi™ Generation," which, in turn, equates the audience as being members of the "Pepsi™ Generation," associated with drinking Pepsi™.

All of this suggests the need to examine the following questions:

1. Who's the intended or target audience?
2. What signs, markers, images, language, or social practices imply that audience?
3. How is the audience linked to use of the product?
4. What are the underlying value assumptions (e.g., having white teeth enhances your popularity; casino gambling is enjoyable)?

Students could also examine the use of advertising and marketing in their own schools (Spring, 2003). Advertisers and corporations provide schools with products or funding in return to being able to place ads on textbook covers or in schools or to sell certain fast-food or beverage products in the school. Because school funding has been cut, schools often need additional funds simply to meet basic needs. For example, Primedia's *Channel One* provides morning in-school "news," now in some 40% of all secondary schools, by providing schools with free video equipment. Forty-two percent of the 12-min "news" broadcasts consist of ads, self-promotions, and filler, thereby using what is assumed to be a pedagogical tool to insert advertising into the curriculum.

One of the most effective ways to study ads is to have students produce their own ads or create parodies of ads, as illustrated in *Adbusters Magazine*. By having to consider techniques and strategies for selling a product, students are having to think about the techniques and strategies they are critiquing in ads.

A Unit on Consumerism.   Central to all of this is a critique of a consumer culture and economy that attempts to create the need for consumer goods—the fact that one's life is always inadequate or unfilled without certain products or that products will enhance one's popularity and happiness. For her student teaching, Becca Dalrymple created a unit based on the science fiction, young-adult novel, *Feed*, by M. T. Anderson (2002). In this novel, adolescents live in a future world in which they are continually fed consumer messages into their brains. Becca began the unit by having students identity their consumer habits—what they buy and what influences what they buy. The students then read popular teen magazines and identified teen consumer norms. Students then went to a shopping mall and interviewed store employees about their teen patronage; students also reflected on their feelings about being in the mall—whether they found it stressful, rejuvenating, exciting, boring, anxious, or calming.

Students then responded to the first section of *Feed* (Anderson, 2002), entitled "Eden," which portrays a world dominated by large corporations. Students discuss their attitudes about large corporations, particularly Clear Channel, Fox News, Disney/ABC, Time Warner, and News Corporation, that control much of the media. For example, the students noted that Clear Channel not only owns nearly 1,200 radio stations, but, until 2005, they also owned SFX Entertainment, the primary concert-venue owner and touring promoter in the country. Clear Channel could therefore choose to promote only certain musicians on their stations that they have also signed up for their concerts.

Students then discussed alternative media texts such as *Utne Reader* and *Mother Jones* magazines that portray alternative perspectives outside of the media conglomerates' texts.

In responding to the second section, "Utopia," students discussed the ways in which the main character, Titus, began to resist the consumer feeds, as he begins to recognize marketing strategies (Anderson, 2002):

> They're also waiting to make you want things. Everything we've grown up with . . . it's all streamlining our personalities so we're easier to sell to . . . they do these demographic studies that divide everyone up into a few personality types, and then you get ads based on what you're supposedly like. They try to figure out who you are, and to make you conform to one of their types for easy marketing. (pp. 80–81)

Students then identified the types of ads they might receive given their own possible "types." They also discussed the ways in which the school in the novel ("School™") is run by corporations to teach students how to consume, and the ways in which adolescents' spending can result in financial debt and depression, as portrayed by the death of one of the characters, Violet, in the novel.

For final activities, Becca's students debated positive versus negative aspects of advertising or "feeds." For final writing projects, students compared the novel to *1984* (Orwell, 1990), created a futuristic society that was similar or different to the society in *Feed* (Anderson, 2002), surveyed their peers' consumer habits and created a "handbook" for responsible teenage consumerism, or addressed an issue associated with media conglomerate control in which they assumed an active role in challenging a corporation's control.

STUDYING FILM AND TELEVISION GENRES

Students could also study film and television genres, analyzing prototypical roles of hero, heroine, sidekick, alien, monster, criminal, cowboy, mentor, detective, villain, talk-show host, and so forth; settings; imagery; plot and story lines having to do with the nature of the problem, who solves the problem, and how they solve the problem; and the themes and value assumptions reflected in the text (Altman, 1999; Mittell, 2004). For example, in analyzing the television crime detective show, students could identify the typical detective and sidekick roles, the setting of the urban world, the imagery of darkness, the story line development based on the problem of crime, the detective as the one who solves a crime, and the means of often tough-minded, even violent actions; and the underlying thematic values that crime doesn't pay. Examining the underlying value assumptions helps students critically examine some of the values that are presupposed in certain genres. As noted in Chapter 7, the crime-detective program often assumes that crime is best solved by control as a deterrent, as opposed to alternative approaches—reducing poverty, providing jobs, instituting drug prevention programs, or enhancing education. Moreover, such shows often invite audiences to position people of color as the "urban criminals" who need to be controlled.

Or, students could study the fantasy film genre's portrayal of the mythic, magical quest journey in which the "good" heroes confront various challenges associated with "evil," challenges that test their tenacity, particularly in the final challenge. In "The Lord of the Rings, The Fellowship of the Ring," Frodo Baggins lives alone in a rural village until he is summoned to lead a group to face a whole series of bizarre, supernatural creatures and worlds, each requiring him and his companions to outwit the enemy in the land of Mordor; the hero therefore triumphs not through greater physical prowess, but through his knowledge of specific details, outwitting the enemy. And, tas also noted in Chapter 7, films such as "Star Wars, The Empire Strikes Back," and "Return of the Jedi," as Joseph Campbell (1991) demonstrates in his volume, *The Power of Myth*, share with fantasy quest films the focus on mythic and archetypal quests, in this case, Luke Skywalker's search for the father represented by Darth Vader, involving the traditional tension between good versus evil—the encroaching power of "the empire," made up of the "Jedi Knights," the "Jawas" who trade "androids," and the "Droids." Science-fiction films dealing with issues of "science" portray threats or challenges to society in the form of technology gone amok—nuclear disasters, mutant insects, computer breakdowns, skyscraper fires, or the threat of environmental destruction, epidemic diseases, mind-control, and genetic manipulation. Students could study how technological devices serve both positive and negative ends in films such as "Contact," in which the main character can travel through space to alien worlds; "Minority Report," in which the police can project themselves into the future prior to people committing a crime; "AI," in which robots assume human-like identities; or "Gattac," in which genetic modification is used to create certain types of persons.

STUDYING MEDIA AUDIENCES' CONSTRUCTION OF MEDIA TEXTS

In studying media, it is important for students to recognize that the meaning of media texts evolves out of the audiences' activity of social participation with media texts (Beach, 2004; Booker & Jermyn, 2003; Steiger, 2005). Audiences engage in fan-club chat exchanges about favorite television programs. They burn music CDs and share those CDs with peers. They participate in "blogging," online exchanges of opinions. They organize viewing events around going to films or viewing at home, such as "Super Bowl" parties. They visit theme parks, attend concerts, or shop in malls, experiences that are highly mediated by media.

Students could analyze audiences' activities of using media texts by studying how audiences or participants construct meaning in television viewing, Internet chat rooms, blogs, online fan-club activities (e.g., soap operas, Star Trek), responses to magazines and e-zines, or participation in media events (e.g., sports broadcasts, rock concerts), playing video games, or surfing the World Wide Web. In observing participants' behaviors, they need to use written field notes and tape-recordings, employing concrete descriptions of behaviors, as well as how group members are using the media for certain social purposes—developing relationships, impressing each other, defining status, and so forth. They could take photos to capture participants' behaviors and interview participants about their personal perceptions of their participation.

For example, Melissa Chiri had her high school students study children watching television. She began the unit by having students study an online photography show by Shawn Michienzi, "If TVs Watched Us" (http://www.iceboxminnesota.com/tvshow/tvshow_i .html). This led to a discussion of the role of television in the culture and how it may shape audiences' beliefs and attitudes—by constantly "watching" audiences.

Students then captured images of older children's television programs by doing searches on Google and creating poster collages of those images. They used these posters to recall their own experiences of watching certain children's television programs and what they may have learned from characters on those programs. Students then studied the history of children's television by visiting the following Web sites:

- http://inventors.about.com/library/inventors/blchildrenstelevision.htm
- http://www.cbc.ca/kids/general/time/history_radio_tv/default.html
- http://www.pbs.org/kids/text_only/did_you_know/back_timeline.html
- http://www.toonarific.com/links.html

Students studied one selected program—its history, target audiences, viewing schedule, genre, and video techniques employed in the program.

Students then observed a young child or group of children watching a children's television show, noting the (a) atmosphere—where, when, and other setting factors; (b) physical and emotional reactions of the child or children and in what part of the program those reactions took place; (c) conversations about the program that took place in the room; and (d) differences to reactions to commercial breaks versus the program itself.

If parents or guardians were available, students interviewed them about their perceptions of their children's responses to these programs and their television-viewing habits. Students then produced a final report of their findings about the children's responses.

STUDYING POPULAR MUSIC

Students could also study popular music in terms of how this music is related to larger social and cultural forces. Students could share or write about their own listening experiences, describing reasons for those experiences in terms of genres, tastes, preferences, quality, performance, and influences of the music industry or radio on their music experiences. And they could identity the characteristics of certain music genres—jazz, be-bop, rock, soul, blues, country, Cajun, calypso, gospel, punk, heavy metal, hip-hop, and rap, and explore the evolution of those genres. For example, they could study how rap music emerged out of a hip-hop culture of the 1960s and 1970s with its emphasis on political expression and resistance through graffiti, modes of dress, language, and social practices. Ernest Morrell (2002) developed a unit on hip-hop music and culture as part of a 12th-grade poetry course. Students first examined the relations between literature and the historical period in which that literature was produced. This led to an analysis of the relation between hip-hop music as a voice of urban youth dealing with the effects of the postindustrial revolution associated with the loss of employment opportunities and the increase in urban blight.

Working in groups, students then selected a poem and a rap song and prepared group presentations on the relations of these texts to their historical and literary periods. Students then completed an anthology of 10 poems and presented five of those poems at a poetry reading. For their final unit project, they wrote a five- to seven-page critical essay on a rap song.

In another related unit for use in his student teaching, Noah Mass had students examine the ways in which music serves as statements of protest. Students began with an exploration of the meaning of protest, both in their lives and in the larger society. The students discussed how individual protest becomes a larger, collective protest. In studying Dr. Martin Luther King, Jr.'s, Letter from a Birmingham Jail (King, 1994), students examine the effectiveness of different protest strategies.

Students then listen to various protest songs such as "Dear Landlord" by Bob Dylan and "Signed D.C." by Love, comparing them to King's letters in terms of purpose and audience. They then listen to Jimi Hendrix's "The Star-Spangled Banner" as an expression of his antiwar attitudes in 1969 at the Woodstock Music Festival. Students then formulate responses to "Black Steel in the Hour of Chaos" by the rap group Public Enemy: "I got a letter from the government / the other day / I opened and read it / It said they were suckers / They wanted me for their army or whatever / Picture me given' a damn—I said never / Here is a land that never gave a damn about a brother like me . . ." (Public Enemy, 1988). Students also studied "Sunday Bloody Sunday" by U2, related to the conflicts in Northern Ireland, and "A Change is Gonna Come" by Sam Cooke, in terms of portrayals of resistance to change.

Students then begin work on a final unit project, in which they write a two-page essay about their protest issue that explores the problem, its historical antecedents and modern and future consequences, and proposed solutions, as well as text or work of art—visual, aural, written, and so forth—that could be used to rally support for their issue.

STUDYING NEWS AND DOCUMENTARY

Much of "news" consists of highly sensational, superficial coverage of trivial events that is not significant for audiences or their communities, whereas issues that are significant are often not reported on because they represent challenges to status quo institutions that often control commercial news broadcasts. Central to studying news is determining what constitutes "news" or "newsworthy events" in terms of whether the event has some significance for certain people; is relevant to audiences' interests, needs, and knowledge; or has some practical, utilitarian value for them or their community's needs and interests.

In a unit for use in student teaching, Erin Grahmann and Erin Warren focused on understanding news through producing their own television newscast. After studying various video techniques, students began by watching a taped news broadcast. Students kept a viewing log to record the topics, number of seconds for each story, sources, use of visuals, and anchor "happy talk" and self-promotions, as well as the amount of time devoted to weather and sports, leading up to the question of what they actually learned in terms of understanding events and issues from this "news" broadcast. They then analyzed the seven "S"s:

1. Stories: What's covered and what's left out?
2. Sequence: What gets priority?
3. Scope: How much coverage and how much time spent?
4. Structure: How organized using what?
5. Style: How presented by writer or anchor?
6. Slant: What bias is evident?
7. Sponsor: How is content shaped by financial supporters?

Students then work in groups to produce different segments for the same newscast: film, music, news, weather, production, camera people, and advertisements. Once each group completes their segments, that material is edited using iMovie™ to create a final production.

Students could also examine the degree to which an editorial or "op-ed" essay clearly formulates their argument and opinion, as well as providing supporting evidence or research. Students could compare the editorial pages of, for example, *The New York Times* and *The Wall Street Journal* to determine differences in their ideological perspectives and how those perspectives influence their editorials. Students could analyze the use of language or style in the news in terms of writers' orientation or objectivity. For example, writers may use metaphors or hyperbolic language to describe an event in a manner that represents a particular attitude toward that event. Students could also participate in news or journalist blogs, examining the ways in which blogs serve to voice perspectives not found in mainstream commercial news.

STUDYING RADIO

Thinking critically about what one is listening to on the radio is an important literacy practice. Part of critical listening is the ability to analyze the rhetorical appeals being employed given different radio stations' target audiences, the types of programs geared for those audiences, and the types of products advertised on those stations (Squirer, 2003). Students could also compare new coverage of the same event between National Public Radio and a commercial news station. Radio also contains a lot of material that can be integrated into a literature curriculum. For example, Adam Kinory (2002) drew on materials from the National Public Radio programs, "This American Life" and "Radio Diaries" (see the Web site for links), in which his 11th-grade students listened to the stories on the program Web site, recorded written reactions based on four types of reactions (text-to-text, text-to-world, text-to-self, questions), and then posted their comments on the program's bulletin boards, leading up to writing their own narratives for sharing with peers.

SHOWING FILMS AND VIDEOS IN THE CLASSROOM

In selecting films, videos, and DVDs that are copyrighted, you a need to follow the guidelines associated with "fair use" of media texts for educational, noncommercial, classroom use (see the PBS Fair Use Guidelines for Off-Air Recording of Broadcast Programming for Educational Purposes: http://www.pbs.org/teachersource/copyright/copyright_fairuse .shtm).

Action Research: Studying Students' Media Uses

To find out about your students' media uses, ask them to complete some surveys of time devoted on a daily or weekly basis to film, television, radio, music, Web browsing, chat, e-mail, magazines, popular fiction, and so forth, as well as particular media texts they enjoy and reasons for their enjoyment. Then, analyze the results in terms of certain patterns according to gender, race, class, age, and access. These results should help you consider ways of integrating popular texts into your teaching and to understand your students' leisure-time activities.

Online Additional Activities, Links, and Further Reading

Go to the textbook Web site, Chapter 11, and "media/technology," for additional activities, links, and further reading.

12

Assessing and Evaluating Students'
Learning: How Do I Know What
Students Have Learned?

Chapter Overview

- Defining what you value in literature instruction.
- Different notions of learning literature.
- Alternatives to "correct answer" tests.
- Use of criteria in judging student work.
- Using feedback to foster students' revision and perspective-taking.
- Determining student learning in your classroom.
- Using portfolios to evaluate growth and reflection.

CASE NARRATIVE: COPING WITH ISSUES OF EVALUATION

In sharing her experience with student teaching, Nicole notes that her cooperating teacher typically gives objective tests at the end of each unit:

> One hundred questions or whatever it is where they really have to know the text, and walking into that situation in the student teaching, I thought, "Oh my gosh." You know, because when I was a student, we never took tests on literature. It was always writing papers so my philosophy before going into this atmosphere was that I'd rather give students some more varied assessment and evaluation strategies. Maybe have them write a paper about one novel, and then you take maybe just a straight essay test on another novel, um, and then maybe an objective test with another novel. So that there will still be an assessment but maybe not objective testing. Um, but I found actually that the students are used to objective testing and they like that. They don't like the word "essay." I've talked with my cooperating teacher about this. She said that students remember things better and they learn more when they are tested on the details of the novel. And that that really benefits them more than maybe writing a paper and as far as teaching to the thirty students, that's the best strategy. You know there might be four or five students in there that would rather write papers while the majority of them would not be successful in that atmosphere. But on the other hand, I know that I have at least four

or five students that are really comfortable taking objective tests as well, so I guess what might be shaping some these behaviors is that's the way they've done things in the past.

If you were in Nicole's shoes, what would you do in this situation? If you wanted to employ alternative assessments other than objective testing, what justifications would you make for these alternatives in terms of fostering learning of literature?

In your student teaching, you devote a lot of time to preparing and then implementing your teaching activities. However, once you've taught those activities, how do you know if your students have really learned anything from what you've taught them? How do you know if you've made a difference in what they learn? And, how will you evaluate students on what they have learned? In this chapter, we discuss ways to determine what students have learned in your literature classes and how you can evaluate their learning.

In this chapter, we use some key terms associated with assessing and evaluating learning. For the purposes of this chapter, when we use the term assessing, we mean use of various tools for collecting data on students' learning—quizzes, journals, discussions, portfolios, and so forth. When we use the term evaluating, we mean making judgments about the degree and level of student learning based on your assessing.

DEFINING WHAT YOU VALUE IN LITERATURE INSTRUCTION

In evaluating students, you are judging their performance based on what you value in their ability to understand and produce literature and media texts. If you value knowledge of factual information about literature, you will evaluate students very differently than if you value their ability to critically analyze texts.

As described in Chapter 3 on planning instruction, you are also evaluating them based on your goals and learning objectives. As we argued, you use "backwards" planning to define your goals and objectives in terms of the specific types of learning that you will be assessing. Because she believed in the value of writing as a learning tool, one of Nicole's goals was to help her students learn to use freewriting and journaling as a means of engaging with texts and grappling with characters' motivations:

> I want them to understand that reading and writing can be fun, um when its approached the right way and when you're involved in some activities through free writing that we do nearly every day and journaling activities and then some form of writing project that can make it relevant to them, if I can make the topic relevant to them, then they seem to be more interested and engaged as well. For example when we worked on the short story, *On The Rainey River* by Tim O'Brien, where the journal question was, you know, if you were in Tim O'Brien's position trying to decide whether to fight in the Vietnam War or flee to Canada, what would you do if you were in that position? And what factors would influence your decision? And if you left, who would you want to say goodbye to or what would you say to your friends and your family if you chose to flee or if you chose to fight?

Then, she would evaluate their writing in terms of the degree to which they were engaged with the text and were able to explain characters' actions.

In specifying your goals and criteria consistent with those goals, you are attempting to demystify the evaluation process by making explicit your expectations or ground rules. Making explicit your criteria with students provides them with an understanding of "what counts" in your classroom. For example, for her journal entries, Nicole told her students that she was not evaluating them on organization, spelling, or mechanics because she wanted them to understand that they were doing informal writing.

DIFFERENT NOTIONS OF LEARNING LITERATURE

In evaluating students' learning of literature, one of the key questions that you need to continually address is what does it mean to "learn literature." Your definition of what it means to learn literature will influence the kinds of assessment tools you will use to evaluate student learning. For example, you may define learning literature to mean acquiring facts and knowledge about literature—the characteristics of the short story or Romantic poetry—or critical concepts used to analyze literary text—the difference between metaphor and simile. If this is your conception of learning literature, as did Nicole's cooperating teacher, you may then turn to quizzes, worksheets, or tests to assess student knowledge about literature or critical concepts. You may ask students to identify the names of certain characters or authors, settings for texts, or definitions for certain concepts—point of view, setting, symbol, theme, and so forth.

One limitation of this conception of learning literature is that it focuses simply on a "knowing that" aspect of learning literature—whether students know that there is a difference between a first person and a third person point of view. Although students need to have certain knowledge about the texts they are reading and critical concepts, what is more important is their ability to apply that knowledge to texts—the "knowing-how" aspect of learning literature. Although a student can demonstrate that she can define the difference between a metaphor and a simile, it doesn't necessarily mean that she knows how to apply that knowledge to texts. Moreover, if you employ assessment tools that focus primarily on recall of knowledge about literature, then you may end up focusing your instruction on covering information or concepts.

Furthermore, "correct answer" quizzes, tests, or worksheets provide little or no opportunity for the expression of individual open-ended responses. Because students know that they will be tested for "correct" and "incorrect" answers to questions such as "who are the main characters" and "what is the setting," they respond to texts by attending primarily to facts. By focusing their attention on trying to retain the "facts," students perceive their own unique responses as irrelevant to "getting a good grade" and becoming more dependent on you for the "right answer," positioning you as the knowledge dispenser.

It is often the case that tests are typically graded according to a group norm. This means that half of the students, unlike Lake Wobegone, in which all of the students are "above average," presumably score "below average." As a result, the less-able students remain at the bottom relative to the "top" students. They may then adopt negative self-images as students, believing that they are "poor readers" or "poor writers"—negative self-images that undermine their confidence in their ability to respond. Evaluating students according to "correct answers" on a bell-curve system based on group norms may undermine your attempts to engage students who assume that they are not "good students" or "good readers."

In contrast to norm-based evaluation in which students are evaluated as "below average," "average," or "above average" in their peer group, you may employ criterion-based evaluation in which students evaluate against themselves over time based on specific criteria. For example, if students who are not all that motivated or engaged with literature know that they will be evaluated in terms of the improvements they make over time based, for example, on the amount they write in their journal, they may then be more motivated to improve over time.

What, then, should be the purpose of evaluation? We believe that evaluation should provide students with (a) a description of what they are doing and how well they are doing when they respond to literature, (b) a blueprint for potential improvement in their responses over time, and (c) ways of self-assessing so that they determine what they need to do to improve.

ALTERNATIVES TO "CORRECT ANSWER" TESTS

One important purpose for evaluating literature is to determine students' ability to formulate and develop their own interpretations. There are several assessment tools you can use to evaluate students' formulation and development of their interpretations as alternatives to "correct answer" tests.

Journal Responses.   You can evaluate students based on informal journal responses to texts. In evaluating their entries, you need to stress the disparity between informal and formal writing, focusing on characteristics fostered by informal writing. If you are simply using journals to foster fluency or expression of ideas, you may not want to evaluate students' journals because to do so may undermine their willingness to express themselves if they are concerned about being evaluated. If you are going to evaluate journals, you need to make it clear to students that you are using journals as "academic journals" for the purposes of evaluation. As we discuss later in this chapter, you then need to specify the criteria you are using to evaluate their responses. With younger students, you may simply want to focus on entry length, whereas with older students, you may emphasize their development or elaboration of their entries, as well as the originality or insightfulness of their interpretations and their ability to define connections between texts or apply certain critical lenses. If you give students specific journal writing prompts, you can base your criteria on that prompt. For example, if students are responding to a short story, you may ask them to describe the characters' motives or reasons for their actions in the story and what those motives or reasons suggest about their larger agendas or plans. You could then evaluate students' entries in terms of the number and specificity of their descriptions of characters' motives or reasons and their ability to use those descriptions to define characters' agendas or plans. If students are engaged in dialogue-journal exchanges, you may evaluate the amount and quality of their partner's responses.

Formal Essay Writing.   You may also evaluate students using essay tests or interpretive essays that determine their ability to employ certain types of interpretive strategies or critical lenses. For example, if asked to infer a story's thematic meaning, students would then be evaluated on whether they actually infer a theme or hypothesis, as opposed to simply summarizing the story, and then develop that theme or hypothesis in terms of material from the text as well as other related ideas, perspectives, and texts.

As we noted in Chapter 6, your prompts for such essays should clearly specify the type of skill or strategy you want students to employ. For example, if you want students to infer the theme of a story, you may word your prompt as "Formulate what you perceive to be the thematic meaning of this story," as opposed to "Interpret the story." You could provide students with the criteria by which you would evaluate their answers, for example, telling them that, "I will be evaluating you on your ability to go beyond simply retelling the story to infer the story's theme."

You may also evaluate students on the amount and quality of their self-assessment and revision. For example, students' use of extensive revision and self-assessing represents learning to critically examine their own drafts, learning that needs to be included in evaluating their writing.

Creative Writing and Hypermedia Productions. You may evaluate students' creative writing of stories in terms of the students' development of characters or events through the use of specific descriptive details or dialogue that serves to portray these characters or events. You could evaluate their poetry in terms of their uses of titles, originality, voice, figurative language, rhythm or rhyme, or white space, as well as their amount and degree of revisions. And, in evaluating their hypermedia productions (PowerPoint™ presentations, Web sites, etc.), you could evaluate students' ability to link together images, texts, music, sounds, and video clips in ways that reflect an original interpretation of the text or a critical stance on the themes or topics examined in the hypermedia production.

Classroom Discussions. You may also evaluate students' classroom discussions in terms of students' use of certain discussion skills—their frequency of participation, their ability to formulate an interpretation, provide support for their interpretation, restate others' interpretations, pose counterinterpretations to these others' interpretations, ask questions to the group, define an emerging consensus, define links to other texts or resources, and adopt certain critical lenses. You can also evaluate their ability to function in different discussion-literature circle roles—as facilitator, leader, critic, and so forth, as well as the frequency, originality, and insightfulness of their contributions.

To evaluate her students' use of inquiry strategies in large-group literature discussions, Sharon Eddleston whose discussion techniques were described in Chapter 5, employed the following rubric (Beach, Eddleston, & Philippot, 2004):

5: This discussant accepts responsibility for making meaning out of literature. He/she consistently demonstrates a careful reading of the text and makes insightful comments that significantly contribute to our understanding of a reading. The discussant refers to specifics from the class text and compares and contrasts that text to related texts, personal experiences, and social and cultural issues. A respectful listener who avoids monopolizing the conversation, he/she sometimes pulls together and reflects on ideas that have surfaced in the inquiry discussions and may also ask relevant follow up questions, thereby pulling other students into the discussion.

4: Although speaking less frequently than the discussant described above, this discussant shows growth in the willingness to express responses. He/she has the ability to explain ideas clearly and to connect those ideas to others being discussed. This discussant may clarify a specific point being discussed or elaborate on specific examples from the text. Body language and eye contact also indicate a substantial involvement in the discussion.

3: Speaking occasionally, this discussant may primarily respond on a personal level to the text ("I liked it," "I didn't . . ."), perhaps supplying some textual evidence for this point of view. The discussant's remarks may be insightful but they tend to be brief. Or, the discussant may speak often but say little that adds significantly to our understanding of a text, and may, in fact, primarily repeat what others have already said or be difficult to follow.

2: This class member says little. This discussant's few remarks may be inaccurate, unclear, or too brief to be helpful. Little textual support is offered; there is little evidence that the student has read the text carefully or at all. Or, the student may belittle other speakers' remarks, monopolize the conversation, interrupt other speakers, ignore their remarks when speaking, or talk to those seated nearby rather than to the whole group.

1: The student says nothing and appears uninterested in the class discussions, according to his/her body language. Or, the students may appear interested in the discussion, but, for whatever reason, does not join in it. (pp. 149–150)

Drama Activities.   You can evaluate students' ability to employ skills in their drama activities, for example, their ability to use language and nonverbal behaviors associated with adopting different roles, spontaneously improvise new directions, interact with peers based on the drama's unfolding development, draw on interpretations of a text to create a drama, and reflect on the meaning of a drama in a postdrama discussion.

USE OF CRITERIA IN JUDGING STUDENTS' WORK

Underlying any evaluation of students' work is some implied judgment about quality. Unfortunately, many of the judgments made about student work in the form of grades or statements such as "good work" mean little to students. Students therefore have no clear sense of how to improve their work because they have no clear sense of the ground rules on which they were judged. When Olympic divers receive scores on their dives, they know the reasons for a high or low score based on very specific criteria associated with the type of dive they attempt and the degree of difficulty associated with that dive. To help demystify judgments about students' work, you need to provide them with reasons for your judgments—why, for example, their interpretation of *Of Mice and Men* did not measure up to your expectations.

Your reasons for your evaluations are based on specific criteria as to what constitutes effective versus less effective work particular to a specific assignment (Broad, 2003). Rather than drawing on generic criteria often readily available on the Web, it is important to define specific criteria based on the unique demands of your assignment.

These criteria communicate to students what you value in their responses—what you hope your students will achieve in your classroom based on a hierarchy of effective versus less-effective responses. For example, based on what they value in journal responses, Kooy and Wells (1996) formulated criteria that range from "Stage I" responses in which students simply summarize the text, make improbable predictions, fail to pose questions, cite stereotyped responses, and confuse the text and the story; to Stage III responses in which students explore different levels of meaning, formulate interpretations and predictions based on textual analysis, explore character motivation, draw connections to other texts, recognize reasons for writers' choices, and examine the relations between their own beliefs and those expressed in the text.

To define criteria for a specific assignment, you consider how you would judge their use of particular interpretative strategies or applications of critical lenses. For example, in an assignment on Herman Melville's (1967) story, "Bartleby the Scrivener," you ask students to explain why Bartleby consistently rejects any and all requests to do certain things with the response "I would prefer not to" by citing a number of different reasons for his actions related to both his traits, beliefs, and goals, as well as his role in his workplace and town. Because you are asking students to explain a character's actions based on specific types of reasons, you would also provide them with the criteria based on your expectations: "You will be assessed according to your ability to formulate a number of *different reasons* based on *specific evidence* from the story related to both Bartleby's traits, beliefs, and goals, and his role in his workplace and town." Note that the criteria contains two indicators of success—the number of different reasons—students need to provide more than one reason, and the level of specificity of their evidence or examples—students need to cite specific evidence or examples from the text in formulating their reasons.

In giving assignments to his high school students at Hopkins High School, Hopkins, Minnesota, David Williams employs what he describes as template writing assignments that specify criteria unique to writing in a particular form or genre. David argues that providing students with a template actually fosters students' exploration:

> A template writing assignment is a stylized writing task that dictates form. The assignment handout gives students itemized expectations, which will also be used as the grading criteria, clearly articulating the writing task through narrative expectations that may include an outline or prompts for specific paragraphs or sections. Because the form is dictated, the teacher is able to focus responses to the students' writing on their content—summary, analysis, interpretations and insights—using margin notes to credit insightful interpretations and pose questions which may urge new ways of thinking or perspectives on their thesis.

American Dream Unit Project.   For a final project in a unit on the American dream in a joint social studies and American literature course, David's students had to create a narrative piece of historical fiction. In that writing, students explored the concept of the "American Dream" by looking at a period and an event in U.S. history through the eyes of a fictitious first-person narrator character, portraying how that event affected the lives of the people who lived through it.

The students portrayed their narrator's version of the event as a witness or participant in the event, as well as how the historic event affected their lives, and how their experiences were related to the concept of the American Dream. Students therefore had to provide historic references to the period and location, and capture in a compelling manner the narrator's direct or indirect experience of the event.

Because this was a relatively complex assignment, David provided students with specific criteria that would be used by five different readers evaluating their writing—the social-studies teacher, David, two classmates selected at random, and the student writer reading with an adult outside of school. Criteria related both to the story and use of the writing process: unity of protagonist, antagonist, conflict, and climax; use of characterization; development of characters; a plot—introduction, development, and resolution; a discernable theme; a consistent narrative voice; original fiction; title which is relative to the story; use of varied text types—narrative, descriptive, expository, dialogue; purposeful use of language, word choice; and a wholistic image of the story from the reader's perspective.

Evaluators then judged the stories based on the following weighted point system on a scale of 1 (*low*) to 4 (*high*); these ratings were then multiplied by the points for a particular feature; for example, if a feature had 3 points, students could receive a maximum total of 12 points. (The points and possible totals are noted as follows):

WRITING PROCESS

1. points from Benchmark Quality Checks: Note taking and Organization (× 10) 40
2. drafts with evidence of revisions and proofreading corrections; drafts attached to one copy of the final draft (× 2) 8

STORY CONTENT

1. clear and direct thematic connection to the American Dream concept (× 7) 28
2. the narrator character is developed throughout the text of the story (× 5) 20

3. accuracy of historical information (× 3) 12

4. quantity of historical information is sufficient to create full, believable, and appropriately germane images of setting, context, and events (× 4) 16

5. weaving fiction and history together: fictional narrator character and information fit together into an historical context (× 3) 12

6. reflects aspects of a narrative text: characters, plot, conflict, climax (× 3) 12

READER RESPONSE CRITERIA

1. unity: narrative story maintains focus (× 5) 20

2. compelling nature of the story (ho-hum vs. wow) (× 5) 20

COMPOSITION CRITERIA

1. purposeful use of language; word choice (e.g. dialect in dialogue) (× 3) 12

2. appropriately balanced use of text types: narrative, descriptive, expository, dialogue (× 2) 8

3. complete sentences organized into paragraphs with a focus (× 3) 12

4. transitions and flow of storyline (× 2) 8

5. composition mechanics: spelling, punctuation, grammar & usage (× 3) 12

FORMAT CRITERIA

1. story is presented from first person perspective (× 1) 4

2. bibliography: list of at least 4 sources of 3 different types—1 copy attached to one final draft (× 2) 8

3. title (and subheadings within text if appropriate) (× 1) 4

4. passages of paper that reflect historic information from your research are italicized (× 1) 4

5. final drafts of paper are turned in on time (× 2) 8

6. appropriate length (minimum 4 pages / 1500 words) (× 2) 8

7. typed / double spaced, 1" margins, 12 point type, readable font (× 1) 4

Well-designed template writing assignments should clearly articulate to students what is expected and how they will be evaluated. By itemizing content grading criteria, and the possible points assigned to each, students can see what aspects of the writing task are most important. The grading criteria for a writing task and the rubric for the task should be essentially identical, using the same narrative language; by clearly articulating each criteria, and by using the same language on the grading rubric, the teacher can align the assignment with the evaluation.

A prescribed template for written responses to literature can minimize the students' anxiety in using forms and can free the student to express ideas within the template; the student is no longer trying to demonstrate mastery of forms but instead is able to express ideas more freely. Using template writing assignments frees students to engage in critical thinking, constructing their own meaning from their interaction with the text, and considering the relation and connections between their personal stories and experiences and the external stories of literature or history. This shifts the focus of the writing task to one of exploration and self-expression rather than on adherence to form.

Devising Scoring Rubrics.   Based on your criteria, you may also develop scoring rubrics that specify particular aspects or dimensions of responses associated with an assignment. These different dimensions are usually set up as a hierarchy of three or four performance levels based on a continuum with descriptors such as (3) *exemplary/distinguished/ exceeds expectations*, (2) *meets expectations/proficient/competent*, or (1) *novice/emerging/ need more work*. To ensure that students understand these descriptors, it is important to specify attributes in the work that represent these different levels of performance related to a specific assignment. (Although you can draw on some of the many prepackaged, generic criteria available on the World Wide Web, e.g., http://www.Rubicon.com, or use the "six-trait scoring system," one limitation of these rubrics is that they are too generic—they are not based on criteria operating for your specific assignment.) To assess his students' writing of a short story, in another course, David Williams developed the following rubric:

> 4—exceeds expectations: demonstrates ingenuity; internalization of concepts; usage of story aspects is strong, accurate, original, detailed, clear, logical, and explored; understanding of nuances
> 3—fulfills all expectations: demonstrates thorough knowledge of concepts; usage of story aspects is accurate, studied, clear, and logical
> 2—falls short of expectations: demonstrates competent knowledge of broad concepts; usage of story aspects is accurate, general, implied, and obvious
> 1—meets minimal standards: demonstrates awareness of broad concepts; usage of story aspects is absent, unclear, misused

To formulate rubric dimensions for a particular assignment, define what would represent a superlative performance on that assignment, and then what would represent the poorest performance on that assignment. These can serve as your four- (or three- with three levels) and one-level dimensions. Then, define what represents one step down from superlative, but still meets your expectations—this serves as your three-level (or two-) dimension. Finally, consider what represents one step up from a one-level—a reflection that a student is going beyond a poor performance, but still has not met your expectations or needs more work on the assignment.

Developing Criteria and Rubrics for Interpretive Strategies

The following are examples of some criteria and rubrics related to formulating and verify interpretations:

Defining Consistent Patterns in Characters' Action.   Students interpret certain consistent patterns in characters' actions implying those characters' beliefs, traits, and goals. For example, in responding to *I Know Why the Caged Bird Sings* (Angelou, 1969), students learn to infer Angelou's beliefs, traits, and goals—that she believes that she has a certain sense of agency, that she is highly persistent and determined, and that she wants to achieve success against all odds.

> Criteria—Students are able to define patterns in characters' actions and infer related beliefs, traits, and goals.
>
> 3: Exemplary: Notes consistent patterns in actions; infers detailed descriptions of beliefs, traits, and goals based on those patterns.
> 2: Proficient: Notes some patterns; infers some beliefs, traits, and/or goals based on those patterns.
> 1: Needs work: Infers actions, but few patterns; does not infer beliefs, traits, or goals.

Contextualizing Characters' Actions.   Students interpret the meaning of characters' actions within larger historical and cultural contexts. Interpreting these contexts requires the ability to define certain norms or expectations operating in text worlds that suggest the influence of certain historical or cultural forces. Students learn to infer Angelou's (1969) actions within the larger context of a segregated, racist culture by noting how, for example, the segregated school system, employment, and housing discriminate and marginalize African Americans resulting in inferior schooling, poverty, and substandard or segregated housing. They infer norms reflecting these historical and cultural forces by noting characters' adherence to or resistance of these norms, for example, her experiences in a substandard school, her parents and grandmother's economic status, and her housing situation, as well as the ways in which White male adolescents taunt her grandmother and how her grandmother defies the boys' attempts to position her as an inferior:

> Criteria—Students are able to contextualize actions within larger historical and cultural contexts based on inferences about characters' reactions to norms operating in those contexts.

> Exemplary—Defines the norms operating in the historical and cultural contexts of the texts based on detailed descriptions of characters' adherence to or resistance of these norms; clearly explains characters' actions in terms of these historical and cultural contexts.

> Proficient—Defines the norms operating in the historical and cultural contexts of the texts based on some descriptions of characters' adherence to or resistance of these norms; explains characters' actions in terms of these historical and cultural contexts.

> Needs work—Does not infer norms operating in historical and cultural contexts; explains characters actions only in terms of traits, beliefs, or goals without references to contexts.

Interpret Thematic Meanings. Students interpret thematic meanings based on the value assumptions underlying the story development related to the norms operating in the text world, for example, that Angelou's (1969) grandmother's challenging the racist system represents the ways in which acts of defiance result in historical changes—that change in systems occurs through challenging those systems.

> Criteria—Students are able to interpret larger themes by inferring the underlying value assumptions inherent in characters' actions related to the norms operating in the text world.

> Exemplary—Interprets a theme(s) by clearly defining the value assumptions inherent in detailed descriptions of characters' actions related to the norms operating in the text world.

> Proficient—Interprets a theme(s) by defining a value assumption inherent in characters' actions related to the norms operating in the text world.

> Needs work—Infers characters' actions, but does not define a value assumption inherent in those characters' actions.

Verifying the Validity of Interpretations

In formulating these interpretations, students also learn to verify the validity of those interpretations. Students certainly need to be able to provide supporting evidence for their interpretations because they often simply assume that their interpretative hypothesis is self-evident. Or, their supporting evidence may not actually support their interpretation; it may be irrelevant or insufficient. Or, a student may provide plenty of supporting evidence, but their interpretation could still be invalid. They may mount a lot of evidence to argue that Hamlet is mentally ill, but that doesn't mean that this is a valid interpretation of Hamlet's character.

How then can you determine if interpretations are valid? There are several approaches to verifying or exploring the validity of interpretations. One that is typically voiced by literature teachers is that "you can formulate any interpretation, as long as you back it up with evidence from the text."[1]

As we have argued through this volume, textual meaning evolves out of a transaction between the reading and a text in a context, meaning that resides more than simply "in the text." A student may therefore apply knowledge and experiences that are not, strictly speaking, "in the text" to verify his or her interpretation. This suggests that the familiar admonishment that students need to support their interpretations with evidence "from the text" needs to be modified to include knowledge and experiences from sources other than just the text.

Authorial Intent.   One criterion often used to determine the validity of interpretations is whether an interpretation is consistent with the perceived authorial intent. Readers infer perceived authorial intent or "authorial meanings" by applying their knowledge of literary conventions to determine that an author is deliberately implying certain meanings through the use of textual clues, literary techniques, or narrator's thematic statements (Rabinowitz & Smith, 1998). For example, readers apply "rules of notice"—the ability to notice that an author is using a title, character descriptions, repetitions, dialogue, or endings to signal that these text features are essential for inferring a particular interpretation (Rabinowitz, 1987). They may note that Maya Angelou (1969) is deliberately implying that her grandmother serves as a role model for her through consistent references to Angelou's perceptions of her grandmother's actions. By citing different instances of her perceptions of her grandmother, they are verifying the validity of their interpretation that her grandmother functions are a role model.

However, critics of the notion of using authorial meanings as the basis for verifying the validity of interpretations (Lewis, 2001) note that relying primarily on textual clues implying authorial intent leaves out how readers apply their literary, historical, and cultural knowledge to construct meaning, knowledge that goes beyond simply attending to authorial meanings. In interpreting Angelou's (1969) actions, students draw on their construction of how attitudes toward race, class, and gender in the South influenced characters' practices.

Rather than framing this debate as an either-or binary, we believe that readers rely on both authorial meanings as well as larger literary, historical, and cultural knowledge. But, consistent with our constructivist orientation, we believe that they should not rely solely on authorial meanings as the ultimate test of validity.

How then do you evaluate the validity of a student's interpretation based on his or her use of related knowledge and experience? There are a number of criteria that you can consider.

---

[1]One reason that teachers rely on this maxim is that they may employ only the traditional thesis or support essay assignment typically associated with the five-paragraph-theme format. This familiar thesis or support essay encourages students to focus simply on format—on whether they have formulated a thesis or provided supporting evidence, as opposed to the quality, depth, validity, or relevancy of their thesis or supporting evidence. They may think—"I've stated my thesis and given some evidence, so I must be done." Limiting evaluation of students' interpretive ability solely to thesis or support essays forecloses use of a range of writing tools described in Chapter 6 for exploring texts. Moreover, as Sheridan Blau (2003) found after examining published essays by literary scholars, these scholars rarely if ever employ this thesis or support format, largely because they are exploring a range of alternative, competing interpretive perspectives.

Clarity of an Interpretive Thesis.   In formulating their interpretations, students need to clearly state an interpretive thesis or position. Students may simply state an opinion about a text without framing that opinion in the form of a hypothesis or position statement that will serve as the basis for their essay. Formulating an interpretive thesis serves as the blueprint for organizing the essay. For example, in writing about the play, *Death of a Salesman* (Miller, 1998), a student goes beyond his opinion that Willy Loman is deluded about the reality of his status as a salesperson to formulate a thesis that Willy Loman is deluded by the myth that individual effort and hard work brings success in American society:

Criteria—Students can clearly formulate an interpretive thesis as a hypothesis or position that serves as the basis for developing arguments in their essays.

Exemplary—Students can formulate a clearly-defined, original interpretive thesis that serves as a hypothesis or position for developing arguments in their essays.

Proficient—Students can formulate an interpretive thesis that serves as a hypothesis or position for developing arguments in their essays.

Needs work—Students can formulate an interpretive thesis that is not clearly defined enough to serve as a hypothesis or position for developing arguments in their essays.

Analysis of Purposes for Uses of Literary Techniques.   Students may also be interpreting or evaluating an author's uses of literary techniques, for example, Shakespeare's uses of metaphors to portray love in his sonnets. In doing such analysis, students often simply cite examples of uses without interpreting the purposes for why those techniques are being employed to develop characters, story lines, settings, or themes. They may catalogue the metaphors of love in Shakespeare's sonnets, but not examine the purposes for using those metaphors to portray the complex ambiguities associated with love. Defining the purposes for using techniques requires students to connect the uses of techniques with the larger themes and ideas portrayed in a text. In evaluating students' uses of literary techniques, you are determining their ability to interpret the purposes for those uses related to the larger themes and ideas portrayed in a text:

Criteria—Students clearly define reasons for use of certain literary techniques related to developing characters, story lines, settings, or themes.

Exemplary—Students define specific reasons for use of a certain literary technique(s) related to detailed descriptions of how those techniques contribute to developing characters, story lines, settings, or themes.

Proficient—Students define a reason for use of a certain literary technique(s) related to descriptions of how those techniques contribute to developing characters, story lines, settings, or themes.

Needs work—Students describe the use of a certain literary technique(s) without reasons for the use of those techniques related to developing characters, story lines, settings, or themes.

Relevancy of Evidence, Knowledge, and Experience.   Another criterion has to do with the extent to which the evidence, knowledge, or experience cited is relevant to building their argument. Students need to consider the degree to which their evidence, knowledge, or experience is relevant to formulating their case—what counts as relevant evidence in terms of their ability to select relevant evidence, knowledge, and experience and then connect it to their claim. For example, a student is arguing that Taylor Greer, the main character in Barbara Kingsolver's (1998) *The Bean Trees*, is seeking a sense of stability in her life that was lacking in her youth through creating bonds with friends as part of an extended family network. To support her argument about Taylor's need for an extended family, the student draws on her own experience about the need for a supportive family relationship to bolster her case for Taylor's need for an extended family. You then would determine whether that related experience is relevant to the student's building her case:

> Criteria—Students provide supporting evidence, knowledge, or experience that is relevant to and clearly connect to their claims.

> Exemplary—Students provide ample supporting evidence, knowledge, or experience that is highly relevant to and explicitly connected to making their claims.

> Proficient—Students provide supporting evidence, knowledge, or experience that is relevant to and is connected to making their claims.

> Needs work—Students provide supporting evidence, knowledge, or experience that is often not relevant to or not connected to making their claims.

Sufficiency of Evidence, Knowledge, or Experience.   Students may cite supporting evidence or related knowledge and experiences for their arguments either from the text or from their knowledge and experience, but not cite enough evidence to build a convincing case for their position. For example, a student is arguing that Gatsby in *The Great Gatsby* (Fitzgerald, 1991) believes that he can use his "new wealth" to buy his way into the "old wealth" moneyed society of Daisy by citing one instance of Gatsby purchasing cars and clothes under the assumption that these would impress Daisy. Although the student's argument may be valid, this one bit of evidence is not sufficient to support her argument.

Similarly, students may apply knowledge about the world of the "Roaring 20s" to argue that Gatsby's actions were shaped by a capitalist economic system in which the "new wealth" was supplanting the traditional "old wealth" of Tom and Daisy. However, if they fail to fully explicate their description of that time period, then they are not able to adequately use that knowledge to build their case:

> Criteria—Students provide sufficient supporting evidence, knowledge, or experience to build their case.

> Exemplary—Students provide ample, sufficient supporting evidence, knowledge, or experience to clearly build their case.

> Proficient—Students provide enough supporting evidence, knowledge, or experience to build their case.

> Needs work—Students provide insufficient supporting evidence, knowledge, or experience so that they do not adequately build their case.

Defining the Significance of an Interpretation.   Students also need to be able to frame the significance of their interpretation, generalizing about what they have learned from a text to the larger world. Rather than simply defining a didactic lesson, students formulate reasons for the significance or importance of their interpretation. For example, a student argues that Nora Zeale Hurston's (1998) novel, *Their Eyes Were Watching God*, demonstrates how Janie, the female protagonist, learns to reject male authority and patriarchy, leading her to develop her own beliefs about the world. The student also argues that her interpretation of the text applies to the larger value of understanding people's development in terms of their ability to formulate their own beliefs about the world. In evaluating students' ability to define the significance of their interpretation, you are determining their ability to generalize about the importance of their interpretation to understanding the world:

> Criteria—Students define the significance of their analysis by applying that analysis to the larger world context.
>
> Exemplary—Students clearly define the significance of their analysis by explicitly and extensively applying that analysis to the larger world context.
>
> Proficient—Students define the significance of their analysis by applying that analysis to the larger world context.
>
> Needs work—Students do not define the significance of their analysis by applying that analysis to the larger world context.

USING FEEDBACK TO FOSTER STUDENTS' REVISION AND PERSPECTIVE-TAKING

In this volume, we have emphasized the value of fostering perspective-taking through drama, talk, art work, or writing. In assessing students' written responses, you are encouraging them to exploring alternative perspectives so that they are continually interrogating their own interpretations, leading to rethinking, elaborating, reformulating, or rejecting their interpretations.

Providing "Reader-Based," Descriptive Responses.   In responding to drafts of students' writing through written, audiotaped, or conference feedback, it is important to provide specific "reader-based" feedback that describes how you are processing and engaged with the students' writing (Elbow, 1998; Johnston, 1983). In providing "reader-based" feedback, you describe the experience of

1. Being engaged, entranced, moved, involved, disturbed, struck by, intrigued, puzzled, and so forth: "When I read the description of the . . .".
2. Acquiring too much information, description, or different ideas or points associated with being overwhelmed, lost, besieged with, drowning in, swimming upstream, and so forth.
3. Not having enough information or description associated with being underwhelmed, missing something, or wanting more.
4. Predicting or expecting subsequent text development associated with being "caught-up-in," anticipating events, expecting support or evidence, and so forth.

Based on your reactions, the student then uses your or a peer's perceptions to identify problems and formulate possible revisions that address these problems. This means that rather than judging the student's writing, as in, "this part isn't well organized—it lacks coherence," you are letting the students make that judgment through reader-based feedback like, "I'm confused here—are you saying that Odysseus was not a true hero?" In some cases, if students have difficulty making that judgment, you may then need to step in and identify what you perceive to be the problem, for example, noting that they haven't clearly defined their overall interpretive thesis.

You also need to prioritize your feedback, selecting those aspects of the text that need more work, for example, a consistent inability to providing supporting evidence for claims (Ferris, 2003). Focusing on a few specific aspects that need the most work is preferable to overwhelming students with a lot of feedback about a lot of different aspects. Students can then concentrate on those aspects, for example, their ability to infer characters' goals based on defining patterns in their actions.

And, you need to frame your feedback by considering a student's ZPD (Vygotsky, 1981) so that you are not overwhelming students with overly-sophisticated responses, but, at the same time, you are challenging them in ways that lead to seminal changes. To determine a student's ZPD, in addition to information from a log or record about their difficulties making interpretations, in a writing conference, you can pose some questions asking them to interpret the text about which they are writing, questions that reflect different levels or difficulty of interpretation: "What is happening in the story?" "What are some reasons for the characters' actions?" "What do the characters' actions suggest about that character or that character's world?" "What do you perceive to be a theme of the text?" Once you sense that a student is having difficulty answering these questions, for example, questions about the larger meaning of the characters' actions, you can then make a rough estimate of the student's upper level of his or her ZPD. By defining that upper level, and, knowing that he or she can readily make relatively less difficult interpretations, you can focus on challenging that student and encourage him or her to exceed that level. At the same time, you need to recognize that the student's ZPD may vary across different texts and assignments.

In giving reader-based feedback, you are also providing students with a metacognitive vocabulary for reflecting on what they are doing in their writing by using certain concepts or descriptions of interpretive strategies that they use to self-evaluate their responses. For example, when you note "I really liked the way you make a connection between the world of *1984* and the world of *Brave New World* to develop the theme of how people can be easily controlled by propaganda," you are providing students with a vocabulary such as "make a connection" or "develop the theme" that they may use in self-evaluating their responses. You may also describe instances in which you are having difficulty with understanding a student's responses or interpretation by stating "I'm having difficulty following your argument" or, "when I read your thesis, I normally expect some supporting evidence, but I'm not finding any." When students reflect on their writing on their own, they may then think about the expectations that they need to add supporting evidence.

It is also important that you provide positive comments about specific aspects of students' interpretation. Your praise serves to bolster students' confidence in their ability to formulate their interpretations. Vague statements such as "good interpretation" do not provide students with information as to their effective use of particular interpretative strategies. Rather, you want to identify specific aspects of a student's interpretation worthy of praise, for example, evoking the sufficiency criterion, "I liked the fact that you provided a number of different reasons for your position."

Fostering Self-Assessment. By providing feedback on the relevancy, sufficiency, and significance of their interpretations, as well as their analysis of literary techniques and exploration of alternative perspectives, you are modeling criteria for use in evaluating their interpretations. By recognizing the limitations of their interpretations, particularly as they are composing, they perceive the need to revise their interpretations, by, for example, adding more supporting evidence or analysis of the purposes for using literary techniques. For example, a student is reflecting back over her rough draft of an essay arguing that there are differences between the adults in the novel, *Holes*—that they are not all evil characters driven by greed to find the buried treasure. She realizes that for those characters whom she identities as "good" characters, she has not provided enough explanations as to why they are "good"—that they actually care about the boys or want to support them. This leads her to revise her draft, adding in material about positive aspects of these "good" adults.

To foster self-assessment for high school students, you can ask students to review specific sections of their drafts and address questions such as the following:

1. Is the evidence, knowledge, or experiences you cite relevant to your position?
2. Have you provided more than one bit of evidence to support your claims in this section?
3. What is the larger significance of your interpretation?
4. What are some alternative perspectives to your position and how would you refute those perspectives?

Teaching Peers to Give Feedback.   Many students, particularly middle school students, are unlikely to self-assess on their own unless they receive some feedback from teachers or peers suggesting the need to self-assess. This points to the importance of having students engage in one-to-one or small-group peer feedback during the composing process. Unfortunately, without some instruction, students have difficulty providing productive peer feedback. They may not focus on specific aspects of a draft, providing only generalities such as, "You're making a good point about the story." Or, they are reluctant to say anything that might be interpreted as a negative judgment, out of concern for their social relationships with peers. Or, they do make judgments that are counterproductive and undermine a writer's confidence.

To train peers to give feedback, you first need to practice giving specific, reader-based feedback, training that coincides with your literary response instruction:

1. Model your own use of reader-based feedback by using short texts, poems, or drafts, showing students how to use think-aloud or descriptions of your interpretations of a text.
2. Have students practice doing think-alouds in pairs with one member of the pair serving as the audience who provides encouraging prompts.
3. Model your own use of feedback questions designed to foster a writer's self-assessing related to defining his or her intended meanings, aspects of the text that do not convey their intended meaning.
4. Have the entire class practice giving feedback to one student's draft, with the student responding to peer feedback by self-assessing his or her draft and noting possible revisions; have the student note which comments were particularly useful in fostering self-assessing.
5. Model ways of concluding conferences with some clearly-agreed-on revisions that they will make in their draft.
6. Have students work in pairs or small groups on giving feedback, concluding these conferences with a written list of further revisions.

In modeling feedback techniques, you also note reader's and the writer's techniques in the conference:

Reader techniques

1. Let the writer begin the conference so that the writer discusses his or her concerns and questions (e.g., "what works?" or "what needs work?").
2. Make a positive comment about some specific aspect of the writing; all writers need praise.
3. Discuss the paper topic itself so that the students can share their ideas that might be used in the paper.
4. Determine the phase of development of specific parts of the draft—some parts may need a lot more prewriting; other parts may require major revisions, whereas other parts are at the editing phase.
5. Consider the writer's basic interest in or attitude toward the assignment or writing in general; if there's a problem with the assignment or the context, deal with that broader problem.
6. Provide "reader-based," descriptive comments about your reactions and experiences so that you let the writer make the judgments.
7. If writers are having difficulty judging or predicting revisions, you may need to model that process or make the judgment for the writer.
8. Don't overwhelm writers with too much feedback; they will be able to process only so much.

Writer techniques

1. Listen to the feedback without being defensive or without trying to rationalize what you did; take in the information, using helpful comments and discarding less helpful comments.
2. Share your intentions, goals, and perceptions of the social context to help define disparities and dissonance between intentions and text.
3. Use the reader descriptions to assess how your text is being processed to judge its effectiveness and predict necessary revisions.
4. Share your revision ideas with the reader to "test the water"; determine what you will do to improve the draft after the conference is over.

Responding to Response Journals or Online Chat.   In responding to students' journals or their online chat, you may frame reactions to create an ongoing dialogue with the student, reactions that can also serve to model the dialogue-journal or chat-room sharing between students. In responding to her eighth-grade students' letters to her, Nancie Atwell (1998), for instance, reacts with her own return letters. She notes that in her letters, she responds on a personal level:

> The letters I write to my kids about their reading and mine are *personal* and *contextual*: what I say in my half of the dialogue comes from my knowledge of how a student reads and thinks, or what a student understands or needs to know. My responses also grow from my own experiences as a reader. When I categorize my letters to kids, they seem to do three things, *affirm*, *challenge*, or *extend* a reader's response. (p. 283)

Atwell avoids responding about personal topics or posing a lot of questions that could be perceived as test questions. Instead, she tries to ask genuine questions based on her own curiosity:

> When I ask questions, they're sparked by curiosity, not a sense of obligation. If we really want to take kids inside books, our one good question will probably be some variation on the questions that are implicit or explicit in our conversations with friends about literature: How did you feel about the book? Why? What did you think of the writing? What was the author up to? (p. 284)

In posing these questions, you are also modeling question-asking strategies for students, which they internalize over time, leading them to pose questions about their writing on their own, leading to elaboration of their writing.

All of this involves assessment as a form of inquiry in which your feedback serves to further engage students in inquiry about their beliefs, ideas, concepts, and strategies. In addition to writing comments on students' journals, you can also respond to students' journals with audiotaped comments on cassette tapes or digital files (using digital recorders) or through online chat exchanges. Using oral feedback or online chat encourages you to adopt a more conversational feedback mode in which you pose questions or provide your own insights about a text than does responding simply to students' interpretations. One advantage of online feedback is that students can save copies of feedback to refer back to at a later point when revising their drafts. (Free, noncommercial chat room sites such as http://www.tappedin .org, http://www.nicenet.org, or http://www.moodle.org, that create or e-mail transcripts of online feedback to students, provide them with a record of comments that they can then use for working on their revisions.)

DETERMINING STUDENT LEARNING IN YOUR CLASSROOM

In engaging in assessment as inquiry, you are continually reflecting on what you hoped your students would learn from participating in your class activities, and if not, what things you might have done differently to improve or change those activities. One technique for determining what students actually did learn is to ask them to write "exit memos" in which they freewrite for 5 min at the end of your class—"what did you learn today in class?" Or, in their journal entries, you could ask students to reflect on what they learned on a daily or weekly basis.

You can then analyze the students' writing or reflect on your observations to ascertain what students learned. You may note a wide variation in students' perceptions of their learning, variation that reflects difference in their preferred learning styles, interest, attitudes, agendas, and social connection to others. You could then use your analysis of these individual differences to shift subsequent activities to accommodate for these variations in learning. For example, if you notice that a high percentage of your students responded positively to your use of drawing or art work in response to a text, reflecting a visual and artistic "learning intelligence" (Gardner, 1993, 2000), you may then continue to include drawing or art work in future activities.

You can also have students write about their learning goals. In her reading workshop approach, Nancie Atwell (1998) asks students to set goals for their reading each term. At the end of the term, students complete a written self-evaluation that asks questions about those goals and students' breadth of reading as well as asks questions about the specific literature activities they did. For example, students are asked, "What will you take away from our study of Shakespeare's life and times, from the plays and sonnets?" (p. 308). Students also set goals for the new term at this time, which may include reading more often independently, expanding the list of favorite authors or genres, understanding more about a particular literary element, or many others.

Students could also write "entrance memos" in the beginning of a class or unit in which they freewrite about their learning goals: "What do you want to learn from engaging in this project or activity?" For example, in a short story unit, students may formulate a goal of learning to write a stream-of-consciousness story based on their reading of similar stories by James Joyce and others. The students would then be asked to specify the ways in which they plan to demonstrate how they have achieved their goal, by, for example, writing a story that contained specific instances of stream-of-consciousness writing techniques. You can then use students' goal statements for devising criteria to evaluate their work. For example, if a student noted that he or she wanted to learn to write a stream-of-consciousness story to show how a narrator was thinking about events, you could devise the following criteria:

- Criteria—Students will write a stream-of-consciousness story that portrays a narrator's beliefs and attitudes through the ways in which the narrator was thinking about events.

USING PORTFOLIOS TO EVALUATE GROWTH AND REFLECTION

In addition to evaluating students' individual writing, you are also evaluating changes over time based on comparisons of their work in the beginning, middle, and end of a course or your student teaching period.

One assessment tool for evaluating student growth is the portfolio (Kent, 1997, 2000; Sunstein & Lovell, 2000; Yancey & Weiser, 1997; Yancey, 2004). Portfolios can take two forms. One is a working or process portfolio which is intended to help students keep track of materials and assignments as they move through your course. Students put all of their written work or essay drafts, journal entries, records of books read, and so forth, into a folder.

The product or showcase portfolio is a more formal collection of work chosen by the student with an introduction written by the student explaining his or her growth and reflections about his or her learning over time. Students are increasing their use of digital, Web-based portfolios to display relations among different aspects of their work and that can be readily accessed by you and other students (with the student's permission) (Hewett & Ehmann, 2004). For example, they may display themselves in a Quicktime™ video clip reflecting about a text that also appears on the screen.

One purpose for the product or showcase portfolio is to foster reflection on their learning. It is therefore useful to provide students with prompts for reflecting on what they have learned, how they have changed, and ways to improve. Students also need to formulate their reflections in ways that point to specific evidence in their written responses that document their learning. Because students may have difficulty reflecting on their learning, you need to model that process for them using your own professional portfolio reflections. You also need to recognize that students may not reflect in a genuine, authentic manner, but rather simply go through the motions of reflecting simply to complete an assignment (Sunstein & Lovell, 2000).

For their product or showcase portfolio, students can compare their initial work with later work to describe changes in their learning in terms of growth in their ability to employ interpretive strategies or critical lenses, define connections between texts, or recognize how their beliefs and values are shaping their responses. They may also select certain written responses they consider to be their most insightful or effective and compare those to less insightful or effective responses. And, they may compare their perceptions of different texts read in your course—which texts they most versus least preferred or were most versus least challenging and reasons for those preferences or challenges.

Advantages of Digital Portfolios. One of the primary advantages of using digital portfolios is that students can readily create links between material in their portfolios; the linking itself leads to further reflection (Yancey, 2004). Students can make links between their writing about one text to their other essays or Web pages that lead to reflections about similarities in themes, issues, critical analyses, use of interpretive strategies, or interests in certain authors or genres, as well as changes over time. And, students can create what Yancey describes as a digital gallery with hypermedia links to images, video clips, music, Web sites, or texts that invites multiple ways of reading a student's work by teachers and peers, a different literacy mode from that of print portfolios. Yancey notes the following:

> Digital portfolios can right branch, and then right branch again; they left branch, and they left branch again. Cumulatively and literally, the right and left branches produce a layered literacy that is different from the thesis-and-support literacy of the print model. Depth of thought is created and demonstrated through multiple contexts: evoked verbally, evoked visually, evoked through internal links, evoked through external links. (p. 92)

Unit Portfolios. Students may also create a portfolio for a single unit, in which the portfolio serves as the final project for that unit. For these unit portfolios, students reflect on how they applied the unit topic, theme, or issue to the text(s) read and what they learned from doing so.

Individualized or Free-Reading Portfolios. For students engaged in individualized or free-reading programs, they can record the different books completed, responses to those books, evaluations of the most versus least enjoyable or challenging books, and reflections on growth in their reading interests and responses.

Anthology Portfolios. Students can also create portfolios as selected anthologies of texts they choose as portraying particular topics, themes, or issues, along with commentary or reflections on those texts.

Evaluating Portfolios. You also need to tell students how and why you are evaluating their portfolios as a record of their abilities and development. As with individual essays, you therefore need to provide them with a set of criteria for how you are evaluating their work. By employing a relatively simple category system, you can record information about the students' performances for one or more of the categories listed later. To evaluate an actual student's web portfolio, go to the Chapter 12 link on the Web site and click on activities and "student portfolio":

1. Amount of oral and written response—As represented by the degree of participation in group discussions or the length of journal entries (none, little, some, extensive).

2. Attitude toward expressing response—As represented by the degree of students' perceived enthusiasm about or interest in expressing responses (little, some, high).

3. Ability to use talk or write tools—Mapping, listing, free-writing, role playing, and so on, to express their responses (ineffective, effective, highly effective).

4. Ability to employ interpretive strategies and critical lenses—As represented by students' ability to formulate insightful interpretations or apply critical lenses to texts (ineffective, effective, highly effective).

5. Level or depth of response—As represented by the degree to which students explore or elaborate on their responses or adopt a "point-driven" interpretative orientation (little, some, extensive).

6. Amount of voluntary reading—As represented by the number of books or pages recorded in an individualized reading program (little, some, extensive).

7. Attitude toward voluntary reading—As represented by students' willingness to and expressed enthusiasm about actively seeking out books (unenthusiastic, positive, highly enthusiastic).

8. Degree of defined reading interests—As represented by students' ability to define the nature of their reading interests and their willingness to seek out books consistent with those interests (vague, somewhat defined, clearly defined).

It is also important that students include writings and artifacts in their portfolios that grow out of what happens in the classroom—for example, photos of a drama activity with written captions that describe what they were doing or thinking for each of the photos. By comparing students' performances over time, you could then determine the degree to which students were changing. In so doing, you are helping them reflect not only on their growth up to the present, but also their future potential direction—how they could continue to improve. Having students set learning goals for their future improvement gives them some direction for improving their work.

DEVISING LITERATURE TESTS AND ASSESSMENTS

Beginning in the mid-1990s, with increasingly vocal calls for more "standards" and "accountability" from politicians and business people, schools often opted for test scores on standardized multiple-choice tests as a means of demonstrated "accountability." From the National Assessment of Educational Progress to statewide assessments to the Bush Administration initiative, the No Child Left Behind Act (United States Department of Education, 2002), assessment has permeated all levels of the educational system. Many teachers have found that increased large-scale assessment has had a negative effect on their day-to-day classroom life, particularly when they believe that they have to "teach to the test" in ways that limit exploration of alternative meanings and critical analysis of texts (Kohn, 2000, 2004; Sacks, 2001; Meier et al., 2004).

It is important that you have a solid understanding of testing so that you understand issues of validity and reliability in tests and assessments and the limitations of psychometric models of assessment. It is also important to know how differences in prior knowledge, level of interest or engagement with the text and task, and familiarity with test-taking strategies, influence performance on these tests. And, in exploring options, you also need to understand the purpose and characteristics of portfolio evaluation in writing and reading, as authentic assessment tools for determining students' development and ability to reflect on their learning.

Although devising tests and assessments involves similar concerns, it is important to distinguish between the two. For the purpose of this chapter, we are defining tests (or exams) as measures of students' individual performances. In contrast, assessments attempt to measure the performance of groups of students within a school, district, or state without reference to the identity of individual students. Knowing how well students perform as a school, district, or state provides some indication of how well schools are teaching. However, given the increased use of assessments as part of the "accountability" movement, there are also limitations to these assessments that you should understand.

THE STANDARDS MOVEMENT

The standards movement received the blessing of the federal government in the 1990s and was codified into law with the No Child Left Behind legislation (United States Department of Education, 2002). This legislation required states to formulate standards for different subject matter areas and to conduct annual assessments in reading, math, and science to determine if students were achieving these standards. Schools need to demonstrate "annual yearly progress" in test scores in all demographic areas and also document that teachers are "highly qualified" to teach in their subject matter area. Schools that do not demonstrate progress must then send students to private tutoring services or other schools. Many schools and districts, as of 2005, had difficulty making progress because of cuts in funding at the state and federal levels.

One problem with the standards movement is the potential standardization of teaching literature according to one homogenized model of instruction. Although teachers may have always attempted to achieve certain implicit standards, they were given the professional autonomy to devise their own curriculum that reflected their particular interests or engagement with literature. Although such individuality can be problematic, mandating that all teachers adhere to the same standards, about which they may have had little input, may undermine teachers' sense of their own professional autonomy to experiment with their own unique instructional methods (Meier, 2003; Ohanian, 2001).

Variations in State Standards.   It is important that you become familiar with your state standards in English and language arts because your school and district in which you are student teaching will need to align their curriculum and assessments to those standards. Different states have formulated standards in quite different ways, reflecting differences in philosophies for what they want students to demonstrate.

In some cases, state standards attempt to specify particular content or objectives that students are expected to acquire or achieve, formulations that are more appropriate for local district or classroom curriculum guides that provide teachers with activities for implementing larger standards. These standards can be read as prescriptions for how to achieve standards, but without a clear sense of the larger purposes or objectives. They also encourage teachers to adopt a transmission model of instruction in which the teacher's role is to simply provide students with information or concepts and then test students on whether they have acquired that information or particular concepts. (See, for example, the Virginia Standards of Learning versus the NCTE Standards for high school literature on the Chapter Web site under "activities," as well as in Chapter 3.) One reason that standards are sometimes formulated in terms of low-level thinking is the assumption that standards need to be "measurable" on some assessment instrument. That means that standards that involve complex, higher order thinking skills that are difficult to assess are often not included, not because they may not be valued, but because they are not "measurable," particularly on multiple-choice tests of students' knowledge of facts and concepts. As a result, much of what remains are "content" standards having to do with the ability to "identify" or "know." This use of high-stakes testing places heavy emphasis on objective measures such as test scores that are then used to determine the success or failure of schools in an impersonal mode that avoids the complexity and values operating in those schools. However, these seemingly "objective" measures such as multiple-choice standardized reading tests may not necessarily be valid measures of a range of different reading practices or abilities; they may also be measures of students' cultural capital associated with social class background (Kohn, 2000).

Classroom Testing.   In devising a test for use in your classroom, you need take into account what you have taught the students and develop a test based on what you hope they have learned. In evaluating tests like these, you may compare students' individual performances with their previous performances to note changes. In an assessment, comparisons with previous performances are generally based on combined group scores. However, remember that in a large-scale district or state-wide assessment, what your own students may have learned from you cannot always be taken into account.

Many classroom literature tests consist of factual-recall, multiple-choice, or short-answer questions. Students are asked to identify the "main character," "setting," or "theme." The purpose for these tests is often to determine whether a student has read a text. As we previously argued, these tests undercut a response-centered orientation. They encourage students to adopt an "information driven" orientation in which they read primarily to extract information rather than for enjoyment or for formulating their own responses. And, having to answer a series of short-answer questions may actually fragment students' attention rather than encourage them to formulate global hypotheses (Marshall, 1987).

Another purpose for tests such as the "weekly quiz" is to determine if students are doing the reading or to provide students with continuous rewards for their performance, assuming that students will not read or perform without such rewards. As we discussed in the first part of this chapter, students can be evaluated on a range of phenomena other than tests—their journals, papers, classroom performance, and so on.

We therefore recommend that tests be used sparingly. When they are used, such tests should encourage students to formulate their own responses, rather than recalling "correct answers." Tests should also, as often as possible, be open-book in format. These shift the focus from memorization to formulation of response. In developing open-ended test questions, consider employing "essential questions" that focus on basic aspects of learning literature such as "What makes a great book?" (Wiggins & McTighe, 2005). These essential questions can lead to what Wiggins and McTighe (2005) describe as "unit questions" such as "Is science fiction great literature?"

LARGE-SCALE LITERATURE ASSESSMENTS

In contrast to classroom tests, school, district, or state assessments are designed more to determine if students are learning in ways that are consistent with school, district, or state standards. However, if those assessments are "high-stakes" assessments, then they are also used to determine if students can graduate from high school. One rationale for conducting an assessment is the need to base decisions about curriculum and instruction on some rela-tively objective information. If an assessment indicates that students are having difficulty responding, teachers can justify the need for instruction in formulating responses. Another rationale for conducting assessments is the need to justify the benefits of a literature pro-gram. If administrators, school board members, or parents want to know what students are learning or gaining from the literature program, teachers may cite assessment results docu-menting the fact that students are learning to express their own responses, employing a range of response strategies, or developing positive attitudes toward reading.

Issues of Validity and Reliability in Literature Assessments. In examining different types of literature assessment, you need to consider two basic aspects of these assess-ments—their validity and reliability. There are a number of different forms of validity, and considerable debate about the meaning of the validity of an assessment having to do with, for example, whether the assessment actually captures students' "literary understanding." Rejecting earlier notions of validity as a property of an assessment itself, Samual Messick (1998) argued that there are actually different aspects of validity associated not with the property of an assessment, but with what the results generated by that assessment mean (Brualdi, 1998). Messick is particularly concerned with whether these results adequately represent the knowledge, interpretive strategies, or attributes being measured by the as-sessment related to what is currently known about, for example, students' ability to under-stand or interpret literature. If, for example, an assessment consists of multiple-choice items having to do with identifying uses of literary techniques, it could be argued that this assessment focuses too narrowly on just one aspect of interpreting literature, and that there is a need for a wider range of different assessment tasks that match up with all of what is currently known about students' knowledge, interpretative strategies, and attributes (for examples of some items, go to the Chapter Web site under "activities").

One major limitation of these multiple-choice items is that they are based on a simplistic model of understanding texts that ignores the complexities of a reader's purposeful trans-action with a text. A reading test may involve an artificial, invalid version of the complexi-ties of real-world reading, serving more as a measure of students' test-taking skills or their prior knowledge than something called "reading ability." It is often the case that students can apply their prior knowledge to select the "correct answer" without even attending to the test item passage. And, as some minority groups change, some of these tests may also be biased in favor of the background cultural knowledge of White, middle-class students.

And, when these assessments are developed to determine norms for what constitutes high versus low scores, the student population used to norm the test may not represent the particular balance of students in many schools and districts taking these assessments. How-ever, the much larger group of students could be scored as "failures" because they are com-pared with the much smaller, limited, initial sample group used for the development of norms (Farr & Tone, 1994).

Given these and other limitations, some states have included more open-ended tasks. For example, in the Massachusetts assessment, students are asked to write an open-ended response to a particular question, like the question designed for the 2003 assessment: "Cre-ate another title for 'Sonnet 26' and explain why your title is appropriate. Use information from the poem to support your answer."

Another major limitation is that faulty generalizations are made about students or schools based on test results. Students may be labeled as "low level" or "struggling read-ers" based on one test score on one kind of reading text in one, highly artificial testing con-text. Although they may have difficulty reading that kind of text in testing context, when they are reading the sports page or instructions for a computer game, they may not be "struggling." And, if a school's average test scores do not improve, that school may then be labeled as "failing," when in fact, test scores often fluctuate for reasons that have little to do with students' actual performances or are due to population size. And, if school districts adopt a "pay for performance" plan and determine teacher salaries based on increases in their students' assessment scores, such plans assume that it is possible to judge the quality of teachers' instruction based on these assessment scores. Given the pressure to avoid being labeled as "failures," administrators may pressure teachers to focus more on preparation for specific tests, a focus that may result in teaching how to give "correct answers" (Taylor, Shepard, Kinner, & Rosenthal, 2003). This focus on test preparation based on a standardized approach to learning can have adverse effects on ELL or special needs students who need alternative learning approaches (Horn, 2003).

In focus-group discussions with teachers in an urban and a suburban high school in Massachusetts, Catherine Luna and Cara Turner (2001) asked teachers to reflect on the influence of the 10th-grade Massachusetts Comprehensive Assessment System English test on their teaching. One teacher, Jane, noted that the test "doesn't reward students for creativity. It does for prescription and formula in their answers . . . I know the rubric they use for grading is in some ways skewed toward formulaic writing rather than creative writing" (p. 84). Another teacher, Stanley, argued that doing poorly on the test has a negative influence on students' self-concept: "I don't think it's a good thing to tell students that because there are some things you can't do that; you can't have a diploma, that your sole value is wrapped up in succeeding on a test that says you can basically do college work. . . . These students will be dropping out" (p. 84). Ronald noted that the test "has become a monster already, an absolute monster in the minds of students" (p. 84). Although the teachers noted that the tests did not necessarily change the way they teach, they noted that they had to give up important material to make time for content that would be on the test. For example, Sarah noted that she focused more on literary definitions: "I'm taking the work that's being done around literary terms much more seriously in my reading classes, and I'm not spending the same amount of time to help kids get an understanding of what they're reading" (p. 84). They were also concerned that the teachers or their schools were being blamed for low test scores, scores that could result from factors beyond their control.

One of the basic assumptions behind the use of high-stakes tests is the need to enforce sanctions on "failing schools" and to no longer let students "fall through the cracks." The further assumption is that by adopting high-stakes testing, schools will improve, that is, more learning will occur. If states' high-stakes testing actually improves student learning, then one would expect that test scores on other national tests would also be increasing. However, a study of the impact of high-stakes testing in 18 states found no increase in Scholastic Assessment Test, American College Testing, National Assessment of Educational Progress, or Advanced Placement test scores over a 4-year period (Amrein & Berliner, 2002).

In arguing that testing actually lowers standards, Donald Graves (2002) said that testing should not be equated with teaching:

> Testing is not teaching. Testing has deprived teachers of the time they need to teach the skills that will enable children to become better readers. Teachers know that the curriculum is already inflated and testing itself has become a major subject. Many systems have layers of tests (local building, system, state, national). The time lost while taking tests does not include the preparation for taking them. How can reading, learning, or any other aspect of curriculum be improved with such a significant loss of teaching time? I repeat: *Testing is not teaching.* Teaching is choosing the right skills based on astute observation of the child's needs. Further,

good teachers know the interests and passions of their students and know how to put good books in their hands. Observe the language used to discuss the teaching of reading. Notice the emphasis on scores and standards with very little discussion about the ideas that can open the lives of children. We have forgotten the purpose behind reading and have treated it as an end in itself. (p. 9)

The Relation Between Assessment and Instruction.   All of this points to the importance of relating assessment and instruction in a positive, productive manner, so that assessment is "authentic" to the kinds of learning occurring in classrooms (Bauer & Garcia, 2002; Wiggins, 1990). The National Council of Teachers of English (1996) posited that "authentic assessment is derived from what students are doing daily in the classroom. At a minimum, it includes samples of students' work, recorded observations of their learning processes, and students' evaluation of their own processes and products, along with teacher evaluation" (p. 6). These "authentic assessments" should also provide information about "student strengths and weaknesses, regardless of performance level, in contrast to standardized tests, which typically highlight the strengths of high performers and the weaknesses of low-performers" (Bauer & Garcia, 2002, p. 464).

Some states, such as Kentucky, Nebraska, and Vermont, have successfully demonstrated that performance assessment and portfolios of student classroom work can be used to provide teachers and parents with valid profiles of student progress. One advantage of the Kentucky portfolio-assessment model is that the teachers' instruction is directly aligned with how students are assessed. The Kentucky program should serve as a model for devising assessments that are consistent with higher order standards.

George Hillocks's (2002) research on the impact of states' writing tests on writing instruction in those states indicates that the type of assessment determines the focus and type of instruction employed. He found that in the four states (New York, Texas, Illinois, and California) that were employing a traditional writing assessment, teachers were teaching the five-paragraph format, with little attention to the composing or thinking processes, audience analysis, inquiry strategies, or writing across the curriculum. In contrast, in Kentucky, which employs a portfolio writing assessment, teachers were focusing more on teaching process writing, rhetorical strategies, revision skills, and writing in different contexts.

Reliability.   Another consideration in examining assessment is that of reliability—does the same assessment generate the same results for the same students across time? If students take an assessment at time A and then again at time B, do they yield the same results? If, not then, serious questions could be raised about validity, whether the assessment provides a valid measure of students' performance if the results vary markedly across time. Related to scoring of writing, reliability also refers to whether judges agree on their scores, agreement generally set at 75%. Without agreement, the final scores may not be considered reliable.

Performance assessments that include open-ended writing tasks or portfolio assessment are typically questioned as lacking reliability—both in terms of reliability across time and being generalizable and are therefore perceived as not useful for determining accountability. Reliability in classroom assessments can be increased if teachers ask other teachers to score several random assessments from a batch. Furthermore, results of the Vermont and Kentucky portfolio scoring reliability indicate that decent reliabilities can be achieved. The limitations of performance assessment need to be weighed against the positive influences of assessments that are consistent with the kinds of instruction promoted in this book.

Portfolio Reflection: Evaluating Student Work

Based on your experiences in being evaluated for your work and evaluating students in your microteaching or practicum work, list some assessment tools for evaluating students' written and oral responses to literature. Reflect on how you will use these tools to help students develop in their literary interpretation and production. Then, in your teaching portfolio, include a draft of a student's work, your comments on that draft, and the student's revised draft, indicating the revisions made due to your feedback. Then, reflect on how your feedback led to these revisions; if possible, include the student's comments about how your feedback helped him or her revise the draft.

Online Additional Activities, Links, and Further Reading

Go to the textbook Web site, Chapter 12, and to the generic link, "assessment," for additional activities, links, and further reading.

13

Text Selection, Censorship, Creating
an Ethical Classroom Environment,
and Teacher Professionalism:
How Do I Stay in Control,
Out of Trouble, and Continue
to Develop as a Teacher?

Chapter Overview

- The complications of choice.
- The ethical classroom.
- Issues of censorship.
- Teachers' professional development.

CASE NARRATIVE: TRINA TEACHING THE NOVEL *SPEAK*

In a message to the members of her student teaching Listserv, Trina writes about Laurie Halse Anderson's (2001) book *Speak*, which deals with the social rejection that follows when a young girl calls the police after being raped at a party by a popular upperclassman. Trina begins as follows:

Can we please have a spot on Dialogue (the electronic discussion server) for a discussion about *Speak*? I finished it last week and it is sooo frustrating because I have no one to talk about it with! Anyway, this weekend I went to Target and just by chance saw the book *Cut* on the shelf. It is a YA book about a high school girl in an institution because she is a cutter. I read the back of the book and the review excerpts mentioned *Speak*, so I thought it might be interesting to read as a companion piece. (I am about halfway through it and it is good . . .)

So when I was checking out, the cashier, an older woman, scans the book and remarks about how good it is. I am not one for small talk, especially in a crowded Target, but I am a sucker for book talks, so I mentioned *Speak* and that I am in an English Education program. I thought she might be a teacher or something . . . She looked at me and said, "Well, I do that, so that book was really helpful for me in therapy." It took me a minute to understand what she was saying and about a million images passed through my head. Like I said, I'm not one for small talk, but then again this wasn't exactly a small issue now was it? I had to find out more, though I didn't know really what I expected to learn in thirty seconds at Target . . . so I said, "I know this is kind of personal, but did reading that help you deal with it better?" I know that's why she told me the book was good, but I needed to say something! She said that it opened up dialogue between her and her therapist, and even though she was older than the main character, she related well to the situation.

I learned in about 3 minutes just how much books help people. I think it's something I take for granted because I enjoy reading so much, but I never really considered how they can inspire healing . . . My experience also proved the importance of giving kids things to read with which they can relate! I know it's something we always talk about as literacy educators, but I sometimes thought that maybe kids might feel depressed or angry if a book hit too close to home. This woman helped me realize that sometimes that risk could prove vital to a student's survival.

See you Wednesday, Trina

Later that week, Kelly, the director of the weekly student teaching seminar, responded with her own suggestions on another topic:

Two YA texts on teenage pregnancy that I like are: *Make Lemonade*, by Virginia Euwer Wolff and the title story in Cynthia Rylant's collection, *A Couple of Kooks and Other Stories about Love*. Students read the former in literature circles on several occasions, including once with the school nurse as a co-participant (an article about this is in the ALAN Journal from a while back—I believe it's online). I gave the latter, which is about a teenage couple preparing to give their baby up for adoption, to an 11th grade student who had announced her pregnancy, and she liked it a lot and found it realistic. In that case, I made it clear that my decision to give her the story was not a veiled suggestion to give the baby up—not a decision I wanted to be involved with—but rather a way to provide her with access to others' thoughts about anticipating a baby (one of the most beautiful aspects of that piece is the way the couple shares what is special about them with the unborn child). For more recommendations of young adult lit. related to particular issues/problems, you may want to check out Joan Kaywell's *Using Literature to Help Troubled Teenagers Cope with Family Issues*. There's a series of these books from Greenwood Press—some of them are more focused on particular topics. While I'm a little uncomfortable with the bibliotherapy approach some of the authors, it does provide a good list of titles. Hope this helps! Kelly

THE COMPLICATIONS OF CHOICE

As this opening conversation reveals, teaching literature involves far more than putting books in the hands of adolescents and hoping they will somehow work their magic. True, books can transform lives. For example, a book such as *Speak* (Anderson, 2001) portrays the rape of a ninth grader, Melinda, at a summer beer party, which results in her retreating into alienation, depression, and silence associated with a fear about speaking out about her rape. Janet Alsup (2003) argues that a book such as *Speak* can serve as a basis for discussing the difficulty of speaking out about issues such as rape, silencing, and power:

> Students may raise the point that if Melinda had spoken about her rape earlier, she might have received help sooner and hence avoided some pain. They might also mention that her peers, her supposed friends, did not try very hard to talk to her or understand her plight. They might also discuss whether they have ever seen anything violent occur at parties, and if so, whether alcohol was a factor. . . . In the most extreme of situations, silence not only isolates adolescents, it can actually put their lives at risk. . . . the Discourse of resistance, such as Melinda's loud "NNNOOO!!!" as she fights off Andrew Evans at the end of *Speak*, as well as her eventual decision to narrate her story to her art teacher ("Me: Let me tell you about it," p. 198) has power and can have a positive effect on material reality. (pp. 162–163)

But, as a teacher, you must make thousands of crucial decisions, each one limiting or supporting those transformations in fundamental ways. The literature classroom is a delicate ecosystem of texts, teaching strategies, human circumstances, choice, and constraint. If you were to take a moment to reread the opening dialogue, you'd probably notice many points of tension or conflict. Following are just a few that you may face in your own teaching.

Literature Teaching Is a Zero-Sum Game.
For every text we place on our classroom shelves or show on a screen, there are millions that have not been chosen. In examining what to exclude and include, we wonder the following: are there enough women authors and protagonists? What about people of color? Are a variety of ethnic and cultural perspectives represented? Which texts are safe to teach and which might get us into trouble? These are just a few of the decisions we face each day.

Your Textual Choices Open Your Classroom to a Plethora of Sensitive Issues.
It's perhaps a cruel irony that in this litigious age, books for teenagers now cover such a host of controversial topics. What if a parent or community member decides that teen pregnancy, for example, is an unsuitable topic for an English classroom? Or what happens if a student chooses a text for independent reading that we haven't screened for "objectionable content"? Many times, it's impossible to know just what an outsider might consider objectionable. For example, one middle school teacher had just finished reading the novel *Freak the Mighty* by Rodman Philbrook (2001) with her seventh-grade students. As postreading experience, she showed what she thought was an innocuous film version of the novel, only to be called to the office a day later by an irate parent demanding to know why any teacher would show a film with a "PG" rating to middle school students. Litigation aside, our most important questions always begin with our students. Are they emotionally ready to handle delicate issues? Might a book be a catalyst for an action they could later regret? Although books themselves do not necessarily change students' behaviors, like Kelly in the opening dialogue, we must make sure that, by placing a book in a pregnant student's hands, we are not appearing to recommend an action as life altering as giving a baby up for adoption.

You face powerful consequences when you make books available to vulnerable adolescents. If you decide to sponsor a book about a topic like racism, homosexuality, or rape, how do you manage the delicate, and sometimes dangerous, issues that arise when kids of color, gay kids, and possibly even victims of abuse are right there in our classroom? And, how do you design a curriculum that takes students beyond books, preparing them for the host of ethical and moral decisions they must make each day of their future lives as members of a democratic society? To address these questions, you have to make choices based on considering the larger moral and ethical dilemmas that all teaching must address.

THE ETHICAL CLASSROOM: WHAT IS IT?

In an ethical classroom, you provide literature and other language experiences that teach students to act in socially responsible ways—to recognize differences and challenge discrimination, to read texts critically, recognizing their social and political implications, and to go beyond the texts to challenge and change the world in which they live. Jim Burke (2003) remarks as follows:

> You can't teach a book like *Huckleberry Finn* without asking if the book is racist, if Twain is racist, if I, as the teacher who invited it into the classroom, am racist. It means stopping the class when the Armenian student hurls the insult at the Turkish student, or when one gender generalizes about another in a hurtful way. It means seeing cheating as an opportunity to discuss moral capacity and personal integrity by explaining how they have diminished the currency of their word in my realm from that point on.
>
> I'm not naive about all this. Just because we talk or I say something doesn't mean anything changes. However, it is the discussion of what is right and wrong, the growth of moral intelligence that counts. We cannot make our students act "better," but we can put them at the center of such essential conversations and, by allowing students to occupy the lives of others—through literature—help them develop the habit of asking of themselves such questions. (p. 78)

Burke (2003) is asking you to consider how you can make your English classroom a site of transformation, whether this means using literature and nonfiction to challenge discrimination and stereotypes at the level of individual students or opposing unethical practices in the larger community and world. This is a tricky and complicated process, requiring you to address some of the following questions.

WHAT IF I GET INTO TROUBLE? CENSORSHIP AND TEXT SELECTION

In her wonderful essay, "How Mr. Dewey Decimal Saved My Life," Barbara Kingsolver (1996) writes as follows:

> If there is a danger in . . . all the works of . . . authors who've been banned at one time or another, the danger is generally that they will broaden our experience and blend us more deeply with our fellow humans. . . . Most alarming, to my mind, is that we the people tolerate censorship in school libraries for the most bizarre and frivolous of reasons. Art books that contain (horrors!) nude human beings, and *The Wizard of Oz* because it has witches in it. Not always, everywhere, but everywhere, always something. (p. 57)

The American Library Association's Web site (http://www.ala.org) yields a curious and amazing array of books that have been challenged in recent years, from the Harry Potter series (wizardry, magic) to *Roll of Thunder, Hear my Cry* (racism; Taylor, 1991), to *Bridge to Terabithia* (offensive sexual content, occultism and Satanism; Paterson, 1987). (For other links related to censorship, go to the Web site.)

People censor books and other texts for a variety of reasons. They worry, for example, that children will face issues for which they aren't prepared; that they will learn things that get them into trouble or harmful circumstances; that they will encounter provocative or hurtful words, images, stereotypes; or that they will question the religious or moral beliefs of the family.

It is also the case that books for adolescents can be censored by librarians simply by placing these books in "adult" sections of the library, as opposed to the adolescent sections. A study of the reasons for placing these books in the "adult" section found that librarians objected to the following (in rank order): profanity, heterosexual activity, homosexuality, sexual activity deemed immoral or illegal, religion or witchcraft, violence or horror, rebellion, racism or sexism, substance use or abuse, suicide or death, crime, crude behavior, and depression or negativity (Curry, 2001).

One of the basic assumptions behind censorship is that reading books causes adolescents to adopt certain practices or attitudes—that reading about characters engaged in sex will cause adolescents to want to engage in sex, as well as change their attitudes about sex. For example, William Broz (2002) reports on objections to a story "Supper" by Leslie Newman, in a collection of stories about adolescent gay and lesbian experience, *Am I Blue: Coming Out From the Silence* (Bauer, 1994), that was in a middle school library in a small, rural community. He notes that members of the public and parents objected to specific descriptions of a 14-year-old character's first sexual experience with an older adolescent girl. He describes a school board meeting at which objections were voiced by two thirds of the 200 people attending the meeting:

> One speaker was a retired high school English teacher who objected to the book asserting that the statistics it offered of 1 in 10 adolescents contemplating suicide were false and that the book could lead students into a homosexual lifestyle. A local Christian minister stated that children are confused about sexuality because adults are confused. He said that the book promotes the gay agenda. He also said the book misleads children about the potential for family acceptance of a gay family member contending that while there are grandparents and sisters who accept homosexuality, they are not the rule. He closed his remarks by condemning homosexuality as a lifestyle. A middle school parent stated with frustration that she did not think the book was appropriate for her two middle school daughters to read. She went on to say that while she could control her daughters' reading material at home, her daughters could go to the middle school library and check out a book like *Am I Blue* without her knowing. She concluded by saying the book was pornography. One parent of a 13-year-old said that readers visualize what is in books in their minds as if they were watching a film. She asked those present if they would want middle school students to view such a scene on film. She said that she would vomit if she saw the scene on film. One speaker charged that the book could be used as a tool by pedophiles to pray on children. Many other speakers offered similar points of view. (p. 346)

Broz (2002) notes that others at the meeting defended the story. One parent argued that the book was not required reading and that no student was forced to read it. She said that the fear that students would read books and be overly influenced to do what was in them was unfounded, asserting that familial and cultural influences had more effect on children's beliefs and behaviors than the books they read. She contended that the job of adults is "not to keep the world from students but to help students form a value system and live by it" (p. 348). At the end of the meeting, a majority of the school board voted not to remove the book from the library.

The persons at the meeting who objected to the story are assuming a cause-and-effect relation between reading about lesbian practices and changes in adolescents' practices or attitudes—as one parent argued that visualizing characters' behaviors means that her daughter may then adopt behaviors she finds objectionable. This argument assumes that readers are highly impressionable blank slates, failing to recognize that what readers bring to a text shapes the meaning of that text. Adolescent readers bring a set of practices and attitudes to their reading that are shaped by their family, peer, community, school, and workplace experiences. However, to assume that reading texts per se causes changes in those practices and attitudes fails to acknowledge that impact of what adolescents bring to texts. As one of the book's defenders noted, adolescents are influenced far more by family and culture than by their reading.

Although censorship is most often associated with conservative groups such as The Eagle Forum, it's important to realize that censorship emerges from the left as well as the right. Witness the spate of challenges to books by authors like Maya Angelou, Mark Twain, and Toni Morrison for "objectionable language" or "racist" content. According to surveys cited by the American Library Association (http://www.ala.org), the vast majority of challenges are by parents for reasons stemming from (in order of frequency) sexually explicit material; offensive language; unsuitability for a particular age group, occult themes or Satanism; homosexuality; and the promotion of "a religious viewpoint." It's easy to see how any text, classic or contemporary, could be challenged by a zealous parent or community member on the basis of one of these concerns. Perhaps this is why many teachers are reluctant to stray very far from texts that have been taught for generations or are on the district's required reading list. As a result, the classic high school canon consists of relatively "safe" books, excluding many more books that might be more engaging for students.

The potential threat of censorship has a strong influence on literature anthology textbooks, particularly those adopted on a statewide basis. Because Texas, a relatively conservative state, is one of the largest of the statewide adoption states, textbook companies are wary of including texts in their anthologies that may evoke the ire of well-organized conservative groups in Texas that monitor the textbook-adoption process. As a result, textbooks rarely contain "controversial" texts that challenge the status quo, White, Protestant, middle class values consistent with those values espoused by these conservative groups. This means that writers of color are often only included as token representatives of certain racial groups. Based on his analysis of textbook content, Arthur Applebee (1994) found little evidence of diverse cultural perspectives: "It is hard to imagine that the handful of selections by African American, Hispanic, Asian, or Native American authors, for example, are sufficient to leave students with a unique sense of the substance and appeal of these alternative traditions, but neither are they well-integrated into a larger, common tradition" (p. 56).

JUST WHAT ARE THE RIGHTS OF PARENTS AND COMMUNITY MEMBERS?

Certainly parents in a democracy have a right to know what their children are reading and to request alternative choices. Although English and language arts teachers are probably opposed to most forms of censorship, there may be occasions where even they might draw the line at another teacher's choice. Consider what you might do if a teacher sponsored a religious text that violated your belief in the separation of church and state or a text with gratuitous sex and violence. Wouldn't it be within your rights to challenge that text and ask for an alternative?

Although parents and community members have a right to know what their children are reading and doing in classrooms, neither they nor we have a right to dictate what happens to all students on the basis of narrow religious or political principles. Perhaps it's helpful to distinguish between text selection and text censorship. The former is based on critical judgment whereas the latter is often born out of exclusion and fear.

The question you must always ask yourself is this: Are my choices made out of sound critical judgment, or out of fear that someone else may challenge my teaching? In an age of mounting litigation, you need to consider the legal and political consequences of your acts. There are horror stories about teachers being removed from classrooms, denied tenure, or sued on the basis of a single "objectionable" text in their curriculum. David Wilson (1997) acutely portrays the dire professional and personal consequences he suffered after publishing an annotated list of books for gay and lesbian teenagers in a national journal. This leads us to the next question.

HOW CAN I PROTECT MYSELF?

In considering this question, your first stop should be at the National Council of Teachers of English censorship page (http://www.ncte.org/about/issues/censorship). Here you will find a host of helpful information and resources, including NCTE and International Reading Association (IRA) position statements on intellectual freedom, action plans and strategies for preventing and confronting challenges, ideas for resolving challenges once they have been made, and contact information for a variety of state, national, and international organizations interested in intellectual freedom. For example, the NCTE currently publishes over 200 rationales for commonly challenged books in CD-ROM format (NCTE, 1998). (See also the Web site for other electronic and print sources for preventing and combating censorship.)

In general, when you decide to sponsor a text that you think might be objectionable (fiction, nonfiction, film, or other nonprint media), you might consider the following strategies:

1. Look for rationales and reviews of the text in sources like NCTE or ALAN (The Assembly on Literature for Adolescents). These rationales and reviews provide a justification for using a book based on its literary quality and significance.
2. Involve others in your decision. Talk with your department chair, principal, and parents about your choices.
3. Consider sending home a reading contract that parents must sign whenever a student chooses a book for independent reading. Encourage parents to read and talk about books along with their children.
4. Organize a book selection committee made up of concerned parents, community members, and other teachers.
5. Be ready to offer alternatives to any text you select for whole class reading.
6. Make sure that your department has developed a formal written complaint form (we've provided a sample on our Web site).

The fact that people need to complete a written complaint form can reduce the emotional aspects of reacting negatively to texts perceived as offensive, sacrilegious, racist or sexist, or sexually explicit. Because most school districts have a formal mechanism for handling complaints, this written complaint should first go to a school administrator who may consult with a parent or you, so that you do not need to initially deal with such complaints.

Self-Censorship.   It's important, however, to understand why teachers commonly, and often unwittingly, act as censors in their own classrooms. In his summary of several large-scale studies of literature teaching in American secondary schools conducted by the National Center on Literature Teaching and Learning, Arthur Applebee (1991) listed the three main reasons why teachers are reluctant to choose books from alternative traditions in their curriculum:

1. Teachers remain personally unfamiliar with specific titles
2. Teachers are uncertain about the literary merit and appeal to students
3. Teachers are worried about possible community reactions. (p. 31)

Self-censorship is a far more insidious form of censorship—one that often lies beneath our consciousness—and that is what Rudolfo Anaya (1991) has called "the censorship of neglect." In an article by the same name, Anaya argues as follows: "Our diverse communities are rightfully demanding to be included in the curriculum of language and literature courses. . . . Our challenge is to incorporate into the curriculum all the voices of our country" (p. 20). He urges us to ask "some tough questions." For example: "Exactly what literature are we teaching in classrooms? Who writes it? What social reality does it portray? Who packaged it for us? How much choice do we really have as teachers to step outside this mainstream packaging and choose books? Who provides the budget? Who calls the shots?" (p. 19).

As Anaya (1991) so eloquently argues, the inclusion of nonmainstream authors into the curriculum is an issue for all teachers—those in ethnically and racially homogeneous schools, as well as those that are more diverse. He concludes as follows: "The issue, of course, is not simply one of insuring that students read works from their own heritage. It is an issue of finding the proper balance among the many traditions, separate and intertwined, that make up the complex fabric of society in the United States" (p. 32).

A fundamental responsibility in creating an ethical classroom is selecting texts that represent this vast and rich heritage for all students, regardless of the cultural, ethnic, and racial makeup of the schools in which we teach. As a student teacher or untenured 1st-year teacher, you may be reluctant to select texts that may be perceived as controversial by your colleagues, parents, or community members. However, you also need to recognize the fact that as a classroom teacher, you are protected by the important legal concepts—students' "right to know" associated with their own and your intellectual and academic freedoms (*Adler v. Board of Education*, 1952). This concept of academic freedom posits the idea that students have the right to know certain things and that teachers have the academic freedom to teach those things (Brown, 1994). The NCTE statement, "The Students' Right to Read" (http://www.ncte.org/about/over/positions/level/gen/107616.htm), grounds students' and teachers' rights based on these legal rights to make choices that should not be limited by others attempting to impose their own parochial perspectives on students' need to learn about the world:

> The right to read, like all rights guaranteed or implied within our constitutional tradition, can be used wisely or foolishly. In many ways, education is an effort to improve the quality of choices open to all students. But to deny the freedom of choice in fear that it may be unwisely

used is to destroy the freedom itself. For this reason, we respect the right of individuals to be selective in their own reading. But for the same reason, we oppose efforts of individuals or groups to limit the freedom of choice of others or to impose their own standards or tastes upon the community at large.

The right of any individual not just to read but to read whatever he or she wants to read is basic to a democratic society. This right is based on an assumption that the educated possess judgment and understanding and can be trusted with the determination of their own actions. In effect, the reader is freed from the bonds of chance. The reader is not limited by birth, geographic location, or time, since reading allows meeting people, debating philosophies, and experiencing events far beyond the narrow confines of an individual's own existence. (National Council of Teachers of English, 1977)

Given the value of the students' right to know about the world, you might ask yourself if you unwittingly participate in what the NCTE The Students' Right to Read (1977) calls "the censorship of neglect." Take a look at your list of classroom texts and ask yourself a few questions:

1. How often do I limit students' access to nonmainstream cultures by sponsoring only one text by an "accepted" author from the traditional literary canon? For example, is Langston Hughes the only African American writer in my curriculum?
2. Do I attempt to balance the gender of authors and protagonists in my textual choices?
3. How often are nonmainstream texts relegated to shorter works like short stories or poems, whereas longer works like novels and plays are by European authors?
4. How often are texts from outside the Eurocentric tradition presented as "alternative" selections for independent reading rather than whole-class texts?
5. Are characters from nonmainstream cultures represented simplistically rather than multidimensionally? If my students see themselves and their cultures represented in my curriculum, what kind of images do they see?
6. What steps do I take to dispel the myth that there is one literature representative of a racial, ethnic, or cultural group (i.e., "African American," "Chicano," "Asian American" Literature) as opposed to a rich and complicated mix of literary, stylistic, and cultural influences?

You may also consider having students themselves explore issues of censorship through a large-group role-play activity in which a parent has lodged a complaint against a book or story your students may be reading or may have read that it should be removed from the library because it is inconsistent with their town's "community values," a legal basis for censorship. The parent brings his or her complaint to a school board meeting at which various participants discuss whether the book should be censored, leading up to a final school board vote. In this activity, students select roles as school board members, parents and students (for or against censorship), a principal, teachers, townspeople, newspaper book reviewer, local minister, priest, rabbi, and so forth. Students prepare their arguments related to the influence of the text on behaviors and attitudes related to their perceptions of the town's "community values." They then each testify in front of the school board, who then votes, giving reasons for their vote. After the role play, students step out of their roles and examine the pro–con reasons for censoring the text, reflecting on the validity of those reasons.

We realize that grappling with issues like censorship and text selection may seem like a difficult and overwhelming task. Most of the time, if you have done your homework, kept parents and administrators involved, collaborated with other faculty members, and offered alternative selections, censorship will not pose a significant problem for you. Similarly, creating an inclusive curriculum is a lifetime process—one that involves constant questioning. And although we'll never completely "get it right," as long as we remain vigilant about whose culture we are excluding and including with our textual choices, we can come closer each day to achieving our goals of equity and inclusion. And then there's another vitally important question.

WHAT ARE YOU WILLING TO GO TO THE MAT FOR?

English language arts teachers often avoid sensitive political and ethical issues for a variety of good reasons. In many ways, our training in literature and language did not prepare us for the Pandora's box of controversial issues that potentially opens each time we sponsor works of literature, whether classic or contemporary. Our visions of the "safe" classroom include rather pastoral images of kids working quietly or collaboratively toward the goal of becoming better readers, writers, and thinkers. Issues like racism, sexism, and homophobia, present a tricky terrain, especially when students who suffer from these abuses and injustices sit in our classroom alongside students who have never experienced them. Yet, consider the cost of not confronting such issues head-on as part of our teaching.

In her graduate course on adolescent literature, one of our authors assigned the book, *Deliver Us From Evie* by M. E. Kerr (1995). The book sparked a lively discussion about what books should be sponsored for whole-class or independent reading and what books should be excluded altogether. As you can imagine, the comments were all over the map. One inservice teacher objected to the book because it portrayed Evie as a "butch." "I would have been more comfortable if she had been less stereotypic," she explained. "I have lots of gay friends, and they're not like Evie. I'd be afraid my students might get the wrong impression of gay people by reading this book." Another argued, "But a lot of my gay friends are *just like* Evie! Stereotypes have some basis in reality or they wouldn't exist, right?" Another remarked, "Yeah, what makes Evie so stereotypic anyway? After all, she works on a farm and has to drive tractors all day. Why wouldn't she be physically strong? And why can't she wear men's clothes? Is the problem with Evie or with society's expectations about what men and women are supposed to look like?" Another remarked as follows:

> Quite honestly, I couldn't see myself teaching this book. By the time my kids get to high school, the costs for appearing to be gay, especially for males, are so high that I'd be afraid this book would only make kids feel uncomfortable and might even incite some violence outside of my classroom. For some reason, the word "gay" is now a synonym for anything weird or unacceptable. I hear kids saying "You're so gay!" and calling each other "faggot" all day long in the cafeteria and in the halls. I'd hate to add to that by sponsoring a book on homosexuality in my classroom. I'd especially worry about kids who are gay or questioning their sexual identity. What will they feel like if somebody uses these derogatory terms in a class discussion?

These concerns reflect the range of sensitive issues that lurk beneath our "official" curriculum. The question is, how willing are you to make them a conscious and visible part of our teaching? Do you really need to confront issues like homophobia head-on, what is the cost of confronting them, and what is the cost of not doing so?

Perhaps the answer to these questions lies in the unsettling comment of Mark, a preservice teacher who is currently observing in a city school: "I hear derogatory terms like 'f—got' and 'n—ger' dozens of times each day by all kinds of kids in the classroom and in the hallways, and I haven't seen one teacher or other adult challenge them since I've been observing in this school." In the discussion that followed, most preservice and inservice teachers felt it was best to either ignore homophobic or racist comments, or, at best, deflect them with humor. As one teacher remarked, "If you make too much of this sort of thing, you'll just make the situation worse." This may be true. But it may be your ethical responsibility to bring issues of hatred and bias to the foreground of your curriculum so that no student is ever forced to suffer for being outside the norm of social stereotypes.

CENSORSHIP AND COPYRIGHT ISSUES WITH MEDIA AND DIGITAL TEXTS

Issues of censorship are not limited to literary print texts. They also apply to media and digital texts: videos and DVDs, Web sites, visual representations, magazines, newspapers, music, and so on. And they apply to students' rights to freedom of expression related to attempts to censor the school newspaper, web pages, drama and video productions, art work, or essays written in a class. Given the importance of including media and digital texts in the curriculum (see Chapter 11), you need to also grapple with ethical issues associated with potential censorship and copyright issues of media and digital texts.

It is important for you to do the following:

1. Learn about your school's or district's policies on use of these texts (see the NCTE "Guidelines for Dealing with Censorship of Nonprint Materials," http://www.ncte.org/about/over/positions/level/gen/107611.htm).

2. Preview materials, particularly videos and DVDs shown to the entire class, so that you are aware of potentially controversial or objectionable material and proactively inform students and parents in writing of your rationale for using this material to achieve your instructional purposes. (Your school district may restrict viewing of R-rated videos and DVDs in the classroom.)

3. Know about district use of filtering software to limit access to Web sites as mandated by the Children's Internet Protection Act (Federal Communications Commission, 2000) that requires all schools and libraries receiving federal funds to use blocking software to restrict access to visual depictions considered to be obscene, pornographic, or "harmful to minors." One study by the Electronic Frontier Foundation (2003) found that for every web page that was blocked correctly consistent with these guidelines, one or more pages were incorrectly blocked.

4. Examine issues of privacy associated with Web use (see "The Parents' and Teachers' Guide to Online Privacy," http://www.classroom.com/community/connection/howto/privacyguide.jhtml). Students need to recognize the risks involved in the sharing of personal information on the World Wide Web, and that it can have negative consequences, particularly when they are engaged in a chat room.

5. Comply with copyright laws related to the use of assigned print texts, as well as media and digital texts consistent with the concept of "fair use." Copyright law limits the degree to which you can make copies of literary texts under the legal concept of "fair use" in educational settings as defined in Section 107 of the Copyright Act of 1976 (United States Copyright Office, 1976). There are four components of "fair use" that you need to consider in determining whether your copying of copyrighted materials constitutes "fair use: (a) the purpose and character of the use, including whether such use is of a commercial nature or

is for nonprofit educational purposes; (b) the nature of the copyrighted work; (c) the amount and substantiality of the portion used in relation to the copyrighted work as a whole; and (d) the effect of the use on the potential market for or value of the copyrighted work (for specific copyright regulations, go to the Web site).

6. Know how to use online literary texts. For more information about literature online, see Browner, Pulsford, and Sears (2000). Most of the texts online are older than 100 years because these texts are now in the public domain; however, there are more recent texts available online (for online literature sites, go to the course Web site).

7. Inform students about ethical issues associated with their own plagiarism of material from the World Wide Web in which they simply lift copyrighted material and insert that material verbatim into their own writing or include material without any citation. Although you can check students' writing for instances of plagiarism using commercial software programs such as Turnitin™, Glatt Plagiarism Screening Program™, MyDropBox™, and Copycatch™, a more productive approach is to make clear the larger principles regarding the problematic use of others' work without acknowledging that use, as well as the dishonesty of pretending that someone else's work is one's own work.

8. Help students critically examine material available on the World Wide Web that is often simply expressions of biased opinions.

9. Recognize that you are still responsible for the kinds of material students access in your classroom, material that parents may find objectionable.

10. Explore with students some of the complex dilemmas associated with limitations of copyright law in a digital age in which users can readily access music, films, and texts for free, raising questions about the role of the music, film, or publishing industry in attempting to protect material weighed against the need to provide artists and producers with remuneration for their work.

Summary.   In grappling with the ethical dilemmas associated with text selection and censorship, it is important to not lose sight of the larger purposes for using these texts—to help students be more aware of the richness and complexity of what Rudolpho Anaya (1991) calls the complex fabric of society in the United States in which expression of a wide range of different cultural and political perspectives and opinions, some of which the mainstream culture will find objectionable, is one of our most cherished values. Barbara Kingsolver (1996) notes the following:

> If there is a fatal notion on this earth, it's the notion that wider horizons will be fatal. Difficult, troublesome, scary—yes, all that. But the wounds for a sturdy child will not be mortal. When I read Doris Lessing at seventeen, I was shocked to wake up from my placid color-blind coma into the racially segregated town I called my home. I saw I had been a fatuous participant in a horrible thing. I bit my nails to the quick, cast nets of rage over all I loved for a time, and quaked to think of all I had—still have—to learn. But if I hadn't made that reckoning, I would have lived a smaller, meaner life. (p. 57)

TEACHERS' PROFESSIONAL DEVELOPMENT

Your success in student teaching and in your first few years of teaching depends heavily on your ability to not only work with colleagues, but to also learn from them as they provide you with support and advice. Doing so involves the following steps:

Find a Teacher or Mentor.   Many schools have mentor programs for new teachers. In fact, some states are requiring that new teachers have a mentor throughout their first years of teaching. If your school does not have such a program, you should seek out an informal mentor.

Mentors are established teachers who know the ropes and how to keep from getting hung with them. Mentors can inform you about the secret unarticulated life of the school, and help you to understand expectations and conventions, like when to hang the attendance sheet outside the door, and that you can't skip a faculty meeting to coach a team, and who the unofficial computer guru is in the school that can help you with your printer problem. The mentor tries to be proactive and to anticipate issues and expectations the new teacher might not understand before the fact.

Peer Coaching.   Peer coaching is a form of mentoring that can work across a school or schools for both established and new teachers (for more information about peer coaching, go to the Web site).

Participation in Professional Organizations and Graduate Training.   There are many other ways to interact with colleagues to share ideas. Attending conferences, both at the local and national level, can be a very exciting and stimulating experience. Taking graduate courses and pursuing advanced degrees gives you the opportunity to interact with college and university personnel as well as other likeminded dedicated teachers.

There are many professional and personal rewards to pursuing advanced studies. All of the authors of this text spent many happy and successful years as school teachers before going on to university careers. We all believe that teachers are the best teachers of teachers, a core belief of the nearly 200 National Writing Project sites across the country that sponsor a summer invitational institute for teacher leaders and a variety of other summer and school-year programs.

Being a student member of the National Council of Teachers of English entitles you to receive journals such as *English Journal* for high school English teachers or *Voices from the Middle* for middle school language arts teachers (http://www.ncte.org/store/membership/new/109491.htm). Being a student member of the International Reading Association entitles you to receive the *Journal of Adolescent and Adult Literacy* for secondary and adult reading or literacy teachers (http://marketplace.reading.org/memberships/IRA_Membership_Main.cfm). And, in joining either of these organizations you are also demonstrating your support for your professional organizations.

Action Research: Conducting Teacher Research

Teacher reflection has been shown to be an essential factor of teacher growth, professionalism, and satisfaction (Burnaford, Fischer, & Hobson, 2001; Lankshear & Knobel, 2004; Sherin & Van Es, 2005; Taggert & Wilson, 2005). Teacher action research is a formalized approach to reflectivity: to learn from your classroom and from your students how better to teach. It is consistent with sociocultural approaches to teaching, because teacher research recognizes that we teach something to somebody in a situation. Although many theories and approaches concentrate on the content (the something) to be taught, only the sociocultural theory looks at all three facets and how they are related. Teacher research also recognizes that teaching is relational and that we need feedback from our students about how to teach them as individuals and in groups. Teaching and learning can't be done through cookie cutter approaches because students, their backgrounds and needs, and the situations in which they learn and are being prepared to participate, are constantly evolving. Therefore, so must your teaching.

Teacher reflectivity really depends on your "learning to notice" by consciously observing students' learning in your classrooms. In addition, many teachers choose to research classroom interactions and teaching techniques by collecting data on a systematic basis to address the question, What is this a case of? (Sherin & Van Es, 2005, p. 477).

Sometimes by posing specific questions, you can then pay attention to particular aspects of students' interpretations, writing, talk, drama, or media productions. Or, you can attend to certain "critical incidents" when something goes very right that you want to be able to repeat, or when something goes very wrong and you wonder how to be proactive about avoiding such problems in the future.

In conducting teacher action research, it is important to keep your study small, focused, and contextualized on your teaching. You should choose research methods that are part of what you do in your everyday teaching, and not something extra.

Once you have identified an important or interesting event, you can then ask the following: How can I understand this? This question might involve exploring why students misunderstood a particular concept or why students seemed unengaged by a particular assignment. Your goal as a reflective teacher is to understand how and why certain things occurred. For what reasons did things turn out the way they did? What is the meaning behind what occurred? What might be learned?

Teacher researchers use various media to focus their attention, or to learn on what they might fruitfully focus attention (Sherin & Van Es, 2005) using the following techniques:

Notetaking. Teacher researchers use notetaking—both "in the midst" of instruction (e.g., when groups are at work) or "after the fact" (immediately after class in the case that you are actively involved in teaching) to record and "placehold" what has happened of importance so that it can be reflected on, studied, and analyzed.

Journal Writing. Keeping a teaching journal a few times a week about what you are noticing or what is bothering you is a useful technique. Another idea is to take a student artifact (an essay, a project) or event and to write about it, reflecting on the specifics of what happened, to reflect on how what was made or occurred furthers your overall goals as a teacher or for a particular class, and to write about ideas that you might try in the future based on what you notice.

Collecting Student Work. Collecting student artifacts or papers and studying them is a powerful technique. Videotaping or audiotaping students as they work allows you to focus on particular events. You can also use a technique called "stimulated recall" by asking students to view a section of tape and to "think aloud" or explain what they were thinking and doing during this segment of class.

Photography and Videotaping. Photographs or videotapes, particularly digital ones that you can store on your computer, give you an efficient retrievable record of student work and interactions. (Note: you will need to get permission to videotape students if you plan to share what you collect with anyone else. Some schools require student and parent permission for any kind of videotaping or audiotaping.)

Videotaping yourself teaching can be a very informative experience, particularly if you can share the viewing of tapes with others. Participants report that viewing videos helps them to take on a "spectator stance" toward their teaching, to achieve the ability to see their teaching as if through a video lens. This helps teachers to not only notice details they might have not have noticed before, but to see alternative actions they could take to improve the learning environment and its possibilities.

Peer Coach Script Taping and Feedback. If you have a peer coaching partner, your coach can observe your teaching and take notes on particular kids, activities, or issues that you identify. You can then discuss these notes and observations to explore what happened and what might have happened if you, as the teacher, had made different kinds of choices.

Analyzing Data. Analyze the data to help you notice and explain patterns. Analyzing data involves the following processes: Collect and Cook and Code, Classify, Explain, Represent, and Share. Collecting is simply getting data. Cooking and Coding is reading through the data and naming what you have noticed. Classifying is seeking out and identifying patterns, and the relations among named events or ideas from the classification. You then try to explain the reasons for the relations in ways that can inform your classroom decision making.

Formulating Beliefs and Theories About Your Teaching. From your results, you formulate beliefs and theories about teaching and learning that help you understand what has actually happened in your classroom and how you can make changes to improve student learning. For example, in Chapter 10, in conducting his study on his literacy lens instruction, Tim Klobuchar recognized that students are better able to employ certain lenses than others based on their prior knowledge of key concepts and his ability to model the use of certain lenses to analyze texts. This served to help him formulate his belief in drawing on students' prior knowledge and the value of modeling.

Beginning teachers often focus only on their own teaching; experienced teachers focus on the connections between their teaching and students by reflecting on student learning in light of acquired beliefs and theories, which leads to improvements in their instruction. Research on teachers who do develop (Guskey & Huberman, 1995; Zeichner, Melnick, & Gomez, 1996) shows that teachers don't change their "grounded theories" and then change their teaching; they change their teaching and what they pay attention to, and this changes their theories and understandings. This in turn fuels the evolution of their teaching practices.

If you want to stay fresh and invigorated as a teacher, then engaging in ongoing inquiry about your teaching serves as a model inquiry-learning for your students and colleagues. We close this volume with the hope that by taking this path, you will discover the rewards that accrue from what can be the most complex, challenging, worthwhile, interesting, engaging, and fulfilling of careers—that of teaching literature to adolescents.

Online Additional Activities, Links, and Further Reading

Go to the textbook Web site, Chapter 13, and to "professional development" for additional activities, links, and further reading.

References

Abbott, H. P. (2002). *The Cambridge introduction to narrative*. New York: Cambridge University Press.

Achebe, C. (1996). *Things fall apart*. Portsmouth, NH: Heinemann.

Achebe, C. (2001). *Hopes and impediments: Selected essays*. New York: Anchor.

Adichie, C. H. (2004). *Purple hibiscus: A novel*. New York: Anchor.

Adler v. Board of Education, 342 U.S. 485. (1952). Retrieved September 15, 2005, from http://caselaw.lp.findlaw.com/scripts/getcase.pl?court=US&vol=342&invol=485

Adler, M. (1992). *The great ideas: A lexicon of western thought*. New York: Macmillan.

Alexie, S. (1994). *The Lone Ranger and Tonto fistfight in heaven*. New York: Perennial.

Alexie, S. (1998). *Smoke signals: Introduction, screenplay, and notes*. New York: Hyperion.

Allender, D. (2002). The myth ritual theory and the teaching of multicultural literature. *English Journal, 91*(5), 52–55.

Allison, D. (1993). *Bastard out of Carolina*. New York: Plume.

Almasi, J. (1995). The nature of fourth-graders' sociocognitive conflicts in peer-led and teacher-led discussions of literature. *Reading Research Quarterly, 30*, 314–351.

Alsup, J. (2003). Politicizing young adult literature: Reading Anderson's Speak as a critical text. *Journal of Adolescent & Adult Literacy, 47*, 158–166.

Altman, R. (1999). *Film/genre*. Berkeley: University of California Press.

Alvarez, J. (1991). *How the Garcia girls lost their accents*. Chapel Hill, NC: Algonquin Books.

Alvermann, D., Moon, J., & Hagood, M. (1999). *Popular culture in the classroom: Teaching and researching critical media literacy*. Newark, DE: International Reading Association/National Reading Conference.

Alvermann, D., Young, J., & Green, C. (1997). *Adolescents' negotiations of out-of-school reading discussions*. Athens, GA: National Reading Research Center.

Anaya, R. (1991). *Aztlán: Essays on the Chicano homeland*. Albuquerque: University of New Mexico Press.

Anderson, D. T. (1988). *The effects of direct instruction in interpretive strategies on students' reading of drama*. Unpublished master's thesis, University of Chicago.

Anderson, L. (1997). The stories teachers tell and what they tell us. *Teaching and Teacher Education, 13*, 131–136.

Anderson, L. H. (1999). *Speak*. New York: Farrar, Straus & Giroux.

Anderson, M. T. (2002). *Feed*. Boston: Candlewick Press.

Angelou, M. (1969). *I know why the caged bird sings*. New York: Bantam.

Anson, C., & Beach, R. (1995). *Journals in the classroom: Writing to learn*. Norwood, MA: Christopher Gordan.

Anzaldua, G. (1987). How to tame the wild tongue. In R. Ferguson et al. (Eds.), *Out there: Marginalization and contemporary cultures* (pp. 204–211). New York: New Museum of Contemporary Art.

Applebee, A. (1978). *The child's concept of story: Ages two to seventeen*. Chicago: University of Chicago Press.

Applebee, A. (1991). *The teaching of literature in programs with reputations for excellence in English microform*. Albany: State University of New York Press, Center for Learning and Teaching of Literature.

Applebee, A. (1994). *A study of high school literature anthologies*. Retrieved September 8, 2004, from State University of New York, Center for Learning and Teaching of Literature Web site: http://cela.albany.edu/reports/antho/index.html

Appleman, D. (2000). *Critical encounters in high school English: Teaching literary theory to adolescents*. New York: Teachers College Press.

Atwell, N. (1998). *In the middle: New understandings about writing, reading, and learning*. Portsmouth, NH: Boynton/Cook.

Austen, J. (1983). *Pride and prejudice*. New York: Bantam.

Austin, J. L. (1975). *How to do things with words* (2nd ed.) (J. O. Urmson & M. Sbisà, Eds.). Cambridge, MA: Harvard University Press.

Avi. (1993). *Nothing but the truth*. New York: HarperTrophy.

Ayers, R., & Crawford, A. (Eds.). (2004). *Great books for high school kids: A teacher's guide to books that can change teens' lives*. Boston: Beacon.

Bakhtin, M. (1981). *The dialogic imagination: Four essays* (M. Holquist, Ed.). Austin: University of Texas Press.

Bakhtin, M. (1984). *Problems of Dostoevsky's poetics* (C. Emerson, Ed. & Trans.). Minneapolis: University of Minnesota Press. (Original work published 1973)

Bakhtin, M. M. (1981). *The dialogic imagination* (C. Emerson & M. Holquist, Trans.). Austin: University of Texas Press. (Original work published 1975)

Baldwin, J. (1985). *Go tell it on the mountain*. New York: Laurel.

Bambara, T. (1999). Raymond's run. In R. Emra (Ed.), *Coming of age* (pp. 21–30). Lincolnwood, IL: National Textbook Company.

Barthes, R. (1974). *S/Z* (R. Miller, Trans.). New York: Hill & Wang.

Bartholomae, D., & Petrosky, A. (2005). *Ways of reading: An anthology for writers*. Boston: Bedford Books of St. Martin's Press.

Bauer, M. D. (Ed.). (1994). *Am I blue: Coming out from the silence*. New York: HarperCollins.

Beach, R. (1993). *A teacher's introduction to reader response theories*. Urbana, IL: National Council of Teachers of English.

Beach, R. (1997). Students' resistance to engagement in responding to multicultural literature. In T. Rogers & A. Soter (Eds.), *Reading across cultures: Teaching literature in a diverse society* (pp. 69–94). New York: Teachers College Press.

Beach, R. (2004). Researching response to literature and media. In A. Goodwyn & A. Staples (Eds.), *Learning to read critically in language and literacy* (pp. 123–148). Thousand Oaks, CA: Sage.

Beach, R., Appleman, D., & Dorsey, S. (1990). Developing knowledge of literature through intertextual links. In R. Beach & S. Hynds (Eds.), *Developing discourse practices in adolescence and adulthood* (pp. 224–245). Norwood, NJ: Ablex.

Beach, R., Eddleston, S., & Philippot, R. (2004). Characteristics of effective large-group discussions. In C. Bazerman, B. Huot, & B. Stroble (Eds.), *Multiple literacies for the 21st century: Proceedings of the 1998 Watson Conference* (pp. 129–150). Cresskill, NJ: Hampton.

Beach, R., & Myers, J. (2001). *Inquiry-based English instruction: Engaging students in literature and life*. New York: Teachers College Press.

Beach, R., Thein, A., & Parks, A. (in press). *High school students' competing social worlds: Negotiating identities and allegiances in response to multicultural literature*. Mahwah, NJ: Lawrence Erlbaum Associates.

Berger, A. A. (1997). *Narratives in popular culture, media, and everyday life*. Thousand Oaks, CA: Sage.

Blackford, H. V. (2004). *Out of this world: Why literature matters to girls*. New York: Teachers College Press.

Blau, S. (2003). *The literature workshop: Teaching texts and their readers*. Portsmouth, NH: Heinemann.

Blau, S. (2004). *The literature workshop*. Portsmouth, NH: Heinemann.

Block, F. L. (1999). *Weetzie bat*. New York: HarperTrophy.

Bloor, E. (2001). *Tangerine*. New York: Scholastic.

Blume, J. (1989). *Wifey*. New York: Pocket Books.

Boal, A. (1985). *Theatre of the oppressed*. New York: Theatre Communications Group.

Boal, A. (2002). *Games for actors and non-actors*. New York: Routledge.

Bolter, J., & Grusin, R. (1998). *Remediation: Understanding new media*. Cambridge, MA: MIT Press.

Bonnycastle, S. (1996). *In search of authority: An introductory guide to literary theory*. Peterborough, Ontario, Canada: Broadview Press.

Booker, W., & Jermyn, D. (Eds.). (2003). *The audience studies reader*. New York: Routledge.

Brashares, A. (2003). *Sisterhood of the traveling pants*. New York: Delacorte Books for Young Readers.

Britzman, D. (1991). *Practice makes practice: A critical study of learning to teach*. Albany: State University of New York Press.

Britzman, D. P. (1998). *Lost subjects, contested objects: Toward a psychoanalytic inquiry of learning*. Albany: State University of New York Press.

Broad, B. (2003). *What we really value: Beyond rubrics in teaching and assessing writing*. Logan: Utah State University Press.

Brooks, G. (1999). We real cool. In G. Brooks, *Selected poems* (p. 73). New York: Perennial.

Brooks, P. (1992). *Reading for the plot: Design and intention in narrative*. Cambridge, MA: Harvard University Press.

Brown, J. E. (Ed.). (1994). *Preserving intellectual freedom: Fighting censorship in our schools*. Urbana, IL: National Council of Teachers of English.

Browner, S., Pulsford, S., & Sears, R. (2000). *Literature and the Internet: A guide for students, teachers, and scholars*. New York: Brunner-Routledge.

Broz, W. J. (2002). Defending Am I Blue. *Journal of Adolescent & Adult Literacy, 45*, 340–350.

Brualdi, A. (1998). *Implementing performance assessment in the classroom*. Document #1.310/2:423312). Washington, DC: ERIC Clearinghouse on Assessment and Evaluation.

Bruner, J. (1986). *Actual minds: Possible worlds*. Cambridge, MA: Harvard University Press.

Bruner, J. (1990). *Acts of meaning*. Cambridge, MA: Harvard University Press.

Bruner, J. (2002). *Making stories: Law, literature, life*. New York: Farrar, Straus & Giroux.

Buckingham, D. (2003). *Media education: Literacy, learning and contemporary culture*. Malden, MA: Polity.

Burke, J. (2002). *Tools for thought: Helping all students read, write, speak, and think*. Portsmouth, NH: Heinemann.

Burke, J. (2003). *The English teacher's companion: A complete guide to classroom, curriculum, and the profession*. Portsmouth, NH: Heinemann.

Burnaford, G. E., Fischer, J., & Hobson, D. (Eds.). (2001). *Teachers doing research: The power of action through inquiry*. Mahwah, NJ: Lawrence Erlbaum Associates.

Buxton, R. (2004). *The complete world of Greek mythology*. London: Thames & Hudson.

Cain, C. (1991). Personal stories. *Ethos, 19*, 210–253.

Campbell, J. (1988). *The power of myth*. New York: Doubleday.

Campbell, J. (1991). *The power of myth, with Bill Moyers*. New York: Anchor.

Campbell, J. (1993). *Myths to live by*. New York: Penguin.

Caro, N. (Director). (2004). *Whale rider* [Motion picture]. United States: Columbia Tristar.

Carroll, L. (1971). *Alice in wonderland*. New York: Norton.

Chandler-Olcott, K., & Mahar, D. (2003). Adolescents' anime-inspired "fanfictions": An exploration of multiliteracies. *Journal of Adolescent & Adult Literacy, 46*, 556–566.

Chang, J. (2005). *Can't stop won't stop: A history of the hip-hop generation*. New York: St. Martin's Press.

Cheever, J. (2000). The swimmer. In J. Cheever (Ed.), *The stories of John Cheever* (pp. 603–612). New York: Vintage.

Chopin, K. (1982). *Awakening*. New York: Avon Books.

Christensen, L. (2000). *Reading, writing, and rising up: Teaching about social justice and the power of the written word*. Milwaukee, WI: Rethinking Schools.

Christian-Smith, L. K. (1993). *Texts of desire: Essays on fiction, femininity and schooling*. London: Falmer.

Christopher, R. (1999). Teaching working-class literature to mixed audiences. In S. L. Linkon (Ed.), *Teaching working class* (pp. 203–222). Amherst: University of Massachusetts Press.

Ciardi, J. (1975). *How does a poem mean?* Boston: Houghton Mifflin.

Clandinin, J., & Connelly, M. (1999). *Narrative inquiry: Experience and story in qualitative research*. San Francisco: Jossey-Bass.

Cobley, P. (2001). *Narrative*. New York: Routledge.

Cole, M. (1996). *Cultural psychology*. Cambridge, MA: Harvard University Press.

Coleridge, S. (1990). Table talk. In K. Coburn (Ed.), *The collected works of Samuel Taylor Coleridge* (Vol. 14, p. 125). Princeton, NJ: Bollingen.

Collier, J. (1943). The chaser. In J. Collier, *The touch of nutmeg, and more unlikely stories* (pp. 45–54). New York: Press of the Readers Club.

Conrad, J. (2000). *Heart of darkness.* New York: Penguin.

Cook, G. (2001). *The discourse of advertising.* New York: Routledge.

Cormier, R. (1986). *The chocolate war.* New York: Laurel Leaf.

Corrigan, T. (1999). *Film and literature: An introduction and reader.* Upper Saddle River, NJ: Prentice-Hall.

Costanzo, W. V. (2004). *Great films and how to teach them.* Urbana, IL: National Council of Teachers of English.

Cowley, M. (1994). *Exile's return: A literary odyssey of the 1920s.* New York: Penguin.

Crane, S. (1990). *The red badge of courage.* New York: Dover.

Crawford, P. (2003). *Graphic novels 101: Selecting and using graphic novels to promote literacy for children and young adults.* Castle Rock, CO: Hi Willow Research & Publishing.

Csikszentmihalyi, M., & Larson, R. (1984). *Being adolescent: Conflict and growth in the teenage years.* New York: Basic Books.

Curry, A. (2001). Where is Judy Blume? Controversial fiction for older children and young adults. *Journal of Youth Services in Libraries, 14,* 28–37.

Cushman, K. (1994). *Catherine, called Birdy.* New York: HarperCollins.

Daniels, H. (2002a). Expository text in literature circles. *Voices from the Middle, 9,* 7–12.

Daniels, H. (2001b). *Literature circles: Voice and choice in book clubs and reading groups.* York, ME: Stenhouse Publishers.

Daniels, H., & Steineke, N. (2004). *Mini-lessons for literature circles.* Portsmouth, NH: Heinemann.

Davis, B. G. (1993). Diversity and complexity in the classroom: Considerations of race, ethnicity, and gender (excerpts from *Tools for Teaching* published by Jossey-Bass). Retrieved September 12, 2005, from http://teaching.berkeley.edu/bgd/diversity.html

Davis, T. (2002). *Vision quest: A wrestling story.* Spokane: Eastern Washington University Press.

Dettmar, K. (1998). What's so great about great books? *The Chronicle of Higher Education, 45,* B6–B7.

Dewey, J. (1974). *On education: Selected writings.* Chicago: University of Chicago Press.

Dickinson, E. (1990). Because I could not stop for death. In E. Dickinson, *Selected poems* (p. 36). New York: Dover.

Didion, J. (2003). *Where I was from.* New York: Knopf.

Dillard, A. (1988). *An American childhood.* New York: Perennial.

Dong, Y. (2004). Don't keep them in the dark! Teaching metaphors to English language learners. *English Journal, 93*(4), 28–33.

Duffy, G. (2003). *Explaining reading: A resource for teaching concepts, skills, and strategies.* New York: Guilford.

Eakin, P. J. (1999). *How our lives become stories: Making selves.* Ithaca, NY: Cornell University Press.

Earthman, E. A. (1992). Creating the virtual work: Readers' processes in understanding literary texts. *Research in the Teaching of English, 26,* 351–384.

Ebert, R. (2001, November 25). The searchers. *Chicago Sun-Times.* Retrieved March 14, 2005, from http://rogerebert.suntimes.com/apps/pbcs.dll/article?AID=/20011125/REVIEWS08/111250301/1023

Eddleston, S., & Philippot, R. (2002). Implementing whole-class literature discussions: An overview of the teacher's roles. In J. Holden & J. Schmit (Eds.), *Inquiry and the literary text: Constructing discussions in the English classroom.* Urbana, IL: National Council of Teachers of English.

Edelsky, C. (1999). On critical whole language practice: Why, what, and a bit of how. In C. Edelsky (Ed.), *Making justice our project: Teachers working toward critical whole language practice* (pp. 7–36). Urbana, IL: National Council of Teachers of English.

Edelsky, K., Smith, K., & Wolfe, P. (2002). A discourse on academic discourse. *Linguistics and Education, 13,* 1–38.

Edgell, D. (1986). *Beka lamb.* Portsmouth, NH: Heinemann.

Edwards, E. (2001). *The genesis of narrative in Malory's Morte Darthur.* Rochester, NY: D. S. Brewer.

Elbow, P. (1973). *Writing without teachers.* New York: Oxford University Press.

Elbow, P. (1998). *Writing with power.* New York: Oxford University Press.

Electronic Frontier Foundation. (2003). *Filtering software overblocks and miscategorizes websites.* Retrieved September 7, 2004, from http://www.eff.org/Censorship/Censorware/net_block_report/20030623_eff_pr.php

Eliot, G. (1981). *Silas Marner.* New York: Bantam.

Elkind, D. (1979). *All grown up and no place to go: Teenagers in crisis*. Reading, MA: Addison-Wesley.

Ellison, R. (1995). *Invisible man*. New York: Vintage.

Ellsworth, E. (1997). *Teaching positions: Difference, pedagogy, and the power of address*. New York: Teachers College Press.

Enciso, P. (1998). Good/bad girls read together: Pre-adolescent girls' co-authorship of feminine subject positions during a shared reading event. *English Education, 30*, 44–62.

Engestrom, Y. (1987). *Learning by expanding: An activity theoretical approach to developmental research*. Helsinki, Finland: Orienta-Konsultit.

Esslin, M. (1987). *The field of drama: How the signs of drama create meaning on stage and screen*. New York: Methuen.

Estes, L. (Producer), & Eyre, C. (Director). (1999). *Smoke signals* [Motion picture]. United States: Miramax Home Entertainment.

Eugenides, J. (1994). *The virgin suicides*. New York: Warner Books.

Fairclough, N. (1989). *Language and power*. New York: Longman.

Farr, R., & Tone, B. (1994). *Theory meets practice in language arts assessment*. ERIC Digest # ED369075. Bloomington, IN: ERIC Clearinghouse on Reading, English, and Communication.

Faulkner, W. (1966). The bear. In M. Cowley (Ed.), *The portable Faulkner* (pp. 227–364). New York: Viking Press.

Federal Communications Commission. (2000). Children's Internet Protection Act. Retrieved September 16, 2005, from http://www.fcc.gov/cgb/consumerfacts.cipa.html

Ferris, D. R. (2003). *Response to student writing: Implications for second language students*. Mahwah, NJ: Lawrence Erlbaum Associates.

Finders, M., & Hynds, S. (2003). *Literacy lessons: Teaching and learning with middle-school students*. Upper Saddle River, NJ: Prentice Hall.

Fitzgerald, F. S. (1991). *The great Gatsby*. New York: Cambridge University Press.

Fleischer, C., & Schaafsma, D. (Eds.). (1998). *Literacy and democracy: Teacher research and composition studies in pursuit of habitable spaces: Further conversations from the students of Jay Robinson*. Urbana, IL: National Council of Teachers of English.

Florio-Ruane, S. (2000). *Teacher education and the cultural imagination: Autobiography, conversation, and narrative*. Mahwah, NJ: Lawrence Erlbaum Associates.

Flower, L., Long, E., & Higgins, L. (2000). *Learning to rival: A literate practice for intercultural inquiry*. Mahwah, NJ: Lawrence Erlbaum Associates.

Frank, A. (1989). *The diary of Anne Frank* (A. J. Pomerans & B. M. Mooyaart, Trans.). New York: Doubleday. (Original work published 1948)

Frank, C. R., Dixon, C. N., & Brandts, L. R. (2001). Bears, trolls, and pagemasters: Learning about learners in book clubs. *The Reading Teacher, 54*, 448–462.

Freccero, C. (1999). *Popular culture: An introduction*. New York: New York University Press.

Freire, P. (1973). *Education for critical consciousness*. New York: Seabury Press.

Freire, P., & Macedo, D. (1987). *Literacy: Reading the word & the world*. South Hadley, MA: Bergin & Garvey.

Frost, R. (1916/1993). The road not taken. In R. Frost, *The road not taken and other poems* (p. 1). New York: Dover.

Frye, N. (1957). *Anatomy of criticism: Four essays*. Princeton, NJ: Princeton University Press.

Fuentes, A. (1998). The crackdown on kids: The new mood of meanness toward children—To be young is to be suspect. *The Nation, 266*, 16–19.

Galda, L., & Beach, R. (2001). Theory and research into practice: Response to literature. *Reading Research Quarterly, 36*, 64–73.

Galt, M. F. (2000). *The story in history: Writing your way into the American experience*. New York: Teachers & Writers Collaborative.

Gardner, H. (1993). *Frames of mind: The theory of multiple intelligences*. New York: Basic Books.

Gardner, H. (2000). *Intelligence reframed: Multiple intelligences for the 21st century*. New York: Basic Books.

Gee, J. P. (1996). *Social linguistics and literacies: Ideology in discourses* (2nd ed.). Bristol, PA: Taylor & Francis.

Gee, J. P. (2003). *What video games have to teach us about learning and literacy*. New York: Palgrave Macmillan.

Gee, J. P., Allen, A., & Clinton, K. (2001). Language, class, and identity: Teenagers fashioning themselves through language. *Linguistics and Education 12*, 175–194.

Gergen, K. (1991). *The saturated self: Dilemmas of identity in contemporary life*. New York: Basic Books.

Giannetti, L. (2004). *Understanding movies* (10th ed.). Upper Saddle River, NJ: Prentice Hall.

Gibbons, K. (1997). *Ellen Foster*. New York: Vintage.

Gies, M. (1988). *Anne Frank remembered*. New York: Simon & Schuster.

Glaspell, S. (1987). *The plays of Susan Glaspell*. New York: Cambridge University Press.

Glaspell, S. (2004). *A jury of her peers*. New York: Kessinger Publishing.

Golding, W. G. (1959). *The lord of the flies*. New York: Perigee Books.

Goodrich, F., & Hackett, A. (1998). *The diary of Anne Frank, The play*. New York: Dramatists Play Service.

Grice, H. P. (1989). *Studies in the way of words*. Cambridge, MA: Harvard University Press.

Guskey, T. R., & Huberman, M. (Eds.). (1995). *Professional development in education: New paradigms and practices*. New York: Teachers College Press.

Guthrie, J. (2004). Teaching for literacy engagement. *Journal of Literacy Research, 36*, 1–30.

Gutterson, D. (1998). *Snow falling on cedars*. New York: Random House.

Haddon, M. (2004). *The curious incident of the dog in the night-time*. New York: Vintage.

Hale, L. A., & Crowe, C. (2001). I hate reading if I don't have to: Results from a longitudinal study of high school students' reading interest. *The ALAN Review, 28*, 49. Retrieved September 15, 2005, from http://scholar.lib.vt.edu/ejournals/ALAN/v28n3/hale.html

Hall, G. S. (1904). *Adolescence: Its psychology and its relations to physiology, anthropology, sociology, sex, crime, religion, and education* (2 vols.). New York: Appleton.

Hamel, F. L. (2003). Teacher understanding of student understanding: Revising the gap between teacher conceptions and students' ways with literature. *Research in the Teaching of English, 38*, 49–84.

Hamilton, E. (1999). *Mythology: Timeless tales of gods and heroes*. New York: Warner Books.

Hammett, R. (1999). Intermediality, hypermedia, and critical media literacy. In L. Semali & A. W. Pailliotet (Eds.), *Intermediality: The teachers' handbook of critical media literacy* (pp. 207–222). Boulder, CO: Westview.

Hammett, R., & Barrell, B. R. C. (Eds.). (2002). *Digital expressions: Media literacy and English language arts*. Calgary, Alberta, Canada: Detselig Enterprises.

Hansen, D. (2001). Teaching as a moral activity. In V. Richardson (Ed.), *Handbook of research on teaching* (4th ed., pp. 826–857). Washington, DC: American Educational Research Association.

Hart, A. (2004). *How to write plays, monologues, or skits from life stories, social issues, or current events: For all ages*. New York: ASJA Press.

Hawthorne, N. (1999a). Young Goodman Brown. In B. Harding (Ed.), *Young Goodman Brown and other tales* (pp. 111–123). New York: Oxford University Press.

Hawthorne, N. (1999b). The maypole of Marymount. In B. Harding (Ed.), *Young Goodman Brown and other tales* (pp. 133–143). New York: Oxford University Press.

Hawthorne, N. (1850/2004). *The scarlet letter*. New York: Barnes & Noble.

Heath, S. B. (1986). What no bedtime story means: Narrative skills at home and school. In B. B. Schieffelin & E. Ochs (Eds.), *Awakening to literacy* (pp. 51–72). New York: Cambridge University Press.

Heller, J. (1996). *Catch-22*. New York: Simon & Schuster.

Hesse, K. (1995). *Phoenix rising*. New York: Puffin Books.

Hesse, K. (1999). *Out of the dust*. New York: Scholastic.

Hesse, K. (2004). *Stowaway*. New York: Aladdin.

Hewett, B. L., & Ehmann, C. (2004). *Preparing educators for online writing instruction: Principles and processes*. Urbana, IL: National Council of Teachers of English.

Higginson, W. (1992). *The haiku handbook: How to write, share, and teach haiku*. Tokyo: Kodansha International.

Hillocks, G. (2002). *The testing trap: How state writing assessments control learning*. New York: Teachers College Press.

Hine, D. (2000). *The rise and fall of the American teenager*. Perennial.

Hipple, T., & Claiborne, J. L. (2005). The best young adult novels of all time, or The Chocolate War one more time. *English Journal, 94*(3), 99–102.

Hirsch, E. D. (1988). *Cultural literacy: What every American needs to know.* New York: Vintage.

Holden, J., & Schmit, J. (Eds.). (2002). *Inquiry and the literary text: Constructing discussions in the English classroom.* Urbana, IL: National Council of Teachers of English.

Holland, D., & Eisenstat, M. (1990). *Educated in romance: Women, achievement, and college culture.* Chicago: University of Chicago Press.

Hubert, K. (2000). *Teaching & writing popular fiction: Horror, adventure, mystery, & romance in the classroom.* New York: Teachers and Writers Collaborative.

Hughes, L. (1994). I, too sing America. In A. Rampersad (Ed.), *The collected poems of Langston Hughes* (p. 46). New York: Knopf.

Hunt, R. (2002). Making student writing count: The experience of "from the page to the stage." In G. Tucker & D. Nevo (Eds.), *Atlantic Universities' Teaching Showcase 2001: Proceedings* (pp. 121–130). Retrieved March 10, 2005, from http://www.stu.cu/~hunt/p2spaper.htm

Hunt, R., & Vipond, D. (1992). First, catch the rabbit: The methodological imperative and the dramatization of dialogic reading. In R. Beach, R. J. Green, M. Kamil, & T. Shanahan (Eds.), *Multidisciplinary perspectives on literacy research* (pp. 69–89). Urbana, IL: National Conference on Research in English.

Hurston, N. Z. (1998). *Their eyes were watching God.* New York: Perennial.

Huxley, A. (1998). *Brave new world.* New York: HarperPerennial.

Ibsen. (1990). *Hedda Gabler.* New York: Dover.

Iser, W. (1960). *The act of reading: A theory of aesthetic response.* Baltimore: Johns Hopkins University Press.

Jackson, S. (1988). The lottery. In J. Pickering (Ed.), *Fiction 100: An anthology of short stories* (pp. 702–708). New York: Macmillan. (Original work published 1948)

Jackson, S. (1999). Louise, please come home. In B. Erma (Ed.), *Coming of age: Fiction about youth and adolescence* (pp. 256–266). Lincolnwood, IL: National Textbook.

Jhally, S. (1997). *bell hooks: Cultural criticism & transformation.* Education Media Foundation.

Johnson, K. E., & Golombek, P. R. (Eds.). (2002). *Teachers' narrative inquiry as professional development.* New York: Cambridge University Press.

Johnston, B. (1983). *Assessing English.* Urbana, IL: National Council of Teachers of English.

Jones, M. K. (1994). *Say it loud!: The story of rap music.* New York: Millwood Press.

Joyce, J. (1993). *Ulysses.* New York: Oxford University Press.

Kappes, D. (Producer), & Dornhelm, R. (Director). (2003). *Anne Frank: The whole story* [Motion picture]. United States: Disney Studios.

Kaysen, S. (1993). *Girl interrupted.* New York: Turtle Bay Books.

Kegan, R. (1994). *In over our heads: The mental demands of modern life.* Cambridge, MA: Harvard University Press.

Kegan, R. (2000). What "form" transforms?: A constructive-developmental approach to transformative learning. In J. Mezirow (Ed.), *Learning as transformation: Critical perspectives on a theory in progress* (pp. 35–70). San Francisco: Jossey-Bass.

Kent, R. (1997). *Room 109: The promise of a portfolio classroom.* Portsmouth, NH: Heinemann.

Kent, R. (2000). *Beyond room 109: Developing independent study projects.* Portsmouth, NH: Heinemann.

Kent, T. (1993). *Paralogic rhetoric.* London: Associated University Press.

Kerouac, J. (1991). *On the road.* New York: Penguin.

Kerr, M. E. (1984). Do you want my opinion? In D. Gallo (Ed.), *Sixteen: Short stories by outstanding writers for young adults* (pp. 93–100). New York: Dell.

Kerr, M. E. (1995). *Deliver us from Evie.* New York: HarperTrophy.

Kincaid, J. (1997). *Annie John.* New York: Farrar, Straus & Giroux.

King, M. L. (1994). *Letter from a Birmingham jail.* New York: HarperCollins.

Kingsolver, B. (1996). How Mr. Dewey Decimal saved my life. In B. Kingsolver (Ed.), *High tide in Tucson: Essays from now or never* (pp. 54–63). New York: Perennial.

Kingsolver, B. (1998). *The bean trees.* New York: HarperTorch.

Kingston, M. H. (1989). *The woman warrior: Memoirs of a girlhood among ghosts.* New York: Vintage.

Kinory, A. D. (2002). *Teaching practice: "Film at 11!"—iMovie™ makes essays come alive.* NBPTS Digital Edge Learning Exchange. Retrieved September 15, 2005, from http://ali.apple.com/ali_sites/deli/exhibits/1000751

Kirby, D., & Kuykendall, C. (1991). *Mind matters: Teaching for thinking.* Portsmouth, NH: Heinemann.

Klein, N. (2000). *No logo: Taking aim at the brand bullies.* New York: Picador.

Koch, K. (1973). *Rose, where did you get that red? Teaching great poetry to children.* New York: Random House.

Koch, K. (1980). *Wishes, lies, and dreams: Teaching children to write poetry.* New York: HarperCollins.

Kohn, A. (2000). *The case against standardized testing: Raising the scores, ruining the schools.* Portsmouth, NH: Heinemann.

Kohn, A. (2004). *What does it mean to be well educated?: And more essays on standards, grading, and other follies.* Boston: Beacon Press.

Kojima, G. (1996). *Mai, the psychic girl.* New York: VIZ LLC.

Kooy, M., & Wells, J. (1996). *Reading response logs: Inviting students to explore novels, short stories, plays, poetry and more.* Portsmouth, NH: Heinemann.

Kozol, J. (1991). *Savage inequalities: Children in America's schools.* New York: HarperPerennial.

Kress, G. (2003). *Literacy in the new media age.* New York: Routledge.

Krueger, E., & Christel, M. T. (2001). *Seeing and believing: How to teach media literacy in the English classroom.* Portsmouth, NH: Boynton/Cook.

Kudo, K. (2000). *Lone wolf and cub 1: The assassin's road.* New York: Dark Horse Comics.

Labov, W. (1972). *The language of the inner city.* Philadelphia: University of Pennsylvania Press.

Lacey, N. (2000). *Narrative and genre: Key concepts in media studies.* New York: St. Martin's Press.

Lakoff, G., & Johnson, M. (1980). *Metaphors we live by.* Chicago: University of Chicago Press.

Landsman, J. (1993). *Basic needs: A year with street kids in a city school.* Minneapolis, MN: Milkweed Press.

Langer, J. A. (1995). *Literacy understanding & literature instruction.* New York: Teachers College Press.

Lankshear, C., & Knobel, M. (2002). Do we have your attention? New literacies, digital technologies and the education of adolescents. In D. Alvermann (Ed.), *New literacies and digital technologies: A focus on adolescent learners* (pp. 19–39). New York: Peter Lang.

Lankshear, C., & Knobel, M. (2003). *New literacies, changing knowledge and classroom learning.* Philadelphia: Open University Press.

Lankshear, C., & Knobel, M. (2004). *A handbook for teacher research.* New York: Open University Press.

Lave, J. (1988). *Cognition in practice: Mind, mathematics, and culture in everyday life.* New York: Cambridge University Press.

Lazar, A. (Producer), & Junger, G. (Director). (2004). *Ten things I hate about you* [Motion picture]. United States: Touchstone Video.

Lee, C. (1993). *Signifying as a scaffold for literary interpretation: The pedagogical implications of an African American discourse genre.* Urbana, IL: National Council of Teachers of English.

Lee, H. (1988). *To kill a mockingbird.* New York: Warner Books.

Lemke, J. (2003, December). *Towards critical multimedia literacy.* Paper presented at the meeting of the National Reading Conference, Scottsdale, AZ. Retrieved January 5, 2005, from http://www-personal.umich.edu/~jaylemke/webs/nrc_2003.htm

Lensmire, T. (2002). *Powerful writing, responsible teaching.* New York: Teachers College Press.

Lesko, N. (2000). *Act your age: A cultural construction of adolescence.* Philadelphia: Falmer.

Lewis, C. (2001). *Literacy practices as social acts: Power, status, and cultural norms in the classroom.* Mahwah, NJ: Lawrence Erlbaum Associates.

Livingstone, S. (2002). *Young people and new media.* London: Sage.

Lloyd, C. V. (2003). Song lyrics as texts to develop critical literacy. *Reading Online, 6.* Retrieved January 5, 2005, from http://www.readingonline.org/articles/art_index.asp?HREF=lloyd/index.html

Lorde, A. (1983). *Zami: A new spelling of my name.* Trumansburg, NY: Crossing Press.

Lowry, L. (1998). *Number the stars.* New York: Laurel Leaf.

Lynn, S. (2000). *Texts and contexts.* New York: Longman.

Lyons, N., & Laboskey, V. K. (Eds.). (2002). *Narrative inquiry in practice: Advancing the knowledge of teaching.* New York: Teachers College Press.

Malchow, R. (2002). *Different types of film adaptations.* Unpublished manuscript, University of Minnesota, Minneapolis.

Malchow, R. (2004). *Talking books: Gender and the responses of adolescents in literature circles.* Master's thesis, Department of Curriculum and Instruction, University of Minnesota, Minneapolis.

Marshall, J. (1987). The effects of writing on students' understanding of literary texts. *Research in the Teaching of English, 21,* 30–63.

Marshall, J., Smith, M., & Smagorinsky, P. (1995). *The language of interpretation: Patterns of discourse in discussions of literature.* Urbana, IL: National Council of Teachers of English.

Martino, W., & Mellor, B. (2000). *Gendered fictions.* Urbana, IL: National Council of Teachers of English.

Mathabane, M. (1998). *Kaffir boy: The true story of a Black youth's coming of age in apartheid South Africa.* New York: Free Press.

McBride, J. (1997). *Color of water: A Black man's tribute to his White mother.* New York: Riverhead Books.

McCormick, K. (1999). *Reading our histories, understanding our cultures: A sequenced approach to thinking, reading, and writing.* Boston: Allyn & Bacon.

McCourt, F. (1999). *Angela's ashes: A memoir.* New York: Scribner's.

McMahon, R. (2002). *Thinking about literature: New ideas for high school teachers.* Portsmouth, NH: Heinemann.

McMahon, S., Raphael, T., Goatley, V., & Pardo, L. (Eds.). (1997). *The book club connection: Literacy learning and classroom talk.* New York: Teachers College Press.

Mehan, H. (1979). *Learning lessons: Social organization in the classroom.* Cambridge, MA: Harvard University Press.

Meier, D. (2003). *In schools we trust: Creating communities of learning in an era of testing and standardization.* Boston: Beacon Press.

Meier, D., et al. (2004). *Many children left behind: How the No Child Left Behind Act is damaging our children and our schools.* Boston: Beacon Press.

Mellor, B. (1999). *Reading Hamlet.* Urbana, IL: National Council of Teachers of English.

Mellor, B., & Patterson, A. (2001). *Investigating texts: Analyzing fiction and nonfiction in high school.* Urbana, IL: National Council of Teachers of English.

Mellor, B., Patterson, A., & O'Neill, M. (2000a). *Reading fictions: Applying literary theory to short stories.* Urbana, IL: National Council of Teachers of English.

Mellor, B., Patterson, A., & O'Neill, M. (2000b). *Reading stories: Activities and texts for critical readings.* Urbana, IL: National Council of Teachers of English.

Melville, H. (1967). Bartelby the scrivener. *Billy Budd, sailor, and other stories* (pp. 258–292). Baltimore: Penguin.

Méndez, T. (2004). 'Hamlet' too hard? Try a comic book. *The Christian Science Monitor, 96,* 11. Retrieved January 5, 2005, from http://www.csmonitor.com/2004/1012/p11s01-legn.html

Messick, S. (1998). *Consequences of test interpretation and use: The fusion of validity and values in psychological assessment.* Princeton, NJ: Educational Testing Service.

Michaels, L. (Producer), & Waters, M. S. (Director). (2004). *Mean girls* [Motion picture]. United States: Paramount Home Video.

Milner, J., & Milner, L. (2003). *Bridging English* (3rd ed.). Upper Saddle River, NJ: Merrill.

Minnesota Department of Education. (2003). *Language arts standards.* Retrieved September 13, 2005, from http://education.state.mn.us/mde/Academic_Excellence/Academic_Standards/Standards_in_Language_Arts/index.html

Mittell, J. (2004). *Genre and television: From cop shows to cartoons in American culture.* New York: Routledge.

Momaday, M. S. (1977). *The way to rainy mountain.* Albuquerque, NM: University of New Mexico Press.

Monroe, B. (2004). *Crossing the digital divide: Race, writing, and technology in the classroom.* New York: Teachers College Press.

Moon, B. (2000). *Studying literature: New approaches to poetry and fiction.* Urbana, IL: National Council of Teachers of English.

Moon, B. (2001a). *Literary terms: A practical glossary.* Urbana, IL: National Council of Teachers of English.

Moon, B. (2001b). *Studying poetry: Activities, sources and tests.* Urbana, IL: National Council of Teachers of English.

Morrell, E. (2002). Toward a critical pedagogy of popular culture: Literacy development among urban youth. Retrieved January 5, 2005, from http://www.readingonline.org/newliteracies/lit_index.asp?HREF=/newliteracies/jaal/9-02_column

Morrell, E., & Duncan-Andrade, J. (2002). Promoting academic literacy with urban youth through engaging hip-hop culture. *English Journal, 91*(6), 88–92.

Morrison, T. (2000). *The bluest eye.* New York: Plume Books.

Morrison, T. G., Bryan, G., & Chilcoat, G. W. (2002). Using student-generated comic books in the classroom. *Journal of Adolescent & Adult Literacy, 45,* 758–767.

Mosenthal, P. B. (1998). Reframing the problems of adolescence and adolescent literacy: A dilemma-management perspective. In D. E. Alvermann et al. (Eds.), *Reconceptualizing the literacies in adolescents' lives* (pp. 325–352). Mahwah, NJ: Lawrence Erlbaum Associates.

Murray, D. M. (1968). *A writer teaches writing: A practical method of teaching composition.* Boston: Houghton Mifflin.

Myers, G. (1999). *Ad worlds: Brands, media, audiences.* New York: Oxford University Press.

Myers, J., & Beach, R. (2001). Hypermedia authoring as critical literacy. *Journal of Adolescent & Adult Literacy, 44,* 538–546.

Myers, W. D. (1988). *Fallen angels.* New York: Scholastic.

Myers, W. D. (1999). *Monster.* New York: HarperCollins.

National Council of Teachers of English. (1977). *The students' right to read.* Retrieved September 15, 2005, from http://www.ncte.org/about/over/positions/category/cens/107616.htm

National Council of Teachers of English. (1998). *Rationales for challenged book.* Retrieved September 8, 2004, from http://www.ncte.org/about/issues/censorship/five/108603.htm

National Education Association. (2001). *Teens "get it"—Reading matters.* Retrieved September 12, 2005, from http://www.nea.org/nr/nr010302.html

Naylor, G. (1983). *The women of Brewster Place.* New York: Penguin.

Neelands, J. (2000). *Structuring drama work: A handbook of available forms in theatre and drama.* Cambridge, MA: Cambridge University Press.

Norris, F. (1994). *The octopus: A story of California.* New York: Penguin.

Nystrand, M. (1997). *Opening dialogue: Understanding the dynamics of language and learning in the English classroom.* New York: Teachers College Press.

Nystrand, M. (1999, Spring). The contexts of learning: Foundations of academic achievement. *English Update: A Newsletter from the Center on English Learning and Achievement, 2,* 8.

O'Brien, D. (2003). Juxtaposing traditional and intermedial literacies to redefine the competence of struggling adolescents. Retrieved January 5, 2005, from http://www.readingonline.org/newliteracies/lit_index.asp?HREF=obrien2/

O'Brien, D. (2004). *Instructions for conducting think-alouds.* Unpublished report, University of Minnesota, Minneapolis.

O'Brien, T. (1998). *The things they carried: A work of fiction.* New York: Broadway Books.

O'Donnell-Allen, C., & Hunt, B. (2001). Reading adolescents: What book clubs are teaching us about collaborative inquiry, young readers and YA literature. *English Journal, 90*(3), 82–89.

Ogdon, R. (2001). Why teach popular culture? *College English, 63,* 500–516.

Ohanian, S. (2001). *Caught in the middle: Nonstandard kids and a killing curriculum.* Portsmouth, NH: Heinemann.

Olney, J. (1998). *Memory & narrative: The weave of life-writing.* Chicago: University of Chicago Press.

Olson, C. B. (2003). *The reading/writing connection: Strategies for teaching and learning in the secondary classroom.* Boston: Allyn & Bacon.

Ondaatie, M. (1996). *The collected works of Billy the Kid.* New York: Vintage.

Orwell, G. (1990). *1984.* New York: Signet.

Otsuka, J. (2003). *When the emperor was divine.* New York: Anchor.

Pace, B. (2003). Resistance and response: Deconstructing community standards in a literature class. *Journal of Adolescent and Adult Literature, 46*(5), 408–412.

Paterson, K. (1987). *Bridge to Terabithia.* New York: HarperTrophy.

Paterson, K. (1990). *Jacob have I loved.* New York: HarperTrophy.

Peschel, L. (2002). *Ramping up to text analysis in theater.* Minneapolis, MN: University of Minnesota Center for Interdisciplinary Studies of Writing, *Write @ U.* Retrieved September 14, 2005, from http://writing.umn.edu/home/write@u/Fall_2002.html#Theater

Petrosky, A. (2005). *The reading difficult text example.* Unpublished report, University of Pittsburgh, Pittsburgh.

Philbrook, R. (2001). *Freak the mighty.* New York: Scholastic.

Pini, W., & Pini, R. (2003). *Elfquest Archives Vol. 1.* New York: DC Comics.

Pipher, M. (1995). *Reviving Ophelia: Saving the selves of adolescent girls.* New York: Ballantine.

Pirie, B. (1997). *Reshaping high school English.* Urbana, IL: National Council of Teachers of English.

Pirie, B. (2002). *Teenage boys and high school English.* Portsmouth, NH: Boynton/Cook.

Plath, S. (1999). Initiation. In B. Emra (Ed.), *Coming of age: Fiction about youth and adolescence* (2nd ed., pp. 256–266). Lincolnwood, IL: National Textbook.

Pogrow, S. (2004). The missing element in reducing the learning gap: Eliminating the "blank stare." *Teachers College Record, 105*(1), 78–81. Retrieved October 7, 2004, from http://www.tcrecord.org/search.asp?kw=Pogrow&x=34&y=8

Pope, R. (1995). *Textual intervention: Critical and creative strategies for literary studies.* New York: Routledge.

Pope, R. (1998). *The English studies book.* New York: Routledge.

Powell, J., & Halperin, M. (2004). *Accent on meter: A handbook for readers of poetry.* Urbana, IL: National Council of Teachers of English.

Pressley, M., & Afflerbach, P. (1995). *Verbal protocols of reading: The nature of constructively responsive reading.* Mahwah, NJ: Lawrence Erlbaum Associates.

Public Enemy. (1988). *Black steel in the hour of chaos.* Retrieved September 15, 2005, from http://www.publicenemy.com/index.php?page=page5&item=9&num=5

Pugh, S. L., Hicks, J. W., & Davis, M. (1997). *Metaphorical ways of knowing: The imaginative nature of thought and expression.* Urbana, IL: National Council of Teachers of English.

Quigley, J. (2000). *The grammar of autobiography: A developmental account.* Mahwah, NJ: Lawrence Erlbaum Associates.

Rabinowitz, P. J. (1998). *Before reading: Narrative conventions and the politics of interpretation.* Columbus: Ohio State University Press.

Rabinowitz, P. J., & Smith, M. W. (1998). *Authorizing readers: Resistance and respect in the teaching of literature.* New York: Teachers College Press.

Radway, J. (1984). *Reading the romance: Women, patriarchy, and popular literature.* Chapel Hill: University of North Carolina Press.

Radway, J. (2002). Girls, reading, and narrative gleaning: Creating repertoires for self-fashioning without everyday life. In M. Green, J. Strange, & T. Brock (Eds.), *Narrative impact: Social and cognitive foundations* (pp. 183–204). Mahwah, NJ: Lawrence Erlbaum Associates.

Raphael, T. E., & McMahon, S. I. (Eds.). (1997). *The book club connection: Literacy learning and classroom talk.* New York: Teachers College Press.

Reif, L. (1992). *Seeking diversity: Language arts with adolescents.* Portsmouth, NH: Heinemann.

Rekrut, M. (2003). Thinking about literature [Review of the book *Thinking about literature: New ideas for high school teachers*]. *Journal of Adolescent & Adult Literature, 46*, 531–532.

Rennison, L. (2001). *Angus, thongs and full-frontal snogging: Confessions of Georgia Nicolson.* New York: Harper Tempest.

Ritchie, J. S., & Wilson, D. E. (2002). *Teacher narrative as critical inquiry: Rewriting the script.* New York: Teachers College Press.

Rohd, M. (1998). *Theatre for community conflict and dialogue: The hope is vital training manual.* Portsmouth, NH: Heinemann.

Romano, T. (2000). *Blending genre, altering style: Writing multigenre papers.* Portsmouth, NH: Boynton/Cook.

Rose, D., & Meyer, A. (2002). Teaching every student in the digital age: Universal design for learning. Retrieved September 10, 2005, from http://www.cast.org/teachingeverystudent/ideas/tes/

Rose, M. (1999). *Possible lives.* New York: Penguin.

Rosen, H. (1984). *Stories and meanings.* Portsmouth, NH: Boynton/Cook.

Rosenblatt, L. (1978). *The reader, the text, the poem.* Carbondale: Southern Illinois University Press.

Ross, E. P., & Roe, B. D. (1977). Creative drama builds proficiency in reading. *The Reading Teacher, 30*, 383–387.

Rozema, R. A. (2003). Falling into story: Teaching reading with the literary MOO. *English Journal, 93*(1), 33–38.

Rubin, R. A. (1995). *Poetry out loud*. Chapel Hill, SC: Algonquin Books.

Ryan, M. (1999). *Literary theory: A practical introduction*. Malden, MA: Blackwell.

Rymes, B. (2001). *Conversational borderlands: Language and identity in an alternative urban high school*. New York: Teachers College Press.

Sacks, P. (2001). *Standardized minds: The high price of America's testing culture and what we can do to change it*. New York: Perseus.

Said, E. (1978). *Orientalism*. New York: Vintage.

Salinger, J. D. (1991). *The catcher in the rye*. New York: Little, Brown.

Santiago, E. (1994). *When I was Puerto Rican*. New York: Vintage.

Schaffer, J. (1995). *Teaching the multiparagraph essay: A sequential nine-week unit*. San Diego, CA: Jane Schaffer Publications.

Schank, R. C., & Morson, G. S. (1995). *Tell me a story: Narrative and intelligence*. Evanston, IL: Northwestern University Press.

Scholes, R. (1983). *Semiotics and interpretation*. New Haven, CT: Yale University Press.

Scimone, A. J. (1999). At home with poetry: Constructing poetry anthologies in the high school classroom. *English Journal, 89*(2), 78–82.

Sebold, A. (2002). *The lovely bones*. New York: Little, Brown.

Shah, A. (2005, March 12). A spotlight on college prep. *Minneapolis Star Tribune*, pp. B1, B4.

Shannon, P., & Crawford, P. A. (1998). Summers off: Representations of teachers' work and other discontents. *Language Arts, 75*, 255–264.

Sheehy, M. (2003). The social life of an essay: Standardizing forces in writing. *Written Communication, 20*, 333–385.

Sherin, M. G., & van Es, E. A. (2005). Using video to support teachers' ability to notice classroom interactions. *Journal of Technology and Teacher Education, 13*(3), 475–491.

Short, K., & Kauffman, G. (2000). Exploring sign systems within an inquiry curriculum. In M. Gallego & S. Hollings (Eds.), *What counts as literacy* (pp. 42–61). New York: Teachers College Press.

Showalter, E. (2002). *Teaching literature*. Malden, MA: Blackwell.

Simon, R. K. (1999). *Trash culture: Popular culture and the great tradition*. Berkeley: University of California Press.

Singer, P. (Ed.). (1991). *A companion to ethics*. Cambridge, MA: Blackwell.

Smagorinsky, P. (2002). *Teaching English through principled practice*. Upper Saddle River, NJ: Prentice Hall.

Smagorinsky, P., & O'Donnell-Allen, C. (1998). Reading as mediated and mediating action: Composing meaning for literature through multimedia interpretive texts. *Reading Research Quarterly, 33*, 198–227.

Smagorinsky, P., & Smith, M. (1992). The nature of knowledge in composition and literary understanding: The question of specificity. *Review of Educational Research, 62*, 279–305.

SmartGirl and the American Library Association. (2001). *Teen week survey*. Retrieved September 10, 2005, at http://www.smartgirl.org/speakout/archives/trw/trw2001.html

Smith, F. (1997). *Reading without nonsense*. New York: Teachers College Press.

Smith, J. B. (2000). Journals and self assessment. In J. B. Smith & K. B. Yancey (Eds.), *Self-assessment and development in writing: A collaborative inquiry* (pp. 122–136). Cresskill, NJ: Hampton.

Smith, M., & Wilhelm, J. (2002). *"Reading don't fix no Chevys": Literacy in the lives of young men*. Portsmouth, NH: Heinemann.

Somers, A. B. (1999). *Teaching poetry in high school*. Urbana, IL: National Council of Teachers of English.

Spence, D. (Ed.). (2003). *Hip-hop and rap: Complete lyrics for 175 songs*. New York: Hal Leonard.

Spiegelman, A. (1993). *Maus: A survivor's tale: My father bleeds history/Here my troubles began*. New York: Pantheon.

Spring, J. (2003). *Educating the consumer-citizen: A history of the marriage of schools, advertising, and media*. Mahwah, NJ: Lawrence Erlbaum Associates.

Squirer, S. (Ed.). (2003). *Communities of the air: Radio century, radio culture*. Durham, NC: Duke University Press.

Stam, R., & Raengo, A. (Eds.). (2004). *Literature and film: A guide to the theory and practice of film adaptation*. New York: Blackwell.

Stanley, L. A. (1992). *Rap: The lyrics/the words to rap's greatest hits*. New York: Penguin.

Steiger, J. (2005). *Media reception studies*. New York: New York University Press.

Steinbeck, J. (1993). *Of mice and men*. New York: Penguin.

Steinbeck, J. (2004). *The grapes of wrath*. New York: Penguin.

Suhor, C. (2002). Contemplative reading—The experience, the idea, the applications. *English Journal, 91*(4), 28–32.

Sunstein, B. S., & Lovell, J. H. (Eds.). (2000). *The portfolio standard: How students can show us what they know and are able to do*. Portsmouth, NH: Heinemann.

Swift, J. (1994). *A modest proposal and other satires*. New York: Prometheus.

Taggert, G. L., & Wilson, A. (2005). *Promoting reflective thinking in teachers: 50 action strategies*. San Francisco: Corwin Press.

Tajiri, V. (1989). *Through innocent eyes: Teenagers' impressions of WW2 internment camp life*. New York: Keiro Services.

Taylor, M. D. (1991). *Roll of thunder, hear my cry*. New York: Puffin Books.

Teasley, A. B., & Wilder, A. (1997). *Reel conversations: Reading films with young adults*. Portsmouth, NH: Boynton/Cook.

The age of innocence isn't what it once was. (1999, April 30). *New York Times*, p. 3.

Tolkien, J. R. R. (2005). *The lord of the rings*. New York: Houghton Mifflin.

Toriyama, A. (2000). *Dragonball (Volume I)* [DVD]. New York: VIZ LLC.

Twain, M. (1981). *The adventures of Huckleberry Finn*. New York: Bantam.

United States Copyright Office. (1976). Copyright Law of 1976. Washington, DC: United States Copyright Office. Retrieved September 15, 2005, from http://www.copyright.gov/title17/

United States Department of Education. (2002). The No Child Left Behind Act. Washington, DC: United States Department of Education. Retrieved September 15, 2005, from http://www.ed.gov/nclb/landing.jhtml?src=pb

VanDeWeghe, R. (2004). Research matters: Teachers understanding of students' understanding. *English Journal, 93*(6), 88–92.

Vygotsky, L. (1978). *Mind in society: The development of higher psychological processes*. Cambridge, MA: Harvard University Press.

Vygotsky, L. (1981). The instrumental method in psychology. In J. V. Wertsch (Ed.), *The concept of activity in Soviet psychology* (pp. 134–143). Armonk, NY: M. E. Sharpe.

Wagner, B. J. (Ed.). (1999). *Building moral communities through educational drama*. Stamford, CT: Ablex.

Wakatsuki Houston, J. (1990). After the war. In J. C. Thomas (Ed.), *A gathering of flowers: Stories about being young in America* (pp. 153–174). New York: HarperCollins.

Walker, A. (1994). *Everyday use*. New Brunswick, NJ: Rutgers University Press.

Walker, M. (1999). *Jubilee*. New York: Mariner Books.

Wardrip-Fruin, N., & Harrigan, P. (Eds.). (2004). *First person: New media as story, performance, and game*. Cambridge, MA: MIT Press.

Watson, L. (1993). *Montana, 1948*. Minneapolis, MN: Milkwood Press.

Wertsch, J. (1998). *Mind as action*. New York: Oxford University Press.

West, C. (1994). *Race matters*. New York: Vintage.

West, D., & West, J. M. (1998). Sending cinematic smoke signals: An interview with Sherman Alexie. *Cineaste, 23*(4), 28–33.

Who are these people anyway? (1998, April 29). *New York Times*, p. G1.

Wiesel, E. (1982). *Night*. New York: Bantam.

Wiggins, G. P., & McTighe, J. (2005). *Understanding by design*. Washington, DC: Association for Supervision & Curriculum Development.

Wilder, A., & Teasley, A. B. (1999). Making the transition to lifelong reading: Books older teens choose. *The ALAN Review, 27*, 42–46.

Wilhelm, J. D. (1999). Reading and writing workshop: Focus on drama. *Instructor, 109*, 43–48.

Wilhelm, J. D. (2001). *Improving comprehension with think-aloud strategies*. Jefferson City, MO: Scholastic Professional Books.

Wilhelm, J. D., Baker, T., & Dube, J. (2001). *Strategic reading: Guiding students to lifelong literacy, 6–12*. Portsmouth, NH: Heinemann.

Wilhelm, J. D., & Edmiston, B. (1998). *Imagining to learn: Inquiry, ethics, and integration through drama*. Portsmouth, NH: Heinemann.

Wilson, R. J. (1997). Censorship, anti-Semitism, and "The Merchant of Venice." *English Journal, 86*(2), 43–45.

Woodson, J. (2003). *From the notebooks of Melanin Sun*. New York: Scholastic Paperbacks.

Wortham, S. (2001). *Narratives in action: A strategy for research and analysis*. New York: Teachers College Press.

Wright, R. (1998). *Black boy*. New York: Perennial.

Yancey, K. B. (2004). *Teaching literature as reflective practice*. Urbana, IL: National Council of Teachers of English.

Yancey, K. B., & Weiser, I. (Eds.). (1997). *Situating portfolios: Four perspectives*. Logan, UT: Utah State University Press.

Zancanella, D. (1998). Inside the literature curriculum. In A. Goodwyn (Ed.), *Literary and media texts in secondary English: New approaches* (pp. 98–109). London: Cassell.

Zeichner, K., Melnick, S., & Gomez, M. L. (Eds.). (1996). *Currents of reform in preservice teacher education*. New York: Teachers College Press.

Zipes, J. (Ed.). (2000). *The great fairy tale tradition: From Straparola and Basile to the Brothers Grimm*. New York: Norton.

Author Index